SEASONALITY, RURAL LIVELIHOODS AND DEVELOPMENT

Seasonality is a severe constraint to sustainable rural livelihoods, and a driver of poverty and hunger, particularly in the tropics. Many poor people in developing countries are ill-equipped to cope with seasonal variations which can lead to drought or flood and adverse consequences for agriculture, employment, food supply and the spread of disease. The subject has assumed increasing importance as climate change and other forms of development disrupt established seasonal patterns and variations.

This book is the first systematic study of seasonality for over 20 years, and it aims to revive academic interest in and policy awareness of this crucial but neglected issue. Thematic chapters explore recent shifts with profound implications for seasonality, including climate change, HIV/AIDS, and social protection. Case study chapters explore seasonal dimensions of livelihoods in Africa (Ethiopia, Malawi), Asia (Bangladesh, China, India), and Latin America (Peru). Others assess policy responses to adverse seasonality, for example through irrigation, migration and seasonally sensitive education.

The book also includes innovative tools for monitoring seasonality, which should enable more appropriate responses.

Stephen Devereux holds a doctorate in economics from the University of Oxford and has worked for over 20 years on food security, seasonality, famine and social protection. He is a Research Fellow at the Institute of Development Studies, UK.

Rachel Sabates-Wheeler holds a doctorate in agricultural economics and development from the University of Wisconsin-Madison, USA. She is a Research Fellow at the Institute of Development Studies and Director of the Centre for Social Protection.

Richard Longhurst is currently a Research Associate at IDS. He has a doctorate from Sussex University in development economics and a masters in agricultural economics from Cornell University, and over thirty years experience working on development policy issues, including food, nutrition and child health.

SEASONALITY, RURAL LIVELIHOODS AND DEVELOPMENT

Edited by Stephen Devereux,
Rachel Sabates-Wheeler and
Richard Longhurst

publishing for a sustainable future

LONDON AND NEW YORK

First published 2012
by Earthscan
2 Park Square, Milton Park, Abingdon, Oxon OX14 4RN

Simultaneously published in the USA and Canada
by Earthscan
711 Third Avenue, New York, NY 10017

Earthscan is an imprint of the Taylor & Francis Group, an informa business

British Library Cataloguing in Publication Data
A catalogue record for this book is available from the British Library

Library of Congress Cataloging in Publication Data
Seasonality, rural livelihoods, and development / edited by Stephen Devereux,
Rachel Sabates-Wheeler, and Richard Longhurst.
    p. cm.
    Includes bibliographical references and index.
    1. Seasonal variations (Economics)—Developing countries. 2. Rural
    poor—Developing countries. 3. Rural development—Developing countries.
    4. Developing countries—Rural conditions. I. Devereux, Stephen.
    II. Sabates-Wheeler, Rachel, 1971– III. Longhurst, Richard.
    HC59.7.S3658 2011   338.9009172'4—dc23
    2011028117

ISBN: 978-1-84971-324-5 (hbk)
ISBN: 978-1-84971-325-2 (pbk)
ISBN: 978-0-203-13982-0 (ebk)

Typeset in Bembo and ITC StoneSans
by Bookcraft Ltd, Stroud, Gloucestershire

CONTENTS

PART 2
Seasonal livelihoods 93
Anirudh Krishna

PART 3
Seasonal awareness 161
Robert Chambers

PART 4
Seasonal policies 235
Stephen Devereux

CONTRIBUTORS

Zemede Abebe (MSc in agricultural economics) is a Program Director for the Hararghe Catholic Secretariat in Ethiopia and the RiPPLE programme (Research-inspired Policy and Practice Learning in Ethiopia and the Nile region). He has over 15 years of experience in research, emergency and rehabilitation and rural development programmes.

Hélène Berton is an agronomist with nine years' experience in food security in emergency and development contexts. She has worked for various organizations, notably Save the Children and Oxfam, mainly in west Africa and Afghanistan. She is now the regional food assistance expert for DG-ECHO for the Middle East, north Africa and central Asia.

Tanya Boudreau is a co-founder of the Food Economy Group, a consultancy firm specializing in the use of livelihoods analysis in famine early warning systems design, emergency assessment, programme planning, and monitoring and evaluation.

Robert Chambers is a Research Associate in the Participation, Power and Social Change team at the Institute of Development Studies, University of Sussex, UK. He is an undisciplined social scientist with field experience mainly in east Africa and south Asia. He works on Community-led Total Sanitation and other aspects of development.

Yuping Chen is Professor in Agricultural Economics at Zhongnan University of Economics and Law, China. She received her PhD from Huazhong Agricultural University, China, and her Master's degree from Poznan Agricultural University, Poland. She specializes in agricultural technology extension and poverty reduction in rural China.

Ephraim W. Chirwa is Professor of Economics at Chancellor College, University of Malawi. His research interests include agricultural development, farming household economics and agricultural systems, food security, farmer organizations, microfinance and small- and medium-scale enterprises.

Kate Conroy is a development practitioner, with expertise working in monitoring and evaluation, social protection and livelihoods on a number of DFID-funded poverty reduction programmes in sub-Saharan Africa and south-east Asia. Kate currently works as Principal Consultant: Monitoring and Evaluation & Social Development for a leading development consultancy in London.

Lorraine Coulter is a water and livelihoods specialist with the Food Economy Group (FEG). Her work has focused on the linkages between access to water and food and livelihoods security, as well as on disaster risk mitigation, particularly in Ethiopia and the horn of Africa. She currently lives in Washington, DC.

Stephen Devereux is a development economist who works on food security, famine, rural livelihoods and social protection in Africa. He is a Research Fellow at the Institute of Development Studies, University of Sussex, UK, and Honorary Research Fellow at the School of Development Studies, University of KwaZulu-Natal, South Africa.

Shijun Ding is Professor in Agricultural Economics and Rural Development at Zhongnan University of Economics and Law, China. He received his PhD from Huazhong Agricultural University and a two-year PhD course-training programme certificate from Winrock International, USA. His research interests include household economics and poverty reduction in rural China.

Andrew Dorward is Professor of Development Economics in the Centre for Environment, Development and Poverty in the School of Oriental and African Studies, University of London, UK. He has a long-term interest in the importance of seasonality in the livelihoods of rural people.

Sierd Hadley is Policy Advisor, Budget and Economic Affairs in Swaziland's Ministry of Finance. He graduated in Governance and Development from the Institute of Development Studies, University of Sussex, UK and has experience working for, among others, HM Treasury, Action Against Hunger, and the Integrated AIDS Programme, Ndola.

Jennie Hilton is a public health nutritionist who has worked in Africa and south Asia with a focus on linking nutrition outcomes to livelihoods interventions and infant and young child feeding. She is currently the Nutrition Adviser for Save the Children in Myanmar.

Steve Jennings has a background in tropical rainforest ecology and natural resource management. He joined Oxfam shortly after the Indian Ocean tsunami, and has worked on livelihoods and climate change adaptation. In 2010, he was appointed Director of Programme Policy, where he leads Oxfam's research, technical advisory and publications functions.

Dee Jupp is a freelance social development consultant who has lived and worked for extensive periods in Bangladesh and Jamaica. Her recent work has focused on enhancing citizens' voice and understanding the perspectives of people living in poverty through Reality Check Approaches which involve immersion in villages in Indonesia, Bangladesh and Mozambique.

Seifu Kebede is Assistant Professor of Hydrogeology at Addis Ababa University. His research focuses on using isotope and geochemical tools in tracing the origin of groundwater and its flow and recharge as well as groundwater–surface water interaction. He is also interested in groundwater management in arid, semi-arid and mountain settings.

Anirudh Krishna is Professor of Public Policy and Political Science at Duke University. His research investigates how poor communities and individuals in developing countries cope with the structural and personal constraints that result in poverty and powerlessness. His most recent book is *One Illness Away: How People Escape Poverty and Become Poor.*

Mark Lawrence is a co-founder of the Food Economy Group, a consultancy firm specializing in the use of livelihoods analysis in famine early warning systems design, emergency assessment, programme planning, and monitoring and evaluation.

Michael Loevinsohn, a Research Fellow at the Institute of Development Studies, University of Sussex, UK, is an ecologist and epidemiologist. Issues at the intersection of environmental change and health have long held his interest, including the impact of pesticides on farmer mortality in Green Revolution Asia and of climatic warming on malaria in the east African highlands.

Michael Lokshin is a Lead Economist in the Poverty and Inequality team in the Development Research Group of the World Bank. His research focuses on applied micro-economics and econometrics. He has published numerous papers on the analysis of poverty and inequality, health and labour economics, migration and applied econometrics.

Richard Longhurst trained as an agricultural economist at London and Cornell Universities, starting a longstanding interest in food policy, nutrition and development, followed by a DPhil in development economics at Sussex University. He has been a staff member for FAO, Ford Foundation, Commonwealth Secretariat and ILO. He is now a Research Associate at the Institute of Development Studies, University of Sussex, UK.

Eva Ludi is a Research Fellow at the Overseas Development Institute. She has over fifteen years of experience in policy-oriented research on sustainable rural development, natural resource governance, climate change adaptation, and climate change, water and food security. She has done extensive research in Ethiopia, east Africa and central Asia.

John Magrath is a writer and researcher who has worked for Oxfam for 26 years in a variety of roles including Press Officer, Executive Assistant to the Director and researcher on climate change impacts and implications for Oxfam's work. As Programme Researcher he is currently working on renewable energy issues.

Edoardo Masset is a Research Fellow at the Institute of Development Studies, University of Sussex, UK. He is an agricultural economist with interests ranging from poverty analysis to hunger and malnutrition, rural development and the impact evaluation of development interventions.

Sergiy Radyakin is an economist in the research department of the World Bank, with interests in labour, family and development economics. He holds an MA degree in economics from the University of British Columbia and since joining the World Bank in 2007 has worked primarily on developing software for economic analysis.

Charles Rethman has worked in southern Sudan, Somalia, Tanzania and Malawi, and is presently a consultant with Masdar, seconded to the Southern African Development Community's Regional Vulnerability Assessment and Analysis Programme. He provides technical support for measuring hunger and poverty to SADC's 15 member states and their Vulnerability Assessment Committees.

Rachel Sabates-Wheeler is a Research Fellow and the Director of the Centre for Social Protection at the Institute of Development Studies, University of Sussex, UK. With over 15 years of experience working on themes of rural development, social policy and migration, she has published on issues of rural institutions; poverty, vulnerability and agriculture; and social protection.

Anna Taylor is the Senior Nutrition Adviser at the UK Department for International Development, providing support to scaling up the UK's multisectoral programme to tackle undernutrition. She was previously Head of Hunger Reduction for Save the Children UK, leading a team of experts to deliver the organizational hunger strategy across development and humanitarian contexts.

Cecilia Turin, professor at the Universidad Nacional Agraria La Molina, Peru and PhD candidate in the Department of Rural Sociology, University of Missouri, USA, holds degrees in animal and social sciences. Her interdisciplinary research over 15 years focuses on the governance of natural resources, collective action, gender, and livelihood strategies in peasant communities of the Andes.

Corinne Valdivia is Associate Professor in the Department of Agricultural and Applied Economics, University of Missouri, USA. Her research and outreach, informed by sustainable livelihoods, focuses on changing rural communities, with interdisciplinary collaborative and participatory research on knowledge and action for adaptation in the Andes, east Africa and the USA.

Marcella Vigneri is a development economist specializing in the empirical analysis of smallholder livelihoods, with a focus on cash-crop production and food security issues in west and southern Africa. She is currently affiliated with the Centre for the Study of African Economies at Oxford University, where she collaborates with IFPRI-Ghana.

Catherine Vignon is a development practitioner with management experience of livelihoods programmes in sub-Saharan Africa, south and central Asia, financed by DFID, the European Commission and the World Bank. Her expertise covers social protection, rural development and climate change adaptation. She currently works for an environmental consultancy in Lyon, France.

Haitao Wu is a lecturer in agricultural economics at Zhongnan University of Economics and Law, China. He received his PhD from the same university. His research specializes in the analysis of poverty dynamics.

Belay Zeleke is a water resource engineer, who has received his first degree from Arba Minch University, Ethiopia, and is currently pursuing an M.Tech in Water Resource Engineering at IIT-Roorkee, India. He has also worked in the Ethiopian Ministry of Water and Energy for four years.

ACRONYMS AND ABBREVIATIONS

ACF	Action Contre la Faim
AMP	Alaba-Mareko lowland Pepper livelihood zone
BGS	British Geological Survey
BMI	body mass index
BPA	Bale Pastoral livelihood zone
BRAC	Bangladesh Rural Advancement Committee
CDO	Community Development Organizer
CFW	Cash for Work
CHF	Community Housing Fund International
CLP	Chars Livelihoods Programme
CoD	Cost of the Diet
CRSP	Collaborative Research Support Programme
DHS	Demographic and Health Survey
DRMFSS	Disaster Risk Management and Food Security Sector (Ethiopia)
ECD	early childhood development
ERHS	Ethiopian Rural Household Survey
FEWS NET	Famine Early Warning Systems Network
HABP	Household Asset-Building Programme (Ethiopia)
HAZ	height-for-age-score
HEA	Household Economy Approach
IDS	Institute of Development Studies
IEP	Infrastructure and Employment Programme
IFAD	International Fund for Agricultural Development
IHS	Integrated Household Survey
IMO	Implementing Organization
ISDR	International Strategy on Disaster Risk
ITCZ	Inter-Tropical Convergence Zone

LBSS	Livelihood Baseline Storage Spreadsheet
LIAS	Livelihood Impact Analysis Spreadsheet
LIU	Livelihoods Integration Unit
MoARD	Ministry of Agriculture and Rural Development (Ethiopia)
NCO	National Classification of Occupation codes
NFHS	India National Family Health Survey
NSSO	National Sample Survey Organization of India
OLS	ordinary least squares
ORT	oral rehydration therapy
PRA	Participatory rural appraisal
PSNP	Productive Safety Net Programme (Ethiopia)
RiPPLE	Research-inspired Policy and Practice Learning in Ethiopia and the Nile Region
SANREM	Sustainable Agriculture and National Resource Management
SAP	Lowland Shinile Agro-Pastoral livelihood zone
SDC	Swiss Agency for Development and Cooperation
SIMI	Systeme d'Information sur les Marches Agricoles (Niger)
SMC	Sorghum, Maize and Chat livelihood zone
SNNPR	Southern Nations, Nationalities and Peoples Region
SRM	Social Risk Management
USAID	United States Agency for International Development
WBP	Wheat, Barley and Potato livelihood zone
WELS	Water Economy for Livelihoods
WFP	World Food Programme
WIAS	Water Impact Analysis Sheet
WSS	water and sanitation sector

ACKNOWLEDGEMENTS

This book draws on papers presented at the conference 'Seasonality Revisited', which was convened by the Future Agricultures Consortium, together with the Centre for Social Protection, on 8-10 July 2009, at the Institute of Development Studies in Brighton. Funded by Ukaid from the Department for International Development (DFID), the Future Agricultures Consortium is an international partnership of research institutions, working together to encourage critical debate and policy dialogue on the challenges of establishing and sustaining pro-poor agricultural growth in Africa. The editors thank Judy Hartley for expert proofreading, Lance Bellars for improving several diagrams, and Tim Hardwick, our patient and supportive publisher.

FOREWORD

As a dimension of poverty, seasonality is as glaringly obvious as it is still grossly neglected. Attempts to embed its recognition in professional mindsets, policy and practice have still a long way to go.

There is some history here. The discovery in a seminar at the Institute of Development Studies (IDS), University of Sussex in the mid-1970s that births peaked towards the end of the rains both in rural Bangladesh and in northern Nigeria, raised intriguing questions and opened up the whole subject. Many seasonal deprivations and stresses were recognized to coincide during the tropical rains – hard work, lack of food, shortage of money and vulnerability to debt, sicknesses, isolation and lack of access to services and markets, among others. To explore and learn more about these and other dimensions, and how they inter-linked, a conference was held at IDS in July 1978. This was convened jointly by Richard Longhurst and myself from IDS and David Bradley and Richard Feachem from the London School of Hygiene and Tropical Medicine. *Seasonal Dimensions to Rural Poverty* (Chambers *et al.*, 1981) brought together the edited papers. These were contributions mainly from specialized professional perspectives with sections on climatic seasonality, energy relationships and food, economic relationships and the seasonal use of labour, the seasonal ecology of disease, patterns of births and death, family health and seasonal welfare, and the social distribution of seasonal burdens. The overarching concerns were to see how these coincided and were connected, and to identify what might be done. We saw that the rains were when many people were poorest and most vulnerable to becoming poorer.

We hoped that once and for all *Seasonal Dimensions to Rural Poverty* would place seasonality firmly in the minds of professionals and on the agenda of policy and practice. The hope was in vain. Several books and an *IDS Bulletin* with seasonality as a theme were indeed published (Longhurst, 1986; Sahn, 1989; Chen, 1991; Gill, 1991; Ulijaszek and Strickland, 1993), but their impact was limited. Throughout the three decades since the 1978 conference seasonality remained largely a professional and policy blind spot. By 2008, however, work on food security and social protection was again placing seasonality on the agenda, notably through *Seasons of Hunger* (Devereux *et al.*, 2008) with its insight that 'seasonal hunger is the father of famine'.

It was time for another conference – to review changes, introduce new perspectives, propose actions, and more decisively and lastingly, if possible, to raise professional awareness and enhance policy relevance. The Seasonality Revisited conference was convened at the Institute of Development Studies in July 2009. The chapters that follow are edited from the papers presented.

The 1978 conference and book were strong on health and technical aspects of nutrition, and much of that still applies. With the second conference, old topics like migration were updated and new topics reflected changes that have taken place since – notably HIV and AIDS vulnerabilities and disabilities, policy interventions such as social protection, and innovations in monitoring livelihoods for enhanced understanding of seasonality. In the 2009 conference, social protection and food security moved centre stage. Neither of these terms was in use in 1978. But the most fundamental new topic is climate change-affecting seasons, threatening radical changes for agriculture and possibly almost everything else.

Changes since 1978

Generalizations about adverse seasonality have always been open to exceptions. As recognized in 1978, conditions and experiences of seasonality vary by location, occupation, gender, wealth and poverty, age, caste and class, and control of resources. Further, generalizations seem more difficult now than they were in 1978. There have been major demographic changes, not least in increasing urbanization and the rising numbers of poor people in urban areas. But in its many varied forms, seasonality for poor people – urban or rural, farmers, labourers or in other occupations – remains both significant and neglected.

Significant trends and changes have affected adverse seasonalities since the 1970s. On the positive side, access to markets and health services has improved in many countries. Seasonal isolation is still prevalent but has diminished: networks of all-weather roads in many countries penetrate further into rural hinterlands. Mobile phones have dramatically improved communications with many innovations: M-Pesa in Kenya and neighbouring countries, for instance, enables instant transfers of money even to 'remote' areas. Where people are now less poor, so they are less vulnerable to seasonal stresses. Counter-seasonal and relief programmes for poorer and more marginalized people, and social protection more broadly, have improved, transformed and spread, as evident in this book – not least the employment guarantee schemes of India, now spreading to other countries. Immunization programmes have achieved wider coverage. Polio and Guinea worm disease, the latter so devastating to communities precisely when they need to cultivate, have been eliminated or nearly eliminated in most of the world. Malaria, for all that it remains a scourge, has sharply declined on the east African coast.[1] And when stresses and shocks are so interlinked, the weakening or elimination of any one can diminish vulnerability to others and enhance resilience.

All the same, much has not changed. Seasonal shortages, stress and price scissors still screw poor rural people down in poverty, and shocks of accidents and illness have sudden downward ratchet effects from which people may not recover. In rural areas during tropical rainy seasons, many of the adverse factors continue to interlock: hard work, sickness, lack of food, poverty of time and energy, shortage of money, isolation and lack of access to markets and services still combine to make these times of multiple stresses and vulnerability for poor people.

Other conditions for poor rural people have worsened. Structural adjustment in many countries reduced rural access to education and health services, and led to a decline in maintenance of roads. Liberalization policies imposed on African countries reduced or eliminated subsidies and uniform pricing regimes. These had supported farmers and rural people throughout the year and had moderated adverse seasonal price scissor effects for selling crops and purchasing food. Liberalization in one country made it unviable for its neighbours to maintain subsidies and price supports because of cross-border leakage. Though these trends have been partially reversed, for example in Malawi, they still generally prevail. In many parts of Africa, a seasonal increase in theft is reported. Climate change has already had an impact, not just through warming, but also as shown in this book through rainy seasons becoming less reliable in their onset and end, and by bringing more intense rainfall at wider intervals. The long-term implications of these trends for agricultural livelihoods, especially in the semi-arid tropics, are serious. Even with adaptations of farming and cropping systems, they will make agriculture more risky and less viable for many, and are liable to reduce the production of food and non-food crops. For climatic seasonal effects on other dimensions of seasonality like disease, the patterns will be varied and are not always easy to foresee.

For the future

Past neglect means present and future potential. In 2011 we are in a stronger position to exploit that potential than we were in 1978. Three points stand out to put seasonality higher on the agenda and keep it there.

The first is better recognition that it can be more cost-effective as well as more humane to use counter-seasonal measures to prevent poor people becoming poorer, rather than trying to help them struggle back up again once they have become poorer. But more research needs to be done to identify those measures that are most effective, and most cost-effective.

The second is social protection. There is now much discussion of counter-seasonal programmes (Hauenstein Swan et al., 2009) such as price-indexed cash transfers and seasonal employment programmes. Social protection as a concept can also be extended to transport infrastructure, access to markets, and livelihoods.

Given the seasonality of sickness and the frequency with which seasonal sickness makes poor people poorer, effective, accessible and affordable health services can be recognized for what they are – a critical form of social protection.

The third, paradoxically, is climate change and its meteoric rise as a concern and priority. The links between climate change, seasonal disruption and agriculture can serve to draw attention to related seasonal vulnerabilities like sickness, hunger, isolation, stress and becoming poorer.

So this book is a standing invitation to development professionals, policymakers and academics. It is an invitation to enhance the relevance of their work to the reduction of poverty and illbeing. It is an invitation to explore seasonal dimensions in many disciplines, domains and specializations. It is an invitation to share the excitement of aha! moments on discovering how different dimensions interlink. Seasonality, like sustainable livelihoods, is a common ground for many disciplines. It can sharpen the relevance of research and action. Poor rural people who experience negative and positive seasonalities know a great deal about them. Those of us who are neither rural nor poor have much to learn. Let me hope that many will be inspired by these pages to be sensitive to seasonal realities and join in the learning, and to see things and do things differently. May seasonality never again be so overlooked. And may this book inform and inspire many to work to banish avoidable seasonal suffering and poverty from our world.

Robert Chambers
2 April 2011

Note

1 The incidence of malaria in Kilifi District on the Kenya coast has dropped to one-fifth of its level five or six years ago and there have been declines all along the east African coast (conversation at the Kenya Medical Research Institute, Kilifi, February 2009).

1

Seasonality revisited

New perspectives on seasonal poverty

Stephen Devereux, Rachel Sabates-Wheeler and Richard Longhurst

What is seasonality and why does it matter?

Seasonality refers to any regular pattern or variation that is correlated with the seasons. 'Adverse seasonality' describes the potentially damaging consequences for human wellbeing of seasonal fluctuations in the weather, and the full range of its associated impacts on lives and livelihoods. Seasonality was a fashionable theme in development studies from the late 1970s to early 1990s, a period when policy-makers and researchers were more interested in tropical agriculture and rural development than they are today. A landmark event was the conference on 'Seasonal Dimensions to Rural Poverty' held at the Institute of Development Studies (IDS) in Brighton in July 1978, which resulted in an eponymous book (Chambers *et al.*, 1981) and an *IDS Bulletin* (Longhurst, 1986a). Several other books on seasonality followed, including *Seasonal Variability in Third World Agriculture* (Sahn, 1989), *Seasonality and Agriculture in the Developing World* (Gill, 1991), and *Seasonality and Human Ecology* (Ulijaszek and Strickland, 1993).

All these publications identified and provided evidence for a similar set of insights: that climatic seasonality shapes and structures rural lives and livelihoods in the tropics in profound but often negative ways; that consistent patterns in these impacts can be discerned across countries as diverse and distant as Bangladesh and Zambia; and that development interventions must account for seasonality in their design and implementation, or they will be compromised and could even fail.

Sometime in the early 1990s, research and policy interest in seasonality faded away. Perhaps the main reason was a precipitate decline (recently partly reversed) in public investment in agriculture, as governments were discouraged by the prevailing neoliberal orthodoxy from intervening directly in the productive economic sectors, and policymakers shifted their focus to the social sectors instead. A related factor may have been the challenges of implementing effective interventions to counteract the adverse effects of seasonality – especially in the constrained public policy space of the 1990s. On the one hand, factoring seasonality into policy design adds to the complexity of project planning and implementation, requiring inter-sectoral collaboration and joint programming (between agriculture and health, for instance) which is notoriously difficult to achieve. On the other hand, many counter-seasonal measures that were already in place (such as price stabilization and grain reserves) were abolished by the liberalization policies of the 1980s and 1990s, which left governments with very few levers to protect lives and livelihoods in households vulnerable to seasonality. In retrospect, advocacy for seasonality may have had a stronger impact if there had been more sustained efforts to draw attention to the problems that followed the withdrawal of these seasonally sensitive policies.

Of course, just because policymakers forgot about seasonality does not mean it went away. Many of the lessons learned three decades ago remain relevant and accurate today. So what did we learn from the seasonality research of the 1980s?

A defining insight of *Seasonal Dimensions to Rural Poverty*, edited by Robert Chambers, Richard Longhurst and Arnold Pacey (1981), was that several seasonal aspects of life in tropical countries contribute to creating and reproducing poverty, especially among smallholder farming families. These 'dimensions' were summarized in a scenario that was found to be generalizable across regions that have pronounced – especially unimodal – seasonality in rainfall.

> most of the very poor people in the world live in tropical areas with marked wet and dry seasons. Especially for the poorer people, women and children, the wet season before the harvest is usually the most critical time of year. At that time adverse factors often overlap and interact: food is short and food prices high; physical energy is needed for agricultural work; sickness is prevalent, especially malaria, diarrhoea and skin infections; child care, family hygiene, and cooking are neglected by women overburdened with work; and late pregnancy is common, with births peaking near harvest. This is a time of year marked by loss of body weight, low birth weights, high neonatal mortality, malnutrition, and indebtedness. It is the hungry season and the sick season. It is the time of year when poor people are at their poorest and most vulnerable to becoming poorer.
>
> (Chambers *et al.*, 1981, p*xv*)

Evidence for seasonal fluctuations in food prices, agricultural wage rates, infectious diseases, birth weights and other indicators was presented from several countries of Africa and south Asia. Affected households were shown to adopt damaging 'coping mechanisms', including seasonal migration and taking high-interest loans. Robert Chambers argued that seasonality is 'unobserved' by officials and researchers because of 'tarmac bias', 'activity bias', 'irrigation bias' and 'dry season bias', but he expressed the hope that the book would raise awareness and 'help to identify feasible measures [to address] seasonal hardship and impoverishment' (Chambers *et al.*, 1981, p6).

A workshop that followed up the 1978 conference resulted in an *IDS Bulletin* titled 'Seasonality and poverty' (Longhurst, 1986a). This *Bulletin* focused on how seasonality affects poor people, how they respond to it and how they can be assisted. One lesson for policymakers was that seasonal 'coping strategies' need to be better understood, since effective policies should build on what people do already. The role of women in 'coping' was found to be vital. Ownership of assets – broadly defined to include land, livestock, crops in store, trees, jewellery and social assets such as membership of food-sharing networks – was also identified as crucial for negotiating seasonality, because 'asset buffers' can lift families above a threshold level that protects them against seasonal poverty ratchets. Finally, researchers were advised to take an interdisciplinary perspective and exploit the linkages that exist between our knowledge of natural resources, economic phenomena and social relationships. Rural people experience seasons in a holistic manner, and professional outsiders should do the same.

A conference focusing on seasonality in household food security produced a book titled *Seasonal Variability in Third World Agriculture*, edited by David Sahn (1989), which documented research on grain marketing and price variability, employment, and the role of technology. Findings confirmed the scenario identified in the 1978 IDS conference. Seasonality creates imbalances between energy intake (food consumption), energy expenditure (on-farm and off-farm labour) and food availability (in granaries and local markets), causing seasonal hunger and malnutrition. Contributors emphasized the need to ascertain what policies need to be pursued to reduce variations in food production, work, incomes and prices. Policies were considered in two groups: untargeted projects and policies that address problems of transitory food insecurity, including price stabilization, infrastructure and technological change and agricultural research; and targeted interventions, generally designed to mitigate directly the consequences of household food insecurity. The latter group were clustered as those policies that generate income through productive work (e.g. labour-intensive public works and home gardens), those that transfer income directly to the household (food stamps and food rations), and those that affect prices faced by market-dependent consumers (e.g. food price subsidies).

Seasonality and Agriculture in the Developing World (Gill, 1991) offers a multidisciplinary 'systems' approach. Gill develops an analytical model for examining the impact of seasonality on household income and consumption. Seasonality affects the variance around the mean of incomes, which are respectively higher and lower in developing countries than in richer countries. Moreover, a high variance occasionally trips a mechanism that pushes down mean income, and a falling mean income tends to increase intra-annual variance. Gill suggests that two basic linkages are at work. First, seasonal variations in income impose costs, reducing the proportion of gross income available to meet basic consumption needs. The second linkage is less direct: people who are better off in terms of wealth or social status are able to pass on seasonal stresses to those who are worse off, either temporarily (by appropriating consumption goods in the hungry season) or permanently (by acquiring investment goods). Finally, Gill discusses biases in policy formulation and the problems of collecting suitable seasonally disaggregated information. He examines land reform, mechanization, labour migration and market failures, all from a seasonal perspective.

Seasonality and Human Ecology, edited by Stanley Ulijaszek and S.S. Strickland (1993), is a collection of edited papers from a symposium at Cambridge University of the Society for the Study of Human Biology, which examined the ways in which seasonality influences human biology and behaviour. Contributions from biologists, physiologists, nutritionists and anthropologists confirm that human groups are 'enormously sensitive' to seasonal cycles within their ecosystems. Systematic seasonal effects are observed in fertility, physical growth in children, infectious diseases (including malaria, measles, dysentery and diarrhoea) and mortality rates (in temperate as well as tropical climates). Finally, several chapters explore seasonal aspects of food security and nutrition. Globally, seasonal nutritional stress was found to be highest in parts of Sahelian Africa (Burkina Faso, the Gambia, Sudan, Ethiopia, Kenya) and India, where the rainfall seasonality index is highest and nutrition status at that time was lowest.

Fifteen years later, *Seasons of Hunger* (by Stephen Devereux, Bapu Vaitla and Samuel Hauenstein Swan, 2008) drew attention to the fact that seasonal hunger persists but continues to be neglected, even though it is predictable and the causes are well understood. This monograph focuses on policy responses to hunger, from the Famine Codes in colonial India to emergency relief in Africa, and proposes a set of social protection measures to combat seasonal hunger and prevent the need for emergency interventions. The 'minimum essential package' includes community-based management of acute malnutrition, seasonal employment guarantee schemes, social pensions, and child growth promotion. Where feasible, these interventions should be complemented by weather-indexed agricultural insurance schemes, price banding and strategic grain reserves. The authors conclude by arguing that freedom from hunger should be legally enforced at the global level through a justiciable international right to food.

Insights from the last 20 years

Evidence of the damaging consequences of seasonality continued to be reported during the 1990s and 2000s, although not as systematically as in the 1980s. Most of this newer evidence reinforced earlier findings on the seasonality of poverty (Dercon and Krishnan, 1998; Dostie *et al.*, 2002), of nutrition status (Hoorweg *et al.*, 1995), of infectious diseases (Ferro-Luzzi *et al.*, 2001; Kale *et al.*, 2004), and of interactions between illness and poverty (Chuma *et al.*, 2006). Several studies concluded that the adverse consequences of seasonality fall disproportionately on women (Hopkins *et al.*, 1994; Devereux *et al.*, 2006) and children (Masudi *et al.*, 2001; Beegle *et al.*, 2005; Macours and Vakis, 2010). Behavioural responses to seasonality include migration (Hampshire, 2002; de Haan *et al.*, 2002; Deshingkar and Start, 2003; Smita, 2008), anti-social behaviour such as theft (Osborne, 2000; Chiwona-Karltun *et al.*, 2009), and the adoption of potentially harmful 'coping strategies' (de Merode *et al.*, 2003; Orr *et al.*, 2009). Note that this review is not exhaustive; the intention instead is to highlight new evidence on selected themes.

Poverty

A study from Madagascar in the early 2000s reported the same patterns of adverse seasonality that were identified by researchers in many other countries during the 1970s and 1980s. An estimated one million Malagasy are pushed below the poverty line during the lean season each year, joining nine million who are chronically poor. Most of this seasonal poverty is concentrated in rural areas, where food prices fluctuate by about 45 per cent over the year compared to just 17 per cent in Antananarivo, the capital city. Seasonal food shortages, high food prices and infectious diseases (especially diarrhoea and malaria) interact to increase rates of malnutrition and mortality. Over a 12-year period, infant mortality was consistently lowest after the harvest (May–June) when food is abundant and prices are lowest, but it more than tripled by December–January 'when the lean and rainy seasons converge' (Dostie *et al.*, 2002).

Disaggregated data on seasonal poverty are hard to find. This is because there are significant costs to collecting data throughout a year, then analysing and reporting the findings by season. Also, policymakers prefer a single poverty headcount figure to several. A rare exception is a panel survey in Ethiopia which measured poverty at three different times within a one-year period, revealing pronounced variability between seasons. The poverty headcount among 1411 rural households stood at 34.1 per cent in the lean months before the 1994 main harvest, fell by a quarter to 26.9 per cent around harvest time, but rose again to 35.4 per cent in the 1995 lean season (Dercon and Krishnan, 1998). Seasonal fluctuations in poverty were lower in communities near to towns and with better access to roads, and among households with more physical assets and human capital – confirming that seasonality affects poor and isolated rural households most severely. This sensitivity of poverty prevalence to the time of year that surveys are conducted – let alone to harvest variability between years – highlights the often overlooked fact that seasonality complicates reporting on 'average' poverty rates and, especially, estimates of trends in rural poverty over time.

Health and nutrition

A study of 'Seasons and nutrition at the Kenya coast' (Hoorweg *et al.*, 1995) found that seasonal variations in nutritional status were most pronounced among children and the elderly. Intriguingly, although poorer individuals had the lowest energy intakes, seasonal weight loss was only weakly affected by wealth (lower-income households were actually better able to smooth consumption across the year), but was strongly determined by cropping patterns (food consumption varied more among maize producers than cassava producers) and by access to wage employment at critical times of year. Local farming families depend on market purchases of food in seasons when their granary stocks are low, and they earn income to buy food mainly from wage employment. Household labour power and availability of employment opportunities dictate the effectiveness of this diversification strategy – relying on market purchases to compensate for diminishing food stocks late in the agricultural year – across households and between years.

Diarrhoeal diseases remain a major health risk in tropical countries, especially for children. A study in Ethiopia found that, 'for young children, seasonal weight loss appears to be much more strongly associated with seasonal patterns of diarrhoeal disease than with seasonal changes in food availability in the household' (Ferro-Luzzi *et al.*, 2001, p*ix*). Bacterial diarrhoea occurs mainly during wet and warm seasons. Rotavirus infections cause acute watery diarrhoea, which kills between 600,000 and 870,000 infants in developing countries every year (Kale *et al.*, 2004), though this might be falling due to increased uptake of oral rehydration therapy (ORT). Undernutrition raises susceptibility to infection, so child deaths from diarrhoea are concentrated in the hungry season and in poor families.

Cross-country data reveal that malaria and poverty are mutually reinforcing. Average GDP per capita is five times higher in countries where malaria is not endemic, and economic growth rates are 1.3 per cent lower in countries where malaria is endemic, after controlling for factors such as human capital and initial income (Chuma *et al.*, 2006). At the household level, poor people are least able to take preventive measures and to access effective treatment. One study in Kenya found that poor households that experienced major malaria episodes fell deeper into poverty, whereas wealthier households were better able to cope without damaging losses of assets and income (Chuma *et al.*, 2006).

Gender

The adverse effects of seasonal variation are gendered. A survey of 960 farming households in highland Ethiopia in 2006 found that self-reported food shortage peaks during the pre-harvest months of June–August and drops to its lowest level following the main annual harvest in October–November. Moreover, food insecurity is consistently higher among female-headed households, peaking at 68 per cent in July 2006, when it also affected 57 per cent of male-headed households, but dropping to 9 per cent of female-headed and just 3 per cent of male-headed households in November (Devereux *et al.*, 2006).

At the intra-household level, survey data from Niger, disaggregated by season and by gender, reveals that the gender of income earners is an important determinant of seasonal spending on food and non-food items. Spending on food peaks in the pre-harvest rainy season, and is the responsibility of both women and men. Women's incomes are lower than men's, and men also have access to stored grain and to dry season income from seasonal migration. Conversely, women are constrained in their access to credit and savings. This means that women in rural Niger are less able than men to smooth food consumption across seasons (Hopkins *et al.*, 1994, p1225).

Children

Adverse seasonality is bad for children's health, education and nutrition. A study from rural Tanzania found that children are especially susceptible to malaria and diarrhoea, but also to typhoid and cholera, during the rainy season, and to colds, coughing and influenza during the dusty dry season. Drinking water is contaminated during the wet season and scarce during the dry season, causing water to be rationed, with adverse consequences for health and hygiene. School attendance drops during the rains, because paths and roads become degraded making it difficult to get to school, because granaries are empty so children are too hungry to learn, and because children are needed to work on the farm. In tobacco-growing areas, the agricultural labour force is dominated by children, who can work up to 18 hours a day during the picking and curing season (Masudi *et al.*, 2001). The combination of seasonal malnutrition, illness and disrupted education compromises the lifetime potential of affected children and contributes to the intergenerational transmission of poverty.

Seasonality increases the demand for child labour. Poor households and those facing significant income variability are more likely to draw on family members (including children) than hired labour for farming, small business and domestic work. Children in poor rural households with no access to credit are more likely to be withdrawn from school (Beegle *et al.*, 2005).

Migration

Seasonal migration, especially by young men in search of work, is often a response to a lack of local employment opportunities in the dry season, but it is risky and expensive. In West Africa, the income remitted by the poorest migrants is sometimes outweighed by the travel and search costs, as well as weakened social networks back home (Hampshire, 2002). Migrants from middle-income and better-off households are more likely to be successful, because they can invest more in looking for work, their households tend to be larger and have labour capacity to spare, and they can draw on relatives and friends in destination communities for advice and support (de Haan *et al.*, 2002). A study of seasonal migration in India focused on the challenges that this creates for access to services and to support from government programmes: 'outside their home areas, migrants have no entitlements to livelihood support systems or formal welfare schemes' (Deshingkar and Start, 2003, p*vi*; see also Sabates-Wheeler and Feldman, 2011).

Seasonal migration is an important response to seasonal underemployment, but evidence suggests that it can undermine early childhood development (ECD). An empirical study found 'a negative correlation between seasonal migration and ECD outcomes for children of pre-school age', implying that 'children of seasonal migrants tend to have a human capital disadvantage even before entering primary school' (Macours and Vakis, 2010, p861). 'Distress seasonal migration' affects an estimated nine million children in India (Smita, 2008).

'Coping strategies'

Seasonal stress can provoke anti-social behaviour, such as stealing from neighbours. Theft of beans from fields during the pre-harvest hungry season has been observed in Ethiopia (Chiwona-Karltun *et al.*, 2009). But this is not a recent phenomenon. Crime statistics from nineteenth-century England reveal that winter was associated with spikes in criminal activities related to food. Most people prosecuted for poaching were seasonal agricultural labourers, and poaching occurred mostly between October and March, when 'demand for farm labour was slackest and therefore poverty most acute' (Osborne, 2000, p28).

Earlier publications on seasonality drew attention to the role of 'coping strategies' to mitigate its worst effects (Longhurst, 1986a). A recent study points out that rigorous empirical evidence for the existence of seasonal poverty traps is 'surprisingly hard to find in development literature' (Orr *et al.*, 2009, p228), and argues that this might be because affected people have developed effective mechanisms for adjusting to seasonality. For instance, farmers in Bangladesh who have no draught animals nonetheless manage to prepare their rice fields on time during the planting season, because an efficient market exists that allows them to borrow or hire draught power from others. In the Democratic Republic of Congo, consumption of bush meat doubles during the lean season when supplies of harvested crops are exhausted, and selling wild foods becomes an important source of supplementary income (de Merode *et al.*, 2003). Of course, not all behavioural adjustments are as effective as these, and not all vulnerable people have access to them. There are also costs. If Bangladeshi farmers have to labour in other people's fields in return for access to draught power, they might still plant later and harvest lower yields. Counter-seasonal interventions should aim to ensure that people do not have to resort to such damaging 'coping strategies'.

New drivers of adverse seasonality

Despite the persistence of adverse seasonality, a great deal changed in the three decades between the 'Seasonal Dimensions' conference in 1978 and the 'Seasonality Revisited' conference in 2009, and many of these changes have had profound implications for rural livelihoods and development. Three of the main drivers of 'adverse seasonality' that became prominent after the 1980s are:

1   climate change;
2   HIV and AIDS;
3   economic liberalization.

First, climate change might be causing the seasons to become more erratic and less favourable to farming families, whose livelihoods depend on predictable rainfall through the growing season (see Magrath and Jennings, this volume). Most climate change scenarios generate pessimistic projections for agricultural yields in tropical and subtropical regions. Lower and more variable rainfall will lead to falling aggregate crop production, which will increase food insecurity in the absence of effective adaptation. Sub-Saharan Africa is especially sensitive to climate change, partly because less than 10 per cent of arable land is irrigated, while poverty and seasonality limit the capacity of smallholder households to self-insure or to invest in strategies to smooth consumption. One calculation estimates that falling rainfall and rising temperatures since 1960 already explain two-thirds of the gap in agricultural production between sub-Saharan Africa and other regions (Barrios *et al.*, 2008).When harvests fail due to erratic rainfall or extreme weather events, the food crises that follow are seasonal in that they peak just before the next harvest – they are severe 'hungry seasons' that differ from famines only in scale and intensity (Devereux, 2010). Climate change is likely to increase the frequency and intensity of seasonal food crises, especially but not only in Africa.

A second vulnerability factor that emerged in the 1980s is HIV and AIDS, which cuts lives short and compromises livelihoods in multiple ways (see Loevinsohn, this volume). Although seasonality is a 'short-wave dynamic' while the AIDS epidemic is a 'long-wave phenomenon', AIDS has enormous potential 'to amplify the adverse short-term effects of seasonality on food security' (Gillespie and Drimie, 2009, p5). Mutually reinforcing negative interactions between AIDS and seasonality have been observed in individual nutritional status, energy requirements from work and infection, time and resources for childcare, presence of infections and parasites (which decrease immune response in HIV-negative persons and increase viral load in HIV-positive persons), and access to health clinics. Smallholder agriculture is labour-intensive, and loss of food and income from farming due to HIV infection can lead to increased dependence on casual work and damaging 'coping strategies' such as asset sales or transactional sex. A consolidated response to the coexistence of HIV and seasonal hunger requires greater coordination between health, food security and social protection policies.

Third, during the 1980s, structural adjustment programmes that required governments to deregulate and liberalize agricultural production and marketing systems had complex effects on national and household food security. One damaging consequence was that farmers in many countries lost their access to input and output markets at guaranteed prices through parastatal marketing agencies. Input prices rose, often to unaffordable levels, and seasonal food price spikes were magnified. Seasonal hunger worsened in families that were unable to secure their subsistence in the face of weak or missing markets. The removal of government interventions extended to many food security measures, including 'seasonal safety nets' such as: **strategic grain reserves** (parastatals used to store grain and release it to stabilize food supplies and prices during the hungry season); **food pricing policies** (a 'floor' price was set below which parastatals would not purchase produce from farmers and a 'ceiling' price was set above which they would not sell food at any time of year ('pan-seasonal' pricing)); and **input subsidies** (food production was effectively subsidized with below-market prices for fertilizer, seed and credit). The abolition of this 'old social protection agenda' (Devereux, 2009a) raised the vulnerability of smallholders throughout Africa and Asia, at least until markets deepened or governments reasserted their mandate to intervene to protect food security, for instance with the re-emergence of input subsidies in some countries in the mid-2000s. On the other hand, as Turin and Valdivia (Chapter 9) remind us, these interventions were not always pro-poor or pro-rural – in Peru, for instance, they 'systematically supported cheap food for urban centres at the expense of the rural communities'.

Implications for managing seasonality

The regular patterns that seasonality introduces, especially for rural livelihoods, suggest numerous opportunities for interventions. New policy agendas include 'climate-proofing' agriculture, addressing seasonal nutrition and health vulnerabilities, and seasonally sensitive social protection.

'Climate-proofing' agriculture

Given the climate change predictions of increasingly unpredictable rainfall, should investment in agriculture aim to maximize or to stabilize crop yields – or, in Gill's (1991) terminology, raise the mean or reduce the variance? The consensus view seems to be that stabilizing farmers' incomes to smooth their consumption through the year should be prioritized. Christiaensen and Boisvert (2000) argue that instead of investing to increase crop production, policy should focus on irrigation to stabilize agricultural income, and on income diversification to spread seasonal risk. Irrigation has the dual benefit of raising yields and reducing income and consumption variability, for instance by allowing a second crop to be cultivated (JBIC Institute, 2007; Longhurst and Kgomotso, 2009; Masset, this volume).

But irrigation is not always feasible or affordable. In Madagascar, results from field studies and a seasonal multi-market model found that raising the productivity of secondary food crops such as cassava was the most effective intervention to combat seasonal food insecurity (Dostie et al., 2002). The crucial role of cassava as a 'famine crop' that can be stored in the ground and harvested when needed to mitigate seasonal or acute hunger is well known (McKay and Lawson, 2002; Strange, 2009; Loevinsohn, this volume). The International Fund for Agricultural Development (IFAD) endorses a focus on diversification of crops and livelihoods. 'Diversifying income sources, either through production and marketing of non-traditional crops or by more fully exploiting off-farm opportunities, is also necessary as it reduces risk to farmers and can help even out seasonal fluctuations in income and consumption' (IFAD, 2001, p76).

Some writers believe that formal and informal credit markets can play a positive role in seasonal consumption smoothing, while acknowledging the risk that poor households could become indebted (Jacoby and Skoufias, 1998; Pitt and Khandker, 2002). Agencies such as IFAD have promoted seasonal credit through mobile banks in West Africa and elsewhere (Devereux and Longhurst, 2009). Any initiatives to alleviate seasonal cash constraints – both for purchasing agricultural inputs and for meeting essential consumption needs – should be encouraged, provided they do not lead to dangerous levels of indebtedness.

A growing literature on 'climate change adaptation' identifies activities that reduce the risks that climate change introduces into people's lives and livelihoods, especially in rural areas. These range from strategies to reduce climate vulnerability (such as livelihood diversification in drought- or flood-prone areas) or to build household resilience and response capacity (such as improved natural resource management), to managing climate risk at the local level (e.g. by devising community adaptation plans). Mortimore (2009) argues that farmers and pastoralists respond and adapt to four timescales of variability: decadal (long-term), inter-annual (year-to-year), inter-seasonal (rainy and dry seasons) and daily (short-term). With this in mind, 'adaptive social protection' argues that social protection interventions in climate-vulnerable contexts should not simply replace or reinforce reactive coping mechanisms, but should adopt a longer-term perspective that takes into account the changing nature and severity of climate shocks and stresses over time (Davies *et al.*, 2009).

Addressing seasonal nutrition and health vulnerabilities

Ferro-Luzzi *et al.* (2001, p59) identify three interventions to address seasonal under-nutrition. The first is to reduce diarrhoeal disease, which is a primary cause of child wasting and stunting, by improving hygiene practices, infant feeding, water quality and sanitation. Second is to raise awareness of the impact of seasonal energy stress on the incidence of low birth weight. Third is supplementary feeding for pregnant women during the hungry season, which can raise birth weights above the threshold below which the physical and cognitive development of infants is irreversibly impaired.

An empirical study in Ethiopia found that seasonal undernutrition is less prevalent among educated than uneducated adults. 'This result supports investment in education as a long-term solution to seasonal undernutrition' (Ferro-Luzzi *et al.*, 2001, ppix–x). Policy responses in the education sector to support children adversely affected by seasonality include providing school meals or take-home rations during the hungry season to protect their nutrition and promote school attendance (Burbano and Gelli, 2009), and adjusting the school calendar so that it is better synchronized with rural livelihood activities (Hadley, this volume).

As discussed above, undernutrition and disease are inextricably connected, and AIDS is no exception. Gillespie and Drimie (2009, p9) write about 'the vicious cyclical interaction between malnutrition and HIV'. Nutritional support for poor people on HIV treatment needs to recognize the seasonal cycles of food insecurity and other diseases, such as malaria. Social protection mechanisms such as cash transfers could be adjusted seasonally, to compensate for food price spikes and intensified needs for healthcare. Finally, migration is a common response to seasonal livelihood stress, but mobility facilitates the spread of HIV, mainly by increasing risky sexual behaviour. Providing seasonal employment opportunities in rural communities, or a 'right to work' like India's National Rural Employment Guarantee Scheme (discussed below), could reduce HIV transmission by removing the need to migrate.

Seasonally sensitive social protection

The evolving social protection agenda has enormous potential to address seasonality, since adverse seasonality is a predictable risk and social protection aims to deliver predictable assistance for predictable needs. Mechanisms include seasonal employment schemes, weather-indexed crop insurance, village grain banks, and seasonal cash transfers. An unresolved question is whether to provide social assistance all year round or only during the hungry season. For instance, timing public works employment for the pre-harvest months delivers food or cash when it is most needed, but this is also when farmers are working in their fields. A legally enforceable 'right to work', as introduced by the National Rural Employment Guarantee Act in India, addresses this concern by offering every rural household up to 100 days of paid work, whenever needed. Apart from ensuring that an effective and guaranteed employment-based safety net is available on demand, this innovative intervention recognizes that poor rural families face numerous shocks and stresses, not only seasonality (Freeland, 2009).

Some social protection interventions do respond directly to seasonal cycles. In Malawi, grain prices can double within six months of the annual harvest, but poor farmers are often forced into selling their produce for cash needs at low prices immediately after harvest, only to buy it back for food consumption needs at higher prices later in the year. One mechanism to counter this impoverishing food price seasonality is a commodity warranty scheme, which allows farmers to sell their produce to a farmers' organization for a guaranteed higher price that the organization will recover when it resells this produce after storing it for several months (Magombo *et al.*, 2009). If operated at sufficient scale, warranty schemes can help to stabilize local food supplies and prices across seasons. Nonetheless, the 'new social protection agenda' has been criticized for replacing 'old social protection' interventions that corrected for failures of markets to ensure food security (such as strategic grain reserves or price subsidies) with targeted assistance to individuals that compensate for market failures but do not address the structural causes of rural poverty, which include weak markets and adverse seasonality (Devereux, 2009a).

Chapter summaries

This book is structured around four themes: seasonal lives, seasonal livelihoods, seasonal awareness, and seasonal policies. Thematic chapters explore developments since the 1980s that have profound implications for seasonality – climate change, HIV and AIDS, social protection. Case study chapters explore seasonal dimensions of livelihoods in Africa (Ethiopia, Kenya, Malawi), Asia (Bangladesh, China, India) and Latin America (Peru), and policy responses to adverse seasonality (irrigation, migration, seasonally sensitive education). The book also discusses innovative tools for monitoring seasonality for improved response. A summary of each chapter follows.

Seasonal lives

In Chapter 2, John Magrath and Steve Jennings ask a provocative question: 'What happened to the seasons?' The impacts of climate change on agricultural harvests are potentially devastating, but this aspect remains relatively unexplored in the literature. This chapter reports on widespread and consistent perceptions of smallholder farmers from Africa, Asia and Latin America that the timing and distribution of rains are becoming more unpredictable almost everywhere, and that some formerly distinct seasons are disappearing altogether. Recognizing that human memories can be fallible and prone to romanticize the past, the authors present scientific evidence for southern Africa and Bangladesh that these perceptions are supported by meteorological records and by predictions from climate models. 'We conclude that changing seasonality may be one of the major impacts of climate change faced by smallholder farmers in developing countries over the next few decades'. Several adaptation responses are suggested to assist farmers to cope with these changes, including: ensuring farmers have access to reliable weather forecasts; making quick-maturing, heat-tolerant and drought-resistant crops readily available and affordable; improving water management systems; improved food storage systems; gendered adaptation measures (recognizing that women often face the brunt of climatic and environmental stresses); and appropriate social protection interventions.

According to Michael Lokshin and Sergiy Radyakin, 'Research has consistently shown that the month of birth is an important predictor of health outcomes, morbidity and mortality'. In Chapter 3, these authors explore the relationship between birth month and child health, analysing data from India's National Family Health Survey. Significant differences are found in nutrition outcomes between children born in different seasons, with 'monsoon babies' recording persistently worse nutritional deficits than autumn or winter babies. Four possible explanations are tested. The 'nutrition-disease' hypothesis relates birth month to seasonal variations in availability of nutritious foods: poorly nourished mothers have low birth weight babies, while the 'hungry season' monsoon months are also associated with debilitating diseases such as diarrhoea and malaria. The 'socioeconomic' hypothesis suggests that annual cycles related to agriculture – e.g. prevalence of marriages in post-harvest months – might result in conceptions being concentrated at certain times of year. The 'selective survival' hypothesis argues that children born during high mortality months will thrive better – if they survive – than children born at other times. Finally, the 'unplanned pregnancy' hypothesis assumes that parents try to plan births for 'good' seasons, so underweight children are likely to have been unplanned. The authors find convincing evidence only for the 'nutrition-disease' hypothesis. Policy implications include family planning campaigns to time births for seasons when food is abundant and diseases are less prevalent, and adjusting nutritional programmes to account for seasonal variations in environmental conditions.

The synergistic relationship between major communicable diseases such as AIDS and seasonal cycles of livelihood insecurity and hunger has been inadequately researched. In Chapter 4, Michael Loevinsohn explores these complex interactions in the case of Malawi, which has one of the world's highest HIV-prevalence rates and suffered a major seasonal food crisis in 2001–03. Data from health clinics and household surveys reveal that several HIV risk factors intensified during the famine, including distress migration in search of work, early marriages and 'survival sex' by women for cash or food. Just as the famine was unequally distributed across areas and population groups, so was the heightened risk of HIV transmission, which fell disproportionately onto young women from poor rural families in famine-affected districts. HIV prevalence among women attending rural antenatal sites increased by 20 per cent during the crisis, with the steepest rises recorded in districts where hunger was most severe. Loevinsohn concludes that efforts to alleviate seasonal food insecurity and bolster resilience to shocks, such as growing cassava to stabilize food supplies across seasons and in years of low rainfall, could contribute not only to improved household food security but also to AIDS prevention, in Malawi and throughout southern Africa.

Robert Chambers has long argued that seasonality is and remains a neglected topic in development thinking and policy, even though seasonal interlinkages between food shortages, diseases and farm labour requirements were identified as 'ratchets' that perpetuate rural poverty back in the 1970s. Seasonal variability affects most aspects of rural life in the tropics, from food prices to transport to social festivals and access to services. In Chapter 5, Chambers adds several new domains to the list, including accidents (e.g. snake bites), animal sickness, disasters (e.g. cyclones), school absenteeism, funerals, shelter, and open defeca-tion, arguing that seasonal concentrations of these events or issues contribute to illbeing and poverty traps. Reasons for persistent 'season-blindness' in books, journal articles and policy responses include the facts that middle-class urban-based development professionals live 'season-proofed' lives – 'Our roofs do not leak' – and that statistics are rarely disaggregated by season. Opportunities for raising, sustaining and intensifying seasonal awareness among policymakers include visiting rural communities during the rains, ensuring that analyses reflect seasonality (e.g. multidimensional seasonal calendars), monitoring indexed refer-ences to seasonality in publications, and commissioning research into various aspects of seasonality.

Seasonal livelihoods

Seasonality affects farmers' incomes and food security through several effects, including fluctuating food stocks and prices, which often translate into fluctuating food consumption in poor households. These effects even affect the prevalence of poverty – a fact that poverty analysts often fail to take into account. By analysing several rounds of household expenditure survey data in Malawi, Ephraim Chirwa, Andrew Dorward and Marcella Vigneri confirm in Chapter 6 that the timing of interviews is crucial. For farmers who earn most of their income (including food production for subsistence) in a single annual harvest, expenditure and consump-tion measures of poverty rise steadily in the pre-harvest months and fall quite dramatically immediately after the harvest. Interestingly, the range of poverty estimates across seasons is lowest in the tobacco-producing districts of Malawi, implying that cash crop income buffers households against rising food prices, but is highest in urban areas, probably because households that do not produce food are most exposed to seasonal food price fluctuations. The authors conclude that any headcount of poverty or projection of food insecurity that is based on a model that does not take seasonality, location and sources of income into account may lead to biased and unreliable estimates.

The positive effects of irrigation on agricultural production and incomes are well documented. Irrigation allows for increases in cultivated areas and crop yields, both of which raise farm incomes, stimulating local economic activity and reducing rural poverty. In Chapter 7, Edoardo Masset argues that the stabilizing effect of irrigation on seasonal incomes and consumption has been less well analysed. Irrigation protects the main harvest against low or variable rainfall, and can allow a second harvest each year, which smooths income and food consumption across the seasons and enables poor farming households to avoid adopting damaging coping strategies to survive the 'hungry season'. Drawing on household survey data from Andhra Pradesh, Masset finds that expenditure (a proxy for income) is both higher on average and smoother throughout the year for farmers with irrigation. Conversely, 'rural households without access to irrigation are not fully able to insure against seasonal fluctuations', and remain vulnerable to the impoverishing effects of seasonality – though this vulnerability is partly offset by a relatively effective state social safety net. By introducing multiple cropping, irrigation also raises and smooths the incomes of agricultural labourers. 'These results suggest that irrigation generates positive welfare effects by reducing the cost of seasonality'.

Seasonality in China is complicated by the size of the country – there are several agro-climatic zones, from the tropical south to the temperate north. Rural Chinese households have developed strategies to adapt to seasonal variations in agricultural production and economic opportunities, including on-farm and off-farm livelihood diversification, but these strategies have economic and social consequences that are inadequately understood. In Chapter 8, Shijun Ding, Haitao Wu and Yuping Chen explore these issues in subtropical southern China, where a single agricultural season results in seasonal underemployment. Drawing on household diaries and a panel survey of 3300 households over four years, the authors first identify seasonal patterns in household income and expenditure, then analyse the effects of labour migration – an increasingly important counter-seasonal strategy – on patterns of income and consumption. Interestingly, rural–urban or rural–rural migration in search of work reduces seasonal variations in household income, but raises seasonal variations in household expenditure, probably because migrants have higher consumption spending while away from home. Implications are drawn for designing appropriate interventions to smooth seasonality and strengthen rural livelihoods. These include 'policies encouraging seasonal migration for casual work during the agricultural slack season', timely provision of agricultural input loans, and more investment in irrigation.

Shifting the focus to Latin America, in Chapter 9 Cecilia Turin and Corinne Valdivia analyse the relationship between agriculture and seasonal migration in Peru's southern highlands ('Altiplano'). Poverty is widespread in this region, and seasonal labour migration is a forced response to the inability of agricultural livelihoods to generate sufficient food and income for household subsistence all year round. Migration is dominated by men but differentiated by age and location – young adults tend to look for work in towns, but older adults work mainly in agriculture in other rural areas. Women and the elderly, who have fewer income-generating opportunities, are more vulnerable to seasonality. The authors also disaggregate their analysis between lakeside farming communities and mountain pastoralists. Lakeside families are generally less poor, less food insecure and have more options for livelihood diversification, because of their proximity to urban centres. Government policy has generally ignored these poor communities, favouring investment in export-oriented agriculture along the coast – which attracts seasonal workers from the Altiplano and perpetuates underinvestment in that region. The authors also make the interesting point that the absence of men for much of the year debilitates local organizations and undermines community governance – so seasonality also has negative social effects.

Seasonal awareness

The global economic crisis of 2008/09 pushed millions of families into poverty and highlighted the vulnerability of poor people to food price volatility, including seasonal fluctuations in purchasing power and access to food. In Chapter 10, Helene Berton, Jennie Hilton and Anna Taylor point out that market access to food for poor households varies by season, for two reasons: fluctuations in incomes and fluctuations in food prices. High food prices during the pre-harvest 'hungry season' undermine access to food, by reducing the purchasing power of cash and the exchange value of assets, including labour. Save the Children has developed a methodology called 'Cost of the Diet' that monitors market access to food through the year. The 'survival threshold' – the cost of a basic diet – evolves over time to reflect changes in the price of staple foods, often doubling within a single agricultural year before reverting to post-harvest baseline. This indicator forms part of a 'Hunger Monitoring System' that helps to identify who is vulnerable to drops in purchasing power, and when. Systematic monitoring also facilitates appropriate and timely counter-seasonal interventions, such as cash or food transfers, insurance mechanisms, food price management, labour market regulation, and micronutrient supplementation during high-risk months.

Chapters 11, 12 and 13 are conceptually linked by the 'Household Economy Approach'. In Chapter 11, Charles Rethman explains how livelihoods-based vulnerability analysis, notably the 'Household Economy Approach' (HEA), can be used for modelling seasonality in household incomes and access to food. HEA draws data from household surveys as well as participatory techniques, including community timelines and seasonal calendars, to capture data on the different strategies that families from different 'wealth groups' living in distinct 'livelihood zones' pursue to secure their basic needs. Forecasts of 'missing entitlements to food' based on these data tend to be aggregated over a year, but can be – and increasingly are – disaggregated by season, reflecting the reality that many livelihood activities and food sources are seasonal, such as crop production, agricultural labour and livestock trading. For timely interventions, reporting on 'peaks' and 'troughs' is more useful than averages. HEA analysis from Malawi finds that the hungriest time of year for poor rural households is not just before the harvest but at the end of the dry season, before agricultural employment and 'green maize' become available but after own-produced food and income from cash crop sales have dried up. One implication is that interventions to protect food security (e.g. food aid) should be delivered before the 'hungry season' begins.

In Chapter 12, Tanya Boudreau and Mark Lawrence point out that definitions of food security that include the phrase 'at all times' implicitly recognize seasonality. It follows that understanding the annual cycle of rural livelihoods is fundamental for effective programming to promote food security and protect vulnerable lives. In Ethiopia, where seasonality (intra-annual variability) and disasters (inter-annual variability) are closely interrelated, the 'Livelihood Impact Analysis Spreadsheet' (LIAS) was developed to track changes in food and livelihood security on a seasonal basis, and to integrate this enhanced understanding of livelihoods into emergency assessment and response. The LIAS builds on the 'Household Economy Approach', which combines baseline information on livelihoods and coping strategies with hazard analysis, to project vulnerability outcomes. Specifically, the LIAS compiles data on the relative importance of different sources of food and income, season by season, for rural households in 170 livelihood zones in Ethiopia, analyses the seasonally variable impact of hazards across these zones, and draws recommendations for improved accuracy, appropriateness and timing of emergency assistance. Implications for seasonally sensitive programming include customizing interventions for needs at different times of year, subsidizing transport and protecting rights and welfare for seasonal migrants, and boosting health services during months of high disease risk.

In Chapter 13, Lorraine Coulter and associates introduce the 'Water Economy for Livelihoods' (WELS) approach, which analyses and models the interlinkages between water security and livelihood security. Complementing the food security emphasis of the 'Household Economy Approach', WELS focuses attention on how people secure access to sufficient safe water to meet their consumption and livelihood needs. The authors note that water-related diseases cause more fatalities in Ethiopia than starvation during famines. WELS analyses begin by compiling 'water baselines' that quantify water availability and access in each livelihood zone, by source and by season, for different wealth groups and different water uses. Next, an interactive 'Water Impact Analysis Sheet' (WIAS) models the impact of seasonal hazards on household water access and livelihoods, providing a forecasting tool for timely policy interventions. A WELS analysis in pastoralist areas of Ethiopia found that poorer households that lack access to sufficient water have lower-quality animals, and lower milk yields and earnings from livestock sales. Lengthy water collection times for women and children, especially during dry seasons, also impact negatively on childcare. One implication is that interventions to protect pastoralist livelihoods should focus on stabilizing access to water throughout the year, for both human and animal consumption.

Seasonal policies

Even when seasonality is recognized as influencing poverty and wellbeing, it is too rarely factored into the design of policy responses. National development plans and poverty reduction strategies invariably prioritize economic growth, rather than reducing seasonal hunger or smoothing incomes and consumption in the face of seasonal cycles. Economic growth is conceived as a linear pathway out of poverty, and is often associated with urbanization and diversification away from smallholder agriculture – in effect, a shift towards 'de-seasonalized' lives and livelihoods. For the foreseeable future, however, millions of the world's poorest people will continue to depend for their survival on rainfed crop farming, and policymakers must ensure that their policies are attuned to the seasonal cycles that dictate production, employment and consumption, especially in rural areas.

In Chapter 14, Kate Conroy and Catherine Vignon demonstrate how planning for seasonality can reduce extreme poverty, by examining the Chars Livelihoods Programme (CLP), which targets extremely poor households in northwest Bangladesh, an area characterized by severe seasonal hunger (*monga*). Analysis of local livelihoods finds that households most vulnerable to seasonal drops in employment, income and food security are those that depend on seasonal agricultural labour. Annual floods cause crop failure, labour market collapse, livestock death and the spread of water-borne diseases. The CLP therefore designed its interventions around seasonal climatic events, and focused on risk reduction, asset protection and consumption smoothing. CLP interventions included: asset transfers (mostly livestock) to generate alternative streams of income; monthly cash transfers to prevent distress sale of assets; veterinary voucher subsidies to safeguard livestock health; cash-for-work programmes to offset seasonal fluctuations in employment; and improvements in infrastructure (e.g. raising houses) to secure homes against seasonal flooding and disease. A critical reason for the success of these interventions was their responsiveness to seasonality and shocks. For instance, a 'Temporary Food Transfer' was introduced in 2008 as a response to seasonal food price spikes, and phased out when prices fell back to pre-crisis levels.

Seasonality in agricultural production implies that demands for working capital peak pre-harvest – when food prices in local markets also spike – whereas income from farming peaks post-harvest. This imbalance between agricultural costs and income can create a seasonal poverty trap, especially for poor rural households with limited access to financial services, while seasonality and poverty in themselves inhibit the emergence and development of fully functioning financial markets (savings, borrowing and insurance services). In Chapter 15, Andrew Dorward points out that farm household models are very useful for understanding resource allocation decisions by poor rural people, but that these models typically fail to take into account seasonal capital constraints. The consequence is a misdiagnosis of the problems that smallholder farmers face, and the design of inappropriate policy interventions to address their production and consumption constraints. Dorward develops an extension of the standard farm household model to take account of constraints in seasonal finance, and argues that this provides important insights for policymakers who are concerned with assisting poor farmers to escape low productivity and seasonal poverty traps. Dorward concludes by arguing that 'seasonal farm household models' should become the default approach for analysing rural economies and designing more effective anti-poverty interventions.

Discussions of seasonality have focused on agriculture, food security and health, but have tended to overlook linkages with other sectors. In Chapter 16, Sierd Hadley develops an argument for making education policy more sensitive to seasonality, by drawing together evidence on seasonality in livelihoods and the direct and indirect costs of education. Seasonal fluctuations in income affect the ability to afford school expenses, while increased demand for child labour at certain times of year (e.g. harvesting) reduces enrolment and attendance. Similarly, seasonal migration can compromise children's schooling directly, if they accompany their parents, or indirectly, if they are required to stay home to care for livestock or younger siblings. Simply getting to school is more difficult during the rains. Recognizing seasonal barriers in access to education is a prerequisite for making education more accessible to poor children. Making education policies seasonally sensitive includes aligning the school calendar with local livelihood cycles (e.g. holidays should coincide with peak on-farm labour requirements and heavy rains) and synchronizing fee payment schedules with local cycles of income (e.g. asking for fees after the harvest, not during the pre-harvest hungry season). Education should be an opportunity for families stressed by seasonality, not an additional burden.

In this book's concluding chapter, Rachel Sabates-Wheeler and Stephen Devereux endorse earlier critiques of the notion that regular fluctuations in the weather are the primary cause of negative seasonal outcomes, and argue that the analysis should be reframed in terms of wealth differentials, because the fundamental drivers of 'adverse seasonality' are the politics of access and distribution. Seasonality is a given. It is the interaction of cyclical stresses with chronic deprivation, limited opportunities and weak fallback positions that leaves poor people unable – unlike wealthier people – to attain 'a-seasonal' levels of consumption and wellbeing. Inequalities in access and opportunities are structural, which explains why conventional development policies and programmes – even those that aim to stabilize production or consumption – are unable to 'solve' the problems that seasonality highlights, only to ameliorate its worst consequences. Analysis of panel data from Ethiopia concludes that interventions such as public works must be carefully timed and flexible, to achieve positive counter-seasonal effects in term of consumption smoothing, risk management and building resilient livelihoods. Moreover, 'graduating' people from seasonal lives towards a-seasonal living requires linking these interventions to broader agendas of rights and redistribution, implying that a seasonally sensitive analysis and response must be political, not just technical.

Conclusion

This book is part of an effort to revive academic and policy awareness of the adverse effects of seasonality on rural livelihoods and development. This chapter concludes by offering ideas as to how awareness of seasonality as a significant driver of poverty and illbeing can be enhanced, with the goal of improving seasonally sensitive policy interventions across the world.

Poverty statistics should reflect seasonal variation

In countries where seasonality significantly affects people's wellbeing, indicators of poverty are likely to vary within as well as between years.

> If seasonal consumption smoothing is less than perfect, for example due to variable food prices or imperfect credit and asset markets, then comparing different survey years may reveal apparent welfare changes over time, which are in fact due to seasonality. One simple way to avoid this problem is to compare results on welfare using as closely related periods as possible.
>
> (Dercon and Krishnan, 1998, p4)

Alternatively, instead of reporting a single poverty headcount for a given year, indicators should be collected and reported by season – at the very least, two figures should be reported, for the best and worst time of year.

New tools should be developed to analyse seasonality

Several chapters in this book, summarized above, propose innovative techniques for understanding the causes and impacts of seasonality. Another methodology presented at the 'Seasonality Revisited' conference is the 'Rural Basket', which monitors seasonal fluctuations in food availability and prices and is used by NGOs in Zambia as an advocacy tool to address the structural causes of rural poverty, including seasonality (Chibuye, 2009). These tools, often devised in specific country contexts, should be adapted and promoted to ensure widespread uptake in other countries.

Seasonality assessments should be routinely incorporated into the design of all rural development projects

A seasonality assessment requires generating a detailed understanding, drawing on the innovative methods discussed in this book, of how local lives and livelihoods are affected by seasonal cycles, and the responses that poor people adopt to protect themselves against the worst consequences. How will the project address the range of risks, vulnerabilities and stresses that seasonality creates or exacerbates? How are these risks differentiated across types of people – farmers, pastoralists and landless labourers, or men, women and children? How might project outcomes be compromised by seasonality, and how can the project be better designed to mitigate these risks?

Agricultural projects should aim to stabilize, not only raise, food production and consumption

Since seasonality can introduce damaging fluctuations to the livelihoods and food security of poor rural people, agricultural projects should strive to reduce food insecurity, which means ensuring that subsistence needs are met in a sustainable way, rather than simply raising average yields or incomes. Introducing irrigation for a second cropping season in unimodal rainfall systems, for instance, is more likely to stabilize income and smooth food consumption throughout the year than is investing in high-yielding but more risky crop varieties.

Seasonality should be factored into project planning and implementation

Access to seasonal inputs such as fertilizer, seed and credit should be provided on a timely basis. Education policy must allow for seasonality in livelihoods, by adjusting (and possibly decentralizing) school calendars to account for local agricultural activities and seasonal migration, collecting school fees after rather than before the harvest, and delivering school meals during the hungry season. Social protection interventions such as public works programmes should either be implemented or scaled up during the hungry season, or alternatively made available on demand, or permanently. Year-round access to health and other services should be facilitated by building all-weather roads.

Although it remains puzzling and disappointing that seasonality has never become mainstreamed in development policy, it is important and appropriate to conclude on a positive note. The renewed policy and research interest in agricultural livelihoods, the challenges posed by climate change and its implications for the seasons, the increasing sophistication of the social protection agenda and the emergence of 'adaptive social protection' – all these trends offer new opportunities for the seasonal dimensions of rural poverty to be fully recognized and systematically addressed. The chapters that follow provide fresh evidence of the complex impacts of seasonality, and of how poor people struggle to overcome cyclical fluctuations in food prices, access to water, employment, and disease. But many contributions to this book also provide fresh ideas for monitoring and analysing seasonal variability, and examples of innovative policies and programmes that can support poor rural people in their efforts to survive the most difficult times of year.

PART 1

Seasonal lives

A rainy day

On the third day of my five-day stay with a poor family in rural Bangladesh, the heavens open. It rains hard and continuously for more than 24 hours and life for 'my' family comes to a standstill. Rain in Dhaka is a nuisance: the drains overflow, traffic grinds to a halt and unpleasant smells permeate the air. Rain in the village is something else and I had never realized before living this for myself just how big an impact it has.

'My' family live in a one-roomed bamboo and corrugated iron sheet house. The rain pounds on the tin roof relentlessly. The bamboo walls soak up the rain and sweat dampness. The father (Ali), a rickshaw driver, is unable to work all day. One day's income lost means that he buys 5kg less rice this week. His wife (Salma) works in the garment industry some five miles away. There was no way she could miss a day at the factory so she leaves home at 6am and paddles through the rain, works her 10-hour shift in the dry clothes she had carried with her and then returns home in her wet ones. She shivers all evening and starts sneezing and snuffling next morning. Their three children, two girls and a boy, are aged between two and seven years. The eldest attends a government school one and a half miles from home. She usually walks to school in bare feet with her friend but there was no way she could go this day. So she stays with her two siblings and their father, cooped up in the house all day. They have no warm clothes. The outside stove is soaked and unusable and so there is no cooked food to be had. The four of them eat handfuls of *moori* (dried puffed rice) periodically throughout the day. At night, we can't go out to use the toilet – I don't know what they did but I had to resort to a bottle. It is very cold … a cold I have never, in 22 years of Bangladesh experience, ever felt before.

We play games, sing songs, read books together but the novelty of having the *bideshi* [foreigner] play Incy Wincy Spider over and over soon wears off. We simply have to sit out the rain. Cooped up together in 200 square feet, it is unsurprising that we all succumb to Salma's cold.

I am due to leave soon … back to Dhaka and the inconvenience of waterlogged streets and the comfort of my echinacea tablets. 'My' family, meanwhile, will take several days to recover from this rainy day.

Dee Jupp

2

What happened to the seasons?

Farmers' perceptions and meteorological
observations of changing seasonality

John Magrath and Steve Jennings

Introduction

This paper explores the impacts of climate change on the timing and characteristics
of seasons, and how this in turn is affecting the phenomenon of 'seasonality'.

Climate change is the alteration of global climates, persisting for decades or
longer, arising from human activity that alters the composition of the atmosphere.

In terms of meteorology the basic pattern of seasons is set by the tilt of the Earth
in its orbit around the Sun, which changes the amount of solar radiation striking
the surface of northern or southern hemispheres and hence day length. However,
different species of plants and animals emerge or behave not only according to day
length but to such things as warmth, lack of frost, differences between daytime and
night-time temperatures, rainfall patterns, air movements, etc. Climate change has
the potential to affect all of these things, and thus alter the timing of interactions
between species, including pollination (IPCC, 2007: figure 1.2). Phenology is the
study of life cycles of plants and animals and such interrelationships (Sparks, 2007).

In the field of development, seasonality describes the experience of regular
peaks in hunger, malnutrition, disease and poverty linked to the agricultural cycle,
notably the recurring 'hungry season' in rural communities in tropical developing
countries (Devereux *et al.*, 2008).

In developing countries the timing of rains, and intra-seasonal rainfall patterns,
are particularly critical to smallholder farmers. Upon these depend their decisions
about when to sow and harvest, and ultimately the success or failure of their crops.
Worryingly, therefore, farmers are reporting that the timing of rainy seasons and the
pattern of rains within seasons are changing; temperatures are rising and the appearances and behaviours of plants and animals are being altered. These perceptions
of change are striking in that they are geographically widespread and described in
remarkably consistent terms. In this paper, we relate the perceptions of farmers from
several regions and impacts on agriculture, livelihoods, psychology and culture.

This information comes from explorations of change amongst people with whom Oxfam and partner agencies work. These testimonies and case studies have been written into a series of reports on specific countries (see Oxfam research reports in References) and a research report focusing on changes to the seasons (Oxfam: Jennings and Magrath, 2009). This present chapter builds on that research.

We go on to ask two critical questions. Firstly, do meteorological and other observations support farmers' perceptions of changing seasonality? We explore this with particular reference to southern Africa and to Bangladesh. Secondly, to what extent are these changes consistent with predictions from climate models?

We conclude that changing seasonality may be one of the major impacts of climate change faced by smallholder farmers in developing countries over the next few decades and, indeed, may already be so. If such is the case then the annual seasonal hunger gap is liable to get longer, and there is less room for farmer 'error' within the shorter growing period that provides the following year's food.

The impacts are likely to be differentiated. One factor is wealth – such as how many times a farmer can afford to sow or hire labour, or employ potentially adaptive technologies such as irrigation or improved seed varieties. Another is geography – it makes a big difference whether 20 days are trimmed from a growing season of 100 days, or from a growing season of 70 days. Without appropriate action these causal pathways could increase and intensify poverty, food insecurity and inequality in many of the world's poorest communities.

Finally, the connections between climate change, changing seasons and seasonality are almost unexplored in the literature. We urge further exploration and also suggest some of the key adaptation responses that might help farmers and rural dwellers cope with changes to seasons.

Observations of climatic changes

In Durban, South Africa, Mr Siga Govender says:

> As a little boy I could distinctly see the different seasons, but now I do not understand why when it's hot it's killing, and when it rains it sweeps everything away. We used to have four seasons in a year but these days you can have four seasons in one day and you cannot plan. If you put your pesticide down in the morning it will soon be washed away by a storm in the afternoon, and the insects do not die. If the floods come as they did recently I lose the entire crop. This is very costly for me.

Mr Govender employs 16 labourers, mainly women. If it rains very heavily they do not come to work and if it is extremely hot they are constantly sick. In almost 40° Celsius the women suffer from heat exhaustion, sweating, dizziness and headaches. Mr Govender's wife gives them paracetamol, but this does not help much. He says: 'Production is much less when people are uncomfortable and sick, you cannot push people'. He says he used to make 30,000 rand (£2,500) per month or more, but is now only making about half that and it is a struggle to pay his workers.

Mr Govender's story is typical. Although the emphasis varies from country to country, in our studies the following observations are reported consistently.

The seasons appear to have shrunk in number and variety, in that relatively temperate 'transitional' seasons are truncated or have disappeared altogether, being replaced by a more simplified pattern of predominantly hot (hotter) and dry or hot (hotter) and wet seasons. The appearances and behaviours of animals, plants and insects have likewise shifted.

Julius Nkatachi, from Tsite village near Phalula in Balaka, southern Malawi, says: 'Originally there were very distinct seasons and we were very sure when things would happen. Now the seasons are not distinct, especially the hot and cold seasons … Now it's only cold for a few days'. Comments from elsewhere echo his, such as: 'The summer now is winter' (Nicaragua); 'There is no stability in the seasons, now Margha (January/February) is becoming Falgun (February/March) and Falgun is becoming Chaitra (March/April)' (Nepal); 'Spring comes 2–3 weeks earlier than before' (Arctic Russia).

Temperatures have increased overall, particularly in winters and also at nights. Seken Ali, from Pangsha, Rajbari, Bangladesh, says: 'The temperature is changed greatly. Summer times never used to be so hot five years back but this year, we can hardly work in the fields in the morning. It is so hot that we get blisters all over our body'. Binita Bikrar from Kapala village in Nepal said, 'Before, it used to snow during the winter, and the winter was much colder. But in the last three years there has been no snow'.

Rain is more erratic, coming at unexpected times in and out of season. In particular, there is less predictability as to the start of rainy seasons. Generally, rainy seasons are shorter. In mountainous areas there is considerably less snowfall. Dry periods have increased in length and drought is more common. Communities in Nepal particularly say the summer monsoons are much shorter, lasting for only three months instead of five and their starts are more unpredictable. There is less regular drizzle and the period of particularly intense rain within the monsoon that used to last one to two weeks now lasts only a few days.

Within recognisable seasons unusual and 'unseasonal' events are occurring more frequently, such as heavy rains in dry seasons, dry spells in rainy seasons, storms at unexpected times, dense and lingering fogs and temperature fluctuations. When rains do come they are felt to be more violent and intense and punctuated by longer dry spells within the rainy seasons. Dry spells and heavier rain increase the risk of flooding and crop loss. Winds – and storms – have increased in strength. They may come at unusual times. Prevalent wind directions have also shifted. 'The most disturbing thing that agonises me is that storms are no longer arriving from the usual direction for the past five years at least. This is how our ancestors have known it – why is it changing?', asks Shahida Begum in Bangladesh. In Malawi farmers commonly say that the winds no longer blow from the right direction, are 'mixed up' and more destructive.

Observations of the effects on agriculture

Changing seasonality seems to be having major effects on agriculture, encouraging widespread changes in crops grown, in farming practices and livelihood choices in many rural areas.

In Tete province in Mozambique people say that until the early 1990s, the rains usually started in October and it would usually rain fairly consistently for three months or so. Maize was sown in early November and harvested in March. Now the rains seem to be starting later and come in a few intense downpours with dry weather in between that can last several weeks. Maize is sown later, germinates when the rains come but then dies for lack of moisture in the dry spell, or gets battered down in the next heavy rains. As the maize is sown later it is also more vulnerable to flooding when the Zambezi River overflows. People say that windstorms are also becoming increasingly common. Florence Madamu in Bulirehe, Bundibugyo, western Uganda, says:

> We've stopped even adopting seasonal planting, because it's so useless. Now we just try all the time. We used to plant in March and that'd be it [finished]. Now we plant and plant again. We waste a lot of seeds that way, and our time and energy. Sometimes you feel like crying. Sometimes you've hired labour and you end up losing all that money for preparing your land.

Baluku Yofesi from Kasese, western Uganda, says the March to June rainy season is no longer reliable. He says:

> Because of the shortened rains you have to go for early maturing varieties and now people are trying to select these. That's why some local varieties of pumpkins and cassava that need a lot of rain, even varieties of beans, have disappeared. We need things that mature in two months – maize needs three months of rain to grow so two months is not enough.

In Nepal, Maya Devi Sarki, from Tartar village, Dhaldendura district, says:

> We used to have wheat and maize, but now the harvest is low and we have to spend more money on seed and labour. This year all the wheat is dry in our field. The raspberries have ripened two months early. The quantity of rainfall is decreasing and the monsoon is changing – now we don't know what to plant and when.

Gagane Bhul from the same village observes that, 'Before, the main fruit we had was oranges, now these are gone. But instead mangoes are growing well – before, these used only to grow in the *terai* [the subtropical plains]'.

In Nepal the altitude at which crops can be grown is rising so that farming is being extended uphill. In Peru too communities report 'crops are growing further up'. There appears to be more rain on the higher ground (*puna*) and less in the lower *Quechua* area. Crops that previously only grew well in the *Quechua* area now grow up in the *puna*. The *puna* was previously only suitable for natural grazing and this encroachment is causing clashes with the stock farmers there.

The biggest problem for farmers is probably unpredictability. The more unpredictable the climate, the greater investment of time, energy and resources required in order to seize the right moments for crucial farming activities, notably planting or transplanting, and to maintain crops (and animals) through dry spells. More erratic weather tends to more erratic outcomes in terms of harvests.

Wider changes to rural livelihoods influenced by climate change

Shifts in crops and livelihoods have social implications, as some groups of people are able to take advantage of such opportunities, while others are increasingly disadvantaged. The poorest people have least access to water, land, capital and expertise to change their crops to what might grow better, such as fruit and vegetables.

In Bangladesh, Afazuddin Akhand from Mymemsingh district says:

> Due to irregular rainfall every year and random floods, growing rice has become a big risk. Many farmers switch to fish farming or sell their land to industrialists, which is more profitable but overall rice production is shrinking, which is our staple food.

Prawn farming in Vietnam has become a byword for a high-risk boom-and-bust industry that has sucked in many small farmers who have switched from rice cultivation. The decline of prawn farming can be put down to many factors, including non-climatic ones, but temperature fluctuations, intense rainfall and floods have all taken their toll.

Nguyen Thanh Nhan, from Binh Loc Commune, Binh Dai District, Ben Tre, said:

> Too much rain and too much sun make the prawns get sick easily. The owner lost the prawns so I lost my job. Earlier this year my wife and eldest daughter had to go to Ho Chi Minh City to find jobs because I don't get a regular income.

Such changes are strengthening social and economic trends, including: shifts away from subsistence agriculture towards aggregation of land holdings and use for cash crops; migration out of rural areas both towards urban centres and across borders, particularly by men; and changes in gender relations. It appears probable that in most cases women's workloads have increased.

In Nepal, male migration leaves women alone to look after families. Physical labour is one of the few resources they control, hence women are doing more daily waged labour. This is often extremely onerous, such as portering construction materials, and badly paid – women are paid only three-quarters of what a man would earn for the same work.

Effects on psychology and culture

These changes in the seasons also create existential shocks to individuals and to societies, by threatening belief systems, cultural practices and, as a result, social relationships.

The noted Indian environmental writer Richard Mahapatra has written movingly about 'the death of seasons' in his native Orissa,[1] explaining how his mother's generation described a year of six distinct seasons, each of two months duration (see Table 2.1). Each was reckoned to arrive on a specific date and was accompanied by the appearance of certain flowers, birds or insects and each was marked by cultural events. According to Mahapatra, the six seasons have now effectively shrunk to two or three – a hot summer for close to eight months of the year, a 30-day rainy season and a truncated and warmer winter forming a transition between the two. The seasons of spring, the dewy season and autumn have almost disappeared, as have many of the animals, insects and 'wisdom birds' whose appearances marked each season and, as a result, sayings, proverbs and ceremonies associated with these events are also dying out.

Many rural communities, and especially marginalized minorities, gain a sense of strength and cohesion from their relationships with the natural world and bewilderment, disorientation and a sense of loss are often palpable in interviews.

Interaction with local environmental stresses

The impacts of changing seasonality are often hard to separate from the results of stresses on ecosystems due to demographic, social and economic pressures.

People interviewed have little or no knowledge of the global causes of climate change but almost always express acute awareness of environmental changes and see these as connected to climatic changes. Farmers commonly point to deforestation and excessive use of fertilizers, pesticides and insecticides for causing the disappearance of fish and animal life. Rising populations are commonly cited as causing increased demand for fuel, farmland and water.

TABLE 2.1 Changing seasons in India (from Mahapatra)

Previous status		Present status
Season	No. of months	No. of days (approx.)
Grishma (summer)	2 months (56 days)	250
Barsha (rainy)	2 months	30
Sarata (autumn)	2 months	5–10
Hemanta (dewy)	2 months	5–10
Sisira (winter)	2 months	30
Basanta (spring)	2 months	5–10

Nevertheless, changes to seasons score highly in people's perceptions as distinct phenomena.

Testing perceptions of change

Some of these perceived changes – and the causes of them – are well understood globally (Table 2.2).

Writing in the *Guardian* (Stott, 2010), Peter Stott, head of climate monitoring and attribution at the UK's Met Office, says:

> Analysing the observational data shows clearly that there has been a rise in the number of extremely warm temperatures recorded globally and that there have been increased numbers of heavy rainfall events in many regions over land. Evidence, including in India and China, that periods of heavy rain are getting heavier, is entirely consistent with our understanding of the physics of the atmosphere in which warmer air holds more moisture.

While this suggests that the perceptions of the people we have interviewed may be broadly in line with observed meteorological changes, it says little about the changes that may (or may not) be occurring in a particular geographical area. Nor do these global observed changes tell us much about some of the more subtle changes of the timing of seasons and intra-seasonal patterns.

TABLE 2.2 Relevant global trends from 1900–2005

Perceived change	*Global trend*
Increasing temperature	Warming of the climate system is unequivocal, with a 100-year linear trend (1906–2005) of 0.74°C
	[very likely] that hot days and hot nights have become more frequent over most land areas
	[likely] that heat waves have become more frequent over most land areas.
Earlier onset of northern spring	[very high confidence] that recent warming is strongly affecting … earlier timing of spring events
More intense rain	[likely] that the frequency of heavy precipitation events (or proportion of total rainfall from heavy falls) has increased over most areas
Wind patterns	Anthropogenic forcing is likely to have contributed to changes in wind patterns

Source: Intergovernmental Panel on Climate Change (2007) *Climate Change Synthesis Report*. 'Very high confidence' denotes that there is at least a 9 out of 10 chance of a finding being correct; 'very likely' denotes a >90% probability of occurrence, and 'likely' a >66% probability.

Meteorological evidence from Malawi and Mozambique

The climate of Malawi and Mozambique is tropical (to subtropical in Mozambique) and highly influenced by topography. The main rainfall season is November to February (to April in northern Malawi and Mozambique). Wet season rainfall is highly influenced by variations in Indian Ocean sea surface temperatures, and especially the variations in this caused by El Niño Southern Oscillation (ENSO).

Communities in Malawi and Mozambique consistently report hotter temperatures, delayed onset of the rainy season (longer dry season), more intense rains with longer dry spells between rainfall, and stronger winds (from unusual directions). How well do these perceptions accord with analysis of meteorological records, and how consistent are they with the robust simulations of Global Climate Models (GCMs)?[2]

Mean annual temperatures have increased by 0.9°C in Malawi (McSweeney et al., undated, a) and 0.6°C in Mozambique (McSweeney et al., undated, b) between 1960 and 2006. Over 1961 to 2000, the averaged occurrence of extreme hot days and nights increased by 8.2 and 8.6 days/decade, respectively, over southern Africa as a whole, including significant changes in both Malawi and Mozambique (New et al., 2006).

There are also indications that the maximum dry spell duration (corresponding in southern Africa to length of dry season) has increased, although this is not statistically significant (New et al., 2006; see also Tadross et al., 2005). Climate model simulations show a coherent picture of decreasing dry season rainfall (June to August and September to October), offset partially by increases in wet season rainfall (December to February and March to May), which suggests that a delayed onset of rains is potentially consistent with global climate change (McSweeney et al., undated, a & b).

New et al. (2006) also provide some evidence that rainfall intensity is increasing over southern Africa: namely, a significant increase in maximum annual 5-day and 1-day rainfall. The proportion of rainfall falling in both heavy events[3] and 5-day maxima has increased in Mozambique from 1960–2005 (McSweeney et al., undated, b). No trend was found for Malawi (McSweeney et al., undated, a). In nearby eastern South Africa, Groisman et al. (2005) found statistically significant increases in the frequency of extreme precipitation events, even though there was no significant change in annual rainfall.

In summary, in Mozambique and Malawi, there appears to be a high level of correspondence between communities' perceptions of local change and observed changes in the meteorological record. These same changes are also robustly simulated by GCMs to increase with anthropogenic forcing of the atmosphere.

Meteorological evidence from Bangladesh

Bangladesh has a tropical monsoon climate. Three seasons are generally recognized: a hot, muggy summer from March to June; a hot, humid and very rainy monsoon from June to September; and a dry winter from November to February.

The climate is one of the wettest in the world, with 80 per cent of the rain occurring during the monsoon. The south Asian monsoon is highly variable, making the detection of trends difficult. The *Aman* harvest is in December to January and the *Boro* (dry season) harvest is in March to May.

Farmers in Bangladesh have highlighted changes including higher and fluctuating temperatures, and erratic and 'unseasonal' rains. Temperatures in Bangladesh have increased in recent decades, by 0.6–1°C in May and 0.5°C in November (Cruz *et al.*, 2007). Over much of Asia, heatwaves are lasting longer (Cruz *et al.*, 2007). The number of cold nights[4] has decreased significantly in Bangladesh over the period of 1961–2000, with a corresponding though greater increase in warm nights (Klein Tank *et al.*, 2007). Maximum monthly temperatures have increased faster than monthly minima from 1961–2000 (Sheikh *et al.*, undated).

There is considerable evidence that annual rainfall has increased in recent years almost everywhere in Bangladesh (Egashira *et al.*, 2003, Cruz *et al.*, 2007, Sheikh *et al.*, undated). Seasonal changes in rainfall are harder to determine, but Egashira *et al.* (2003) indicate a reduction (not statistically significant) in winter and pre-monsoon rains (except for Chittagong), while late (October) monsoon rains have increased since 1979 in south Asia (Syroka and Toumi, 2002). These observations of a drier winter and pre-monsoon period, with increased rain in the rest of the year, are consistent with the predictions of most climate models (Christensen *et al.*, 2007). A recent study indicates that anthropogenic climate change may cause a delay in the onset of the monsoon and increase monsoon precipitation over most of Bangladesh (although rainfall will decrease over most of India – Ashfaq *et al.*, 2009).

Rainfall extremes have shown clear trends over Bangladesh. The frequency of days of heavy rainfall has increased significantly over the period 1961–2000 (Goswami *et al.*, 2006, Klein Tank *et al.*, 2007).

In summary, there appears to be some consistency between communities' perceptions of local change and observed changes in the meteorological record regarding increasing temperatures and subtle shifts in the pre-monsoon and late monsoon and winter rains.

Perceptions *vis-à-vis* measured change

It can be objected that human memories and perceptions are unreliable and cannot be taken at face value: farmers' perceptions of 'normality' and deviations from it may be actually based on quite short-term memories, the prevailing patterns of just the last few years. Yet in our experience what farmers say seems remarkably consistent across (often widely dispersed) localities within countries and, indeed, across the globe.

The evidence cited from the meteorological record for Mozambique and Malawi, and for Bangladesh, does not contradict what farmers say and to some extent supports it, but it clearly paints a less dramatic picture than emerges in testimonies. How may we account for this?

Farmers and meteorologists may be essentially measuring 'real' but different things. A study in Nepal (Gill, undated) describes how farmers articulate the mode – the most frequent or typical pattern – while meteorologists use the arithmetic mean. Farmers measure the 'amount' of rain not in isolation but according to what it is supposed to do, i.e., in relation to the water requirements of certain crops. Small amounts of rain in the dry season may be described as large, because the rain is assessed in relation to what it will grow, such as dry season wheat rather than rice. Even if the total amount of rain has not changed, a perception that a particular season is becoming 'drier' might be a summation of hotter temperatures (reduced soil moisture through increased evaporation), changed patterns of rain (greater run-off caused by a higher proportion of rain falling in intense events) and changes in water storage capacity of land and soils.

There are also huge constraints on analysing the meteorological record in many parts of the developing world, not least the paucity of long-term records. There is a global inequality in meteorological station coverage between rich and poor countries and in the human resources available to process, analyse and forecast weather. This is exacerbated in many parts of sub-Saharan Africa by the high rates of absenteeism in government agencies, caused to a large degree by HIV and AIDS.

In the absence of extreme changes to mean annual rainfall and temperature, subtle changes in the timing and the intra-seasonal patterns of rain will have a significant impact on smallholder, rainfed agriculture. Yet the vast majority of analyses of meteorological records and climate model data focus on mean annual temperature and precipitation change, rather than the timing of rains and intra-seasonal rainfall patterns. We argue that there is enormous potential, and utility, in examining meteorological and model data with a 'farmer's eye'.

Similarly, predictions of the impact of climate change rarely take into account seasonal and intra-seasonal changes and variation. This is likely to lead to an under-estimate of the adverse impacts. Given the severity of the predicted impacts on smallholder farmers, especially in sub-Saharan Africa (Boko *et al.*, 2007), this is a truly frightening proposition.

Perceptions *vis-à-vis* phenology

Observations of plant and animal life cycles, especially the first appearances of plants, animals and insects, demonstrate how the biological cycles of organisms are influenced or governed by a variety of stimuli such as warmth or dwindling days of frost. Seasons – such as spring – begin for different organisms at different times. In turn, the appearance of particular plants or animals provides much of the cultural and psychological definition of a 'season' for human observers.

Historical records for the United Kingdom, for example, show that in the most recent 25 years plants are flowering between 2.2 and 12.7 days earlier than in any other consecutive 25-year period since 1760 (Amano *et al.*, 2010). It would be reasonable to suppose that farming systems are not unaffected by similar disruptions, exacerbated by many other stresses on ecosystems.

Oxfam research in Pakistan shows that the length of the cropping period has shrunk by between 15 and 20 days, with a forward shift in the sowing time and an earlier harvest (Oxfam: Abbass, 2009). A recent scientific field study finds that diurnal temperature variations have contrary impacts on rice production, with less cool nights wiping out gains from higher daily temperatures (Welch et al., 2010). The differential responses of plants and animals to various stimuli are disrupting the synchronicity of hitherto interdependent ecosystems, with impacts on pollination. Farmers we have interviewed often note how certain animals have disappeared, like frogs or snakes, while new pests are appearing. Mohamad Abdul Kadir, from Mymensingh district in Bangladesh, observes, 'I have 30 mango trees, there are flowers but no fruit. There are various types of insects which cause heavy losses in the mango harvest which wasn't the case just a few years ago'.

Summary of effects

We do not claim here that farmers' perceptions of local change are universally consistent with meteorological observations and with the robust predictions of climate models. Clearly, farmers, meteorologists and climate scientists often 'measure' different things. But what is clear is that:

- Local perceptions of changing seasons are remarkably consistent around the world.
- Farmers widely hold these perceived changes accountable for significant crop loss and degradation of their livelihoods, as well as psychological stress and 'cultural bewilderment'.
- These perceptions of the changing timing and character of seasons seem often to find support both in the meteorological record and in phenology.

The precise effects of climate changes on seasonality are very geo-specific, but broad patterns are:

1 Unpredictable weather has always presented serious problems for smallholder farmers and fishing communities in poor countries, but farming is becoming even more difficult and risky because of the greater unpredictability in seasonal rainfall patterns. Heat stress, lack of water at crucial times and pests and diseases are serious problems that climate change appears to be exacerbating. These all interact with ongoing pressures on land, soils and water resources that would exist regardless of climate change. The most common observation is that the changes are 'shortening' the growing season.

2 Unpredictability requires greater investment of time, energy and resources in order to seize the right moments and to maintain crops (and animals) through dry spells.

3 Rising temperatures and unpredictability together can be an incentive to diversification – whether desired or as a matter of necessity. But the ability to diversify is highly dependent on many factors and generally requires support to succeed.

4 Seasonality difficulties are strengthening trends within rural societies for people to move out of agriculture to a greater or lesser degree and to migrate, especially to urban areas. These movements are gendered, although exactly how depends very much on each society.

5 Seasonality difficulties are likely to increase inequalities between those who are in a position to diversify – including taking advantage of the ability to grow new crops – and those who are not.

6 Women are particularly badly affected by the combination of climatic and environmental stresses, but their particular needs and wishes for adaptation are less likely to be heard or acted upon.

Responding to seasonal change

Most of the changes in seasonality are simulated to become worse under climate change scenarios, so farmers will increasingly have to adapt to them. And indeed, they already are; within their limits of knowledge and resources, farmers are experimenting with new crops and varieties.

Some of the key strategies for helping farmers adapt to changing seasonality would be:

Access to forecasts

Many of the changes described above are essentially issues of (un)predictability. Traditional 'calendar' or local 'indigenous' forecasting systems will increasingly become less useful for decision-making. Access to reliable, appropriate forecasts is an essential step, and particularly when farmers themselves are intimately involved in the process (e.g. Hellmuth et al., 2007). It may be useful to develop simple community-level phenological indicators – such as the onset of harvest – to measure the impacts of climate change (Amano et al., 2010).

Access to crops and varieties

There is a particular demand for quick-maturing, heat-tolerant and drought-resistant crops. These must be available, reliable and affordable. Above all, they need to be appropriate and this means that they need to be co-created with the end users. In many cases a suite of crops and varieties is already available within a country or district, but not necessarily widely grown. For example, for the communities that live close to the Zambezi River in Tete province, Mozambique, fast-maturing maize varieties would reduce the chance of flood losses. At the same time, government is resettling communities to higher land. Existing drought-tolerant crops that are sometimes grown but not yet widely available (such as sweet potato, manioc, and local cowpea), as well as more drought-resistant varieties of sorghum, are all promising alternatives for these areas.

Water management

A range of options that could help farmers work with more erratic rains and higher temperatures includes soil management for greater moisture retention (e.g., increasing soil organic matter); water harvesting and physical barriers against flooding.

Food storage

Greater unpredictability increases the need to be able to store crops for longer periods to even out more violent fluctuations in supply and protect stocks against pests, whether animal, insect or fungal.[5]

Gendered adaptation

Adaptation thinking has reasonably focused on the agricultural sector but that runs the considerable risk of marginalizing non-agricultural livelihood strategies in rural areas and, in particular, of ignoring strategies demanded by women. When women in Malawi were asked what would enable them to adapt to climate change, they said that they wanted a crèche. They argued that until they had help to look after HIV and AIDS orphans they did not have the time or energy to cultivate their gardens, still less carry out conservation measures. They also called for family planning, access to credit to help them to start up small businesses, vocational training and free healthcare (Oxfam: Magrath, 2009).

Social protection

More broadly, if seasons are going to become more unpredictable, then social protection measures that help generate greater certainty throughout the year – insurance for example, or a guaranteed minimum income at regular intervals (such as a pension) – become even more important. Year-round, regular and predictable protection can enable families to budget for seasonal shocks. Onto this framework, specific seasonal interventions, such as employment schemes, can be added as appropriate. Creating alternative livelihoods must be part of long-term plans to deal with climate change. This brings adaptation strategies firmly into the sphere of development policy and practice, not a mere add-on (Oxfam: Pettengell, 2010).

Notes

1   Infochange India May 20, 2009; first published April 2006, see www.infochangeindia. org/200604116870/Disasters/Related-Features/Death-of-the-Seasons.html
2   Climate models are mathematical representations of the interactions between the atmosphere, oceans, land surface, ice and the sun, used by scientists to predict trends in climate.
3   A 'heavy' event is defined as a daily rainfall total which exceeds the threshold that is exceeded on 5 per cent of rainy days in the current climate of that region and season.
4   'Cold nights' ('hot days') are those below (above) the 10th (90th) percentile for the period 1961–90.
5   Dabi and Nyong studied changes in Sahelian agriculture via 27 communities in Northern Nigeria subject to increasing drought. They observe the main strategy has been a revival in food storage methods. See www.iisd.org/pdf/2005/climate_cop11_daniel_dabi.ppt

3

Month of birth and children's health in India

Michael Lokshin and Sergiy Radyakin

Introduction

A large literature in economics, human biology and medicine has been devoted to understanding the effects of early childhood conditions on outcomes later in life (see Martorell, 1999; Glewwe and King, 2001; Alderman *et al.*, 2006). Research has consistently shown that the month of birth is an important predictor of health outcomes, morbidity and mortality. But, so far, no convincing theories have been proposed to explain this association.

In this paper we use data from three rounds of the India National Family Health Survey (NFHS) to (1) quantify the effect of the month of birth on children's anthropometrics, and (2) test four hypotheses that might explain the relationship between the month of birth and children's health outcomes. We find that Indian children born during the monsoon months have worse health outcomes than children born during fall/winter months. The 'month-of-birth' effect persists after controlling for a wide set of observable and unobservable characteristics. The effect is large: the differences in height among children born during the monsoons and other children are comparable to the differences in health outcomes between children born to illiterate mothers and to mothers with completed primary education.

The empirical tests of hypotheses explaining the correlation between children's health outcomes and their month of birth conclude that one of the likely explanations for the observed pattern of changes in children's health by the month of birth could be a higher prevalence of malnutrition and a wider exposure to diseases in the lean monsoon season. Our results show that seasonal climatic variations affect the environmental conditions at the time of birth and determine health outcomes for young children in India. Policy interventions that affect such conditions might be as effective in improving children's health as nutrition and micronutrient supplementation programmes.

Data and descriptive statistics

This analysis uses data from three waves of the India NFHS (1992/1993, 1998/1999 and 2005/2006). The survey structure corresponds to the typical structure of demographic and health surveys (DHS) conducted in several other countries. Our main sample contains information on 45,279 children from the 1992/1993 round, 30,984 children from the 1998/1999 round and 48,679 children from the 2005/2006 round of the India NFHS, residing correspondingly in 33,032, 26,056 and 33,968 households.

We focused our analysis on the age-adjusted measure of height-for-age (HAZ) for children less than 36 months of age, which reflects children's development relative to a reference population of well-nourished children (WHO, 2006).[1] The height-for-age (stunting) is an indicator of the long-term effect of malnutrition (Dibley *et al.*, 1987).

Malnutrition is highly prevalent in India. According to NFHS data, about 80 per cent of children under the age of 3 were underweight in 1992, with minimal changes in 1998 and 2005. In 1992, 72 per cent of boys and 70 per cent of girls were stunted. The proportion of stunted children had decreased to 65 per cent by 2005. The overall averages of height-for-age z-score (HAZ) rose over the years for both boys and girls. The average HAZ had risen for boys from -1.9 in 1992 to -1.5 in 2005. Girls experienced similar improvements in health outcomes between 1992 and 2005.

The distribution of births by calendar month for the three rounds of NFHS is presented in Figure 3.1.[2] The proportions of boys and girls born in each month are similar. The highest birth rates are registered in August, September and October – these children were conceived in winter. Fewest children were born during the winter months of December, January and February – these children were conceived in spring. The wedding season in India, which falls in the months from November to February, could partially explain this seasonality of births (Medora, 2003). Figure 3.2 shows the proportion of children, among all children born in a particular month, who died before the age of three years. Child mortality declined from 1992 to 2005. In 1992, 14.8 per cent of boys and 15.2 per cent of girls died before reaching the age of three years. By 2005, these figures had decreased to 11.5 and 11.8 per cent respectively.

Setting up the problem

Figure 3.3 shows the changes in height-for-age z-scores by the month of birth for boys and girls in the three rounds of NFHS.[3] Anthropometric measures appeared to be the lowest for children born in summer and improving for children born in fall and early winter. This relationship held for both girls and boys. For example, if the average HAZ for boys born in June of 1992 was about -2.27 (standard error of 0.05), the HAZ for boys born in December of the same year was -1.73 (SE 0.06). The average HAZ increased from -2.33 for girls born in June to -1.69 for girls born in December. The differences in health outcomes between summer and fall/early winter months persist in 1992 and 1998 and exhibit a decline in 2005.

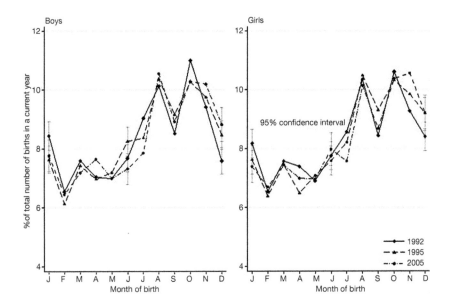

FIGURE 3.1 Share of total number of births in a current year by month of birth

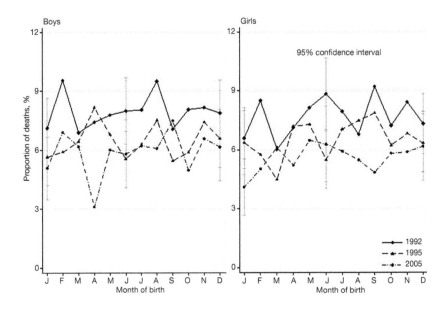

FIGURE 3.2 Proportion of children that died before the age of 36 months among all children born in a particular month

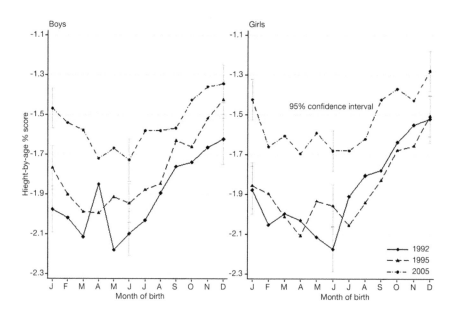

FIGURE 3.3 Health outcomes (HAZ) by month of birth and gender

Would the effect of the month of birth on a child's health be significant after controlling for the characteristics of a household, a mother, and a child? To find the answer to this question we rely on a standard theoretical framework of household utility maximization that incorporates the production function determining a child's health (Behrman and Deolalikar, 1988). According to that theory, the household demand for child health depends on a set of exogenous characteristics of a child X_i, household characteristics X_h, characteristics of its mother X_m, community characteristics X_c, and some unobserved factors captured by random error ε_i (Thomas et al., 1991). The child's characteristics include its age, sex, birth order, and month of birth. The mother's characteristics include her age and educational attainment. Characteristics of a household include household size, socio-demographic composition, household wealth index, religion and caste. Community characteristics include availability of community services and infrastructure.

Table 3.1 shows the coefficients of the linear regressions of HAZ for children younger than 36 months. The 'month-of-birth' effect persists when we control for a wide set of exogenous characteristics. Relative to December, children born in other months have worse health outcomes, with the largest negative difference in May, June and July.

However, in the presence of an unobserved heterogeneity in the parental inputs to the production function of a child's health, the variation in health outcomes by the month of birth could be partially attributed to differences in the parental behaviour (Rosenzweig and Schultz, 1982). For example, parents of children born weak might devote more resources to these children to compensate for the

TABLE 3.1 Regressions of height-for-age z-scores (specification with the state dummies, household characteristics, characteristics of the mother, and characteristics of a child, NFHS 1992, 1998, 2005)

		Boys		Girls		Boys and Girls Fixed Effects	
		Coeff.	SE	Coeff.	SE	Coeff.	SE
1992	January	−0.372***	0.078	−0.324***	0.080	−0.192	0.158
	February	−0.362***	0.083	−0.487***	0.085	−0.692***	0.165
	March	−0.489***	0.079	−0.364***	0.080	−0.580***	0.163
	April	−0.281***	0.082	−0.410***	0.083	−0.502***	0.167
	May	−0.588***	0.082	−0.586***	0.084	−0.704***	0.165
	June	−0.492***	0.079	−0.602***	0.079	−0.482***	0.154
	July	−0.443***	0.075	−0.400***	0.077	−0.366**	0.157
	August	−0.311***	0.073	−0.253***	0.073	−0.447***	0.144
	September	−0.222***	0.076	−0.208***	0.078	−0.341**	0.149
	October	−0.126*	0.072	−0.074	0.073	−0.109	0.145
	November	−0.072	0.075	0.020	0.076	−0.081	0.145
	December	Reference month					
	N Obs.	10,341		9,946		3,686	
	R2	0.167		0.181		0.291	
1998	January	−0.399***	0.065	−0.433***	0.068	−0.581***	0.140
	February	−0.537***	0.069	−0.432***	0.071	−0.506***	0.143
	March	−0.590***	0.065	−0.606***	0.068	−0.551***	0.139
	April	−0.611***	0.067	−0.654***	0.071	−0.625***	0.141
	May	−0.605***	0.066	−0.541***	0.069	−0.632***	0.144
	June	−0.597***	0.063	−0.529***	0.067	−0.876***	0.131
	July	−0.524***	0.063	−0.595***	0.066	−0.737***	0.136
	August	−0.443***	0.060	−0.422***	0.062	−0.608***	0.125
	September	−0.254***	0.062	−0.376***	0.064	−0.553***	0.128
	October	−0.261***	0.060	−0.183***	0.062	−0.525***	0.127
	November	−0.112*	0.061	−0.205***	0.064	−0.145	0.127
	December	Reference month					
	N Obs.	13,023		11,818		4,534	
	R2	0.190		0.228		0.288	
2005	January	−0.171**	0.066	−0.080	0.072	−0.071	0.143
	February	−0.209***	0.071	−0.352***	0.074	0.042	0.154
	March	−0.287***	0.068	−0.328***	0.071	−0.348**	0.141
	April	−0.423***	0.066	−0.431***	0.073	−0.493***	0.148
	May	−0.380***	0.068	−0.347***	0.073	−0.549***	0.148
	June	−0.405***	0.067	−0.457***	0.070	−0.570***	0.141
	July	−0.274***	0.066	−0.392***	0.071	−0.500***	0.143
	August	−0.286***	0.061	−0.353***	0.066	−0.537***	0.133
	September	−0.285***	0.064	−0.196***	0.068	−0.186	0.140
	October	−0.089	0.061	−0.126*	0.065	−0.158	0.126
	November	0.011	0.062	−0.170***	0.065	−0.202	0.131
	December	Reference month					
	N Obs.	12,020		11,085		4,521	
	R2	0.143		0.156		0.193	

Note:
* is significant at 10% level;
** at 5% level;
*** at 1% level. Fixed effects estimation is on the sample of households with two or more children younger than three years of age.

negative conditions at birth. If the unobserved heterogeneity in parental inputs is constant over time (siblings), we can account for the endogeneity of the month of birth by estimating the fixed-effect regression (FE) on the sample of siblings. The third columns in Table 3.1 show that most of the FE coefficients on the 11 dummies for the months of birth are statistically significant.[4] The seasonal patterns in child health are similar to patterns revealed by ordinary least square regression (OLS) estimations: children born in fall/winter months are healthier compared to children born in summer.

The average HAZ of children born during the monsoon season is about 0.5 standard deviations (SD) lower than the average HAZ of children born in the fall/winter months (Figure 3.3). After controlling for the characteristics of the child, the mother and the household they live in, the 'month-of-birth' effects ranged from 0.4 to 0.8 SD (Table 3.1). The magnitude of this effect is similar to the differences in z-scores between children of illiterate mothers and mothers with incomplete secondary education, as observed in our data. Alderman, Hoogeveen and Rossi (2005) report that the anthropometric measures of children born during the 'lean' season in Tanzania are 0.2 to 0.4 SD lower than the measures of children born in other months of the year. These effects are comparable with the effects of nutrition programmes and the estimated elasticities of the changes in the household's and mother's characteristics. For example, in Bangladesh the average HAZ of children with illiterate mothers is about 0.4 SD lower than the HAZ of children whose mothers hold a university degree (Moestue and Huttly 2008). Similar effects of maternal education on children's anthropometrics are found by Alderman and Garcia (1994) for Pakistan and Kassouf and Senauer (1996) for Brazil.

The above estimations demonstrate the consistently strong correlations between the month of birth and children's health outcomes for boys and girls, across different regression specifications, years and for different samples. In the next section we try to establish the causality of this correlation.

Explaining the correlation between the month of birth and health outcomes

Several theories are proposed in the literature to explain the variation in children's health outcomes by season of birth. These theories attribute variations in outcomes by month of birth to seasonal differences in prenatal and postnatal nutrition and the disease environment; social differences in the seasonal distribution of births; the selective survival at birth and during infancy; and planned versus unplanned pregnancies. We discuss each of these theories in turn.

The 'nutrition-disease' hypothesis

We start our analysis by testing the 'nutrition-disease' hypothesis. Both diet and the absence of disease are crucial for the adequate growth of children and may work in synergy (Alderman and Garcia, 1994). Changes in food supply and food quality affect intrauterine growth. In India, mothers who gave birth in the fall or an early winter season had access to better-quality food and fresh fruits and vegetables during most of their pregnancies. Occurrences of infectious diseases that impact the mother, foetus and newborn child are correlated with seasonal climatic changes because of the interaction between climate and the vectors of disease, and the interaction between the nutritional status and immune functions of a mother and her child. Other seasonal factors that might affect the health of children include the effect of exposure to sunlight on the children's and mothers' metabolisms, and the seasonal variations in availability and rates of vitamin absorption.

The monsoon is a climatic event that separates seasons and is essential for agriculture in India. The deprivation of nutrients and other health-related intakes during the monsoon was shown to have a considerable effect on the health status of women and children in India (Chambers, 1982; Sahn, 1987). The monsoon is associated with heavy rains that bring a multitude of diseases (water-borne gastrointestinal infections; cholera, asthma; dengue; malaria and others). The National Nutrition Policy developed by the Department of Women and Child Development in India (1993) indicates that children of poor households are at risk of malnutrition during the monsoon season and recommends giving special rations to 'the seasonally "at risk" population'.

The NFHS provides no data on the nutritional intake of mothers during pregnancy or of children during the first months of their lives. In the absence of such information we use household wealth and the education of the mother as proxies for the nutritional status and disease environment into which the children were born. We argue that wealthier households have better means to smooth consumption for their children during the lean season and can obtain better healthcare if their children become sick. Maternal education has a strong positive impact on children's nutrition and health outcomes via modern attitudes towards healthcare and reproductive behaviour (Caldwell, 1979; Thomas *et al.*, 1991; Glewwe, 1999).

To test the 'nutrition-disease' hypothesis, we regress the HAZ of a child on a set of variables that include the socio-demographic characteristics of a household, a household wealth index, characteristics of the mother, location dummies, the month-specific level of precipitation in a district, month-of-birth dummies, and interactions of the month of birth with the wealth index and years of mother's education. A significance of coefficients on month–wealth interactions or month–education interactions would point to the presence of seasonal differences in the effect of wealth and maternal education (as a proxy for nutrition and healthcare) on children's health outcomes.

Table 3.2 shows the results of the test on the joint significance of coefficients on the interactions of household wealth and maternal education with the month of birth (separately for boys and girls and for three waves of NFHS). The table is based on two econometric specifications. Specification 1 is an OLS regression based on the unrestricted sample of observation. Specification 2 is a fixed effect regression estimated on the sample of siblings. Because of a strong correlation between maternal education and household wealth, we show three tests for each specification/year/gender combination. The first group of tests is based on regressions where we include the interaction between wealth and month of birth only. The second group is based on the regressions with interactions of years of maternal education and the month of birth. The last group of tests includes both interactions and tests the joint significance of the coefficients.

These estimations demonstrate that household wealth and the education of mothers have significant effects on children's health outcomes by month of birth. The seasonal variations in HAZ for children living in wealthier households and with better-educated mothers were smaller compared to the variation in health outcomes of other children. The formal tests strongly reject the null hypotheses of no heterogeneity by maternal education and household wealth for both genders. The majority of tests point to the joint significance of the interaction in terms of household wealth and maternal education with child's month of birth.

The 'socioeconomic' hypothesis

If, during certain seasons, more children are born in better-educated and/or wealthier families, the correlation between children's health outcomes and their months of birth can be attributed to the difference in resources available to the

TABLE 3.2 Tests of the joint significance of coefficients on the interactions of household wealth and maternal education with the month of birth in HAZ regressions (F-test for Specification 1 and c2-test for Specification 2)

		Specification 1		Specification 2
		Boys	Girls	Boys & Girls
	Wealth			
	1992	2.313***	1.992**	21.476**
	1998	2.944***	3.478***	36.454***
	2005	3.091***	2.070**	15.274
Height-for-age	*Education*			
	1992	1.457	1.922**	27.169***
	1998	3.156***	2.595***	19.100*
	2005	2.818***	2.584***	15.654
	Wealth and education			
	1992	1.794**	1.664**	35.285**
	1998	2.350***	2.458***	45.753***
	2005	2.463***	2.632***	32.968*

Note:
* is significant at 10% level;
** at 5% level;
*** at 1% level. Standard errors are adjusted for clustering on a village level.

children (Bronson, 1995). In the less developed countries, women's involvement in agricultural activities, food availability, the seasonality of marriages and male migration are more important determinants of the seasonality of birth. Panter-Brick (1996) demonstrates that, in Nepal, seasonal rates of pregnancies are determined, among other things, by seasonality of marriage (which, in turn, is determined by agricultural cycles), and marital disruptions related to out-migration of males and agricultural activities; the peaks of conception are observed at the beginning of the monsoon season of June–July and during rice harvesting in December. Rajagopalan *et al.* (1981) documented the strong effect of agricultural cycles on births in Tamil Nadu in India, emphasizing large differences in the seasonality of birth between urban and rural areas. Better-off families and families less dependent on maternal labour have fertility patterns more beneficial for their children's survival.

To test the 'socioeconomic' hypothesis, we estimate the relationships between the month of birth and household wealth and maternal education, controlling for the characteristics of a household and a mother. Given an unordered structure of the month-of-birth variable we applied the multinomial logit specification for this estimation. A significance of the coefficients on household wealth and maternal education would indicate that household wealth and education of the mother affect the probability of a child being born in a certain month of the year, thus supporting the 'socioeconomic' hypothesis.

Table 3.3 shows the multinomial logit estimates of the coefficients on the wealth index and maternal education for 11 month-of-birth categories for boys and girls and for three waves of NFHS. In 1992, the coefficients on the wealth index and maternal education are significant only for boys born in October; for girls, household wealth and education of the mother have no significant effect on the probability of being born in a particular month. For boys in the 1998 sample, the effects of wealth and mother's education on the month of birth are significant. But the pattern of this significance differs from the patterns we would expect to observe based on Figure 3.3. For example, in the 1998 sample, better-off households are more likely to have their children born in the months of February, May, August, October and November. But May and August are the 'bad' months to be born in, in terms of health outcomes. We find no effect of wealth and maternal education on girls in the 1998 sample and for children surveyed in 2005. The results of likelihood ratio tests (the bottom part of Table 3.4) confirm that both wealth index and maternal education contribute little to determining the month in which a child will be born.

Thus, we can conclude that our empirical results provide no support for the 'socioeconomic' hypothesis.

The 'selective survival' hypothesis

The third hypothesis postulates that if mortality at birth is higher in a certain season than mortality in other seasons, children who survived during the high-mortality season might be more robust and would have better outcomes later in

TABLE 3.3 Multinomial logit of the probability of a child being born in a certain month of the year (coefficients on household wealth and maternal education variables)

	1992 Boys		1992 Girls		1998 Boys		1998 Girls		2005 Boys		2005 Girls	
	Coeff.	SE	Coeff.	SE	Coeff.	SE	Coeff.	SE	Coeff.	SE	Coeff.	SE
Household wealth index												
January	0.113	0.086	-0.011	0.086	0.069	0.085	-0.114	0.090	-0.012	0.085	-0.010	0.089
February	0.161*	0.092	-0.155	0.092	0.127	0.090	-0.005	0.093	0.073	0.089	-0.167	0.091
March	0.120	0.088	-0.097	0.089	0.108	0.088	-0.056	0.091	0.125	0.087	-0.032	0.088
April	0.147	0.090	-0.030	0.090	0.066	0.089	0.048	0.095	-0.078	0.086	-0.025	0.090
May	0.163*	0.091	-0.018	0.090	0.180**	0.088	-0.051	0.092	-0.011	0.087	0.042	0.090
June	0.189**	0.088	-0.058	0.090	0.082	0.086	-0.076	0.090	0.133	0.086	0.085	0.087
July	0.230***	0.086	-0.055	0.087	0.084	0.084	0.053	0.088	0.088	0.085	0.024	0.088
August	0.097	0.084	-0.069	0.083	0.217***	0.081	-0.016	0.085	0.042	0.081	-0.028	0.084
September	0.147*	0.086	-0.095	0.088	0.032	0.083	-0.086	0.088	0.110	0.082	-0.058	0.086
October	0.332***	0.083	-0.095	0.083	0.192**	0.081	-0.034	0.085	-0.018	0.081	0.073	0.083
November	0.085	0.085	-0.094	0.085	0.186**	0.083	0.010	0.086	-0.043	0.081	-0.070	0.084
December	Reference Month											
LR Test	22.313***		5.510		15.560		6.883		14.449		12.354	
Education of the mother												
January	-0.012	0.013	-0.006	0.013	-0.002	0.012	0.004	0.013	0.005	0.012	-0.001	0.013
February	-0.012*	0.014	0.003	0.013	-0.012	0.013	-0.001	0.014	-0.004	0.012	0.020	0.013
March	-0.019	0.013	-0.004	0.013	-0.015	0.013	-0.011	0.013	-0.011	0.012	0.020	0.013
April	-0.022	0.013	-0.003	0.013	-0.003	0.013	-0.009	0.014	0.006	0.012	0.010	0.013
May	-0.017*	0.013	-0.019	0.013	-0.024**	0.013	0.012	0.013	0.002	0.012	0.011	0.013
June	0.003**	0.013	-0.019	0.013	-0.017	0.012	-0.003	0.013	-0.006	0.012	0.009	0.013
July	-0.023***	0.013	-0.016	0.013	-0.003	0.012	0.006	0.013	-0.011	0.012	0.002	0.013
August	-0.018	0.012	-0.015	0.012	-0.024***	0.012	-0.006	0.012	-0.000	0.011	0.013	0.012
September	-0.008*	0.013	-0.016	0.013	0.009	0.012	0.004	0.013	0.007	0.012	0.024	0.012
October	-0.012***	0.012	-0.018	0.012	-0.024**	0.012	0.000	0.012	0.007	0.011	-0.000	0.012
November	0.003	0.012	0.009	0.012	-0.013**	0.012	0.000	0.013	0.003	0.011	0.006	0.012
December	Reference Month											
LR Test	11.918		12.032		17.673*		4.625		6.230		9.471	

Note:
* is significant at 10% level; ** is significant at 5% level; *** is significant at 1% level. Standard errors are adjusted for clustering on a village level.

life (Samuelson and Ludvigsson, 2001). In other words, weak children born in high-mortality seasons die and only the strong children survive.

To test whether selective child mortality during the first months after birth explains the variation in health outcomes, we estimate the probability of a child surviving past the age of one as a function of the characteristics of: a household, a mother, and a child; month-of-birth dummies; and the interaction between the month of birth and weight at birth. The significance of the coefficients on the interactions between the month of birth and weight at birth rejects the null hypothesis that the survival probabilities of weak and robust children born in a certain month of the year are the same.

The top panel of Table 3.4 shows the coefficients on the interaction in terms of the month of birth and child's weight measured at birth. In different samples, interaction terms are significant for some months, but the pattern of this significance is inconsistent with the observed variation in children's health outcomes. For example, in the 1992 sample, a higher birth weight increases the probability of survival for boys born in April, and decreases this probability if boys were born in September. Overall, the estimations shown in Table 3.4 provide no evidence in support of the 'selective survival' hypothesis.[5] However, the information on measured weight at birth could be imprecise or registered with an error. We use an alternative measure of child weight at birth to address the problem of potential attenuation bias in the estimated coefficients due to such imprecision.

The NFHS asks mothers to categorize the weight of their children at birth as large, average or small.[6] We use this subjective assessment as a proxy for health endowments at birth. The weight of a child at birth influences his/her health and prospects for survival (Rosenzweig and Schultz, 1982; Behrman and Rosenzweig, 2004). Similarly to the results in the top panel, the pattern of survival shown in the bottom panel of Table 3.4 is inconsistent with the observed monthly variation in children's health outcomes. For example, in the 1992 sample, boys who were weak at birth were less likely to survive if they were born in April, May, July, and October. According to the 'selective survival' hypothesis this would result in better health outcomes for children born during these months, which is not the case. The probability of survival for weak children appears to be unaffected by their month of birth for the sample of girls in 1992 and the sample of boys from 1998.

Based on this evidence, our results do not support the 'selective survival' hypothesis.

The 'unplanned pregnancy' hypothesis

Assume that parents *believe* that certain months are 'bad' for their children to be born in. Then, in order to improve their children's health outcomes, parents would plan their pregnancies to give birth during the 'good' months. Under this assumption, children born during 'bad' months would more likely be a result of unplanned pregnancies and thus to have disadvantaged health status

TABLE 3.4 Probability of child surviving to 1 year of age (Sample of children born no more than 36 months prior to the date of interview. Coefficients on the interactions of month-of-birth dummies and the weight of a child measured at birth.)

	1992 Boys		1992 Girls		1998 Boys		1998 Girls		2005 Boys		2005 Girls	
	Coeff	SE	Coeff	SE	Coeff	SE	Coeff	SE	Coeff	SE	Coeff	SE
Interactions of month-of-birth dummies and child's weight as measured at birth												
January	-0.251	0.315	0.763*	0.456	0.351	0.357	0.122	0.329	-0.167	0.261	1.005***	0.349
February	0.508	0.352	0.224	0.551	-0.165	0.252	0.176	0.351	-0.362	0.223	0.168	0.312
March	-0.257	0.251	-0.614	0.488	0.521**	0.255	-0.220	0.397	-0.445**	0.214	0.930***	0.293
April	0.588*	0.347	0.214	0.496	0.528*	0.319	0.551	0.522	-0.452*	0.240	-0.443	0.274
May	0.220	0.314	-0.713*	0.412	0.489	0.308	0.402	0.250	-0.257	0.245	0.276	0.283
June	-0.079	0.283	0.260	0.558	0.316	0.232	-0.017	0.363	-0.305	0.218	0.038	0.310
July	-0.363	0.307	-0.246	0.455	0.391	0.317	-0.149	0.268	0.339	0.268	0.866***	0.294
August	-0.213	0.295	0.205	0.662	0.207	0.240	-0.068	0.330	0.095	0.207	0.380	0.241
September	-0.467*	0.252	0.004	0.406	0.271	0.354	0.225	0.325	-0.254	0.184	0.349	0.308
October	0.042	0.262	0.445	0.382	0.293	0.271	-0.142	0.289	-0.340	0.216	0.348	0.243
November	-0.056	0.280	0.073	0.540	0.928***	0.310	1.140**	0.444	-0.149	0.197	0.257	0.259
December	Reference Month											
N Obs.	1,902		1,517		2,890		2,455		4,291		3,630	
Interactions of month-of-birth dummies and mother-assessed weight at birth												
January	-0.182	0.196	0.173	0.195	0.401*	0.212	-0.326	0.217	-0.442*	0.251	-0.427	0.269
February	-0.227	0.205	-0.270	0.201	0.390	0.239	-0.182	0.226	0.122	0.267	0.056	0.270
March	-0.235	0.202	0.096	0.206	-0.022	0.212	0.188	0.243	-0.092	0.255	0.010	0.265
April	-0.289	0.201	0.163	0.202	0.249	0.221	-0.566**	0.226	0.003	0.284	0.265	0.295
May	-0.273	0.206	0.064	0.202	0.293	0.211	-0.403*	0.216	-0.068	0.267	-0.379	0.260
June	-0.057	0.203	0.177	0.197	0.276	0.214	-0.058	0.225	-0.127	0.253	-0.090	0.262
July	-0.524***	0.196	0.166	0.197	0.059	0.205	-0.318	0.213	-0.461*	0.243	-0.474*	0.258
August	-0.283	0.188	-0.077	0.184	-0.045	0.190	-0.116	0.203	-0.194	0.231	-0.499**	0.242
September	-0.291	0.198	0.173	0.187	0.138	0.207	-0.071	0.206	-0.288	0.235	-0.012	0.281
October	-0.391**	0.186	0.104	0.186	0.216	0.198	-0.289	0.201	-0.352	0.237	0.115	0.249
November	-0.228	0.192	0.183	0.187	0.041	0.189	-0.028	0.203	-0.034	0.236	-0.133	0.245
December	Reference Month											
N Obs.	1,902		1,517		2,890		2,455		4,291		3,630	

Note: * is significant at 10% level; ** is significant at 5% level; *** is significant at 1% level. Standard errors are adjusted for clustering on a village level.

(Kost *et al.*, 1998). If this hypothesis were true, the observed variation in children's anthropometrics across the months of the year could be explained by the higher proportion of unplanned births during the monsoon season. The NFHS questionnaire asked mothers whether their pregnancy with a particular child was desirable or not – in the form of this question: 'At the time you became pregnant with (name) did you want (1) to become pregnant then (2) to wait until later (3) no more children at all?'

Across the different rounds of the survey, the birth of about 20 per cent of children could be considered unplanned – that is, the mothers of these children either wanted to have children later or did not want to have more children at all. There are no significant differences in the shares of desirable pregnancies of boys and girls because parents cannot select the sex of the child at the time of conception.[7]

We use these data to test the 'unplanned pregnancy' hypothesis empirically. We estimate the probability of a child being born in a certain month of the year as a function of the 'desirability' of a child and a set of controls. The 'child desirability' is a dummy variable that is equal to one if a mother wanted to have that child when she became pregnant, and zero otherwise. A significance of coefficients on the 'child desirability' dummies would indicate the concentration of unwanted pregnancies in some months of the year.

Table 3.5 with multinomial logit estimates shows that for the 1992 and 1998 samples, 'child desirability' had virtually no effect on the probability of children being born in a certain month of the year. In 2005, boys who were wanted by their parents were more likely to be born in May, June, and September. For girls in the 2005 sample, the 'desirability of birth' increased their likelihood of being born during the summer months and in January, February, April, and November. These patterns of births would result in a variation in health outcomes very different from those observed.

A mother's opinion about the 'desirability' of her child at the time of conception could be subject to recall errors that attenuate the coefficients of interest. To address this issue, we use the method of instrumental variables. We instrument the 'desirability of birth' variable with the gender composition of older siblings in the household. We argue that the gender of siblings would affect the 'desirability' of a child for its parents (Thomas, 1994; Duflo, 2003) and would have no direct effect on the month the child is born in. We simultaneously estimate (by simulated likelihood) a binary probit of 'desirability of birth' of a particular child as a function of the characteristics of its mother, household characteristics and the gender composition of the child's older siblings[8] and the multinomial logit of the month of birth on a set of maternal and household characteristics and the indicator of desirability initially predicted. The bottom panel of Table 3.5 shows the coefficients on the instrumented 'desirability of birth' variable in the multinomial logit estimation. Similar to the first specification, the instrumented 'desirability' variable has no impact on the probability of being born in a particular month. Thus, neither of the estimations supports the 'unplanned pregnancy' hypothesis.

TABLE 3.5 Mlogit and IV Mlogit estimations of the probability of being born in a certain month as a function of 'child desirability' (coefficients on 'desirability' variable)

	1992 Boys		1992 Girls		1998 Boys		1998 Girls		2005 Boys		2005 Girls	
	Coeff	SE	Coeff	SE	Coeff	SE	Coeff	SE	Coeff	SE	Coeff	SE
Specification with 'desirable pregnancy' dummy												
January	0.049	0.096	−0.001	0.092	−0.026	0.103	−0.008	0.102	−0.076	0.104	0.205*	0.107
February	0.004	0.102	0.079	0.099	0.262**	0.115	0.056	0.108	−0.041	0.109	0.142	0.109
March	0.058	0.099	0.036	0.095	−0.107	0.105	−0.065	0.103	0.131	0.111	0.009	0.104
April	−0.004	0.100	0.126	0.097	−0.079	0.106	0.057	0.108	0.068	0.110	0.265**	0.110
May	−0.028	0.102	−0.078	0.097	−0.194	0.106	−0.046	0.105	0.135	0.111	0.134	0.109
June	0.105	0.100	0.111	0.098	−0.066	0.104	0.057	0.105	0.183	0.111	0.151	0.107
July	−0.009	0.096	0.022	0.094	−0.030	0.102	0.030	0.102	−0.085	0.106	0.225**	0.109
August	−0.043	0.093	0.049	0.089	−0.090	0.098	0.097	0.098	0.134	0.102	0.222**	0.102
September	0.096	0.098	−0.117	0.093	−0.078	0.100	0.052	0.101	−0.172	0.101	0.201*	0.105
October	0.055	0.093	−0.028	0.088	−0.066	0.099	−0.035	0.097	−0.005	0.101	0.126	0.100
November	0.028	0.095	−0.056	0.091	−0.030	0.100	−0.016	0.098	0.056	0.102	0.240**	0.102
December	Reference Month											
Specification with 'desirable pregnancy' dummy instrumented by the gender composition of the siblings												
January	0.773	0.986	−2.848	1.295	0.871	0.886	−2.230	1.520	0.150	0.925	0.850	1.548
February	2.363**	1.038	−0.921	1.520	0.687	1.073	−0.693	1.542	1.308	0.870	−0.942	1.409
March	0.803	1.074	−0.668	1.533	−0.650	0.915	−1.465	1.455	0.128	0.920	0.708	1.477
April	0.480	0.988	−0.474	1.491	0.383	0.982	0.667	1.624	−0.112	0.952	1.457	1.543
May	0.122	1.015	0.365	1.534	1.258	0.995	−0.551	1.575	−0.442	0.916	−0.893	1.478
June	1.226	1.057	−3.142	1.429	0.818	0.911	−1.020	1.552	1.348	0.954	0.795	1.501
July	0.236	0.952	−1.799	1.428	1.206	0.887	0.025	1.524	0.672	0.941	−1.490	1.427
August	0.928	0.966	−1.815	1.313	0.664	0.917	0.565	1.320	1.466*	0.862	1.730	1.320
September	−0.086	1.000	0.425	1.612	0.846	0.878	−0.130	1.524	0.413	0.850	−0.938	1.403
October	−1.627	0.906	−2.103	1.412	1.265	0.969	0.890	1.491	0.562	0.805	−0.452	1.424
November	2.166**	0.975	−3.609	1.335	1.390	0.929	−0.814	1.379	0.291	0.841	1.751	1.346
December	Reference Month											
Test 1 stage	36.715***		0.006		27.370***		1.012		46.496***		6.390**	

Note: * is significant at 10% level; ** at 5% level; *** at 1% level. Standard errors are adjusted for clustering on a village level.

Sensitivity analysis

We test the stability of our results using alternative econometric specifications and different samples. First, we replicate all the results presented above using the month of birth relative to the beginning of the monsoon season. The reason for this is that the monsoon season starts in late May/early June in the southern states of India and in late July in north India. Figure 3.4 shows the average HAZ by month of birth normalized to the beginning of the monsoon season. For example, children born in June in the southern states of India would have a normalized month of birth of 0, and children born in November would have a normalized month of birth equal to 6. The trends in health outcomes depicted in Figure 3.4 are similar to those of Figure 3.3: children born during the monsoon months are more likely to be stunted than children born during the six months after the start of the monsoon. The 'month-of-birth' (relative to the beginning of the monsoon) effect persists after controlling for observable and unobservable characteristics of a child and his/her family. As in the case of calendar month of birth, the 'nutrition-disease' hypothesis seems to be most plausible in explaining the variation in health outcomes by month of birth relative to the beginning of the monsoon.

Another concern about the stability of our results is the impact of the deterioration in health outcomes after children are switched from breast milk to solid food (in India this happens 4–6 months after birth) (Barrera, 1990; Olango and Aboud, 1990; Adair and Guilkey, 1997). To address this concern, we repeat our analysis

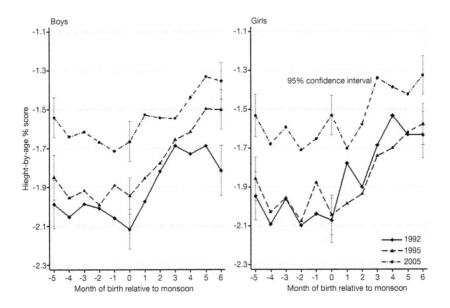

FIGURE 3.4 Health outcomes (HAZ) by gender and the month of birth normalized relative to the beginning of the monsoon season

on a sample of children older than 12 months. Again, our main conclusions remain the same: the environmental conditions around the date of birth play an important role in determining a child's health outcomes in later life.

Conclusions

In this paper, we used data from three waves of the India NFHS to explore the relationship between the month of birth and health outcomes of young children in India. We demonstrated that children born during the monsoon months have consistently worse health outcomes compared with children born in the fall/winter season. The 'month-of-birth' effect persists after controlling for a wide set of observable and unobservable characteristics of a child, its mother and the household they live in. The size of these effects ranges from 0.5 to 0.8 SD of the HAZ and is comparable to or larger than the effects of maternal education and nutrition supplementation programmes on children's health.

We empirically tested four hypotheses to explain the month-of-birth variation in children's health, controlling for a wide range of observable characteristics and using the fixed effect and instrumental variable approaches to account for the effects of unobservable factors. We concluded that one possible explanation for the observed patterns of changes in children's health by their month of birth might be the higher prevalence of malnutrition and wider exposure to diseases in the lean monsoon season.

Our results demonstrate the significance of seasonal changes in environmental conditions in explaining variations in children's health. Interventions to improve these conditions could have a positive impact on the health and achievements of children. Family planning campaigns can help parents optimally time births, thus improving the health of their children. Low-cost modifications to existing nutrition programmes, which take into account the season of birth, may have a large impact on the health of Indian children.

Notes

1   Across the rounds of the NFHS, about 10 per cent of eligible children were not measured, either because they were not at home, or because their mothers refused to allow the measurements (Lokshin et al., 2005).
2   The results shown in Figure 3.1 are calculated from the sample of children younger than 36 months of age ever born in a household. This sample includes children who did not survive.
3   A relatively large gap between the anthropometric measures of children born in December and January persists in all rounds of the NFHS. We observe similar December–January differences in health outcomes in DHS surveys from other countries.
4   The F-tests on the fixed effects (FE) in all regressions in Table 3.2 reject the pooled OLS specification in favour of FE specification.
5   Alderman and Lokshin (2009) demonstrate that selective mortality has only a minor impact on the measured anthropometric status of children or on that status distinguished by gender.

6 We find a good correspondence between the measured weight and the children's weight at birth assessed by their mothers. For example, in 1992, only about 3 per cent of children who were assessed as large at birth had a measured weight in the first quintile of the weight distribution.
7 Although the observed ratio of desired boys and girls could be influenced by selective abortion after conception.
8 We use 'a household already has a male child' and 'the previous child was a boy' as instruments for the desirability of children.

4

Seasonal hunger, famine and the dynamics of HIV in Malawi

Michael Loevinsohn

Introduction

The impact on health of seasonal patterns of livelihood and access to food has not attracted systematic research attention. Investigations in South Asia and sub-Saharan Africa have shed some light on the effect of seasonally restricted nutrition on maternal health and infant and child development (Kinabo, 1993; Maleta *et al.*, 2003; Bang *et al.*, 2005). However, there is very little evidence of how these patterns influence the risks of major communicable diseases such as HIV. Understanding these links is important because many of the countries where HIV prevalence is greatest are also ones where food production and livelihoods are highly seasonal. Moreover, climate change and variability are likely to aggravate food insecurity most in regions that are dependent on seasonal, rainfed agriculture (IPCC, 2007).

Much of what is known about the effect of hunger and other facets of poverty on the epidemiology of HIV comes from cross-sectional or longitudinal studies of limited duration that shed little light on dynamic effects, whether seasonal cycles, longer trends or major shocks (Gillespie *et al.*, 2007; Weiser *et al.*, 2007). The fact that hunger is both a cause and a consequence of HIV further limits the ability of these methods to disentangle the effect of change in either HIV or hunger.

The evidence reported here brings new light to bear on this relationship. It assesses the 2001–03 famine in Malawi – a particularly severe seasonal crisis (Devereux *et al.*, 2008) – as a country-scale 'unnatural experiment' on the effect of hunger on the dynamics of HIV. As described below, the 'intervention' that triggered the famine was 'sharp, well-defined but unplanned' and its effects were unequally experienced among rural areas, between rural and non-rural areas and between men and women – characteristics of a natural experiment (Susser,

1981). However the famine was the consequence largely of human actions that were entirely avoidable. Its analysis suggests important policy opportunities and, in the final section, I discuss the implications for the conception of HIV prevention and that of related health conditions.

The famine

Two poor maize harvests in 2001 and 2002, provoked by bad weather, provided the famine's immediate trigger. While these shortfalls were not exceptional in historical terms, their impact on food security was magnified by three converging trends. First, rural Malawians had become dangerously vulnerable to the fate of the main maize harvest with the erosion of crop and livestock diversity – in part a result of policy favouring maize, and of dry season livelihood opportunities in and outside agriculture. This was exacerbated by prolonged under-investment in human capital and rural infrastructure, notably irrigation. Households affected by AIDS, either through the illness of prime-age adults or taking in orphans, were particularly vulnerable (Devereux, 2002; Frankenberger *et al.*, 2003; Mandala, 2005; Devereux and Tiba, 2007).

Second, increasing numbers of rural households had, in the years leading up to the famine, become unable to feed themselves from one harvest to the next and were forced to rely on casual labour (*ganyu*) and the market (Bryceson, 2002). The poor harvests of 2001 and 2002 exacerbated this trend, pushing larger numbers of farming households, not just the poorest, into the search for *ganyu* while at the same time reducing the number of farmers who were hiring. Consequently, wage rates fell and working conditions deteriorated (Shah *et al.*, 2002; Ellis *et al.*, 2003; MVAC, 2003).

Third, ill-conceived and delayed administrative responses contributed to a steep rise in food prices. By February 2002, a kilo of maize cost 2–6 times what it had the previous year, in most markets considerably more than the daily *ganyu* wage. The harvest of March to May 2002 brought little relief and prices remained high in most areas through the rest of 2002 (Devereux, 2002; IDC, 2003).

Deaths from hunger and cholera were reported in several areas early in 2002 (Devereux, 2002; WHO, 2002). Nationwide surveys begun later that year found that 31 per cent of rural households would need food assistance between December 2002 and March 2003 – the traditional hungry season, unevenly spread but substantial in all regions. Hunger was less severe among wealthier households, those headed by men and those with non-agricultural income (MVAC, 2002; 2003). Though not covered by the surveys, households in the towns and cities evidently felt the crisis less acutely. They were not directly affected by the loss of production and the scarcity of *ganyu* employment while benefiting from more reliable maize supplies and less volatile prices. These differences compounded existing rural/non-rural economic and social disparities (Devereux, 2002; World Bank, 2007).

Hunger and HIV risk

As the famine intensified, rural Malawians increasingly resorted to measures that many, particularly the most vulnerable, had come to rely on in the annual hungry season, such as regularly going entire days without eating and removing children from school. Some of these actions pushed people further into existing 'situations of risk' for HIV. Among these was survival sex – women with few other liveli-hood options selling or exchanging sex for food or cash on an occasional basis (Government of Malawi, 2000; Shah *et al.*, 2002).

A report early in 2002 from Mchinji, one of the hardest-hit districts, spoke of increasing numbers of women engaging in survival sex (Kamowa, 2002). In a rapid survey in ten districts, 15 per cent of young women and 6 per cent of older women acknowledged exchanging sex for food during the famine (United Nations Country Team, 2002), likely underestimates given the difficulty of assessing this sensitive matter through formal interviews. Informants in an ethnographic study in the Central region reported that provision of sexual services was frequently demanded of women seeking *ganyu* employment, a practice that continued after the famine (Bryceson *et al.*, 2004; Bryceson, 2006).

Reports also emerged during the famine of young women being forced into marriage with older men (UNCT, 2002; Munthali, 2006). They would have been at heightened risk of HIV and other STIs because their partners were more likely to be infected than men their age; physiological immaturity would have increased the likelihood of infection following exposure (Bruce and Clark, 2004).

Finally, people moved in search of food or work: among 1,200 rural households surveyed in early 2002, 39 per cent had adult members migrating (Devereux *et al.*, 2003). They moved to towns, cities, neighbouring countries and less affected rural areas – the latter including areas where cassava, more tolerant of drought than maize, was grown (Devereux, 2002; Kamowa, 2002; World Food Programme, 2003). People moving in distress, often facing poor living conditions, sexual abuse and separation, are more likely to engage in non-marital sex and to be HIV-infected than non-migrants (Pison *et al.*, 1993; Decosas *et al.*, 1995; Lurie *et al.*, 2003).

This evidence suggests hypotheses about the famine's impact on HIV infection rates, focusing on women, since regular surveillance has only involved them. Greater involvement in survival sex and early marriage would likely increase HIV incidence and prevalence in rural women in proportion to the extent and duration of hunger locally. Early marriage's effect would be concentrated in younger women while that of survival sex, which apparently involved both older and younger women, would be more even. The unequal experience of hunger by rural men and women may also have contributed to more asymmetrical relationships (e.g. a man able to provide *ganyu* having sex with several workers) and concurrent relationships (e.g. the man maintaining relationships with his wife and one or more workers). Both have been shown to hasten HIV transmission and the latter to increase equilibrium prevalence (Garnett and Anderson, 1996; Morris and Kretzschmar, 1997; Halperin and Epstein, 2004). Malnutrition itself may have increased women's risk of infec-tion once exposed to the virus by suppressing immune function. The evidence for this is clearest with respect to sexually transmitted and parasitic infections that facilitate HIV transmission (Stillwagon, 2006).

The impact of hunger-induced migration on HIV prevalence and distribution depends on how long people remained away from home. There has until now been no information on this but evidence from other famines suggests that not all migration is temporary (von Braun *et al.*, 1998). To the extent this was true in Malawi, one would expect to see changes in the distribution of HIV and population in both source and destination areas, i.e. effects on both epidemiology and demography.

Methods

The prevalence of rural hunger in the district surrounding an HIV surveillance site was taken from a country-wide survey in August 2002 (n=1,128 households). It used an algorithm to estimate whether a household would experience a significant food deficit in the December 2002 to March 2003 period – the lean season in the famine's second year – given its food requirements, stocks and expected income (MVAC, 2002). For Mzuzu city, which is not part of any district, the average of the estimates for the two districts that surround it is used.

Estimates of the prevalence, timing and direction of migration were calculated from a country-wide survey in 2004 and early 2005 (n=10,777 households) which asked when and from where members had moved to their present residence (NSO, 2005).

HIV prevalence estimates from before and after the worst of the famine are drawn from the antenatal surveillance rounds in 1999/2000 (median sample date 7 January 2000, 15–85 per cent completed 30 December 1999 to 24 January 2000), approximately 18 months before the steep rise in maize price, and 2003 (median sample date 11 March 2003, 15–85 per cent completed 16 February 2002 to 13 May 2003), overlapping the lean season in the famine's second year and the post-harvest period when food was more readily available. (The 2001 round cannot be used because it overlaps the rise in maize price.) Eight of the 19 sites are rural, located in village health centres, and 8 are semi-urban, located in hospitals in district administrative centres (*bomas*). These sites were established in randomly selected districts, stratifying for region. One semi-urban site, Nkhotakota, is discarded because its results in 2003 were unreliable (National AIDS Commission, 2003). Three sites are urban, located in hospitals or health centres in the three largest cities – Mzuzu, Lilongwe and Blantyre.

On each surveillance round, a consecutive sample of women on their first antenatal visit were tested anonymously for HIV using a single enzyme-linked immunosorbent assay. Their age, education status, occupation and partner's occupation were also recorded. Because the occupation codes for 1999/2000 are missing, it was only possible to infer the code for 'farmer', by far the most common occupation in Malawi. A woman who gave her occupation or her partner's as 'farmer' is here considered a farmer. Rural clinics attract predominantly farmers, urban clinics mostly non-farmers and semi-urban clinics intermediate proportions (Table

4.1). Figure 4.1 shows the trends in HIV prevalence since 1994. Prevalence has been similar at urban and semi-urban sites since 1999/2000 and these are analysed together as 'non-rural'.

Multilevel, random intercept models are used to analyse the contribution of contextual factors at the surveillance site level (rural or non-rural setting, the extent of rural hunger in the district) and compositional factors at the individual level (age, occupation and education) and their interactions, to the probability of a woman being HIV-infected and to the change in this probability over the course of the famine. The serostatus of the ith woman in the jth site in 2003, y_{ij}, is a binary variate that takes the value 1 (positive) with probability $\pi03_{ij}$. The logit link relates this probability to a linear function of factors and covariates. Individual and site-level residuals are assumed to follow binomial and normal distributions, respectively. A site-level model is first estimated:

$$\text{logit } \pi03_{ij} = \text{logit } \pi99_j + \beta_{0j} + \beta_1 \text{ rural}_j + \beta_2 \text{ rural}_j \cdot \text{hunger}_j + \beta_3 \text{ nonrural}_j \cdot \text{hunger}_j + \mu_{0j} \quad (1)$$

where $\text{logit } \pi03_{ij} = \log [\pi03_{ij} / (1-\pi03_{ij})]$ is the log odds of a woman being positive in 2003 and $\text{logit } \pi99_j$ the log odds of being positive averaged over all women at the jth site in 1999/2000. Subtracting the latter term from both sides makes the dependent variable the log of the odds ratio of being HIV-infected in 2003 vs 1999/2000 (adapting an approach suggested by Ukoumunne and Thompson,

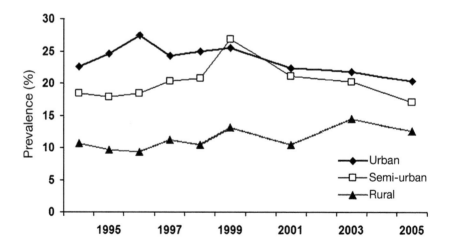

Source: National AIDS Commission (2003)

FIGURE 4.1 Prevalence of HIV in women attending antenatal clinics in Malawi 1994–2005

TABLE 4.1 Characteristics of the women surveyed at antenatal surveillance sites and of the surrounding district

	Rural (n=8)		Non-rural (n=10)			
			Semi-urban (n=7)		Urban (n=3)	
	1999	2003	1999	2003	1999	2003
Number of women	1144	1627	3392	3618	1901	2460
HIV serostatus positive	12.1 (2·4)	14.5 (2.1)	27.6 (2.0)	21.6 (2.3)	25.6 (1.4)	21.8 (3.1)
Age						
15–19 yrs	24.9 (3.1)	22.0 (2.4)	24.0 (1.7)	20.7 (0.7)	20.0 (1.6)	19.7 (0.6)
20–24 yrs	38.9 (3.1)	36.2 (1.0)	39.5 (1.0)	40.3 (1.6)	43.2 (2.3)	44.1 (1.2)
25–44 yrs	36.2 (2.6)	41.8 (2.2)	36.5 (1.8)	39.1 (2.1)	36.8 (2.3)	36.2 (1.8)
Education						
None	23.6 (4.7)	29.8 (6.7)	29.1 (7.6)	31.7 (10.7)	8.8 (2.7)	10.2 (3.2)
Primary	70.6 (3.8)	64.6 (6.6)	58.6 (6.2)	54.8 (8.3)	62.4 (5.8)	63.9 (1.6)
Secondary +	5.8 (1.1)	5.7 (0.9)	12.3 (1.6)	13.4 (2.6)	28.8 (6.3)	25.9 (3.5)
Occupation						
Farmer	76.9 (5.1)	77.2 (4.6)	46.5 (3.5)	40.7 (6.3)	5.9 (4.3)	5.7 (2.9)
Non-farmer	23.1 (5.1)	22.8 (4.6)	53.5 (3.5)	59.3 (6.3)	94.1 (4.3)	94.3 (2.9)
Surrounding district Rural population in need of food assistance Dec 2002–March 2003		32.6 (3.8)		26.0 (4.3)		20.8 (3.8)

2001). β_{0j} is the fixed part of the intercept and μ_{0j} its site-specific residual. *rural$_j$* and *nonrural$_j$* are dummy variables taking the value 1 when the site is rural or non-rural, respectively, and 0 otherwise. β_1 is thus the additional fixed part of the intercept at rural sites, while β_2 and β_3 are the linear coefficients of rural hunger in the district surrounding rural and non-rural sites, respectively. The *hunger$_j$* variable was arc sine-transformed and centred on its overall mean. Quadratic terms in *hunger$_j$* were also fitted to test for non-linear relationships.

Model (2) adds the individual-level factors and their interactions with rural hunger. The coefficient associated with a class of a factor, e.g. farmer in occupation, indicates the extent to which change from the 1999/2000 mean log odds of infection was greater or less for farmers than for non-farmers. The coefficient associated with the interaction term indicates the extent to which the difference between farmers and non-farmers varied with the level of rural hunger in the district. In both cases, the coefficients control for other individual and site-level variables.

Change through the famine in the composition of women sampled at the sites was estimated with models (3, 4), of the form of models (1, 2) but with log odds of a woman being a farmer in 2003 as dependent variable.

A model (5) with the individual-level factors and site terms, but without hunger, was estimated to assess the determinants of prevalence in 2003.

These models were estimated with the RIGLS procedure, employing PQL with second-order Taylor series in the MLwiN 2.02 software (Rasbash *et al.*, 2005). Results were confirmed using Monte Carlo Markov chain simulation, which may yield less biased parameter estimates with small samples, employing the WinBUGS program in MLwiN (Browne, 2003).

The dependent variable in these equations is the odds ratio but a better and more intuitive measure of the impact of exposure on risk is the risk ratio – the ratio of prevalence in the two years (Greenland, 1987). Models 1–4 were therefore also estimated using a log probability link, yielding the log risk ratio of infection and the log risk ratio of being a farmer in 2003 relative to 1999/2000 as dependent variables. Here a negative binomial distribution of individual-level errors was assumed. However, as is common with the log link, convergence could only be achieved with one of the models (4) if simplified. The detailed analytical results from the odds ratio models are therefore discussed in what follows but key results from risk ratio models are illustrated in graphic form, noting any substantive differences among the methods and procedures in the text.

Results

HIV prevalence increased 20.2 per cent over the course of the famine at rural surveillance sites but declined by 19.3 per cent at non-rural sites (21.7 per cent and 14.8 per cent at semi-urban and urban sites, respectively – see Table 4.1). The increase at rural sites was non-linearly related to the extent of rural hunger in the district, implying no increase in prevalence below a threshold of about 30 per cent and a steep increase thereafter (Model 1, Table 4.2, Figure 4.2). At non-rural sites, the decline in prevalence was negatively related to rural hunger with no evident non-linearity; urban and semi-urban sites followed a similar pattern. This regression excludes one extreme outlier – the semi-urban site Nsanje (departure from predicted P<0.001; see further below). At the rural and non-rural sites where hunger was greatest, Model 1 estimates that HIV prevalence increased 142 per cent and declined 49 per cent, respectively.

At rural sites, adding individual-level factors and interactions had little effect on the site-level relationship with hunger (Model 2).Women under 25 years were at significantly less risk of infection relative to the pre-famine mean than older women, but this risk and that of the other individual-level factors did not vary with the extent of hunger. At non-rural sites, women under 25 years and those who farmed were at significantly reduced risk while those with at least some secondary education were at increased risk relative to the pre-famine mean. Here, the risk for women farmers declined significantly as rural hunger rose: the log odds ratio fell 0.044 per unit increase in hunger compared to a non-significant 0.018 for non-farmers, controlling for other factors.

TABLE 4.2 Multilevel analysis of change in HIV prevalence at antenatal sites over the course of the famine

	Model 1		Model 2	
	Rural	*Non-rural*	*Rural*	*Non-rural*
Site level:				
Rural hunger				
Linear	-0.251 (-0.514, 0.013)+	-0.029 (-0.047, -0.012)**	-0.293 (-0.610, 0.023)+	-0.018 (-0.050, 0.014)
Quadratic	0.004 (0.000, 0.008)*†	—	0.005 (0.000, 0.009)*	—
Rural (dummy)	0.600 (0.296, 0.905)**	—	0.814 (0.122, 1.506)*	—
Individual level:				
Occupation				
Farmer			-0.235 (-0.690, 0.220)	-0.422 (-0.609, -0.235)**
Non-farmer (ref.)			0	0
Age				
<25 yrs			-0.403 (-0.745, -0.060)*	-0.282 (-0.427, -0.138)**
25+ yrs (ref.)			0	0
Education				
None (ref.)			0	0
Primary			-0.002 (-0.454, 0.450)	0.012 (-0.189, 0.213)
Secondary +			-0.166 (-0.986, 0.655)	0.307 (0.064, 0.549)*
Interaction:				
Occupation × rural hunger				
Farmer			0.002 (-0.066, 0.070)	-0.026 (-0.050, -0.002)*
Non-farmer (ref.)			0	0
Age × rural hunger				
<25 yrs			-0.010 (-0.057, 0.038)	0.006 (-0.012, 0.024)
25+ yrs (ref.)			0	0
Education × rural hunger				
None (ref.)			0	0
Primary			0.035 (-0.027, 0.097)	-0.002 (-0.030, 0.025)
Secondary +			0.043 (-0.069, 0.155)	0.004 (-0.029, 0.036)
Intercept	-0.396 (-0.531, -0.261)**		-0.156 (-0.392, 0.081)	
Between-site variance (se)	0.031 (0.017)		0.048 (0.024)	

Source: Loevinsohn (2009)

Notes: The dependent variable is the log of the odds ratio of a woman being seropositive in 2003 versus 1999/2000. Coefficients (95% C.I.).
+P<0.10; *P<0.05; **P<0.01; †Joint probability linear and quadratic P<0.05.

A

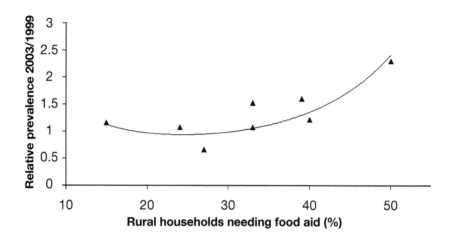

B

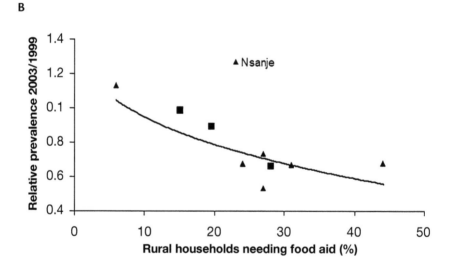

Notes: A = rural sites; B = non-rural sites (triangles = towns; squares = cities). The outlier (Nsanje) is not included in the analysis (see text).

FIGURE 4.2 Change in HIV prevalence at antenatal sites over the course of the famine in relation to the proportion of rural households estimated to be in need of food assistance in the surrounding district in December 2002 to March 2003

The rural site results suggest an increased per capita risk of infection at levels of hunger above the threshold that was not concentrated in any particular group. This is consistent with the reports of women's increased exposure to HIV through survival sex, less so with more frequent early marriage whose effects would have been concentrated in the under-25 age class. Factors that increased the likelihood of infection once exposed might also have contributed.

The non-rural site results suggest selective out-migration by farming women from rural areas. This is consistent with the evidence that the erosion of livelihoods and the effect of the price spike were most keenly felt by those dependent on farming; also that migration in search of food or work was common. Women who moved to towns and cities and who remained long enough to become pregnant (if they weren't already when they moved) and attend antenatal clinics there would have reduced HIV prevalence because they came from a lower-risk environment: in 1999/2000, the probability of a farming woman being HIV-positive at the rural sites was 10.6 per cent (95 per cent CI 6.2–17.5 per cent) but 22.0 per cent (19.5–24.8 per cent) at the non-rural sites. This dilution would have increased the greater the level of hunger-induced migration. As discussed below, this effect is likely to have diminished with time.

Migration may explain the discrepant result at Nsanje. In 2005, a one-off surveillance site was established at a rural health centre in the district. HIV prevalence was 40.5 per cent (n=74), higher than at the district hospital in 1999/2000 (26.0 per cent) or 2003 (33.0 per cent) – indeed, the highest level ever recorded at an antenatal surveillance site in Malawi. If similar infection rates prevailed in rural Nsanje during the famine, migration from the villages would, as observed, have raised rather than lowered prevalence in the town.

This implication, that selective migration of farming women from rural areas underlies the decline in prevalence at non-rural sites, is corroborated by Model 3 (Table 4.3) and Figure 4.3: the proportion of farmers attending non-rural antenatal clinics rose significantly through the course of the famine in proportion to the extent of rural hunger in the district but fell significantly at rural clinics. As hunger pushed farmers into the towns and cities it would have removed farmers from the villages.[1]

Figure 4.3A and Model 3 indicate that at rural surveillance sites where hunger was relatively low, the proportion of farmers in 2003 was greater than in 1999/2000 (ratio >1). This is consistent with the accounts of villagers migrating to other rural as well as urban areas in search of food and work; districts where hunger was low would have been the most attractive.

Similarly, the fact that at the non-rural sites where rural hunger was low, the proportion of farmers in 2003 was less than in 1999/2000 (ratio <1, Figure 4.3B) might result from women farmers resident in or near those towns leaving for the villages. However, this is unlikely to be a sufficient explanation because even at the highest levels of rural hunger the proportion of farmers in 2003 was not much greater than in 1999/2000. The simplest explanation, consistent with the hypotheses, is that, for many, leaving their villages was more than a temporary measure. A village

TABLE 4.3 Multilevel analysis of change in the proportion of farmers at antenatal sites over the course of the famine

	Model 3		Model 4	
	Rural	*Non-rural*	*Rural*	*Non-rural*
Site level:				
Rural hunger	−0.122 (−0.181, −0.063)*	0.053 (0.011, 0.095)*	−0.126 (−0.217, −0.036)**	0.075 (0.024, 0.126)**
Rural (dummy)	0.767 (0.190, 1.345)**	–	0.972 (0.162, 1.782)*	–
Individual level:				
Age				
<25 yrs			0.497 (0.094, 0.899)*	−0.014 (−0.173, 0.144)
25+ yrs (ref.)			0	0
Education				
None (ref.)			0	0
Primary			−0.838 (−1.430, −0.246)**	−0.150 (−0.373, 0.073)
Secondary +			−1.678 (−2.555, −0.802)**	−1.205 (−1.511, −0.899)**
Interaction:				
Age × rural hunger				
<25 yrs			−0.068 (−0.122, −0.014)*	−0.003 (−0.024, 0.019)
25+ yrs (ref.)			0	0
Education × rural hunger				
None (ref.)			0	0
Primary			0.044 (−0.033, 0.121)	−0.021 (−0.054, 0.011)
Secondary +			0.025 (−0.086, 0.136)	−0.051 (−0.092, −0.011)*
Intercept	−0.169 (−0.497, 0.159)		0.096 (−0.282, 0.474)	
Between-site variance (se)	0.227 (0.088)		0.225 (0.088)	

Source: Loevinsohn (2009)

Notes: The dependent variable is the log of the odds ratio of a woman being a farmer in 2003 versus 1999/2000. Coefficients (95% C.I.); *P<0.05; **P<0.01.

A

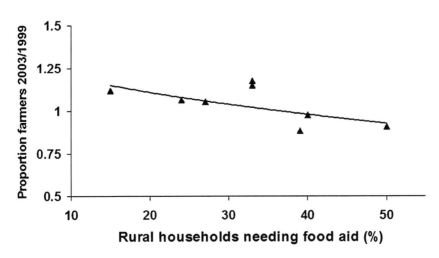

B

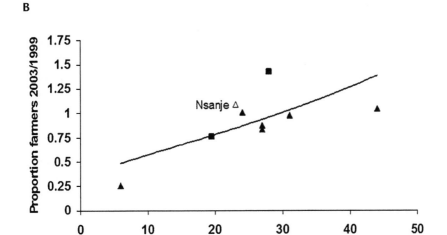

Notes: A = rural sites; B = non-rural sites (triangles = towns, squares = cities). The outlier from Figure 4.2 (Nsanje) is not included in the analysis (see text).

FIGURE 4.3 Change in the proportion of farmers at antenatal sites over the course of the famine in relation to the proportion of rural households estimated to be in need of food assistance in the surrounding district in December 2002 to March 2003

woman attending an antenatal clinic in a town or city in 2003 who had decided to remain there would probably not give her occupation as 'farmer'. In aggregate, such decisions would tend to depress the regression line. They would also lead to the overall decline in the proportion of farmers at non-rural – especially semi-urban – sites evident in Table 4.1. Other evidence bearing on this is presented below.

Model 4 (Table 4.3) indicates that at both rural and non-rural sites, relative to the 1999/2000 mean, farmers were significantly more likely than non-farmers to have less than a primary education and at rural sites to be less than 25 years of age. The interaction coefficients indicate that at the rural sites, compared to the 1999/2000 mean, the proportion of farmers less than 25 years of age decreased significantly relative to older farmers as rural hunger in the district rose; the log odds ratio declined 0.194 per unit increase in rural hunger for the former and 0.126 for the latter, controlling for woman-level factors and other interactions. Note, however, that both coefficients are significant. This suggests that farmers under 25 years had a greater propensity to migrate in response to hunger than older farmers who in turn had a greater propensity to migrate than non-farmers.

At the non-rural sites, compared to the 1999/2000 mean, the proportion of farmers with no formal education increased relative to farmers with a primary or secondary and higher education as rural hunger in the district rose; the log odds ratio increased 0.075 per unit increase in rural hunger for those with no education, 0.054 for those with primary education and 0.024 for those with at least some secondary education, again controlling for woman-level factors and other interactions. Only the first two are significant. This suggests a greater propensity to migrate in response to hunger in less educated farmers and especially those with no formal education than in those with at least some secondary education or in non-farmers.

These analyses suggest that women who left the villages were disproportionately young farmers while those who arrived in the towns and cities were disproportionately uneducated farmers. There is no contradiction because the comparisons are made to different populations – women attending the rural and non-rural antenatal clinics respectively – which differed in composition.

No substantive differences were found between the log probability and log odds forms of the four models. The significance of the MCMC-derived regression coefficients at the site level was lower than with RIGLS but the interpretation would be the same using either method. The significance of the individual-level and interaction effects was unchanged or in some cases enhanced using the MCMC procedure.

Data on migration from the 2004–05 Integrated Household Survey are presented in Figure 4.4. Across the country, 22.3 per cent of women 15–24 years who were interviewed in towns and cities reported having moved to their place of residence from a rural area in the previous three years – roughly the period since the beginning of the famine. Among women 25–49 years, the corresponding proportion was 11.8 per cent ($\chi2 = 41.3$, P<0.01); in men 15–24 years and 25–49 years it was 17.8 per cent and 14.3 per cent, respectively. Figure 4.4A also indicates that migration from rural to non-rural areas in women 15–24 years peaked 1–2 years before the survey, i.e. around the height of the food crisis in 2002–03. No such peak is evident in the other age-gender groups. The varying shape of these curves makes it less likely that some factor other than migration is responsible – such as people recalling recent events better than more distant ones.

A

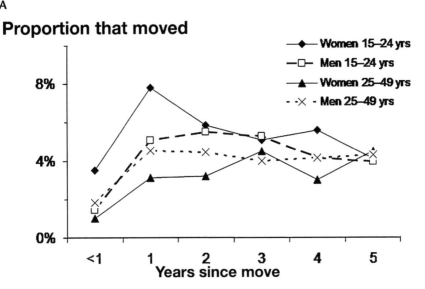

B

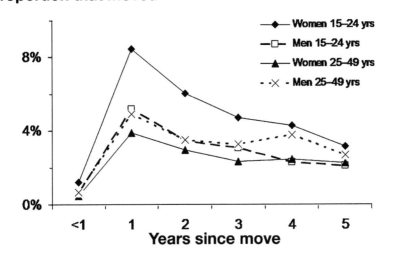

Notes: A = rural to non-rural migration, N=4,427. Non-rural includes cities, towns and the district *bomas* (administrative centres). B = rural-to-rural migration, N=17,722.

FIGURE 4.4 Prevalence of migration in Malawi, assessed in 2004 and early 2005

Figure 4.4B shows a similar pattern for rural-to-rural migration: greater in women 15–24 years than in women 25–49 years (20.4 per cent vs 9.6 per cent, $\chi2 = 212.8$, P<0.01). In men 15–24 years and 25–49 years, the proportions were 12.3 per cent and 12.4 per cent, respectively. There is again a peak in migration 1–2 years before the survey that is most marked in women 15–24 years but also apparent in the other groups.

These results confirm the findings from the multilevel analysis of HIV prevalence and antenatal clinic composition: there is evidence of substantial migration from rural areas to both non-rural and other rural areas during the famine that involved women under 25 years of age significantly more than older women. Given that the IHS was conducted approximately a year after the 2003 antenatal surveillance round, the results also support the suggestion that for many women migration was more than a temporary response to hunger. There is no evidence for significant movement from towns and cities to the villages that might have affected these patterns (1.5 per cent and 1.3 per cent of women aged 15–24 and 25–49, respectively).

Discussion

Taken together, the results suggest that the Malawi famine had a rapid and substantial effect on both HIV prevalence and demography across the country's rural and non-rural areas. The famine's consequences must be considered not just in terms of hunger and malnutrition but also in additional HIV infections, illness and death; the lifelong costs of antiretroviral treatment, as well as the dislocated lives left by widespread migration that was far from voluntary and evidently not always temporary.

The findings of an increased risk of HIV infection at the rural sites where hunger was greatest, broadly shared among age, occupation and education classes, are consistent with hunger leading women into increased involvement in survival sex that raised their exposure to HIV and, with depressed immune function, increased their risk of infection once exposed. Hunger may also have reduced women's ability to insist on their partners using condoms; however the level of use before the famine was relatively low – less than a quarter of rural women in 2000 reported using a condom with their last non-cohabiting partner (NSO and ORC Macro, 2001).

The implication of hunger in the rise in rural HIV prevalence is supported by a single multilevel regression. More robust is the implication of hunger-induced rural out-migration in the decline of HIV prevalence at non-rural sites which is supported by three lines of evidence: the multilevel analyses of changing HIV prevalence and composition of the antenatal population and the analysis of IHS migration data. It also appears to be plausible that rural migration on the scale observed could have produced the observed changes in non-rural prevalence. A full treatment cannot be presented here but a key factor is that the rural areas (84 per cent of the population [NSO, 1998]) exert significant demographic 'leverage' over the cities (12 per cent) and especially the towns (3 per cent).

It bears pointing out that catchment areas for migration are unlikely to have followed district boundaries. Particularly in the case of the cities, migrants may well have been attracted from a much larger distance. The analyses reported above used hunger in the surrounding district as the independent variable; however, neighbouring districts that shared socioeconomic and agronomic characteristics often had similar levels of hunger. Also, the methods employed give no indication of the frequency of transient migration – women who returned to their villages before the 2003 HIV surveillance round or the 2004–05 IHS.

The decline in non-rural HIV prevalence due to 'dilution' by rural women migrating in distress was probably an initial effect, it was suggested, which would diminish over time. The reason is that the women most involved were, before migrating, at relatively low risk of infection and at progressively greater risk as they settled in the towns and cities. A woman attending a rural antenatal clinic in 2003 who was a farmer, under 25 years of age and with less than a primary education, had a 9.9 per cent probability of being HIV-positive (Model 5). She had a probability of 12.9 per cent if she attended a non-rural clinic and a 19.2 per cent probability if her occupation changed to non-farmer, which appears to have been common. Migration nearly doubled her risk of infection, this suggests. This is in line with the widespread evidence, cited above, concerning the hazards a migrant confronts. But she may well have been at increased risk compared to a non-migrant, non-rural woman with similar characteristics because social isolation added to poor education would have left her with few skills or resources to avoid situations of infection risk in her new environment. Whatever the extent of this additional risk, it appears likely that the famine gave rise to an increased burden of HIV infection not just among the women forced into survival sex in the villages but also among those forced into migration to towns and cities.

It is important to consider the relevance of these findings to situations beyond Malawi in 2001–03. Detailed data from neighbouring countries in this period are not available but a preliminary assessment for Zambia using aggregate data suggests a similar pattern of change in rural and non-rural HIV prevalence. Certainly, the underlying situations of risk – particularly distress migration and survival sex – were widely reported in the region and persisted in Malawi in subsequent hungry seasons (Bryceson, 2006). They are also familiar in other developing regions dependent on highly seasonal agricultural production. In semi-arid areas of India, research has paid much more attention to seasonal, distress-linked migration than survival sex, but one study which interviewed male and female sex workers in seven districts of Andhra Pradesh found that many turn to it when employment on-farm or in rural warehouses is not available (George *et al.*, 2005).

Food crises that are not fundamentally seasonal in origin may provoke similar effects. There is evidence that the surge in global cereal prices in 2008 forced people in many parts of eastern and southern Africa, if not elsewhere, further into survival sex and distress migration (Gillespie *et al.*, 2009). Whether a food access crisis produces epidemiologic and demographic consequences comparable to those of the Malawi famine will depend on the frequency with which people are drawn into such situations of risk. At least two aspects of the Malawi context appear to have been critical in driving that frequency. First, the shocks that triggered the famine acted on a rural population whose livelihoods had become increasingly precarious; many had few options left other than the most extreme. Second, hunger was very unequally experienced. That inequality was central to the operation of the main situations of infection risk: economic and social disparities within rural communities drove survival sex (a desperate seller, an able buyer); geographic disparities among rural areas and between them and non-rural areas drove distress migration.

Spurred by the experience of 2001–03 and the return of near-famine conditions in 2004–05, the Malawi government instituted an input subsidy programme in 2005 focused on maize seed and fertilizer and targeted to poor farmers. Evaluations suggest that it has been relatively successful in this and contributed to raising cereal production to historic levels (Dorward and Chirwa, 2010). To what extent this has translated into households better able to bridge the annual hungry period is still unclear (*pers. comm.*, A. Dorward). The structural conditions that underlay the famine persist – dependence on maize and casual labour and the paucity of productive non- or counter-seasonal livelihood alternatives (MVAC, 2007; FEWSNET, 2010). Food insecurity remains chronic for many in areas such as the Middle and Lower Shire Valley, including Nsanje, where the highest HIV prevalence was recorded. The findings suggest that addressing the structures of risk for hunger is likely to have broad and important benefits, including enabling people to avoid HIV infection and related sources of ill-health.

Implications

Poverty, hunger and inequalities are generally considered by public health professionals to be structural determinants of HIV infection and as such slow to change and essentially beyond the reach of near-term intervention in support of prevention. The findings indicate that these factors can in fact change rapidly and substantially, influencing HIV dynamics with little lag. In the Malawi famine, state actions contributed greatly to that change. These included the mismanagement of maize stocks and prices in 2001–02 and policies over a longer term that exacerbated seasonality and left people vulnerable to volatile prices and moderate climatic variability.

Turning these findings on their head suggests opportunities. Avoiding actions that unwittingly undermine food and livelihood security is an obvious one. More positively, efforts that bolster food and livelihood security broadly, across the year, could enable people to avoid situations of risk and escape infection. Indeed, successful such efforts may already be doing just that, yielding an as yet uncounted 'prevention dividend'.

The sites where hunger and change in HIV prevalence were lowest offer clues to what is feasible. Karonga (Figure 4.2A) and Nkhata Bay (Figure 4.2B), are both in the Northern Region, but probably more important in moderating famine and seasonal hunger is the widespread cultivation of cassava, grown by 71 per cent and 83 per cent of households respectively (NSO, 2005). Cassava is a classic famine crop – a perennial, more tolerant of drought than maize, it provides a large caloric yield per hectare.

Over all districts, the prevalence of hunger in December 2002 to March 2003, the independent variable in Figures 4.2 and 4.3, is negatively related to the prevalence of cassava cultivation ($r = -0.57$, P<0.01, Figure 4.5). In many southern districts, sweet potato plays a similar role to cassava (Mandala, 2005) and, as explained earlier, food was more available in the cities. The relationship is closer when southern districts and those surrounding cities are excluded ($r = -0.85$, P<0.01).

Cassava cultivation may have provided a further benefit to all households, whether or not they grew it: by damping demand for maize and other foods, it would have reduced the pressure on prices. There is evidence that this was happening during the famine. The peak maize price in February 2002 in local markets (FEWSNET, 2002) was negatively related to the prevalence of cassava cultivation in the district ($r = -0.63$, P<0.02; Figure 4.6). Again, the relationship is closer when Southern Region districts and peri-urban markets are excluded ($r = -0.81$, P<0.01).

Clearly, these ideas require more detailed attention. At this point, the evidence is suggestive that cassava cultivation provides an HIV prevention dividend – an unintended consequence of people's struggle to secure food and livelihood.

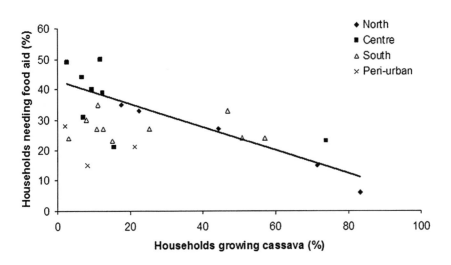

Note: All districts, with and without antenatal surveillance sites are plotted (n=26); the regression is fitted to the non-peri-urban Northern and Central Region districts (n=13).

FIGURE 4.5 Proportion of households estimated to be in need of food assistance, December 2002 to March 2003, in relation to the proportion of households growing cassava, by district

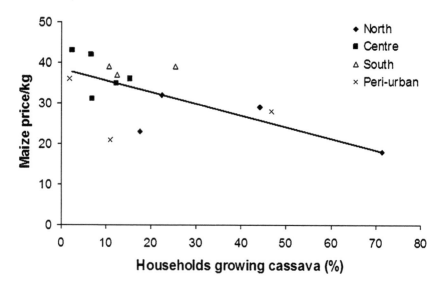

Note: All districts reporting market prices are plotted (n=15); the regression is fitted to the non-peri-urban Northern and Central Region districts (n=9).

FIGURE 4.6 Peak maize price in February 2002 in local markets (Malawi Kwacha) in relation to the proportion of households growing cassava in the district

Cassava may be particularly helpful to poorer households caught in the dilemma of either working their own fields or doing *ganyu* in others: the crop is more forgiving of delay in planting, weeding and harvesting than maize. Farmers in Malawi, Zambia and Mozambique appear to have substantially increased their production of cassava which now plays an important role in regional food security (Haggblade, Longabaugh and Tschirley, 2009). The evidence cited earlier of migration to cassava-growing areas during the famine attests to this role.

Cassava is not a panacea nor is it the only rural innovation that can yield prevention dividends (Loevinsohn, 2006). There is a wealth of ways in which the seasons of hunger and the diseases they entrain can be curtailed.

Acknowledgements

I am grateful to Kathleen Beegle, World Bank, for her assistance in analysing the IHS data, to Tom Snijders, Universities of Oxford and Groningen, for statistical advice and to Ken Maleta, Faculty of Medicine, University of Malawi, for assistance in accessing the surveillance data and to the Malawi National AIDS Commission for permission to use it.

Note

1   The non-rural regression again excludes Nsanje although it is not a significant outlier in this case. Including it would little alter the results aside from increasing significance. The explanation suggested for Nsanje being an outlier in Figure 4.3 – greater HIV prevalence in the villages than in the town – would not be relevant to the movement of women *per se*.

5

Seasonal poverty

Integrated, overlooked and therefore opportunity

Robert Chambers

Integrated seasonal poverty and stress

That for poorer people, especially in tropical conditions, poverty and stress have strong seasonal dimensions is scarcely a new revelation. It has always been known by those who experience it. Hard work in agriculture, infections and sickness, food shortages, quality and prices, nutritional status, household reserves of cash and other assets, communications, transport and markets, social relations, and access to services – these are all interlinked in negative ways. Seasonally poor people are screwed down, and it is often during rains that there are downward ratchet effects of poor people becoming poorer (see Krishna, this book).

Those professionals, not themselves rural or poor, but who have been close to rural life throughout the year, have known this. A classic example quoted by Gerry Gill (1991) comes from Leonard Woolf's novel *The Village in the Jungle*, based on his experiences while an administrator working in Hambantota District in Ceylon. A mother speaks:

> I say to the father of my child, 'Father of Podi Sinho', I say, 'there is no *kurakkan* in the house, there is no millet and no pumpkin, not even a pinch of salt. Three days now and I have eaten nothing but jungle leaves. There is no milk in my breasts for the child'. Then I get foul words and blows. 'Does the rain come in August?', he says. 'Can I make the *kurakkan* flower in July? Hold your tongue, you fool. August is the month in which the children die. What can I do?'
>
> (Woolf, 1913)

In the scenario of an earlier book on seasonality (Chambers *et al.* 1981), many factors interlocked as adverse conditions for poor rural people during tropical rains, not least lack of food, high food prices, lack of money, hard work, sickness and isolation and lack of access. The earlier scenario remains largely valid and the dimensions identified probably remain the most important ones. There was, though, much that we underperceived or missed.

Linkages that interlock

Diagrams can make the points, or state the hypotheses, better than text. Three can illustrate ways of presenting, analysing and reflecting on adverse linkages that do or may operate seasonally. Readers are challenged to draw their own and do better.

Figure 5.1 is a slight adaptation of a diagram used to postulate development as good change, from illbeing to wellbeing. Shifts in either direction can and do occur seasonally.[1] Material lack and poverty, physical weakness, powerlessness and vulnerability are all accentuated in the wet season scenario, and conversely reversed towards wellbeing during early dry seasons.

Figure 5.2 [overleaf] illustrates conditions affecting the state of the body and affected by it, contrasting the syndrome of a hungry, weak, sick and exhausted body linked with reduced food, ability to work, bargaining power and medical access and the syndrome of a well-fed, fit, strong and rested body. Typical wet season stresses accentuate the former while typical dry season conditions sustain the latter.

The third is of unknown provenance but has been in my possession for perhaps 20 years.[2] It shows the effects of three factors on women and children – food shortages, peak agricultural labour, and the rising incidence of some diseases. It can be

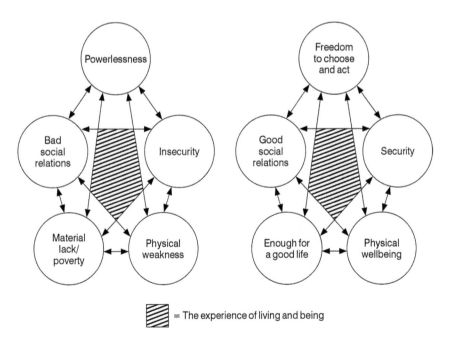

FIGURE 5.1 From illbeing to wellbeing

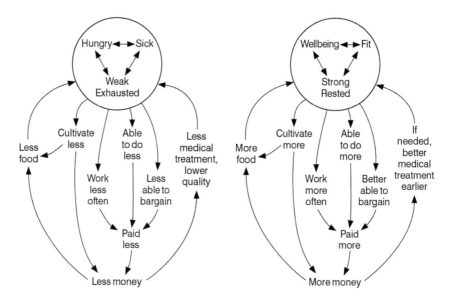

FIGURE 5.2 Body syndromes

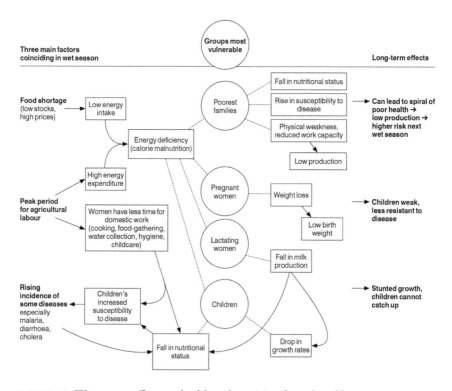

FIGURE 5.3 Wet season effects on health and nutrition for vulnerable groups

looked at together with Susan Schofield's seminal article, 'Seasonal factors affecting nutrition in different age groups and especially preschool children' (1974, pp26–7):

> Reallocation of female labour time (especially where energy expenditure is in excess of calorie supply) will have other effects. *Cooking practices* change, especially where quick easy-to-prepare meals (usually of the nutritionally poorer staples such as cassava) are produced once a day or in bulk and vitamins are destroyed by food kept simmering in the pot. *Intra-family distribution of food* is affected, where the children are asleep before the daily meal has been prepared and women have no time to either prepare special infant foods or effect the proper distribution of available foods. *Food gathering* may be inhibited so that some types of foods (e.g. green leafy vegetables) are suddenly excluded from the diet. *House-cleaning*, essential in overcrowded and insanitary conditions, may be inhibited. *Fuel and water* collection is constrained by lack of time. Finally, mothers devote less time to *care* of their children who are often left in the charge of other siblings or elderly grandparents.

The question can still be asked, and perhaps should always be asked – what else have we missed? What have we tended to overlook? With our professional specializations, and our tendencies to research and write in and to our own disciplines, we miss the interlinkages that are so significant for those who live seasonal poverty and stress.

Reflection, experience and research indicate 11 domains which were overlooked or little considered in the 1978 seasonality conference (Seasonal Dimensions to Rural Poverty, Institute of Development Studies, Brighton, UK, 4–7 July, 1978).

Accidents

Accidents can impoverish. To what extent they are seasonal, and during which seasons they are most common, is for investigation in each environment and for each gender and occupation. Three points can be made. First, rainy season conditions make people more vulnerable. Snake bite is one example. More generally, floods, landslides, and slipperiness can impact. The SDC Views of the Poor study in Tanzania reported of one community that, for fetching water, 'The biggest problem is the terrain which is steep and slippery during the rainy season ... people in the villages have had accidents carrying water' (Jupp, 2003, p36). Second, dealing with accidents is likely to be more difficult and impoverishing during the rains for reasons of access, money and cost, and failing to recover fully for lack of treatment. Third, the opportunity cost of labour can be high. As remarked by a Gambian villager to Margaret Haswell (1975, p44), 'Sometimes you are overcome by weeds through illness or accidents'.

Animal sickness

Animal sicknesses are seasonal. Participatory livestock research with pastoralists in Thiet, southern Sudan, revealed what is reportedly a common pattern of peaks during the rains from May, June or July through to August, September or October, and a healthier period during the dry season. Median scores from groups of pastoralists' analyses sum to:

	Feb–April	May–July	Aug–Oct	Nov–Jan
Rain	0	7	11	1
Cattle diseases	10	22	46	20
Biting flies, ticks, snails	6	41	38	13

Source: Conroy (2005, p65). The original gives a breakdown by disease and by vector.

Disasters

The seasonality of disasters is so evident and obvious that it can pass unrecognized. When seeing how seasonal dimensions interlock as cyclical screws, it is easy to miss shocks which may not come every season, but to which people and communities are vulnerable at certain times of the year. In rural communities most of these are during the rains: floods, landslides, riverbank erosion, storm surges and high waves. Bangladesh has two cyclone seasons, one in early summer and the second in the late monsoon, the latter overlapping with the hard *monga* time (Salahuddin *et al.*, 2009; Neogi *et al.*, 2009) for poor rural people. That also is when floods come: in 1988 two-thirds of Bangladesh's 64 districts experienced extensive flood damage in the wake of unusually heavy rains that flooded the river systems, leaving millions homeless and without potable water, reportedly destroying about 2 million tons of crops, and making relief work difficult.

Funerals

To the extent that mortality is seasonal with a peak in the wet season,[3] the considerable costs of funerals in many cultures come at a bad time for those who are poorer, when money is short and the food required for ceremonies expensive. The opportunity cost of time and energy for those who take part is also often high, leading to loss of earnings for labourers and failure to weed and conduct other operations in a timely and adequate manner for small farmers. In Zimbabwe, attendance at funerals delayed planned activities for all six of the farmers in the study reported to the 'Seasonality Revisited' conference (Dorward *et al.*, 2009, pp1 and 8). In northern Ghana the direct and opportunity costs of funerals can be so high that they could be delayed until a better time of year, or even for years (Devereux, 1992). Where funerals do occur during the rains, and if open defecation is common, the concentration of faeces, which is liable to be more substantial because of the amount of food consumed, may sharply raise the risks of infection.[4]

Powerlessness to bargain

The normal view is that wages rise with demand and so should rise during labour peaks such as weeding and harvest. This may well be the general tendency, depending on conditions, but in most analyses, bargaining power is omitted. Bargaining power is gendered to the disadvantage of women (Jackson and Palmer-Jones, 1999, pp563–4). But all poor people can be affected. The authors of the Bangladesh *Voices of the Poor* report wrote that, 'Due to minimum food intake during crisis period, men and women cannot do labour-intensive work. Consequently they do not get proper wages from the employer in time' (Un Nabi *et al.*, 1999).

This implies that not only did they not get proper wages but that payment was also delayed. Paying labourers in kind at harvest has been a common form of cruel screw, leaving them hungry and vulnerable to debt when they have to work and prices are high, and paying them in food when it is abundant and cheap.

Weak bargaining power when people are hungry or are known to need money badly, can depress wages, as in this lament from Malawi:

> ... the problem is that these boat owners know that we are starving, as such we would accept any little wages they would offer to us because they know we are very desperate ... we want to save our children from dying.
>
> (Khaila *et al.*, 1999, p66)

A Malawian student told me that before Christmas was a very good time. Labourers would do a standard amount of work on his family's fields for only one *kwacha*. After Christmas they had to pay four *kwacha* for the same work. Before Christmas is the bad time for poor people, with shortages of food and money, sickness and the rest. Those labouring for so little may well have been desperate to earn whatever they could so that their families could celebrate Christmas.

The rains can be a good time for those with resources if they are bad enough for others.

School attendance

Many factors may weaken school attendance seasonally. These include priorities for agriculture and agricultural work, lack of money, hunger, and the timing of school fees (Hadley, this book). There is also difficulty getting to school in heavy rain: sickness, getting wet and cold, damage to books and papers, shortage of money if that is required, and being unable to dry an only uniform. A single mother living in a single small hut in Cornwall Barracks, an area of high annual rainfall in Jamaica, gave her inability to dry wet single uniforms as a main reason for her children's substantial absenteeism from school (interview, 10 November 2000).

Shelter

Shelter is not a topic in the book of the 1978 Conference.[5] But a participatory appraisal with very poor families in Tanzania (Jupp, 2003) found that shelter was a higher priority for them than outsiders had supposed:

> Most of the rural study households had houses with grass thatch roofs in poor condition and leaking roofs were nearly always mentioned as one of the worst aspects of their lives ... The urban households either had very old corrugated iron roofs which leaked badly or a crude 'thatch' of plastic bags and cardboard.

Problems of leaking and collapsing roofs, flooding, water and dampness within shelters and wet sleepless nights compound other stresses. The Malawi *Voices of the Poor* reported the problem of collapsing houses made of mud and thatched with grass which could not withstand the heavy rains (Khaila *et al.*, 1999, p82). Also in Malawi, having a house that did not leak was an indicator of wellbeing. A woman said that houses should not make people wake up and stand when it is raining like in a court when the judge is arriving and people say '*khoti liime* – court stand!' (Khaila *et al.*, 1999, p32). There are periods too of seasonal vulnerability to losing dwellings completely. Rivers changing course and flooding can destroy houses: when the Kosi river in Bihar floods and changes course, thousands are displaced; in Bangladesh many, perhaps most, of those in the slums of Dhaka are there because they have lost their land and/or houses to riverbank erosion with seasonal floods in the big rivers; and the Pakistan floods of 2010 are without precedent for scale and devastation.

Theft

The seasonality of theft was not considered in 1978. Indeed in some regions theft was probably less significant then. Seasonal theft of food and animals has been found to be a significant experience and problem for small farmers and livestock keepers. In the *Voices of the Poor* study (Narayan *et al.*, 2000), when focus groups in Ethiopia, Malawi, Nigeria, Somaliland and Zambia used causal-linkage diagramming to identify their perceptions of causes of poverty, the two most common were health and theft: the theft of food is seasonal and it may be surmised that the same will be true of stock theft, whether large-scale or petty. As Tariq Omar Ali points out from his study in rural Bangladesh (Ali, 2004), there is a moral economy of petty pilfering of food crops and small amounts can be tolerated. However, he also reports people going to considerable lengths to protect their crops, camping in their fields and staying up all night, but that even this is not always effective. In Malawi, it is reported that in past years the custom was to keep crops in stores (on stilts to protect against rats) outside dwellings, but that this has been abandoned because of theft: crops are now stored inside. In Ethiopia, theft of fava beans, once tolerated on a small scale, has become so serious that farmers have stopped growing them, with adverse effects on nutrition (Chiwona-Karltun *et al.*, 2009). Heavy rain contributes to the seasonality of theft by first making a noise so that thieves are not heard and then by covering their footprints and those of stolen animals, making them harder to follow (*pers. comm.*, Dave Kuchanny).

Defecation behaviour and infection from faeces

Defecation behaviour is seasonal and plausibly linked with an increase in infections during rainy seasons.

In triggering Community-Led Total Sanitation (Kar with Chambers, 2008), participatory mapping includes villagers putting yellow powder or sawdust on their social map on the ground to show where they defecate. Typically, this is around the edges of their settlement. When asked where they go at night during the rains, a common response is an emotional cocktail of embarrassment and laughter as they put the powder down outside their own or their neighbours' houses. When it is raining, especially when it is raining at night, people and children without latrines evidently and understandably defecate very close by their dwellings. Those most likely to do this will be those suffering from the urgency and pain of acute diarrhoeas. The liquid stools mix with the rainwater and may be trampled bare-foot back into dwellings to infect others. It is then precisely when diarrhoeas are most common that behaviour is least hygienic and reinfections are most likely. Hookworm has also been found to infect during the rains, with a break in the dry season (Nwosu and Anya, 1980). Further, unlined pit latrines often collapse during rains and become unusable and unhygienic when water tables are very high and during floods. A survey in Cambodia has found that many people who use pit latrines during the dry season abandon them during the rains; the reasons given include odour problems, pit collapses, and generally unhygienic conditions (*pers. comm.*, Andy Robinson, 2 May 2009).

Neglected aspects of nutrition and energy use

Food absorption was mentioned in the 1981 book (Longhurst and Payne, 1981, p46) but remains relatively neglected as a subject. Food absorption is reduced by diarrhoeas, other diseases and intestinal parasites. In his keynote address to the Third South Asia Conference on Sanitation in November 2008, M. S. Swaminathan stressed heavily that of the three 'A's' of food – availability, access and absorption – the last had been largely overlooked. It is especially acute among sick infants and small children. Malnourished children are more vulnerable to diarrhoeal infections and have longer episodes, and a frequently quoted statistic is that 80 per cent of deaths from diarrhoeas are in children under the age of five. At least as serious, however, may be more continuous tropical enteropathy with bacterial damage to the gut wall reducing nutrient absorption and the energy demanded to make the antibodies to fight the infections. Malabsorption and nutrient energy consumed in producing antibodies may be more significant even than diarrhoeas as a cause of undernutrition and stunting in children (Humphries, 2009) and would seem likely to have a seasonality similar to other faecal-oral infections.

Urban seasonality

Seasonality of deprivation in urban areas seems to have been little studied. In urban slums there can be seasonal patterns of water and electricity supply, of security and violence, and of access. The *Voices of the Poor* study in Malawi (Khaila *et al.*, 1999, p79) found that the problem of poor roads was particularly acute during the rainy season. Big potholes had forced public and private transport operators to withdraw services. Women said this made their life unbearable: this was because they had to travel into town for their small-scale businesses. More generally, lack of waterproof shelter is perhaps the most pervasive problem.

Taken together, many of the factors that are adverse seasonally combine as integrated seasonal poverty, as seen in Figure 5.4.

Warning: there are many local variations, nuances, paradoxes and exceptions. The inner circle is really an interconnected web. These are stresses which are largely predictable and expected and which regularly and steadily screw people

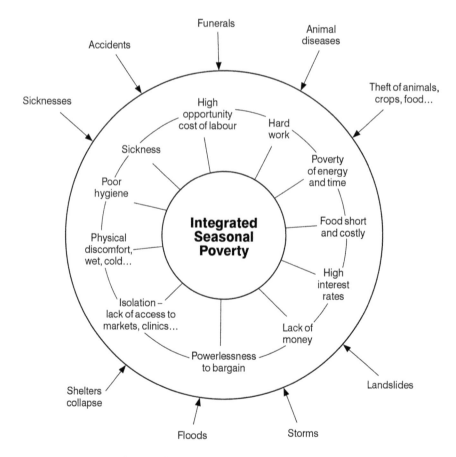

FIGURE 5.4 Integrated seasonal poverty

down into poverty. The outer events are vulnerabilities – shocks which are less predictable, often with ratchet effects, making poor people suddenly poorer.

To conclude, then, the interlocking of many factors points to the lean, hungry and sick seasons as the time when poor people are most likely to become poorer. Anirudh Krishna (see also this book) found this with sickness and related expenditures. His research in five countries has consistently found that sickness, accidents and related expenditures are the most common proximate cause of people becoming poorer (Krishna, 2010). In parts of Bangladesh, the worst season is *monga* – a slack period in the middle of the rains and floods when there is little work. The Bangladesh *Voices of the Poor* study reports that many poor households had sold or mortgaged and later lost their last piece of land during this slack season (Un Nabi *et al.*, 1999, p37).

All this said, the rains are not a bad time for all. Some women in an Indian village startled me by saying the monsoon was their best time of year. That was when there was a lot to do, and they enjoyed the sense of urgency and purpose. But then these were healthy, strong women with good stone houses and by no means poor. It is the poor who live and know the seasonal integration of poverty and stress.

Professionals: season-proofed and season-blind

> Come let us mock at the wise;
> With all those calendars whereon
> They fixed old aching eyes,
> They never saw how seasons run ...
> (W. B. Yeats, 'Come let us mock at the great')

Seasonal biases

The interlocking biases against urban professionals perceiving seasonal rural deprivations during tropical rainy seasons have been repeated almost ad nauseam:[6] they prefer for many reasons to travel during the dry seasons. This is when people are better fed, healthier, stronger and less stressed. Spatial and seasonal biases interlock: during the rains vehicles stick even more to tarmac than in the dry season, reducing contact with precisely those people who are most cut off and most likely to be suffering. Offsetting this, there are now, as noted, often more tarmac roads penetrating further into rural areas than there were. But the biases remain.

There is a bias in international travel from Europe and North America. Those in cold climates north of the equator prefer to travel in their winter:

> The international experts' flights
> fit northern seasons; winter nights
> in London, Washington and Rome
> are what drive them in flocks from home.

In Bangladesh, such visitors from the North are known as *sheether pakhi* – winter birds – who come in January to March. When the Select Committee on Overseas Aid of the British House of Commons wanted to visit India in the winter, the Indian authorities requested postponement as it was near the end of their financial year; but the convenience of the MPs prevailed and they went at what for many poor people in India was their least bad time of year – cool, relatively dry, healthy and after harvest.

Three other factors deter urban-based professionals from exposure to the multiple rainy season deprivations of poor rural people. The first is the incestuous 'capital trap' (Chambers, 2006, pp8–10) in which aid agency and government staff have become increasingly ensnared, holding them fast in capital cities, accentuated by demands for harmonization and policy influence, and career incentives. The second is reluctance to experience discomfort and embarrassment. The third is ethics: the argument is that it is unfair to take poor people's time or disturb them at a time of hardship and poverty of time and energy, when they need to be busy cultivating for their survival. These can be all be answered by pointing to the impacts of immersions (PLA, 2007) and the informed energy, anger and commitment that come from knowing first-hand what poor people are suffering, and becoming personally aware of what seasonal deprivation means to them (Jupp and Krishna, this book).

Our own institutional seasonality and how this relates to that of poor rural people has also been a relative blind spot. The timing of governments' fiscal years is often unrelated to rural seasonal needs. Cases are common in rural areas where authorities to incur expenditure come too late for seasonal needs, and where late releases accentuate crises towards the end of the financial year with unspent funds which cannot be carried forward.[7]

Unseen people – out of sight, out of mind

There is interlocking invisibility too of groups of people. These vary by occupation and environment. However, generically and across almost all environments and conditions, some of those most out of sight and out of mind are:

- Those who are socially and spatially marginalized in any community – not least those who are poorer, disabled, destitute and/or chronically sick.
- Older people, of whom there are growing numbers.
- People who are poor, female (especially widows), young, 'remote' and mobile are not seen by many professionals and often not by the state.
- Seasonal migrants, travelling in distress. They tend to be powerless, exploited and deprived, and their children and old people even more so. The children below 14 years of age involved in seasonal migrations in India are 'a group that has not been on the radar screen of the government or development agencies', a group for whom there are 'no official data' but that may number close to 9 million (Smita, 2008, ppvii and 1). Migrants in India have until recently been unable to use their ration books in the places they go to, and suffer multiple

insecurities – of housing, lack of social protection, vulnerability to abuse by the police, and weak bargaining power for work and wages.

Missing in statistics

And statisticians too declare
they have a seasonal nightmare;
an average is but a dream –-
with seasons, means aren't what they seem

To what extent health and other statistics have seasonal or counter-seasonal biases, tending to over- or underestimate bad things that happen at the worst times for poor people, is a topic for a literature review and then research. It looks likely that the rainy season incidence of sickness will be understated in clinic and hospital statistics not least because of problems of access during rains, lack of cash, and the need to work. Indeed, as Box 5.1 overleaf suggests, many factors may combine. Conversely, these are reversed once the rains are over. So statistics may understate for the rains and overstate for the early dry season after harvest.

All this said, there are honourable exceptions to lack of seasonal statistics. A UNDP Poverty Analysis Manual for Benin measures poverty by trimester and finds that in 1994/95 poverty ranged from 26 per cent in March to May to 43 per cent in September to November (Aho *et al.*, 1998, p160). The title of an IFPRI study 'Seasonal undernutrition in rural Ethiopia' (Ferro-Luzzi *et al.*, 2002) speaks for itself. And there will surely be many others.

Missing in books and journals

That said, there is an intriguing and perhaps important puzzle. Why, given its central significance in the lives of so many poor people, is seasonality so rarely mentioned elsewhere?

The seasonality of nutrition and the nutritional status of children deserves to be a major focus of attention (for an early study showing quite dramatic seasonal changes see Brown *et al.*, 1982). Yet seasonality is not evident in a collection of papers (Haddad and Zeitlyn, 2009) on undernutrition in India. Seasonality simply does not seem to be a category on many professionals' mental maps. Indexers may be one of these. In Michael Lipton's classic *Why Poor People Stay Poor* (1977) which predated the first seasonality conference in 1978, seasonality is not in the index. But I could not believe that Michael Lipton, who had lived almost a year in an Indian village, would have missed this, even though the book is about urban bias. And indeed on pages 243–4, he mentions that rural peaks of effort are likely to be required when food is scarce and expensive and he notes that sickness and shortage of food occur at the same time. So integrated seasonal poverty is there. But it is not indexed: it is not an analytical category. And other classics may well not mention seasonal linkages at all.[8] Taking them in chronological order, Jean Drèze and Amartya Sen in *Hunger*

Box 5.1 Behaviour under rainy season stress

This is a hypothetical question posed to participants in workshops. The question is, 'In the middle of the rains a poor rural family decides not to take their very sick child to the clinic 8km (five miles) away when, had it been the dry season, they would have taken the child. What are the possible reasons?'
There are at least 17:

1   One or both of the parents are themselves sick.
2   They are exhausted, weak and short of food and energy.
3   The mother is in late pregnancy or has just given birth (births tend to peak in the rains).
4   Another of their children is sick.
5   With rain and cold the child would suffer on the journey.
6   They have no waterproofs, umbrella or big banana leaf.
7   Carrying a child in wet and slippery conditions is difficult, even dangerous.
8   There is no transport (bicycle rickshaw, minibus, bus) during the rains, or it is less reliable or costs more.
9   The opportunity cost of not working (especially weeding) is high.
10 It is difficult to ask neighbours to look after their other children because they are in the same state, and it would be asking more as the opportunity cost of their time too is higher.
11 They are short of cash and fear indebtedness.
12 The clinic staff may be charging more for drugs because in the rains demand exceeds supply.
13 The clinic is more likely to be out of drugs because of demand.
14 The clinic may not be open and they cannot know because people are not travelling bringing news.
15 There is a risk of not getting to the clinic or not being able to get back again (flash flood, landslide, etc.).
16 Their shelter is damaged or has collapsed and needs repair.
17 Herbal remedies are more available in the rains.

It may need only a few of these interlocking factors, or sometimes only one, to deter the parents.

and Public Action (1989) are strong on interannual comparisons and droughts but the book has no index entries for disease, seasonality or sickness.[9] It is perhaps less remarkable that the dimension of seasonality is not to be found in Peter Townsend's *The International Analysis of Poverty* (1993) since his major work has been in the UK, nor in Jeffrey Sachs's *The End of Poverty* (2005) given its broad generalizations. It is surprising, though, to find it also missing in four recent otherwise excellent works:

Paul Spicker *et al.* (2007) *Poverty: An International Glossary*, where it is not among the 27 entries under the letter 'S'; Paul Spicker (2007) *The Idea of Poverty*; Duncan Green (2008) *From Poverty to Power*; Potter *et al.* (2008) *Geographies of Development* (except for entries for seasonal migration).

The last two have full sections on climate change but do not touch on the changes to seasonal patterns reported to the 2009 'Seasonality Revisited' conference (Jennings and Magrath, 2009; Mubiru *et al.*, 2009). And with climate change too, seasonal dimensions appear to have been late to be recognized by 'us' (professionals), though experienced by 'them' (in this case farmers).

Season-proofed and season-blind

Perhaps the deepest and most pervasive reason why we professionals underperceive seasonal poverty, suffering and stress is that we do not experience them. Our roofs do not leak. We have fans and air conditioners. We have tarmac and pavements to walk on. We drive in rainproof vehicles. We have umbrellas and raincoats. We do not have to cultivate in the rains. We have access to medical treatment. We have money. Season-proofed, we are season-blind.

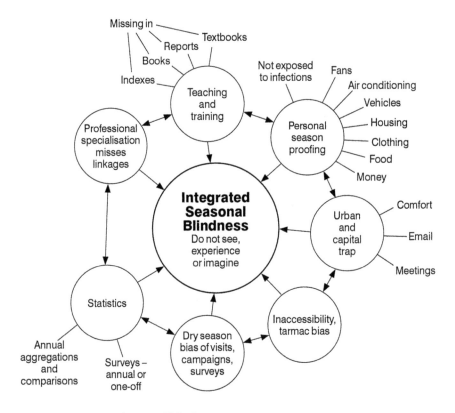

FIGURE 5.5 Integrated seasonal blindness

These many factors interlock and reinforce each other, as others did in Figure 5.4, Integrated Seasonal Poverty. Set against Figure 5.4, we can see two strong syndromes which combine in professional and policy neglect of the significance of seasonality.

The opportunity: awareness and influence

Past neglect is present opportunity. It is precisely because seasonal dimensions have been so often overlooked or underperceived that they now present potential for pro-poor actions. The question is how to raise and sustain awareness of seasonality so that it is permanently and prominently on the agenda of policy and practice.

Thirty years after the 'Seasonal Dimensions' conference we are in a transformed world. We have multimedia, a professional team and means of instant communication.

The big challenge is long-term, to *raise*, *sustain* and *intensify* awareness of how adverse factors interlink and how they affect poor and marginalized people. To this end, there will be actions during and following the 'Seasonality Revisited' conference, from blogs to videos to publications and other uses of the media. Some additional proposals follow.

Personal experience

Making visits during the rains, including immersions (pun regretted). These are stays of a few days and nights in a poor community, living and being with people, and experiencing some of their life. Dee Jupp's immersion (this book) is an example which brings to light, vividly and unforgettably, some of the multiple effects of heavy rain and the integration of the seasonal bad life.[10]

Analysis and presentation

PRA analyses by poor people themselves indicating how adverse and favourable conditions coincide and reinforce each other. These include facilitating PRA-type visual analyses by poor urban as well as rural dwellers, and sharing and discussing the resulting diagrams widely. Such diagrams should be available whenever there is a discussion of programmes or policy, whether at district or higher levels. This requires proactive commissioning and supply of such diagrams, whether by government or NGOs.

Diagramming to be more often a starting point and basis than words. The complexity of local experience and connections and linkages across dimensions, whether seasonal or not, can be better expressed visually than verbally. A diagram is far easier to inspect, analyse and discuss than are words, whether written or spoken. An example is the multidimensional seasonal calendars in use for livelihoods impact analysis in Ethiopia (see Boudreau, 2009, p6).

Behaviour

Nominating one person at every policy meeting to reflect on seasonality and raise seasonal issues.

Alerting publishers, requesting them to ask their indexers to be conscious of seasons and seasonality as categories, and contacting associations of indexers and their members, where such associations exist. Similarly, alerting those who review books to look for seasonality, the absence of which can provide them with just the sort of critical comment they might like to make.

Monitoring mentions – analysing reports and documents and searching them to count the number of mentions of seasons and seasonality, and the context and comprehensiveness of those mentions.[11]

Asking questions – being personally proactive, and encouraging others to do likewise, repeatedly asking questions about seasonal dimensions and realities – in committees, workshops, meetings.

Interrogating research proposals – those who assess research proposals repeatedly asking about seasonal dimensions, and letting it be known that these will be assessed.

Sponsoring and encouraging research on many aspects of seasonality, including:

* multidimensional linkages
* the seasonality of sickness having impoverishing ratchet effects
* the relative pro-poor and anti-poverty cost-effectiveness of enabling people seasonally to avoid becoming poorer compared with, once they are poorer, enabling them to climb back up again

Notes

1   The image that comes to mind is the Inter-Tropical Convergence Zone, with its six-monthly oscillation across the equator, regularly moving one way and then the other and carrying the same conditions with it.
2   If anyone can tell me who drew it, please do, I would like to acknowledge her (I am almost sure it was a woman).
3   A peak in the rains was reportedly common but not universal in the late 1970s (Chambers *et al.*, 1981, pp135–62).
4   Immediately after funerals can be a good time to trigger community-led total sanitation precisely because there are so many excreta lying around (*pers. comm.*, Sammy Musyoki) though not a good time if there is an agricultural labour peak then.
5   Housing is in the index but this refers only to conditions conducive to meningitis which is mainly a dry season disease.
6   For a recent reincarnation of this hoary topic see Chambers, 2006, pp23–5 and 31.
7   As a District Officer in Samburu District, Kenya, I tried to solve this problem by using unspent funds to buy cement just before the end of the financial year on 31 March. Unfortunately this was just before the onset of the rains when cement was vulnerable to becoming an unusably hard currency.
8   This is a tentative generalization. I cannot pretend to have combed these books from cover to cover.
9   Drèze and Sen include in their references *Seasonal Dimensions to Rural Poverty* and the later work by Longhurst (1986), but I do not find this reflected in the content of the text. I should be glad to be shown that this is an oversight on my part.

10 The best recent collection on immersions is 'Immersions: Learning about poverty face-to-face', *Participatory Learning and Action*, 57, December 2007.
11 The number of appearances of a particular term in a document can be counted by using the Find feature in the program Word.

PART 2
Seasonal livelihoods

Dreading the monsoon

Kothari Bai has strong feelings about the monsoon season. 'On the one hand, when it rains our crops get nourished. But no work is available at that time, and there is more need for money'. Wage employment is hard to find in July and August in southern Rajasthan. Those whose livelihoods depend upon receiving a daily flow of wages face a particularly hard time during the monsoon season.

Throughout the year, seasons rule the tempo of life in this village. Many people migrate to nearby Gujarat to work as casual labour. For those who stay behind – children, the elderly, and women – the monsoon season represents the hardest time of the year. Food supplies, stored from the previous harvest, are at their lowest point. Those who left to work in Gujarat have not yet returned, bringing back their savings. With money and food supplies simultaneously running low, families survive by borrowing small or large amounts from local moneylenders. Interest on these loans is calculated at rates ranging from 2 per cent to 10 per cent monthly, with the poorest borrowers having to pay the highest interest rates.

Seasonal illnesses peak at the time of monsoon. Water-borne diseases, such as diarrhoea and gastroenteritis, and others, such as malaria, are most prolific soon after the monsoon showers begin to fall. Additional expenses on account of health-care add to the financial burdens of cash-strapped families. Further loans are taken out to pay for healthcare costs. Quite often, future labour power is pledged against these loans, initiating a cycle that ends in debt peonage for many.

According to one moneylender, Ram Kishore, who lives in Kothari Bai's village, requests for new loans are most frequent in July and August. Distress sales of families' assets also peak during these months. Low cash reserves and emergency expenses combine to deplete the meagre pools of assets that poor families possess.

Many families have fallen into chronic poverty in this village. Of the total of 111 households who live here, 16 households make up the category of the newly impoverished. They were not poor ten years ago, but they are desperately poor at the present time. Not all of them fell into poverty during the monsoon season. Indeed, it is hard to say when exactly they moved across this categorical divide. Unlike statisticians, ordinary people do not think of poverty in terms of some sharply drawn dividing line. Nor is it any single event that usually pitches people into poverty. More often, descents into poverty occur over longer periods of time, the cumulative result of a succession of negative events.

Among the events that contributed to descents into poverty in Kothari Bai's village, ill health and high healthcare costs are most prominent. For a study that I conducted, a random sample of eight households was selected from among all 16 households who fell into poverty in this village. Interviews conducted with multiple household members helped reconstruct detailed event histories, revealing the nature of negative events that were experienced by these households. On average, three negative events were experienced in each such case.

Two-thirds of all negative events involved illnesses, injuries, deaths from diseases, and high healthcare costs. The onset of some of these ailments, such as cancer, cardiovascular diseases, and tuberculosis is hard to date precisely. In other cases, the interviewees were more forthcoming about these dates.

Nearly one half of all related health incidents (7 of 16) commenced or became acute at the time of the monsoons. Kiladevi's 18-year-old son, Ramesh, who went out in the dark to rescue some cows from a rising stream, accidentally stepped upon a live high-power cable set loose by the heavy storm. He was instantly paralysed on one side of his body and died six weeks later, but not before Kiladevi's entire savings were exhausted by medical costs. Gokalnath, a 60-year-old man, fell ill for the first time in his life after drinking contaminated water brought home from a nearby pond. Three years later, he died, reportedly on account of a stomach ulcer. His widow, Tulcchi Bai, had to sell their small agricultural holding in order to meet the doctors' demands for cash. Ramjilal's wife died during the monsoon season. She was carrying their third child. Complications developed after she was bitten by mosquitoes. Because the river, normally dry, could not be easily crossed, especially by a mortally ill woman in her eighth month of pregnancy, Ramjilal arranged, at great expense, for a qualified nurse to be brought across. But fate intervened before the nurse could arrive. The expense was to no avail. Other negative events followed. Ramjilal, like Tulchhi Bai, is desperately poor at the present time.

Floods caused by an unnaturally heavy rainfall destroyed the low-lying fields that Chaturbhuj had patiently nurtured over the previous ten years. As he frantically attempted to repair the breach in the low mud wall, one of his pair of oxen was carried away by the fast-flowing flood. Two years later, Chaturbhuj died, strangely enough during the monsoon season. Although his worsening heart condition had hardly anything to do with the rains, his widow, Kothari Bai, continues to have strong feelings about the monsoon season.

Those who have remained persistently poor narrated similar stories about how suffering due to respiratory diseases, such as asthma and chronic bronchitis, became more pronounced during the monsoon months. Long-lingering diseases are more acutely experienced after the rains begin to fall. Doctors and healers have to deal with their heaviest patient loads during this season. Cattle deaths are also more frequent at the time of monsoon. Despite the efforts that poor and near-poor families make through the rest of the year, setbacks suffered during the monsoon tend to perpetuate poverty.

Anirudh Krishna

6

Seasonality and poverty

Evidence from Malawi[1]

Ephraim W. Chirwa, Andrew Dorward and Marcella Vigneri

Introduction

Many agrarian economies are associated with seasonal patterns of income and consumption expenditure. Chambers (1982) notes that many poor people in developing countries live in tropical environments characterized by wet–dry seasonality with varying levels of income, food availability, incidence of disease and supply of and demand for labour. However, studies that model the determinants of poverty tend to ignore the issue of seasonality in the estimates of poverty even though the household-level data used in the analysis are collected over a long period of time. Several studies looking at the determinants of poverty in different African countries do not account for seasonality (Grootaert, 1997; Geda *et al.*, 2005; Datt *et al.*, 2000; Mukherjee and Benson, 2003; Okwi *et al.*, 2007). Geda *et al.* (2005) acknowledge that the data collection did not take seasonality into account, and therefore could not control for seasonality in the estimation of the determinants of poverty in Kenya. Other studies, however, explicitly discuss the role of seasonality in household welfare. Dercon and Krishnan (2000), for instance, use seasonal price indices and seasonal wages to capture seasonality and these proxies were highly significant with per capita consumption increasing in peak labour periods and decreasing in high price periods. Appleton (2002), using a nationally representative survey in Uganda, controls for the time of interview in regression models and finds it statistically significant in welfare and poverty functions. Similarly, Khandker (2009) controls for a season associated with food deprivation and finds a negative and significant impact on welfare in Bangladesh.

Seasonality effects on income and consumption expenditure are expected in Malawi – by and large an agrarian economy. The agricultural sector remains pivotal for livelihoods in rural Malawi with more than 80 per cent of the population depending on agriculture. Agriculture also accounts for nearly 40 per cent of gross domestic product, 80 per cent of export earnings, and is the main economic activity for 71 per cent of the rural population. Agriculture in Malawi is largely rainfed with less than 5 per cent of the land under irrigated cultivation. According to NSO (2005), about 97 per cent of households are engaged in rainfed agricultural cultivation with only 36 per cent engaging in dry season (*dimba*) cultivation. Recent estimates of poverty reveal that about 52 per cent of the population in Malawi lives below the poverty line. Poverty is largely a rural phenomenon, with 56 per cent of the rural population compared with 25 per cent of the urban population living below the poverty line (NSO, 2005).

Khandker (2009) suggests that seasonality in the consumption pattern of agrarian economies is determined by seasonality in income opportunities and by the absence of credit markets to facilitate consumption smoothing for poor people. Several factors, however, are at play. In Malawi, these factors include seasonal patterns in food stocks and incomes, reliance on seasonal labour markets, seasonal movements in food prices and seasonal patterns in asset prices. For instance, most rural households in Malawi tend to have adequate food stocks soon after harvest, and maize stocks from own production last on average five months after harvest. A food crisis for many households peaks in the lean season, between January and March. Seasonality in the availability of food stocks is also accompanied by seasonality in maize prices, which rise sharply in lean periods, thereby adversely affecting the livelihoods of the poor during the lean season. Devereux (2009a) notes that during food crisis periods the poor cope by, *inter alia,* reducing portions of meals and consuming inferior and less expensive foods. These strategies may reduce consumption expenditures but increase poverty and vulnerability.

Although most rural income is seasonal in Malawi, previous studies on the determinants of poverty in Malawi do not account for seasonality in their models (Mukherjee and Benson, 2003; Government of Malawi and World Bank, 2007). Ignoring seasonality in the estimates of poverty may lead to less efficient estimates of correlates of poverty and may lead to biased estimates of poverty. This chapter seeks to investigate the importance of seasonality in poverty estimates for Malawi. It does so by using data collected over a 13-month period in the 2004/05 Integrated Household Survey. The chapter is organized as follows. The next section presents a review of economic reforms and resulting economic performance in Malawi. The third section presents the methodology and estimation techniques used in the study. The empirical evidence on the relationship between poverty and seasonality is presented in the fourth section. Concluding remarks and policy implications are in the final section.

Seasonality and poverty in Malawi

The seasonal nature of agricultural and agriculture-related incomes, which are dominant in rural Malawi, makes households vulnerable to seasonal variations in consumption and poverty. First, most smallholder farmers are subsistence farmers and produce maize mainly for their own food requirements. However, different studies show that in 2006 about 57 per cent of households had inadequate food consumption. For instance, NSO (2005) find that 81 per cent of the households who grew food crops in the 2004/05 agricultural season (which was a poor season) had run out of staple food stocks by December 2005. Most of these households relied on purchases from the markets to meet their food requirements once their stocks of own food production ran out. Food prices in Malawi are also highly seasonal and tend to be high during the lean season, around January and February. Devereux (2009a) presents case study evidence that about 92 per cent of households in southern Malawi use food expenditure-reducing strategies as coping mechanisms during food shortages.

Poor Malawian households also frequently engage in *ganyu* (casual) labour, partly as a coping strategy. Whiteside (2000) notes that *ganyu* is the most important coping strategy for most poor households in the crucial hungry period between food stores running out and the new harvest. *Ganyu* activities by households tend to intensify during the wet season, between November and February, thereby competing with own labour demand for own farm production (Devereux, 2009a). Thirdly, seasonality in consumption is also exacerbated by the lack of credit for consumption-smoothing among rural households. Most households in Malawi do not have access to credit. Only 13 per cent of households in 2004/05 received a loan (NSO, 2005). Zeller and Sharma (2000) observe that there are several ways in which access to or lack of financial services can influence household income and food consumption (food security). The first is through income generation in which access to credit provides additional capital. This enhances households' existing human, physical and social capital in order to earn more income or to increase the risk-bearing capacity of households to invest in more risky and more profitable income-generating activities. Thus, access to financial services helps poor households diversify their sources of income and reduces their vulnerability to income shocks. Secondly, credit can be used directly to finance immediate household consumption needs. Households may stabilize their consumption in adverse climatic conditions by adjusting their disposable income or liquidity through borrowing for consumption or borrowing for investment where, with fungibility of credit, the borrowed funds may be diverted to immediate consumption.

Data from the 2004/05 Integrated Household Survey (IHS2) reveal seasonal patterns in the proportion of households that are estimated or classified as poor. Figure 6.1 shows that households interviewed soon after harvest (during the peak marketing season in June and July) are less likely to be classified as poor, while those interviewed during the lean season (December to February) are more likely to be classified as poor. Poverty incidence was also higher in March 2005 than in March 2004, consistent with higher food prices and lower food stocks in 2004/5 following a poor harvest in May/June 2004. A similar pattern is observed among the ultra-poor. This suggests that the date of interview matters, and poverty (when measured using expenditure and consumption records at the time of interview) seems to be associated with seasonality in income sources.

In the IHS2, poverty is assessed on the basis of estimated annual household expenditure. This is estimated by extrapolating across the whole year the value

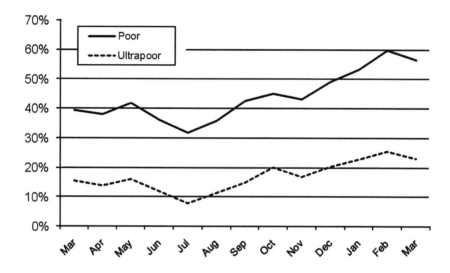

Source: Calculated by authors from IHS2 data

Note: * Simple (unweighted) mean of sample.

FIGURE 6.1 Estimated poverty incidence by date of interview, March 2004 to March 2005*

of food consumed in the week before the interview, and adding this to estimated annual non-food expenditures where some information on some larger and less frequently purchased items is reported for the previous 3 or 12 months. If food expenditure varies seasonally then this will also lead to seasonal variation in estimates of annual expenditure, and hence of poverty incidence, according to the time of data collection. Figure 6.2 shows how estimates of aggregate food and non-food household expenditures in Malawi vary seasonally from March 2004 to March 2005. As one would expect, median annual household total expenditures show a pattern closely related to variation in poverty incidence (Figure 6.1), with higher median expenditures in the post-harvest period and lower expenditures during the lean agricultural season. Again as one would expect, variations in estimated total annual income with time of interview are affected more by changes in food expenditures than by non-food expenditures, as more of the information on the latter is derived from respondents' estimates of annual expenditure and less from extrapolation of respondents' estimates of weekly expenditure at the time of interview. However non-food expenditures are still affected by time of interview.

Figure 6.3 shows the median annual per capita expenditure by region in Malawi. Major swings in per capita expenditure in the northern region are not easily explained, with higher per capita expenditure estimated for households interviewed in July/August, March/April and October, but lower per capita expenditure estimated for households interviewed in February, June, September and December

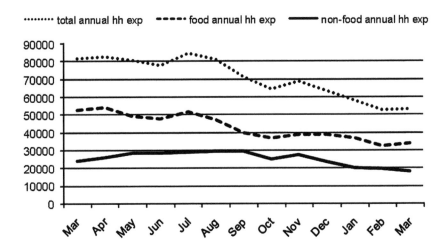

Source: Calculated by authors from IHS2 data

Note: ★ Simple (unweighted) median of sample.

FIGURE 6.2 Median annual household expenditures March 2004 to March 2005★

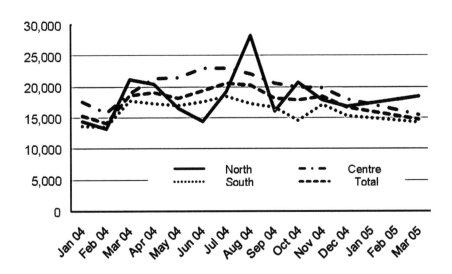

Source: Calculated by authors from IHS2 data

Note: ★ Simple (unweighted) median of sample.

FIGURE 6.3 Median annual per capita expenditure January 2004 to March 2005★

2004. Possible explanations include later timing of rains and a more favourable 2004 harvest as compared with the central and southern regions. These regions do not display major swings, although in all cases their median per capita expenditures tend to be higher in the post-harvest period than in the lean agricultural season.

The poor and food insecure are also at risk due to seasonal variations in food prices. Figure 6.4 shows movements in the domestic food price index using the food consumer price index (CPI).[2] An upwards trend in nominal food prices is evident in Figure 6.4a, with swings in monthly and seasonal prices (Figure 6.4b). The major price increases tend to occur initially around August/September, when most households run out of own food stocks, and again in February/March, the lean season just before the maize harvest. Major falls in prices then occur in April/May/June, just after harvest, when most households have maize from own production. The seasonality index based on the centred 12-monthly moving average of the food price index reveals that the highest index value of 1.11 occurs in February, starts declining in March and reaches its lowest point of 0.90 in August, thereafter rising slowly but remaining below 1.0 by December. This confirms that food prices tend to be high in the hungry season and low in the harvest season.

These changes in prices are not only important in causing poor people to reduce their maize consumption, they also have to be taken into account in estimates of poor people's annual expenditure. Seasonal food expenditures are affected by both changes in quantities consumed and changes in prices, which move in opposite directions. High prices therefore mean that the value of food consumption will fall much less than the quantity of food consumed – and may even increase – during the lean period. It is therefore important that either average annual prices or deflated prices are used in estimating annual expenditure. This was the case for estimates reported in Figure 6.2 and in IHS2 poverty estimates.

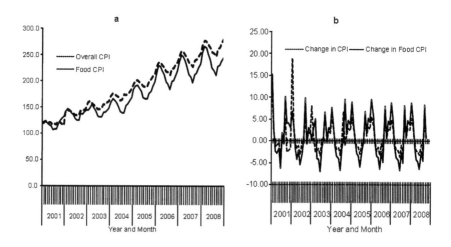

Source: Chirwa (2009)

FIGURE 6.4 Food price trends in Malawi 2001–2008

Variations in poverty, in average per capita expenditures, and movements in prices all underscore the need to account for seasonality in poverty estimates, because the date of interview affects the estimated expenditures and poverty status and may lead to differences in poverty status being significantly determined by the timing of data collection. The importance of this is illustrated by the NSO's use of a poverty model that ignores seasonality in estimating poverty incidence from the relatively low-cost Welfare Monitoring Survey (WMS). From 2005 to 2009, the WMS collected data in different months between June and November (months with relatively high expenditures and low poverty incidence as compared with December to February, as shown in Figures 6.1–6.3). Poverty correlates from a non-seasonally adjusted model based on 2004/5 data are then used to predict household expenditures and hence the incidence of poverty, and poverty estimates based on data collected in different months between June and November are then compared with the 2004/5 poverty estimate, derived from data from interviews in all months from March 2004 to March 2005 (see for example NSO, 2006). Gujarati (2003) notes that if an important variable that is excluded from a model is also correlated with the included explanatory variables, then the parameter estimates for these variables will be biased and inconsistent. However, even if the variables are not correlated, the intercept term will remain biased, and forecasts based on the incorrect model will be unreliable. Hence, failure to include time of data collection in the poverty estimation model could lead to biased and inconsistent estimators.

Model specification and data

We investigate the extent and nature of possible biased and inconsistent estimators from omission of timing of interview from poverty correlate models, using the same specification of the determinants of poverty model as given by GOM and World Bank (2007) in the Poverty and Vulnerability Analysis (PVA) adapted from Mukherjee and Benson (2003), with the addition of various specifications of seasonal dummies (see Appleton, 2002). The welfare model is specified as follows:

$$\ln\ C_j = \beta_0 + \sum_{i=1}^{n} \beta_j X_j + \sum_{k=1}^{m} \alpha_k S_k + \varepsilon_i \qquad (1)$$

where C_j is annual consumption expenditure per capita of household j in Malawi Kwacha (MK); X_{ij} is a set of exogenous household characteristics or other determinants; S_k is a set of seasonal dummies for time of data collection; and ε is a random error term. Our explanatory variables include demographic characteristics, education, employment and occupation, farm and non-farm activities, community characteristics (GOM and World Bank, 2007) and season of data collection.

The model is estimated using data from the second Integrated Household Survey (IHS2) collected from March 2004 to March 2005 by the National Statistical Office (NSO), as discussed earlier. The survey collected information from a representative sample of 11,032 households (9,601 rural households and 1,431 urban households). The sampling design is representative at both national and district level across seasons (i.e. each district contained a balanced sample across all months), and the survey therefore provides reliable estimates for those areas.

The demographic variables include age in years of household head, the sex of the household head, the age of the household head, whether the household head is a widow, the total size of the household and the number of children. The education variables are specified as categorical variables of maximum education level attained by the household head. Education categories include: primary education, secondary education, and tertiary education dummies with a no education dummy variable as the reference category.

The employment and occupation category captures the effects of the distribution of different sorts of occupations at the household level. The variables used include whether the household head is engaged in formal wage employment, and/or whether the household runs a non-farm enterprise.

Agricultural activity variables account for whether the household farms had any rainfed plots, the total per capita landholdings of rainfed land held by the household, whether the household has a *dimba* plot (valley bottom land cultivated in the dry season using residual soil moisture and/or irrigation), and whether the household grew tobacco (in the last cropping season).

We also include community characteristics and access to services at the community level such as the existence of a regular bus service to/from the community, the presence of a health clinic and bank in the community, differential access to markets by including a dummy if the household is in a *boma* (district administrative centre) or trading centre, and the presence of an Agricultural Development and Marketing Corporation (ADMARC) (parastatal) market and a daily market, and a dummy for the presence of a tarmac/asphalt road in the community. We also include dummies representing regions and agricultural development divisions.

We capture the effects of seasonality on poverty by constructing dummies in two ways. First, we include dummy variables for each of the 12 months as the data were collected over a period of 13 months (March 2004 to March 2005). The month of March 2005 is taken as a base category. Second, we group the observations into four farming seasons: March to April 2004 (harvesting season) as base category; May to August 2004 (post-harvesting/marketing season); September to November 2004 (pre-planting season); and December 2004 to March 2005 (farming and lean season).[3]

Empirical results

We investigate the effects of seasonality on poverty by looking at two different measures: the statistical significance of seasonal dummies and the significance of the incremental contribution of seasonal dummies using analysis of variance. We compare the R-squared obtained from models without seasonal dummies (R^2_{PVA}) to that obtained from models with seasonal dummies (R^2_{PVAS}). We use the F-test for incremental contribution of additional variables to determine the significance of seasonal dummy variables in explaining poverty.[4] Chirwa *et al.* (2009) note that there are small changes in the values of the slope parameters with the inclusion of dummies, and the coefficients that were found to be statistically significant in GOM and World Bank (2007) remain statistically significant in all the models. However, the introduction of seasonality variables changes the value of the intercept (Chirwa *et al.*, 2009). In the case of monthly seasonal dummy variables and farming season dummy variables there is a positive shift in the value of the intercept term while the introduction of a continuous seasonal dummy variable leads to a downward shift of the regression line.

Poverty and monthly seasonal dummies

Table 6.1 presents estimates of dummy variables from the determinants of poverty model disaggregated by residence and regions. The full illustrative results and those disaggregated by residence are presented in Appendix Table 6A1. In all the models, inclusion of seasonal dummy variables increases the explained variations compared to the base model without seasonality. The hypothesis that all the coefficients of seasonal dummy variables are equal to zero is rejected at the 1 per cent level in all models. There is a consistent pattern of declining welfare as households approach the lean season. This result is consistent with the findings in Appleton (2002) and Khandker (2009). First, from the national model, we find that the coefficients of the months of April 2004 and August 2004 through to February 2005 are negative and statistically significant. Generally, there is an absolute increase in the size of coefficients from August 2004 through to February 2005. Poverty tends to increase during the months of December, January and February. These are the lean months for food supply among poor households and consumption tends to be lower as households pursue strategies that limit food consumption.

Turning to the model for rural households, we find negative and statistically significant seasonal effects for the months of April and May, and July through to February 2005. Similarly, absolute sizes of coefficients increase from July through to February, and households that were interviewed in the month of January are more likely to be poor. This general picture is also found in the model for urban households. All the seasonal dummies, except May 2004, June 2004 and October 2004, are statistically significant (i.e. different from March 2005) and the absolute value of coefficients increases as we approach the lean food availability season. Regional regression models also depict the importance of the lean food availability season in determining the level of poverty. While the results of the central and southern regions are highly consistent with the national results, for the northern region we also find that households that were interviewed in July were less likely to be poor (as would be expected from Figure 6.3). However, in all the three regions, the period from October 2004 through to February 2005 shows increasing absolute effect of month of interview, with the month of January revealing the highest absolute value.

TABLE 6.1 Poverty and monthly seasonal dummies

Seasonal Dummies	(1) National	Residence		Region		
		(2) Rural	(3) Urban (no tobacco)	(4) North	(5) Centre	(6) South
March 2004	-0.02 (0.02)	-0.00 (0.03)	-0.16** (0.07)	-0.02 (0.06)	0.02 (0.04)	-0.00 (0.04)
April 2004	-0.05* (0.03)	-0.06** (0.03)	-0.18** (0.08)	-0.11 (0.07)	0.11*** (0.04)	-0.12*** (0.04)
May 2004	-0.03 (0.02)	-0.05** (0.03)	-0.02 (0.08)	-0.25*** (0.07)	0.11*** (0.04)	-0.04 (0.04)
June 2004	-0.00 (0.03)	0.01 (0.03)	-0.10 (0.10)	-0.14** (0.07)	0.08* (0.04)	0.05 (0.04)
July 2004	0.01 (0.02)	0.05* (0.02)	-0.30*** (0.07)	0.31*** (0.07)	0.04 (0.04)	-0.04 (0.04)
August 2004	-0.13*** (0.02)	-0.12*** (0.02)	-0.33*** (0.07)	-0.31*** (0.07)	-0.03 (0.04)	-0.12*** (0.04)
September 2004	-0.15*** (0.03)	-0.16*** (0.03)	-0.20** (0.09)	-0.03 (0.08)	-0.07** (0.04)	-0.20*** (0.04)
October 2004	-0.12*** (0.03)	-0.16*** (0.03)	-0.08 (0.08)	-0.32*** (0.07)	-0.02 (0.04)	-0.06 (0.04)
November 2004	-0.20*** (0.03)	-0.19*** (0.03)	-0.41*** (0.08)	-0.27*** (0.07)	-0.13*** (0.04)	-0.19*** (0.04)
December 2004	-0.30*** (0.03)	-0.27*** (0.03)	-0.56*** (0.09)	-0.37*** (0.07)	-0.19*** (0.04)	-0.26*** (0.05)
January 2005	-0.36*** (0.02)	-0.33*** (0.02)	-0.63*** (0.08)	-0.47*** (0.06)	-0.23*** (0.04)	-0.33*** (0.04)
February 2005	-0.31*** (0.02)	-0.29*** (0.02)	-0.42*** (0.07)	-0.42*** (0.10)	-0.31*** (0.04)	-0.24*** (0.03)
N	11032	9601	1431	1637	4219	5176
R^2_{PVAS}	0.50	0.47	0.55	0.50	0.53	0.49
R^2_{PVA}	0.47	0.43	0.51	0.41	0.50	0.47
F-test ($\alpha_i = 0$)	54.87***	60.02***	10.18***	23.72***	22.14***	16.73***
F(Prob.)	(0.00)	(0.00)	(0.00)	(0.00)	(0.00)	(0.00)

Source: Chirwa et al. (2009)

Note: The dependent variable is a natural logarithm of per capita consumption. Robust standard errors are in parentheses. * Significant at 10%; ** significant at 5%; *** significant at 1%. Omitted dummy is date of interview = 1 if March 2005.

Figure 6.5 presents the plot of coefficients of monthly seasonal dummies. There is a general trend showing that per capita consumption falls from around October. However, there is a sharper decline in per capita consumption for urban areas compared to rural areas, suggesting that urban households are more vulnerable to high variability in prices – and hence tighten their belts more than rural households as they cope with food shortages. While the patterns of variation in the centre and the south are largely consistent with the national pattern, the northern region is very different with per capita consumption increasing substantially in August. There are more seasonal variations in per capita consumption in the north compared to other regions. One reason for this may be that generally the north receives rain later and harvest starts around June/July, therefore leaving plenty of food around in August – but this does not explain low consumption in September and November, with higher consumption in October.

Poverty and farming seasons

The agricultural season in Malawi is typically divided into three seasons. The first is the harvesting and marketing season that runs from May to August. During this time many households earn cash from their crop sales and also have adequate food supplies, particularly maize, from their own production. This period is also associated with low maize prices, although food and cereal prices tend to rise sharply in August (FEWSNET, 2009, and see Figure 6.4 earlier). The second season is the

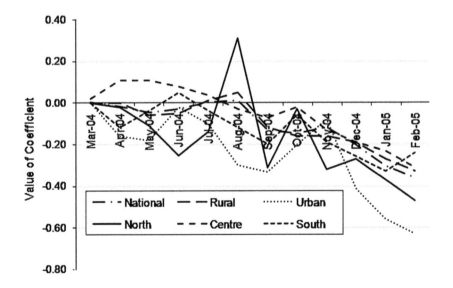

Source: Calculated by authors from IHS2 data

FIGURE 6.5 Values of monthly seasonal dummy coefficients

pre-planting season, between September and November. The major agricultural activity is land preparation, although for some households this is also the time for winter crop harvests. The third season is the rainy season, between December and March. This is also known as the hunger season – as most households run out of their own production during this period, particularly from December to February. This season extends into April, in which food security improves due to consumption of green maize (FEWSNET, 2008).

Table 6.2 presents a summary of the results from modelling the effects of farming seasons on poverty in Malawi. The period from March to April 2004 is taken as a base category. In all models the F statistics show a rejection of the null hypothesis that the inclusion of seasonal dummies does not improve the explanatory power at the 1 per cent level of significance. It is evident that farming seasons affect the level and depth of poverty. In all estimates the coefficients of the September to November and December 2004 to March 2005 periods are negative and statistically significant at the 1 per cent or 5 per cent level.

It is interesting to note that these findings suggest that households interviewed during the hunger season are more likely to be classified as poor compared to the base category and other seasons. The results from the national estimate of poverty in Model 1 show that per capita annual expenditures fell by 25 per cent during December 2004 and March 2005, but fell by only 12 per cent during the pre-planting season.[5] The largest margin in poverty between the base category and the hunger season occurs in the urban areas and in the northern region. In the

TABLE 6.2 Poverty and farming season dummies

| Seasonal Dummies | (1) National | Residence | | Region | | |
		(2) Rural	(3) Urban (no tobacco)	(4) North	(5) Centre	(6) South
May–August 2004	−0.01	−0.01	−0.07	−0.01	0.08***	−0.04*
	(0.01)	(0.02)	(0.05)	(0.04)	(0.02)	(0.02)
Sep–Nov 2004	−0.13***	−0.15***	−0.14***	−0.19***	−0.05**	−0.14***
	(0.02)	(0.02)	(0.05)	(0.05)	(0.02)	(0.02)
Dec 2004– Mar 2005	−0.29***	−0.27***	−0.40***	−0.36***	−0.23***	−0.26***
	(0.01)	(0.02)	(0.05)	(0.04)	(0.02)	(0.02)
N	11032	9601	1431	1637	4219	5176
R^2_{PVAS}	0.50	0.46	0.54	0.45	0.53	0.49
R^2_{PVA}	0.47	0.43	0.51	0.41	0.50	0.47
F-test ($\alpha_i = 0$)	219.64***	176.89***	30.04***	38.55***	88.77***	67.05***
F(Prob.)	(0.00)	(0.00)	(0.00)	(0.00)	(0.00)	(0.00)

Source: Chirwa et al. (2009)

Note: The dependent variable is natural logarithm of per capita consumption. Robust standard errors are in parentheses. * Significant at 10%; ** significant at 5%; *** significant at 1%. Omitted dummy is date of interview = 1 if March to April 2004.

urban areas, poverty estimates increase by 33 per cent and in the northern region by 30 per cent during the hunger period, as compared with rises of 21 per cent and 23 per cent in the central and southern regions, respectively. For the central region, poverty falls by 8 per cent during the harvesting and marketing season. The central region is the main production area for tobacco, which is the main cash crop and main foreign exchange earner in Malawi. The central region is also the main producing area for maize. The positive and statistically significant coefficient of the May to August 2004 dummy also points to the seasonality of tobacco incomes. Nonetheless, poverty still increases during the hunger season in the central region, and per capita consumption falls by 23 per cent.

Effects of seasonality on poverty estimates

Such seasonal variation in poverty incidence also means that estimates of changes in poverty incidence between years may be significantly affected by differences in the timing of data collection. In Malawi, for example, data from annual Welfare Monitoring Surveys conducted in different months between June and October each year from 2005 to 2009 have estimated falling poverty incidence (50 per cent, 45 per cent, 40 per cent, 40 per cent and 39 per cent). This appears to suggest a steady fall in poverty incidence when compared with the IHS2 estimate of 52 per cent in 2004/5. A different picture emerges, however, if we use IHS2 information on seasonal variation in poverty incidence to adjust WMS estimates of poverty incidence.

Figure 6.6 compares three different time series for estimates of poverty incidence: 'WMS unadjusted' shows the time series reported by NSO (2010); 'WMS Adj A' shows the effects of standardizing the WMS estimates of poverty incidence by the ratio of overall annual poverty incidence to average poverty incidence across the months of data collection reported for the WMS each year as given in NSO (2006), NSO (2007), NSO (2008), NSO (2009) and NSO (2010); 'WMS Adj B' is adjusted in the same way as 'WMS Adj A', but using the ratio of overall annual poverty incidence to average poverty incidence across the central months of reported data collection (i.e. assuming the majority of households were interviewed in the middle of the reported data collection period).

The effects of seasonal adjustments on estimated poverty incidence are striking for WMS 2005 and 2006, when data collection occurred in August to September and June to September respectively. Adjusted poverty estimates for 2005 suggest that it has risen by 3.6 percentage points from 2004/5 to 2005, not fallen by 2.4 percentage points. Higher poverty incidence in the second half of 2005 as compared with 2004 is consistent with the effects of the poor 2005 harvest and food insecurity and deprivation in 2005/6 (for example FEWSNET, 2005). The large 2006 difference between 'WMS Adj A' and 'WMS Adj B' further illustrates the potential importance of seasonality for poverty estimates, with a relatively minor change in timing of data collection leading to substantial changes in estimated poverty incidence. The effects of seasonal adjustment are smaller for WMS 2007, 2008 and 2009, when data collection occurred a little later, from

Estimated poverty incidence

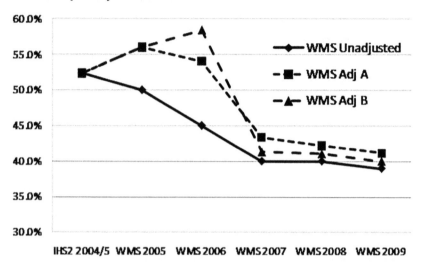

Source: NSO (2005; 2006; 2007; 2008; 2009; 2010) and authors' calculations

FIGURE 6.6 Effects of seasonal adjustments on WMS estimates of poverty incidence

August to October or November, further from the harvest period and closer to the lean period. Nevertheless these lead to estimated falls in poverty of 11–12 percentage points from 2004/5 to 2009 as compared with an estimated fall of over 13 percentage points using unadjusted estimates. (A further potential source of downward bias in estimates of poverty incidence may arise for WMS 2008 and 2009 when sampled households were selected from household listings made in 2007 for the National Census for Agriculture and Livestock (NACAL) – and this will be likely to exclude recently formed households with younger household heads and younger children which tend to have higher poverty rates (GOM and World Bank, 2007) and recent immigrants.)

This analysis illustrates clear dangers in drawing comparative lessons from estimates of poverty incidence over time (or indeed between different population groups or areas) if seasonal influences on poverty estimates are not properly taken into account in data collection, analysis and interpretation.

Conclusions

This chapter has used data from Malawi to examine the impact of seasonality on estimates of poverty incidence and to test the argument that in agrarian economies characterized by seasonal variations in households' incomes and food availability, modelling determinants of welfare and poverty without controlling for seasonality can be misleading and generate incorrect inferences. We find that estimated poverty incidence is significantly affected by seasonality if expenditure values at different times of year are extrapolated to obtain estimates of annual expenditure, without any seasonal adjustment. Estimates of poverty incidence will be higher if expenditure data are collected during the hunger gap, while estimates of poverty incidence for the same population will be lower if expenditure data are collected during the post-harvest period.

These findings have a number of important implications. First, this analysis provides clear evidence that in a poor economy like Malawi, poor people's physical consumption can vary significantly between seasons within a year. This affects poor urban people as well as rural people, and is caused by variation in both food availability and food entitlements - people's ability to afford food purchases as a result of changes in food prices and incomes (although we have not examined the relative importance of seasonal variation in food prices and incomes as determinants of seasonal variation in consumption). Seasonal variation in physical consumption in a poor population leads to seasonal variation in the incidence and also depth of consumption (or income) poverty. Since seasonality is an important correlate and, as argued in this chapter, determinant of poverty, policies attempting to reduce the causes and incidence of poverty must address seasonal issues – both the immediate effects of seasonal stresses on the poor and the underlying causes of seasonal stresses. Insofar as seasonal traps perpetuate poverty across seasons (for example Chambers, 1982; Gill, 1991), such policies should also have wider effects on poverty.

Second, and following on from this, estimates of poverty incidence and depth may be affected by the timing of data collection and methods of data analysis with respect to seasonality. This is important when determining and reporting poverty incidence for a particular time or period. Figure 6.1, for example, shows that within the eight-month period from July 2004 to February 2005 the unweighted mean poverty incidence approximately doubled, from around 30 per cent to around 60 per cent. This poses questions about the correct figure for poverty incidence over this period as a whole. Related, perhaps greater, concerns arise when comparing estimates of poverty incidence over time. Figure 6.6 shows substantial differences in patterns of change in poverty using estimates allowing for and ignoring seasonality of data collection. These issues should be considered in policy analysis, policymaking, and policy implementation to ensure that they are informed by accurate and reliable poverty measures.

The third important finding from this analysis is that although allowance for seasonal factors affects estimates of the incidence of poverty, it does not appear to significantly affect the relationships between other factors and poverty incidence. This suggests, first, that seasonality does not generally have differential impacts on different kinds of poverty or determinants of poverty, at least among those variables included in the determinants of poverty model investigated in this chapter. Second, and of direct relevance to policy, the effectiveness of actions to address poverty through these variables is not affected (strengthened or undermined) by the effects of seasonality, and earlier findings on this remain robust.

Notes

1 This chapter is an abridged version of a paper presented at the Seasonality Revisited International Conference 8-10 July, 2009 at the Institute of Development Studies, Sussex. We acknowledge financial assistance from DFID-UK to the Future Agriculture Consortium (FAC) who sponsored this research work. The usual disclaimer applies.
2 It is, however, important to note that maize is a dominant commodity in the computation of the food price index in Malawi, and the food price index is the main driver of the overall consumer index.
3 MVAC (2005), cited in Devereux (2009a), categorizes the farming season into four periods: April–June, July–September, October–December, and January–March.
4 The full results of estimated poverty models without and with dummies representing seasons of data collection are presented in Chirwa et al. (2009).
5 Since the model is log-lin, the semi-elasticity is obtained by taking the antilog to base e of the estimated dummy coefficient and subtracting 1 from it and multiplying the difference by 100 (Gujarati, 2003).

Appendix

TABLE 6A1 Determinants of welfare with monthly seasonal dummies

	(1)	(2)	(3)	(4)	(5)	(6)
	Baseline – All		Rural		Urban	
Dependent variable is log(pc exp)	PVA	PVA with Month D	PVA	PVA with Month D	PVA	PVA with Month D
Female household head	-0.14***	-0.15***	-0.14***	-0.15***	-0.07	-0.09*
	(0.01)	(0.01)	(0.01)	(0.01)	(0.05)	(0.05)
Age of hh head: 26–35 years	0.07***	0.07***	0.06***	0.06***	0.12***	0.11**
	(0.02)	(0.02)	(0.02)	(0.02)	(0.05)	(0.04)
Age of hh head: 36–45 years	0.09***	0.09***	0.08***	0.08***	0.14**	0.12**
	(0.02)	(0.02)	(0.02)	(0.02)	(0.06)	(0.06)
Age of hh head: 46–55 years	0.03	0.03	0.02	0.03	0.02	0.01
	(0.02)	(0.02)	(0.02)	(0.02)	(0.07)	(0.07)
Age of hh head: 56–65 years	-0.04*	-0.04*	-0.03*	-0.03*	0.01	0.02
	(0.02)	(0.02)	(0.02)	(0.02)	(0.07)	(0.07)
Age of hh head: 66+ years	-0.07***	-0.08***	-0.07***	-0.08***	-0.18*	-0.16*
	(0.02)	(0.02)	(0.02)	(0.02)	(0.09)	(0.09)
Widowed household head	0.06***	0.05***	0.06***	0.06***	-0.07	-0.04
	(0.02)	(0.02)	(0.02)	(0.02)	(0.07)	(0.06)
Household size	-0.28***	-0.28***	-0.29***	-0.29***	-0.32***	-0.31***
	(0.03)	(0.02)	(0.03)	(0.03)	(0.03)	(0.03)
Household size squared (/100)	1.37***	1.35***	1.33***	1.32***	2.02***	1.94***
	(0.21)	(0.21)	(0.22)	(0.21)	(0.24)	(0.24)
Number of children 0–4	-0.08***	-0.09***	-0.06***	-0.07***	-0.14***	-0.15***
	(0.01)	(0.01)	(0.01)	(0.01)	(0.03)	(0.03)
Number of children 5–10	-0.04***	-0.04***	-0.03***	-0.03***	-0.05*	-0.04
	(0.01)	(0.01)	(0.01)	(0.01)	(0.03)	(0.02)
Number of children 11–14	-0.02**	-0.02**	-0.01	-0.01	-0.06*	-0.06**
	(0.01)	(0.01)	(0.01)	(0.01)	(0.03)	(0.03)
Religion: Islam	0.03	0.02	0.00	0.00	0.24***	0.15*
	(0.02)	(0.02)	(0.03)	(0.02)	(0.09)	(0.08)
Religion: Catholic	0.03	0.03	-0.00	0.01	0.21***	0.14*
	(0.02)	(0.02)	(0.02)	(0.02)	(0.08)	(0.07)
Religion: CCAP	0.09***	0.09***	0.06**	0.06***	0.24***	0.18**
	(0.02)	(0.02)	(0.02)	(0.02)	(0.08)	(0.08)
Religion: Other Christian	0.02	0.02	-0.00	0.00	0.16**	0.10
	(0.02)	(0.02)	(0.02)	(0.02)	(0.07)	(0.07)
Highest education: some primary	0.05**	0.05**	0.07***	0.06***	0.05	0.04
	(0.02)	(0.02)	(0.02)	(0.02)	(0.09)	(0.09)
Highest education: completed primary	0.13***	0.12***	0.16***	0.16***	0.13	0.10
	(0.03)	(0.02)	(0.03)	(0.03)	(0.09)	(0.09)

Dependent variable is log(pc exp)	(1)	(2)	(3)	(4)	(5)	(6)
	Baseline – All		Rural		Urban	
	PVA	PVA with Month D	PVA	PVA with Month D	PVA	PVA with Month D
Highest education: post-primary	0.40*** (0.03)	0.40*** (0.02)	0.37*** (0.03)	0.37*** (0.03)	0.67*** (0.09)	0.61*** (0.09)
HH has wage/salary income	0.12*** (0.01)	0.12*** (0.01)	0.11*** (0.01)	0.11*** (0.01)	0.10*** (0.04)	0.08** (0.03)
Household has a non-farm enterprise	0.14*** (0.01)	0.13*** (0.01)	0.15*** (0.01)	0.13*** (0.01)	0.11*** (0.04)	0.07** (0.03)
HH grew tobacco last crop season	0.09*** (0.02)	0.10*** (0.01)	0.10*** (0.02)	0.10*** (0.01)		
HH owns any *dimba* plot	0.07*** (0.01)	0.06*** (0.01)	0.08*** (0.01)	0.07*** (0.01)	-0.19*** (0.05)	-0.13*** (0.05)
HH farms any rainfed plots (0/1)	-0.01 (0.02)	0.01 (0.02)	-0.03 (0.02)	0.01 (0.02)	0.06 (0.04)	0.05 (0.04)
Ln total hectares of rainfed plots	0.08*** (0.01)	0.08*** (0.01)	0.08*** (0.01)	0.08*** (0.01)	0.07*** (0.03)	0.09*** (0.03)
Regular bus service in community	0.01 (0.01)	-0.00 (0.01)	0.01 (0.01)	-0.01 (0.01)	0.08** (0.04)	0.11*** (0.04)
Health clinic in community	0.07*** (0.01)	0.05*** (0.01)	0.06*** (0.01)	0.03*** (0.01)	-0.03 (0.04)	0.04 (0.04)
EA is a *boma* or trading centre	0.15*** (0.02)	0.17*** (0.02)	0.19*** (0.03)	0.21*** (0.02)		
Travel to nearest *boma*: >20–30 mins	-0.00 (0.02)	0.02 (0.02)	-0.02 (0.02)	0.00 (0.02)		
Travel to nearest *boma*: >30–45 mins	-0.10*** (0.02)	-0.08*** (0.02)	-0.11*** (0.02)	-0.10*** (0.02)		
Travel to nearest *boma*: >45–60 mins	-0.04** (0.02)	-0.04*** (0.02)	-0.04** (0.02)	-0.05*** (0.02)		
Travel to nearest *boma*: >60 mins	-0.04** (0.02)	-0.02 (0.02)	-0.03 (0.02)	-0.02 (0.02)		
ADMARC market in the community	-0.04*** (0.01)	-0.04*** (0.01)	-0.04*** (0.01)	-0.03** (0.01)	0.10 (0.07)	-0.05 (0.07)
Bank in community	-0.02 (0.02)	-0.02 (0.02)	-0.02 (0.02)	-0.02 (0.02)	-0.10 (0.07)	-0.16** (0.08)
Daily market in community	0.01 (0.01)	0.02* (0.01)	-0.00 (0.01)	0.01 (0.01)	0.10** (0.05)	0.04 (0.05)

	(1)	(2)	(3)	(4)	(5)	(6)
	Baseline – All		Rural		Urban	
Dependent variable is log(pc exp)	PVA	PVA with Month D	PVA	PVA with Month D	PVA	PVA with Month D
Tarmac/ asphalt road in community	0.13*** (0.02)	0.16*** (0.02)	0.03* (0.02)	0.06*** (0.02)	0.44*** (0.04)	0.46*** (0.04)
North region	−0.06** (0.03)	−0.05* (0.03)	−0.04 (0.03)	−0.03 (0.03)		
Central region	0.24*** (0.02)	0.24*** (0.02)	0.25*** (0.02)	0.26*** (0.02)		
ADD: Karonga	0.00 (0.00)	0.00 (0.00)	0.00 (0.00)	0.00 (0.00)	0.00 (0.00)	0.00 (0.00)
ADD: Mzuzu	0.11*** (0.03)	0.11*** (0.03)	0.10*** (0.03)	0.09*** (0.03)	0.00 (0.00)	0.00 (0.00)
ADD: Kasungu	0.00 (0.00)	0.00 (0.00)	0.00 (0.00)	0.00 (0.00)	0.00 (0.00)	0.00 (0.00)
ADD: Salima	−0.10*** (0.02)	−0.09*** (0.02)	−0.08*** (0.02)	−0.07*** (0.02)	0.00 (0.00)	0.00 (0.00)
ADD: Lilongwe	−0.03* (0.02)	−0.04** (0.02)	−0.04*** (0.02)	−0.06*** (0.02)	0.22*** (0.05)	0.19*** (0.05)
ADD: Machinga	−0.06*** (0.02)	−0.06** (0.02)	−0.06** (0.02)	−0.05** (0.02)	−0.04 (0.06)	−0.00 (0.06)
ADD: Blantyre	−0.04* (0.02)	−0.04* (0.02)	−0.01 (0.02)	−0.01 (0.02)	−0.31*** (0.06)	−0.24*** (0.06)
Urban	0.31*** (0.02)	0.32*** (0.02)				
March 04		−0.02 (0.02)		−0.00 (0.03)		−0.16** (0.07)
April 04		−0.05* (0.03)		−0.06** (0.03)		−0.18** (0.08)
May 04		−0.03 (0.02)		−0.05** (0.03)		−0.02 (0.08)
June 04		−0.00 (0.03)		0.01 (0.03)		−0.10 (0.10)
July 04		0.01 (0.02)		0.05* (0.02)		−0.30*** (0.07)
August 04		−0.13*** (0.02)		−0.12*** (0.02)		−0.33*** (0.07)
September 04		−0.15*** (0.03)		−0.16*** (0.03)		−0.20** (0.09)
October 04		−0.12*** (0.03)		−0.16*** (0.03)		−0.08 (0.08)
November 04		−0.20*** (0.03)		−0.19*** (0.03)		−0.41*** (0.08)

	(1)	(2)	(3)	(4)	(5)	(6)
	Baseline – All		*Rural*		*Urban*	
Dependent variable is log(pc exp)	*PVA*	*PVA with Month D*	*PVA*	*PVA with Month D*	*PVA*	*PVA with Month D*
December 04		−0.30***		−0.27***		−0.56***
		(0.03)		(0.03)		(0.09)
January 05		−0.36***		−0.33***		−0.63***
		(0.02)		(0.02)		(0.08)
February 05		−0.31***		−0.29***		−0.42***
		(0.02)		(0.02)		(0.07)
Constant	10.47***	10.59***	10.52***	10.63***	10.43***	10.79***
	(0.05)	(0.05)	(0.06)	(0.06)	(0.13)	(0.14)
Observations	11032	11032	9601	9601	1431	1431
R-squared	0.47	0.50	0.43	0.47	0.51	0.55

Note: Robust standard errors in parentheses. * significant at 10%; ** significant at 5%; *** significant at 1%. Omitted seasonal variable is March 2005.

7

The stabilizing effect of irrigation on seasonal expenditure

Evidence from rural Andhra Pradesh

Edoardo Masset

Introduction

Irrigation has an obvious positive impact on agricultural production. First, irrigation determines an expansion of the area cropped. This expansion occurs both spatially, by bringing under cultivation previously uncultivated soils, and temporally, by allowing the same area to be cultivated more than once during the same agricultural year. Second, irrigation increases farm yields, because the availability of water allows the adoption of more productive crop varieties and production technologies. Lipton *et al.* (2003) offer an exhaustive review of the evidence on the links between irrigation and income. There is also considerable evidence on the impact of irrigation on income of all sectors of rural society, not just farmers, as well as on the wider economy. By increasing agricultural production, irrigation determines changes in prices, in wages and in the structure of the labour force that result in significant poverty reduction (Datt and Ravallion, 1998; Fan and Hazell, 2001; Palmer-Jones and Sen, 2003; Quizon and Binswanger, 1986). Much less attention has been devoted to the stabilizing effect of irrigation on rural income. By insulating production from weather variability, irrigation stabilizes income both over the years and within each year. This chapter is concerned with the much neglected analysis of the effect of irrigation on seasonal variability of income and consumption.

There are three orders of welfare costs associated with seasonality of income and consumption. First, people have historically responded to the seasonal income cycle by adopting coping strategies, like storing food or borrowing and saving, which have all been found to have economic costs (Fafchamps, 2003). Second, seasonal expenditure fluctuations may interact with health shocks and generate vicious cycles of poverty by progressively impairing households' productive capacity (Behrman and Deolalikar, 1989; Gill, 1991). Finally, unsmoothed consumption fluctuations imply a welfare cost for risk-averse individuals, the size of which depends on the initial household wealth, the size of the consumption fluctuation and the degree of risk aversion (Newbery and Stiglitz, 1981). By smoothing seasonal income, irrigation has a potentially positive welfare impact that needs to be assessed and quantified.

Seasonal poverty analysis has been neglected by researchers, particularly by economists (Gill, 1991). Chambers *et al.* (1981) attribute this neglect to a bias arising from the lack of seasonal data, excessive specialization of researchers, and general ignorance of the main aspects of rural life. Consumption seasonality in developing countries has been the subject of a small number of studies, which include Paxson (1993), Chaudhuri and Paxson (1994), Jacoby and Skoufias (1998), Dercon and Krishnan (2000), and Pitt and Khandker (2002). The main aim of the first three studies is testing the validity of the permanent income model of consumption over the seasonal cycle. Paxson (1993) uses three cross-sectional household surveys collected in Thailand to compare seasonal consumption patterns of household groups with different income patterns. She finds that consumption is independent of seasonal income fluctuations and attributes the observed seasonal expenditure fluctuations to variations in prices and preferences. Chaudhuri and Paxson (1994) use longitudinal household data of rural India and compare consumption patterns of household groups with distinct income patterns. They find that consumption, though varying over the seasons, does not track income over the seasonal cycle, which they attribute to households' ability to build precautionary savings rather than to the use of loans. Jacoby and Skoufias (1998) use panel data of rural Indian households and estimate household responses to anticipated and unanticipated seasonal income fluctuations. They find that, in spite of large income fluctuations, households are able to smooth consumption over the seasonal cycle. They attribute households' smoothing ability to the working of credit markets, and the exchange of gifts between households. Dercon and Krishan (2000) test the dependence of seasonal consumption on income shocks for a panel of Ethiopian households and find that households are unable to insulate consumption from seasonal income shocks. They also observe that households increase consumption in the season in which food prices are low in order to store energy to be released in the season in which returns to labour are high. Pitt and Khandker (2002) analyse expenditure patterns of a short panel of landless Bangladeshi households and find that they are unable to smooth seasonal fluctuations. They conclude that participation in a microcredit programme is strongly motivated by the need to smooth the seasonal pattern of consumption, as individuals tend to self-select into the credit programme during the lean season when consumption reaches its lowest level.

There are some descriptive studies showing the impact of irrigation technology in smoothing crop production and labour demand (see Dhawan, 1988; Gill, 1991). The income and consumption stabilization effect of irrigation, however, has been largely overlooked by the economics literature. An impact evaluation of irrigation projects in India found that areas reached by canal irrigation increased cropping intensity by 40 per cent as a result of the increase in the number of growing seasons (IEG, 2007). Paxson (1993) tests the difference in consumption patterns of single and double cropping farm households in Thailand and finds no significant difference in the seasonal consumption patterns between the two groups, in spite of a large difference in income patterns. The present study is similar to the one by Paxson in that it uses cross-sectional data to compare seasonal expenditure patterns of rural households with and without access to irrigation. The purpose of this chapter, however, is not to test the validity of the permanent income hypothesis over the seasonal income cycle. This chapter empirically investigates the seasonal welfare effects of irrigation for farmers with and without irrigation and for agricultural labourers living in irrigated and non-irrigated areas. Rainfall data are employed to test to what extent consumption decisions are affected by expected seasonal income variability. The empirical analysis suggests that non-irrigated households in rural India are unable to fully smooth consumption fluctuations over the seasonal cycle. Conversely, irrigation has a stabilizing effect on household expenditure. The study also finds that expected seasonal variability of rainfall affects seasonal consumption patterns, suggesting that inter-seasonal precautionary saving is one of the strategies adopted by these households to stabilize their expenditure flows.

A seasonal model of consumption

Descriptive accounts of seasonality in poor rural areas often portray an endless cycle of survival and hunger (see Devereux *et al.*, 2008). Imagine a simplified scenario in which rural households are employed either as small farmers or agricultural labourers in an environment where a dry season follows a wet season. Rainfall patterns allow only one crop per year and poverty follows a seasonal cycle. Food produced and income earned in the wet season are stored for the lean season. Toward the end of the dry season food becomes scarcer and more expensive as stocks are running down. In the pre-harvest period, when rains begin, land must be prepared and crops sown. Households are burdened by exceptional work at a time that coincides with the highest food prices. With the harvest, food becomes available again and cheaper, labour demand drops and a new cycle begins.

In India, where the cycle of production and labour demand is dictated by seasonal rainfall variability, rural life is not too distant from this hypothetical scenario. In most years, 50 per cent of total precipitation falls in just 15 days, and 90 per cent of river flows run in just four months (World Bank, 2005). In Andhra Pradesh, which is the Indian state selected for the empirical analysis, there are two rainy seasons (Chatterji, 1992). The first and most important occurs from June to October, with winds blowing inland from the sea (southwest monsoon), while the second occurs from November to April, with winds blowing from inland towards the sea (northeast monsoon). In the agricultural calendar these are known as the *Kharif* and the *Rabi* seasons. The southwest monsoon is the most important source of rainfall for Andhra Pradesh, bringing more than 75 per cent of total annual rainfall, while rains of the northeast monsoon are not only less abundant, but also more erratic. The amount of rainfall in each season determines the area sown by farmers and the agricultural yields. Therefore, *Kharif* is the most important agricultural season in all areas of Andhra Pradesh. Rice is the main crop produced in the state. It is planted in the period between May and June and harvested between November and December. Depending on rains, and on the availability of irrigation, a second crop is possible in *Rabi*, with sowing in the months of December and January, and harvesting between April and May. Harvesting of main cash crops like groundnut, castor, cotton, sugar cane and chilli takes place in the months between November and March. Occasionally other crops like *jowar* (sorghum), vegetables, and summer pulses are produced between March and June.

In order to build a theoretical model of seasonal consumption, suppose the agricultural calendar is subdivided into three seasons; *Kharif*, in which most annual income materializes with relative stability; *Rabi*, in which some income is produced with high variability; and the lean season, in which no income is produced. The farmer's problem is how best to distribute income earned in *Kharif* and *Rabi* among the three seasons. The problem can be solved using a method of backward induction known as dynamic programming (Masset, 2009). The solution achieved by dynamic programming states that in the lean season nothing is saved for the following season and nothing is earned, and the consumer spends all assets and income previously saved. In the *Rabi* season income is known and is distributed between *Rabi* and the following lean season. In the *Kharif* season, the farmer decides the expenditure level based on his income in *Kharif* and on the expectation of income in the *Rabi* season. An increase in the uncertainty regarding *Rabi* income reduces its current valuation in terms of utility, thus bringing about a reduction in consumption in *Kharif*. A higher variability of expected income induces households to save more for precautionary reasons.

To summarize, the model predicts that (a) seasonal consumption is a function of current income both in *Kharif* and *Rabi*; (b) there is precautionary saving in *Kharif* and savings are higher the higher is *Rabi* income variability; (c) there can be borrowing only in *Kharif*, provided a minimum level of income is expected in *Rabi*. Note that the model finds a precautionary motive for saving in *Kharif* without imposing borrowing constraints. Liquidity constraints are not strictly necessary if consumers self-impose restrictions to borrowing out of worst case scenario incomes. This argument is based again on backward induction and proceeds in the following way (Carroll, 2001). In the third season consumers spend everything. As income in the third season is zero, consumers need to make positive savings in the second season in order to be able to spend in the third season. In order to consume less than income and assets in the second season, farmers need to make sure that they reach the second season with positive assets, because if income is zero in the second season, farmers will not be able to consume anything. So if zero is a possible outcome in *Rabi*, households never borrow. If, on the other hand, income is always positive in the *Rabi* season, however low, farmers can borrow in *Kharif*, but will not borrow more than what they will be able to repay in the case of the worst income outcome in *Rabi*. In these circumstances farmers will borrow in *Kharif*, but never beyond an amount that is limited by their ability to repay in the following seasons. Since income is higher in *Kharif*, it is unlikely that households will borrow in this season unless the *Kharif* income is catastrophically low.

What is the role played by irrigation in this model? First, irrigation allows a second cropping season in *Rabi*, thus stabilizing the relative income difference between *Kharif* and *Rabi*. Second, irrigation can reduce the income variability of *Rabi*, thus decreasing the amount of *Kharif* income that farmers need to save for precautionary reasons. Third, if *Kharif* income is unexpectedly low, irrigated farmers may borrow to fund immediate consumption needs, a possibility that is precluded to non-irrigated farmers because, differently from irrigated ones, they may face zero income realizations in *Rabi*.

By comparing seasonal consumption patterns of irrigated and non-irrigated farms, we would expect these patterns for irrigated farmers to be (a) more stable and (b) less dependent on expected income variability. These effects of irrigation on income are not limited to farmers. Irrigated farms demand more labour because they cultivate larger areas and crops that require more labour. Rice, in particular, is a very labour-intensive crop at the time of transplanting and harvesting. Because agricultural production is more stable in irrigated farms, labour demand and agricultural labour wages over the seasons are also more stable. Irrigation therefore also has a positive impact on employment and wages of agricultural labourers.

Data and methodology

In order to test the hypotheses outlined in the previous section, this chapter uses four of the last cross-sectional rounds of household expenditure data collected by the National Sample Survey Organization (NSSO) of India in Andhra Pradesh: 1987–88 (6,016 households from 602 villages); 1993–94 (4,908 households from 492 villages); 1999–2000 (5,181 households from 432 villages); 2004–05 (5,555 households from 556 villages).

The NSSO data are particularly suitable to the analysis of seasonal expenditure for two reasons. First, the survey is conducted over a 12-month agricultural year, starting on 1 of July and ending on 30 of June of the following year. The data are stratified by three-month sub-rounds, each composed of an equal amount of households and clusters. Each seasonal sub-round is statistically representative of the population at the state level and can be analysed separately from the others. Second, the NSSO questionnaire uses a 30-day recall period for all expenditure items, rather than a 12-month recall, and hence household expenditure can be easily assigned to a particular season.

In the empirical analysis, samples of rural households are used to form sub-samples of farmer and agricultural labour households with and without access to irrigation. Any subdivision by social classes is an oversimplification of rural society. In reality, many farmers do some paid work for other farms, while many labourers cultivate small plots of land. Samples of farm and agricultural labour households were identified using the National Classification of Occupation codes (NCO) used by the NSSO. A distinction was then operated between irrigated and non-irrigated farm households, exploiting a survey question that quantifies irrigated and non-irrigated land cultivated by each household. A farm was considered as irrigated if any share of any size of cultivated land is irrigated at the time of the survey interview. Based on this definition, farmers account for about 25 per cent of the rural population, and between 65 per cent and 75 per cent of the farms are irrigated.

Agricultural labourers are considered as living in irrigated villages if 100 per cent of cultivated land reported in the survey is irrigated in the village where they live. Based on this definition, agricultural labourers account for about 30 per cent of total rural population, 20 per cent of whom live in irrigated villages.

Since the objective of this chapter is the estimation of seasonal consumption, household expenditure figures must not be affected by demographic factors, by seasonal variations that are unrelated to income, or price effects, and must be adjusted accordingly. The demographic adjustment is easily performed by dividing household expenditure by the number of adult equivalents rather than by household size (Deaton, 1997).

Expenditure items whose fluctuations are not related to income were subtracted from seasonal expenditure. There are two main sources of non-income-related seasonal fluctuations in the quantities of goods demanded: climate and custom (ILO, 2004). Seasonal changes in climate affect, for example, the demand for clothing and healthcare, while custom determines the times at which certain payments are made, such as for school fees, ceremonies and holidays. In order to avoid using expenditure data that reflect seasonal consumption patterns related to climate and custom, expenses on education, health, ceremonies and durables were excluded from the computation of total household expenditure.

Seasonal price variations have to be removed from the expenditure data, which can be done by dividing households' expenditure by a price index. Household-specific price indices were calculated from the survey data using the methodology described in Deaton and Zaidi (2002). There are two main advantages in using household-specific price indices. The first is that they adjust expenditure for seasonal and spatial price variation simultaneously. The second is that household-specific indices are tailored to each household, thus reflecting individual households' income and preferences, and do not overstate or understate changes in the cost of living in the way that other price indices do.

In the empirical analysis we compare expenditure patterns of farmers and agricultural labourers with and without access to irrigation. This comparative analysis suffers from two endogeneity problems. First, there is endogeneity in household access to irrigation. Second, there is endogeneity in the occupational choice of farming or working as wage labour against other occupational choices. The first form of endogeneity overstates the impact of irrigation on consumption, while the second tends to understate the impact of irrigation. In order to overcome these endogeneity problems, the empirical analysis employs a variation of the Roy model (Cameron and Trivedi, 2005).[1]

Whether a farm is irrigated or not is partly endogenous. Irrigation might be considered exogenous if it were provided to farms by area only, as in the case of canal irrigation. Even in this case, however, it could be regarded as endogenous to the extent that some farmers, with specific characteristics, might choose to buy or might inherit land in irrigated areas. Moreover, some farmers, for example the most influential and powerful, might have access to irrigation in irrigated areas while others in the same areas do not. Even allocation of irrigation by area could be endogenous, if irrigation investments are made in areas where incomes are already more stable than elsewhere. This might be the case if canal irrigation is provided to areas that are already better off in terms of geographic characteristics and infrastructure (Palmer-Jones and Sen, 2003). More serious endogeneity problems arise if farmers irrigate their farms using water pumps, because farmers investing in water pumps are likely to be different from other poorer farmers with respect to many other characteristics. For example, farmers with water pumps might be less liquidity-constrained. In all these cases, the endogeneity of irrigation implies an overestimation of the impact of irrigation on consumption stability, as the stabilizing role of other factors is erroneously attributed to irrigation.

The occupational choice of farming is also potentially endogenous. Seasonal consumption is modelled as a function of seasonal income and of its expected variance. The variance of future income, however, is not fully independent of water availability. This is true in both dry and wet areas. In dry areas households make production choices to reduce income instability. They may have multiple income sources, and grow a more diversified range of crops in order to reduce total output variability. Conversely, households in wet areas may specialize in farming and in the production of a limited number of crops. Indeed, earlier studies on the impact of the green revolution pointed to a potential increase in income instability rather than a decrease (Hazell, 1984). In this case the impact of irrigation on income and consumption stability is underestimated, because households in irrigated areas may specialize in more risky enterprises, while dry farms diversify their mix of activities and crops in order to reduce the variance of future income.

Empirical results

There are substantial consumption differences between irrigated and non-irrigated farms, and between labourers of irrigated and non-irrigated villages, in terms of both the levels and seasonal patterns. Figure 7.1 shows per capita equivalent expenditure of farmers and agricultural labourers by season. Expenditure is reported on a logarithmic scale, so that the differences between groups can be read in percentage terms. Expenditure of households with access to irrigation is higher in all seasons, and the difference is particularly large between irrigated and non-irrigated farmers. For both farmers and agricultural labourers, expenditure is higher in the second half of the agricultural year (from January to June). Expenditure of farmers seems to follow agricultural output, with consumption picking up in the second season and reaching its maximum in the third season (corresponding to *Kharif* and *Rabi* harvesting respectively). The seasonal pattern of agricultural labour households is less clear. Overall, the seasonal expenditure pattern of irrigated farms and labourers living in irrigated villages appears smoother. These expenditure patterns will now be tested separately for farmers and agricultural labourers within causal regression models.

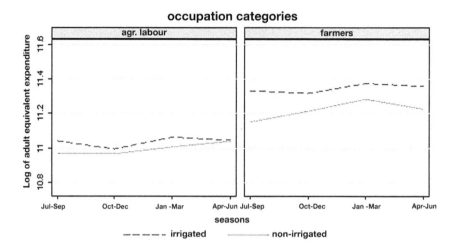

FIGURE 7.1 Seasonal consumption of agricultural labourers and farmers with and without irrigation

Farmers

In order to test the difference in expenditure patterns between irrigated and non-irrigated farms, we regress expenditure on seasonal dummy variables and on a set of determinants of expenditure as control variables. The dependent variable in the regressions is the logarithm of per capita expenditure. Demographic effects are accounted for by including the logarithm of household size and the ratios of five age groups by gender. Education of the head of household and spouse are included. Other control variables include the logarithm of the size of land cultivated during the agricultural year in acres, the social group to which the household belongs, dummy variables for each of the 23 administrative districts into which the state is subdivided and dummy variables for the four survey rounds. The different seasons of the agricultural year are included in the form of dummy variables. Each regression is adjusted by a term that adjusts the selection bias produced by the endogeneity of sub-sampling farmers within the rural sample of households, and further sub-sampling irrigated farms within the sub-sample of farmers.

Table 7.1 contains the estimated coefficients, including the seasonal coefficients that test the significance of the patterns observed in Figure 7.1. The R-squares of the regressions are large (more than 70 per cent of the total variance is explained), and most variables are highly significant. None of the seasonal dummies is significant in the regression of the irrigated farms, while two largely significant values were found in the regression of the non-irrigated farms. A seasonal pattern of consumption seems to emerge among households operating non-irrigated farms. Consumption is higher in the second and third seasons of the agricultural year. This conforms to intuitive expectations, as these are the seasons in which most of the agricultural output is realized through the *Kharif* and *Rabi* harvesting. The size of the consumption fluctuations however is not very large; its maximum fluctuation reaches the value of 11 per cent between the first and the third seasons.

According to our theoretical model the difference in seasonal consumption between irrigated and non-irrigated farms depends on both current and expected income. Irrigation reduces the variability of expected income caused by rainfall variability and irrigated farmers consume more both because they have higher income

TABLE 7.1 Seasonal consumption effects of irrigation: Farmers and agricultural labourers

	Farmers		Agricultural labourers	
	Irrigated	Non-irrigated	Irrigated villages	Non-irrigated villages
Scheduled caste	−0.145***	−0.082*	...	...
	(0.026)	(0.045)		
Scheduled tribe	−0.138***	−0.205***	...	...
	(0.041)	(0.042)		
Age of head of household	0.003***	0.004***	−0.002***	−0.003***
	(0.001)	(0.001)	(0.001)	(0.001)
Female children from 0 to 5	−0.078	−0.056	−0.020	−0.015
	(0.115)	(0.132)	(0.110)	(0.055)
Male children from 5 to 10	0.120	0.155	0.293	0.192***
	(0.086)	(0.133)	(0.103)	(0.050)
Female children from 5 to 10	0.191**	0.106	0.297*	0.191***
	(0.086)	(0.132)	(0.096)	(0.051)
Male children from 10 to 15	0.314***	0.434***	0.727	0.524***
	(0.094)	(0.140)	(0.113)	(0.073)
Female children from 10 to 15	0.298***	0.394**	0.401	0.399***
	(0.091)	(0.157)	(0.120)	(0.064)
Adult male	0.498***	0.394**	0.680*	0.629***
	(0.091)	(0.129)	(0.101)	(0.054)
Adult female	0.409***	0.313**	0.446*	0.400***
	(0.098)	(0.148)	(0.105)	(0.060)
Elderly male	0.302***	0.081	0.591	0.457***
	(0.108)	(0.186)	(0.10)	(0.073)
Elderly female	0.155	0.241	0.329	0.177**
	(0.104)	(0.153)	(0.115)	(0.070)
Logarithm of household size	−0.338***	−0.329***	−0.264**	−0.234***
	(0.021)	(0.033)	(0.025)	(0.017)
Education of head of household	0.078***	0.050***	−0.008	0.000
	(0.009)	(0.016)	(0.016)	(0.010)
Education of spouse of head of household	0.030**	0.087***	−0.010	0.009
	(0.013)	(0.028)	(0.020)	(0.014)

	Farmers		Agricultural labourers	
	Irrigated	Non-irrigated	Irrigated villages	Non-irrigated villages
Logarithm of cultivated land	0.095***	0.030*	0.183***	0.011
	(0.011)	(0.018)	(0.030)	(0.011)
2nd season (Oct–Dec)	–0.020	0.060**	–0.022	–0.006
	(0.021)	(0.034)	(0.023)	(0.012)
3rd season (Jan–Mar)	0.024	0.114***	0.008	0.051***
	(0.022)	(0.037)	(0.024)	(0.013)
4th season (Apr–Jun)	0.020	0.032	–0.023	0.046***
	(0.021)	(0.037)	(0.024)	(0.012)
Urban area	0.168***	0.253*	...	...
	(0.043)	(0.139)		
50th round (1993–94)	0.644***	0.837***	–0.060**	0.056***
	(0.024)	(0.045)	(0.028)	(0.013)
55th round (1999–2000)	1.301***	1.639***	0.097***	0.124***
	(0.036)	(0.063)	(0.027)	(0.012)
61st round (2004–05)	1.235***	1.380***	0.079***	0.103***
	(0.022)	(0.038)	(0.026)	(0.014)
Selection term	–0.501***	0.510***	0.602***	0.614***
	(0.092)	(0.077)	(0.127)	(0.070)
23 district dummies (output omitted)	...	...	...	...
Constant	9.827***	8.474***	10.369***	10.283***
	(0.107)	(0.256)	(0.119)	(0.062)
Observations	4572	1654	1592	5750
R-square	0.73	0.72	0.35	0.28

Note: Standard errors in parentheses. Triple asterisk (***), double asterisk (**), and single asterisk (*) indicate statistical significance at the 1%, 5%, and 10% level, respectively.

and because they save less for precautionary reasons. This hypothesis is tested using rainfall as a predictor of expected income. Income realizations and expectations are modelled using the deviations of *Kharif* rainfall from their historical average, the square of these deviations, and the historical variability of *Rabi* rains. The squares of rainfall deviations are included in the regressions for two reasons. First, the positive impact of rainfall on consumption may be non-linear. Second, excessive rains may damage crops. According to data provided by the Ministry of Agriculture of Andhra Pradesh, heavy rains affected large numbers of households and districts in all years between 1987 and 2000 with the exception of drought years. The historical variability of *Rabi* rains provides an indicator of the variability of future income, and the larger this variability, the lower is consumption in the current season because farmers save for precautionary reasons. In other words, farmers operating in districts where rainfall variability is higher, are forced to set aside some of their current income to prevent the effects of shortfalls in future consumption.

The results are presented in Table 7.2, omitting the output results of the variables already included in the model of Table 7.1. The model estimated is restricted to observations collected in the *Kharif* cropping season and expands the model of Table 7.1 by including rainfall variables. Rainfall deviations do not show an impact on current consumption in the period July–September for either farm category, with the exception of a negative coefficient for the squares of rainfall deviations presumably reflecting the expected negative impact of heavy rains on output. The variability of *Rabi* rains has a slightly significant negative effect on expenditure of non-irrigated farms, but no effect on expenditure of irrigated ones.

Agricultural labourers

Table 7.2 also presents the results of the regression model run for the sample of agricultural labourers. Most variables in the regression are highly significant and the R-squares are large. None of the seasonal dummies is significant for labourers working in irrigated villages, while two highly significant values are found for those living in non-irrigated villages. For these households, consumption is higher in the third and fourth season of the agricultural year. The size of the consumption fluctuation, however, is quite small. Consumption in the second half of the year appears to be 5 per cent higher than in the first half.

The smoother consumption pattern of agricultural labour in irrigated areas is a consequence of the effect of irrigation on labour demand and wages. Irrigation increases labour demand for a number of reasons. First, it expands the net area cropped, as more land is brought under cultivation, thus increasing labour requirements. Second, irrigation may determine a shift from less labour-intensive to more

TABLE 7.2 Rainfall effects on seasonal consumption: July to September

	Farmers		Agricultural labourers	
	Irrigated	*Non-irrigated*	*Irrigated villages*	*Non-irrigated villages*
Rainfall deviation	−0.169	−0.677	0.552	0.648***
	(0.231)	(0.539)	(0.568)	(0.207)
Rainfall deviation squared	−0.268	−1.941*	0.841	1.189**
	(0.489)	(1.020)	(1.078)	(0.439)
Rabi rainfall variability	0.001	−0.001*	−0.001	0.001
	(0.001)	(0.000)	(0.001)	(0.001)
Selection term	−0.715***	0.843***	0.515*	0.631***
	(0.174)	(0.221)	(0.267)	(0.117)
Observations	1163	449	317	1497
R-square	0.51	0.44	0.40	0.35

Note: Standard errors in parentheses. Triple asterisk (***), double asterisk (**), and single asterisk (*) indicate statistical significance at the 1%, 5%, and 10% levels, respectively.

labour-intensive crops. This is certainly the case in Andhra Pradesh, where irrigation promotes the cultivation of rice, which is labour-intensive. Third, as yields increase, labour requirements per acre of land increase, in particular for transplanting and harvesting. Irrigation has a stabilizing effect on labour demand for two main reasons. First, the introduction of double and triple cropping during the same agricultural year generates a more stable demand in the course of the year. Second, multiple cropping may produce a shift in the demand of labour from casual to permanent labour.

In keeping with the analysis performed for farmers, rainfall variables were introduced in the model and a sub-sample of observations collected during the first trimester of the year, corresponding to *Kharif* planting, was selected (see Table 7.2). Rainfall deviations take on a different meaning in the model for agricultural labourers compared to the farmers' model. Rainfall deviations not only represent income expectations, but also current income, as labour demand varies with the amount of rainfall in the planting season. The coefficient of variation of *Rabi* rainfall represents, as it did for farmers, an approximation of the variability of future income, as districts where rainfall variability is higher should display a higher variability in demand for labour in the harvesting season.

Rainfall deviations have a highly significant effect on consumption of labourers of non-irrigated villages, but no effects on labourers of irrigated villages. The square of the rainfall deviation is also positive and very large in non-irrigated villages. No effect is found for *Rabi* rainfall variability on consumption by labourers in the first trimester in either irrigated or non-irrigated villages. These results show that expenditure of labourers in non-irrigated villages is more responsive to current rainfall than is consumption of labourers in irrigated villages. Conversely, seasonal consumption of labourers of irrigated villages is not immediately affected by current and expected income. The absence of an effect of *Rabi* income variability on expenditure in the first trimester suggests that the precautionary motive for saving among both samples is not strong.

Conclusions

This chapter assessed the stabilizing effect of irrigation on expenditure of rural households in Andhra Pradesh. The main findings of the empirical analysis are as follows. First, consumption by households with access to irrigation is more stable over the seasonal cycle. Expenditure of farmers' households without irrigation fluctuates up to 10 per cent in the harvest season compared to the lean season. Expenditure of agricultural labourers living in non-irrigated areas fluctuates up to 5 per cent in the harvest season compared to the lean season. Second, consumption by households with access to irrigation is less affected by expected income variability, approximated by historical rainfall variability. The effect is statistically significant for farmer households but not for agricultural labour households. These results suggest that irrigation generates positive welfare effects by reducing the cost of seasonality. The size of these welfare effects, however, is not easy to quantify because of the difficulty of estimating the three costs of seasonality mentioned in the introduction: the welfare cost, the coping cost, and the cost of seasonal crises.

Irrigation presumably reduces the number of severe seasonal crises that generate poverty traps, as it is likely to reduce the number of distress sales and the impact on very poor households of shocks produced by severe seasonal fluctuations. However, to the extent that seasonal shocks result in family dissolution, death or migration, these effects will not be noticed by standard household surveys. The surveys conducted by the NSSO interview households found in rural areas, thus missing out those households that migrated or disappeared in consequence of seasonal shocks. The fluctuations in income and consumption observed by household surveys are therefore limited to those fluctuations that do not produce seasonal crises and that are smaller in size.

The estimation of the welfare cost produced by income and consumption fluctuations requires a number of assumptions on the structure of consumers' preferences and their attitudes toward risk. The rate of time preference ('impatience') and the degree of risk aversion need to be estimated. Though some estimates for rural India are available (Binswanger, 1981; Pender, 1996), the number of studies performed is too small and the methodologies employed are too questionable to provide reliable estimates of the parameters of interest (Cardenas and Carpenter, 2008). Given the observed size of fluctuations, however, this cost cannot be very large.

The estimation of the cost of coping strategies is constrained by problems of data availability and of empirical identification. The expenditure data of the NSSO, as those of most household surveys, do not contain information on household savings. The elicitation of households' expectations of future income was obtained using rainfall data, but rainfall data are an imprecise measure of the uncertainty faced by households. Finally, the empirical estimation of the size of precautionary savings is a lively area of research and there is no consensus on the way it should be performed (Carroll and Kimball, 2007).

While the present study cannot directly quantify the costs of seasonality and the benefits of irrigation, it does provide qualitative evidence of the facts that (a) rural households without access to irrigation are not fully able to insure against seasonal fluctuations, and (b) farm households hold savings for precautionary reasons, thus implicitly incurring financial losses. Both effects were found to be not very large. There are two possible explanations for the relatively small effect of the seasonal cycle on household expenditure. The first is economic and market development, while the second is the presence of other smoothing mechanisms. Over the last 25 years Andhra Pradesh has experienced a considerable increase in rural household incomes. This progress, however, has not resulted in a reduction in the share of income produced in agriculture, which is the income component more sensitive to seasonal fluctuations (DES, 2005). Nor is there evidence of a significant development of financial markets that justifies an increase in households' ability to save and borrow (Pradhan et al., 2003). It is more likely that the seasonal smoothing of expenditure fluctuations is the result of a multiplicity of welfare interventions by the state government. Andhra Pradesh runs a policy of price support that stabilizes incomes over the seasonal cycle by smoothing price fluctuations (Jairath, 2000). The state also runs an expensive programme of public distribution of main food items. In spite of serious distribution inefficiencies, this system provides most households with staple food at a fixed price over the year (Dutta and Ramaswami, 2001; Ravi and Indrakant, 2003). Devereux *et al.* (2008), who found qualitative evidence of large fluctuations of income over the year but found no evidence of seasonal hunger among children in Andhra Pradesh, also conclude that the impact of the seasonal cycle is likely to be smoothed by the large, though inefficient, safety net system operated by the state.

Note

1   The version of the Roy model adopted here is the one Maddala (1983) defines as 'the switching regression model with endogenous switching'. See Masset (2009) for a detailed discussion of the econometric methods employed.

8

Seasonal dimensions of household wellbeing and labour migration in rural southern China

Shijun Ding, Haitao Wu and Yuping Chen

Introduction

Seasonal patterns of farm households' economic activities and wellbeing have been studied since the 1970s, with most research focusing on tropical agriculture in countries from Africa and South Asia (Chambers *et al.*, 1981; Devereux, 2008, 2009). It has been generally recognized over the last four decades that seasonal variations in household agricultural activities and other types of economic activities explain, to a large extent, rural poverty in low-income countries in general (Harris and Todaro, 1970; Paxson, 1993; Stark and Fan, 1993; De Haan, 1999; Stark, 2007) and in tropical countries in particular, and that there are several negative factors that make the lives of poor households worse during the pre-harvest months every year. Furthermore, the backgrounds or contexts of agricultural development in most developing countries have been changing rapidly over recent decades, and these changes need to be taken into account when designing policy interventions to reduce the negative effects of seasonality in developing countries' agricultural and rural development.

Seasonal variation in agricultural and rural economy is a fundamental phenomenon characterizing rural development in China (Zhao, 1999). The country is located in a wide range of geographic locations, with its southern part in tropical and subtropical regions and the northern part in a temperate region. While patterns of seasonal variation of agricultural and rural economic activities in southern regions may follow what had been studied in African and south Asian countries, patterns of seasonal variation may have their own features in northern regions.

The seasonality of households' production and wellbeing in rural China can be investigated in terms of patterns of income generation from a variety of sources: sales of agricultural products, wages, family-based non-farm enterprises, remittances and transfer payments. While households' income from field crops will be markedly seasonal, production and sale of cash crops may balance the seasonality of agriculture-related activities. In the same way, casual non-farm work may balance the seasonality of a household's productive activities. Small farm households in China have developed different combinations of livestock/grain production and farm/non-farm activities in reducing the negative effects of seasonality. However, seasonal dimensions in agricultural and rural development in China have been less empirically investigated, and the strategies employed by small farm households to cope with seasonal variations are currently poorly understood.

Socioeconomic consequences of seasonal patterns of household income, expenditure and labour mobility need to be understood in order to design appropriate interventions to smooth seasonality and improve livelihoods. For example, policies encouraging seasonal migration for casual work during the slack season will certainly help households improve their economic wellbeing; timely arrangements for production loans during the planting season will help households in purchasing inputs (seeds, fertilizers, etc.) for crop production. This paper aims to describe patterns of seasonal variation in household income and expenditure, to document patterns of seasonal migration from rural areas to urban cities in search of casual labour work, and to investigate the effects of seasonal migration on the changing patterns of households' income and expenditure.

Data for this paper come from the Rural Household Survey (RHS) of the State Bureau of Statistics (SBS) and a household interview conducted by the authors. The RHS is administered directly by SBS through its provincial and county survey network, and this ensures that the data collected are free from local interference. Rather than employing a single-interview approach, each selected household maintains a daily diary over the entire year. An assistant interviewer is supposed to visit each household once every two weeks to check the diary and assist the household in completing it and then transfer the information to the county level. A dataset covering 3,300 households in 33 randomly selected counties (from a total of 75 counties) during 2004 to 2007 in Hubei province, containing variables on household demographics, monthly migration, monthly income and expenditure and others, is used for this paper. A case study from Guangxi province on seasonal variations of household cash income and expenditure is also provided. County-representative rainfall data from ten selected counties come from the Meteorological Bureau in Hubei, containing monthly rainfall data from 1982 to 2001.

The paper is organized into the following sections. Firstly we describe the seasonal variations of household income and expenditure; this will be done by investigating household monthly income and expenditure variations over the year. In the following section we document the patterns of monthly migration, to look at the correlation of migration and monthly agricultural activities; this is done by mapping seasonal migration between peak and slack seasons. We then investigate the effects of monthly migration on the changing patterns of household income and expenditure; this is done by comparing monthly income and expenditure variations between households with and without migrant labour, and modelling how household income and monthly expenditure are affected by seasonal migration. Moreover, a unique farm household case, which we interviewed during a previous study, is analysed in the next section to reinforce the conclusions and get in-depth understanding of the seasonal variation of household wellbeing in rural China. Finally, findings are presented and implications for designing interventions to protect farm households' livelihoods are drawn.

Seasonal variations of household income and expenditure

Rainfall and its seasonal patterns

In subtropical regions, where southern China is located, seasonality seems more intuitive since summer and winter differ distinctly from each other, with most crops harvested in late autumn and a slack season in winter and early spring. To investigate seasonal patterns in agriculture, an attempt is made to define dry and wet seasons in the study province in an absolute sense based on monthly rainfall.[1] The average rainfall in each month from ten randomly selected counties (of 75 counties) in Hubei for the period 1982 to 2001 is shown in Figure 8.1. Rainfall shows a trend increasing from January and reaching its peak in July, and then a trend decreasing until December. An arbitrary approach is used to classify the whole year into dry and wet seasons, in which 100mm of rainfall per month is taken as a threshold. The wet season can be seen as being from April to September while the remaining months are seen as the dry season.

A wide range of crops are grown in the area, with the main crops being rice, maize and cotton in summer and wheat in winter. Rainfall is an important determinant of crop production. Figure 8.1 also depicts a generalized version of cropping calendars in the area. Rice, maize and cotton are generally planted in April and harvested in September and October. Wheat is sown in October and harvested in the following May. It can be concluded that the main agricultural activities happen in the wet season (peak season), and the slack season coincides with the dry season.

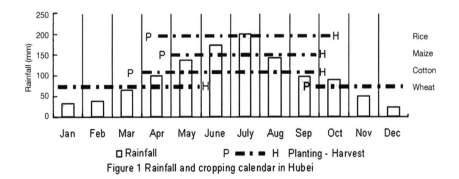

Figure 1 Rainfall and cropping calendar in Hubei

Source: *pers. comm.*, Hubei Meteorological Bureau, 2007

FIGURE 8.1 Rainfall and cropping calendar in Hubei

Seasonal variations of household income and expenditure

Income and expenditure are used to denote household wellbeing in this paper. Household income consists of wage income, family-based enterprise income and other sources, while household expenditure consists of family-based enterprise spending and consumption expenditure.

The seasonal variations of monthly household income, expenditure and balance in 2006 and 2007 show a similar trend, as can be seen in Figure 8.2.[2] Monthly income is lower than monthly expenditure for most of the year and the only exception occurs in December. This can be explained by the fact that agricultural and related productive expenses mainly occurred during spring, summer and autumn when households invested in most of the productive inputs, and that household income is mainly from selling summer crops at the end of the year and migrants' wage income which is mostly received at the end of the year. On the other hand, household income and expenditure in the peak season are generally lower than in the slack season.

To investigate the variations of monthly income and expenditure, income sources and expenditure items are separated out in Figures 8.3 and 8.4, respectively. The varied shares of different income sources and expenditure items show seasonal patterns of variation over the year:

1   Wages are the main income source from January to September, while family-based agricultural enterprise becomes the main income source from September as households would sell their agricultural products in late autumn;
2   The income share of family-based enterprise in the peak season is generally lower than that in the slack season;
3   Consumption is one of the main expenditure items over the year, and is higher in December when the traditional Chinese New Year comes around, this is especially true for food consumption;
4   The expenditure share of family-based enterprise is much higher in the peak season, indicating the higher agricultural inputs use.

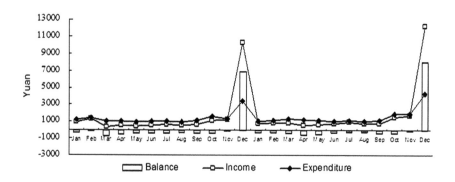

Source: *pers. comm.,* Hubei Statistics Bureau, 2007

FIGURE 8.2 Seasonal variation of income, expenditure and balance, 2006–2007

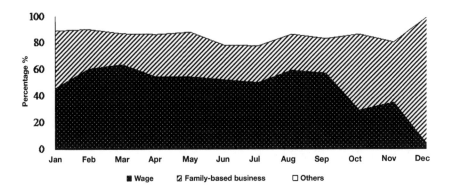

Source: *pers.comm.,* Hubei Statistics Bureau, 2007

FIGURE 8.3 Seasonal variation of income shares from different sources

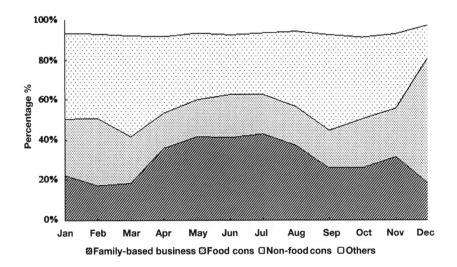

Source: *pers.comm.,* Hubei Statistics Bureau, 2007

FIGURE 8.4 Seasonal variation of expenditure shares for different items

Quantifying seasonal variations of household income and expenditure

To quantify seasonal variations of household income and consumption, a seasonality index (Walsh, 1980) is used in this paper, and it can be expressed as follows:

$$SI = \frac{\sum\limits_{n=1}^{n=12} | x_n - \dfrac{\overline{R}}{12} |}{\overline{R}}$$

where SI denotes seasonality index, x_n means income/consumption of month n, and $\overline{R}$ is the mean annual income/consumption. The seasonality index takes into consideration all months of the year.

Seasonality indices of household income and expenditure from 2004 to 2007 are calculated and listed in Table 8.1. First, overall seasonality indices of monthly total income and total expenditure (except for 2006) show a decreasing trend over the four years, implying that monthly income and expenditure are generally becoming more stable. Second, seasonal variations in total income are generally higher than in total expenditure, and this is because expenditure usually reflects households' long-term wellbeing, and households are more able to smooth their expenditure than income, as evidenced elsewhere (for example, Morduch, 1995). Third, looking at different categories of income and expenditure, the table shows different patterns. Seasonal variations for wage income, in the decreasing trends, are relatively higher, ranging from 1.346 to 1.281, while seasonal variations for consumption expenditure in the decreasing trends, are relatively lower, ranging from 0.928 to 0.816. Fourthly, seasonal variations of income from family-based enterprise are greater than those from wage income, and seasonal variations of expenditure on family-based enterprise are greater than on family consumption. This may be because agriculture as the main kind of family-based enterprise in rural China requires inputs in the peak season (a few months in March, April and May, for example) but income from farming comes mainly after harvest later in the slack season (for example, in October, November and December). Seasonal variations of income from, and expenditure on, family-based enterprise over the four years show increasing trends, and this may need further explanation.

TABLE 8.1 Seasonality index for income and expenditure, 2004–2007

Year	Income			Expenditure		
	Total	Wage	Family-based enterprise	Total	Family-based enterprise	Consumption
2007	1.227	1.281	1.682	0.702	0.975	0.816
2006	1.248	1.285	1.667	0.725	0.945	0.827
2005	1.294	1.305	1.658	0.722	0.926	0.842
2004	1.298	1.346	1.650	0.774	0.907	0.928

Source: *pers. comm.*, Hubei Statistics Bureau, 2007

Effects of migration on changing patterns of household income and expenditure

Seasonal patterns of migration and households' monthly income distribution

Migration from rural areas to urban cities to earn a living has become an important phenomenon in China over the last three decades, with a considerable amount of migration being seasonal. The monthly distributions of the percentage of households with members migrating during 2004 to 2007 are shown in Figure 8.5. There are increasing numbers of households with members migrating over the study time period (from 75 per cent of households in 2004 to 90 per cent in 2007). Patterns of migration show seasonal variation, with fewer going out in the peak season and more in the slack season. Most migration occurs in February when the traditional spring festival is just over.

To further investigate the effects of seasonal migration on household income and expenditure, monthly incomes of different types of household are compared in Figure 8.6: households without migration, with 1–3 months of migration, with 3–6 months of migration and with 6+ months of migration. The log value of income is adopted for intuitive expression. Households with longer migration times generally have higher incomes. When considering separate months, it follows from what we found earlier that household income is lower in the peak season and higher in the slack season, with December having the highest monthly income. This monthly pattern of income generation does not seem to fit intuitively with the migration story above. This can be explained as follows. Monthly wage income as remittances from migrants is sometimes paid by employers at the end of the year (this is especially true for construction migrant workers) and taken back home by migrants themselves when they are back home taking the Chinese New Year (the spring festival) holiday in November and December. Farm households mostly sell

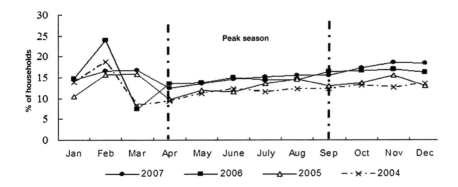

Source: *pers. comm.*, Hubei Statistics Bureau, 2007

FIGURE 8.5 Percentage distribution of number of households with migration by month

their agricultural products at the end of the year, and traditionally it is common that households sell their livestock (mostly pigs) shortly before the Chinese New Year so that they have cash income for the coming festival celebration. As a result, household income can dramatically increase in December.

Determinants of seasonal variations of income and expenditure: an ordinary least squares (OLS) analysis

The ordinary least square regression on determinants of – more specifically, effects of migration on – seasonal variations of household income and consumption expenditure is applied in this section. Considering other factors affecting variations of income and expenditure, variables such as farm size, working time per labourer and percentage of household labourers who have received technical training are included in the analysis. The determinant equation can be expressed as follows:

$$Y = a_0 + a_1 farmsize + a_2 worktime + a_3 training + a_4 migration.dummy + u$$

where Y represents the log value of household income (consumption expenditure) or seasonality index; *farmsize*, *worktime* and *training* represent farm size (hectares of cultivated land), working time per labourer (number of months) and percentage of household labourers receiving technical training, respectively, while *migration. dummy* represents numbers of migration labour dummy variables (0 if no migrant, 1 if 1 migrant, 2 if more than 1 migrant); a_0 is a constant item, a_1 to a_4 are the coefficients of corresponding independent variables, and u is the disturbance term. Using data for 2007, the OLS estimations of four equations are listed in Table 8.2 for income and Table 8.3 for consumption expenditure.

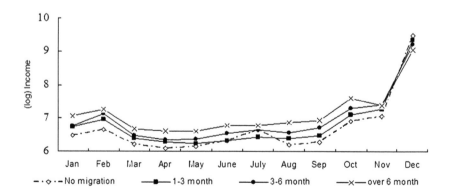

Source: *pers. comm.*, Hubei Statistics Bureau, 2007

FIGURE 8.6 Distribution of monthly income of households with different migration periods

TABLE 8.2 Determinants of income and its seasonality index

Variables	Income		Seasonality index of income	
	Coefficient	T value	Coefficient	T value
Farm size	0.042***	22.11	0.032***	20.80
Migration.dummy=1	0.029	1.32	−0.085***	−5.98
Migration.dummy=2	0.113***	4.88	−0.141***	−9.76
Ωορκτιμε	0.023***	3.45	−0.018***	−3.41
Training	0.229***	8.34	0.016	0.86
Constant	9.251***	148.82	1.208***	29.58
Observations	3300		3300	
R-squared	0.1566		0.1532	

Source: *pers. comm.*, Hubei Statistics Bureau, 2007

Note: *** Statistically significant at 1% level.

TABLE 8.3 Determinants of consumption expenditure and its seasonality index

Variables	Consumption expenditure		Seasonality index of consumption expenditure	
	Coefficient	T value	Coefficient	T value
Farm size	0.018***	9.03	0.005***	4.46
Migration.dummy=1	0.032	1.38	0.010	1.01
Migration.dummy=2	0.018	0.72	0.042***	3.76
Worktime	0.025***	3.59	−0.007*	−1.93
Training	0.220***	7.58	−0.049***	−3.72
Constant	8.809***	134.56	0.834***	29.10
Observations	3300		3300	
R-squared	0.0582		0.0516	

Source: *pers. comm.*, Hubei Statistics Bureau, 2007

Note: *** Statistically significant at 1% level. * Statistically significant at 10% level.

The results show that migration has a positive effect on household income generation, with the effect being statistically significant (at 1 per cent level) when the household has more than one migrant labourer. Other variables, including farm size and percentage of household labourers having received technical training, also have significant positive effects on income. Moreover, migration has a significant negative effect on the seasonality index of income (at 1 per cent level), meaning that migration helps reduce seasonal variation of household income.

Looking at the effect of migration on household expenditure, although it is not statistically significant, the effect shows a positive sign. Other explanatory variables, including farm size, work time per labourer and technical training received, all have statistically significant positive effects on household expenditure (at 1 per cent level). Regarding the effect on the seasonality index of expenditure, while work time per labourer and technical training received have negative effects, farm size and having two or more migrants have statistically significant positive effects (at 1 per cent level), meaning farm size and migration contribute to the seasonal variation of household consumption expenditure. This may be explained by the fact that seasonal migrant labourers actually have higher consumption expenditure when they are away than when they stay at home, as explained earlier.

It is worth noting that higher seasonal variability of household consumption expenditure cannot be interpreted as problematic. Migrant workers have been seen as an important engine for China's economic boom over the last three decades. More than three-quarters of rural households in the sample have at least one member who has migrated to cities for non-farm work. The migrants have far higher productivity than they would have had if they had stayed at home involved in agriculture, while they also have higher consumption expenditure away from home, which contributes to the higher variability of household consumption expenditure.

Seasonal variations of household income and expenditure: a case study

A farm household in Guangxi was interviewed in 2002. The household head voluntarily recorded a detailed cash income and expenditure diary from January 2001 until our visit in March 2002. Figures 8.7 and 8.8 show different items of cash income and expenditure.

The household depends almost entirely on agriculture for its livelihood. Cash inflows include selling various types of agricultural products such as grains, vegetables, animals, and so on. The farmer grows single-season rice but does not sell it at once. Instead, sales are rather scattered across the year, with the largest sales occurring during April to June in the pre-harvest season when the household may be short of cash income, and when there is also intensive labour input. The constant cash inflow over the year comes from selling vegetables. As for cash expenditure, constant cash outflow occurs in items such as food and other daily necessities. The sudden increase in expenditure in June is mainly because the farmer is paying to install a biogas system for agricultural production and for household energy use by his wife, who cooked for the biogas construction technicians every day in June.

The constant cash inflow from vegetable sales may compensate for the expense of daily necessities. However, the farmer pays a large sum of money in October for baby pigs to rear, and this makes him indebted. In November a payment to one of his relatives as a gift for a ceremony makes him indebted again, and the situation is even worse in the subsequent month, when he makes gifts to relatives for other ceremonies (it is common in rural China for farm households to hold their celebrations/ceremonies later in the year, in the slack season). The balance of monthly cash inflows and outflows is shown in Figure 8.9.

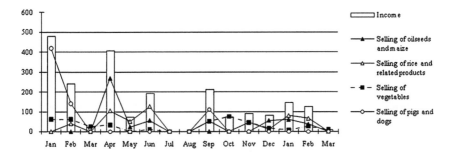

Source: *pers. comm.* with a farm household in China, 2002

FIGURE 8.7 A household's cash income (RMB Yuan) over 15 months, 2001–2002

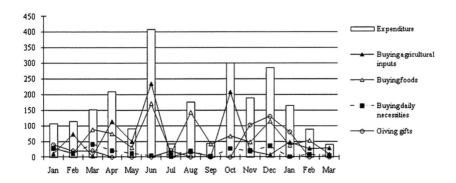

Source: *pers. comm.* with a farm household in China, 2002

FIGURE 8.8 A household's cash expenditure (RMB Yuan) over 15 months, 2001–2002

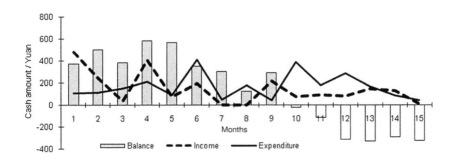

Source: *pers. comm.* with a farm household in China, 2002

FIGURE 8.9 A household's cash flow over 15 months

As can be seen, the fluctuation of the farmer's cash flow in income and expenditure over the year shows no pattern, with the peaks and lows not matching at all. He faces a cash deficit after October (he actually borrows in this month to pay for baby pigs), and gets indebted by some 300 Yuan by the end of the year. Furthermore, his indebted status continues at the same level for the next couple of months. If there were no government support, no social network, and no mechanism for borrowing, he would probably have to sell his productive assets to repay his debts. Alternatively, if he didn't have enough assets to sell, or if a family member suddenly suffered an emergency or accident, he would then not be able to sustain his livelihood.

Concluding remarks

Risks and uncertainties have been seen as fundamental factors leading farm households in rural China into poverty and desperation. Seasonality in subtropical regions, such as in southern China, can be an important source of such risks and uncertainties, leading to great fluctuations in household income and expenditure. This may be seen from the fact that seasonal changes in agricultural production explain, to a large extent, the variations in households' cash income and expenditure. This may be especially true for those households that mostly depend on agriculture for their livelihoods.

In the study areas, wage income is the main income source for most of the year while family-based agricultural enterprise becomes the main income source at the end of the year. Consumption is one of the main expenditure items over the year, and is higher in December and this is especially true for food consumption. The expenditure share of family-based enterprise is much higher in the peak season, indicating higher agricultural inputs use during that time. As income from agricultural production forms a large proportion of overall household income, public policies should be carefully designed to help households mitigate the adverse effects of the seasonal variation in agricultural income. For example, because drought is one of the major risks in southern China, developing an irrigation system may help farm households with additional rice harvests (i.e., increasing rice production from one season to two seasons), and providing drought-tolerant crop varieties may also help to reduce the variability of agricultural income.

Migration from rural to urban areas for non-farm work has made a significant contribution to China's economic boom over the last three decades. Casual labour migration is seen as the main non-agricultural income-generating activity for farm households, and helps a large proportion of rural households climb out of poverty. On the other hand, seasonal migration has been one of the most important factors affecting the fluctuation of household income and expenditure, both positively and negatively.

Variability in household income and expenditure in the study areas may not necessarily be problematic. As discussed earlier, although seasonal migration contributes to variability in household expenditure, it generates higher income and helps smooth household income variability, and consequently, household expenditure can be increased. That no statistically significant variations in seasonal food consumption patterns have been evidenced may indicate that household food supply in the study area has been secured to some extent, and there may be other variables, such as variation in household labour supply and changes in household resource endowment, that explain seasonal variations of household wellbeing. This finding is somewhat different from other studies in African and south Asian regions which found that seasonal hunger is a serious concern (Devereux *et al.*, 2008).

One of the variables that very positively affects income and expenditure and their variability is the technical training provided to the rural labour force. A labourer who has received technical training (especially for non-farm productive skills) on the one hand significantly *increases* both income and expenditure on consumption and on the other hand significantly *reduces* their seasonality. This may have important policy implications. For example, training as a public good should be government-funded and provided more widely to the rural labour force, to develop the labour market and generate a higher return to households who rely heavily on the seasonal migrant labour market. In the same way, household assets play a very positive role in helping to generate income and smooth expenditure, so further policy intervention should encourage household asset accumulation.

Seasonal variations in agriculture and their effects on household livelihoods in rural China have been inadequately investigated, and little evidence has been collected. Further efforts should be made to identify the nature and extent of seasonal variations and their impact on households in rural China. Two arguments can be made:

1   agricultural policies and rural development agendas need to engage more with agricultural seasonality and look more at household-level evidence, which is currently rarely considered in policy interventions;
2   more institutional or integrated interventions (e.g., financial support for agricultural production, subsidies) and technological improvements, rather than ad hoc arrangements (i.e., social relief programmes), are needed to help smooth seasonal variations of household income and expenditure in rural areas.

Acknowledgements

The research projects on which this paper is based received financial support from the National Science Foundation of China (Grants No. 70573122, 70773120). Mr Shu Zhenbin from the State Bureau of Statistics Hubei Branch helped with data analysis. We are grateful to Dr Stephen Devereux and colleagues at the Institute of Development Studies, UK, for comments in revising the chapter and help in editing.

Notes

1 More sophisticated studies may use 'temperature' as well. To take our study as a starting point, only rainfall is used. Further investigation of seasonality in a subtropical region may need to take temperature into account.
2 The Chinese lunar calendar is used in the paper, which is based on the cycles of the moon. In the Chinese lunar calendar the beginning of the year falls somewhere between late January and early February. Chinese farmers mainly base their agricultural activities on the lunar calendar, and it is also used for festive occasions such as the Chinese New Year.

9

Off-farm work in the Peruvian Altiplano

Seasonal and geographic considerations for agricultural and development policies

Cecilia Turin and Corinne Valdivia

Introduction

Rural households in the Peruvian highlands are among the poorest in the country: 60 per cent of this population lives in poverty, and 32 per cent in extreme poverty (UNDP, 2002). Rural households define their livelihood strategies according to the geographic and climatic conditions in which they live, as well as the social, economic and cultural needs and opportunities. They diversify their portfolio of activities to use their limited resources efficiently to deal with poverty, to ensure consumption during shocks or to improve their living conditions (Morduch, 1995; Valdivia *et al.*, 1996; Ellis, 1998; Valdivia and Gilles, 2001). Diversification on the farm is not always possible. It depends on geographic location, environmental characteristics, and labour availability. The Altiplano is a plateau between two mountain ranges in the southern region of the Andes of Peru. Climate conditions are difficult, and the Altiplano landscape is not homogeneous. It presents several agro-ecological zones and geographical characteristics, and climatic conditions that vary according to distance from Lake Titicaca and altitude (Sperling *et al.*, 2008).

Rural households defined as agriculturalist, who rely on crops and livestock and live near the lakeside, enjoy quite favourable climatic conditions. Their proximity to markets reduces participation costs. Their farming systems are mixed, producing crops and livestock for consumption and sale, with more opportunities to diversify within agriculture. Pastoralist households of the dry *puna*[1] zone, located in the highest and remote areas, face more difficult climatic conditions and exclusively graze livestock for the market. They have little or no opportunity for diversification, due to the high elevation and type of land they access. They are more vulnerable to market and climate changes and food insecurity and have fewer development opportunities. Households of both zones intensify their activities during the rainy season, a period of high on-farm labour demand.

Off-farm work is a common livelihood strategy in the Andes, as in other parts of the developing world. However, off-farm work patterns differ according to seasonal on-farm labour needs and labour market opportunities that depend on location. These characteristics are especially important when deciding where and when to work off-farm. Determinant in defining on-farm livelihood strategies is the allocation of family labour. Moreover, because of variable labour market conditions, Altiplano households have to evaluate the pros and cons when deciding whether or not to work off-farm.

Government development policies have encouraged off-farm work as a strategy for poverty alleviation, but they have not considered the differences in livelihood strategies according to agro-ecological zone, nor its impact on Altiplano rural households. Thus, understanding differences in off-farm work in distinct agro-ecological zones can provide new insights for policy in the Altiplano region. The objective of this study, therefore, is to explore and describe off-farm work patterns according to seasonal variation in two rural communities from two different agro-ecological zones of the Peruvian Altiplano.

This chapter is organized into seven sections. The second section presents a brief literature review of seasonality and the geographic implications for off-farm work. The third section describes the seasons and geographic conditions of the Altiplano. Section four provides a brief review of agricultural and development policy and its impact on rural households of the Andes. The fifth section describes the source of empirical research, the sixth presents the findings, and section seven presents the conclusions.

Seasonality and geographic considerations for off-farm work

According to Ellis (2000), off-farm work is a way to diversify income. It includes all activities that rural households get involved in beyond their own farm. Migration refers to off-farm work that happens when one or more family members leave home for varying lengths of time to work and contribute to the welfare of the household. Temporary migration could be either seasonal, when it depends on the agricultural season or calendar, or circular, when it responds to cyclical needs for labour in non-farm markets. Off-farm work includes migration and other off-farm income-generating activities. Off-farm work takes place because of different factors, defined as 'push' and 'pull'. Push factors include seasonality, risk, market failures, erosion of assets, landlessness and disasters. Pull factors are the result of income differentials and development opportunities that attract people (Ellis, 2000).

Seasonality is also a determinant of the livelihood strategies of rural households, whether on-farm or off-farm. On-farm it defines production cycles for crops and livestock; thus, rural households arrange crop and livestock cycles according to the seasons. They define the moment (when), the destination (where) and the off-farm activity to engage in (what) according to the seasons. Seasonality also determines the intensity of labour needs, such as for planting, harvesting, or transformation to add value. Seasonality impacts on income by influencing the economic returns to labour – a function of peak demand and low demand cycles. And seasonality affects rural households' consumption, because it fluctuates throughout the year according to food abundance and scarcity. Thus, there will be moments during the year (post-harvest) when food is more available and affordable but there will be other moments (planting) when food will be scarce and pricey. To smooth consumption throughout the year, households diversify their livelihood strategies to even out income across seasons (Valdivia *et al.*, 1996; Valdivia, 2004).

Geographic location is another factor that determines off-farm work opportunities for rural households. Reardon et al. (1992) found that, in sub-Saharan Africa, there are different development opportunities according to the specific locations of rural households. Thus, in three agro-ecological zones of Burkina Faso – Sahelian, Sudanian and Guinean – with different agro-climates and distances to markets, households with unfavourable agro-climatic conditions and less agricultural development had fewer opportunities for wage labour and self-employment off-farm than those with more favourable agro-climatic conditions. Reardon *et al.* concluded that policy intended to promote non-farm activities should consider both seasonality and geographic location.

However, Timmer (1998) argues that policies have failed to incorporate seasonality and geographic differentiation because policymakers have limited understanding of how agriculture functions in different countries. Policies do not only dismiss the natural characteristics of agricultural production (seasonality and geographic location) but do not include social aspects of agricultural production which are also affected by seasonality – such as the presence of several decision-makers in the household and the dual behaviour of farmers as producers and consumers. Geographic location in remote areas limits the access of rural households to input markets (labour and credit) and increases transaction costs in participating in output markets (Omamo, 1998; Key *et al.*, 2000). In addition, seasonality could increase these costs during certain times of the year. Therefore, it is important to understand seasonality and geographic location in order to inform policy design and government interventions when developing off-farm opportunities and markets (Timmer, 1998).

Non-farm rural employment in Latin America has proven to be an effective way of improving incomes when it is linked to other industries in the region (Reardon *et al.*, 2001). In Peru, non-farm income diversification in rural areas has benefited from increasing access to credit, education and infrastructure (Escobal, 2001). Provisioning of public goods, public rural investments, and innovations are also seen today as basic in supporting the future of small farms (Wiggins *et al.*, 2010), and require understanding of the diversity of contexts of these farms.

Seasonality and geographic considerations in the Peruvian Altiplano

The Peruvian Altiplano is located in the southern region of Peru, near the border with Bolivia. Two ethnic groups live in this region, the northern part being more influenced by the Quechua ethnic group and the southern part by the Aymara. The main livelihood is small-scale rainfed agriculture that depends on family labour. The dominant political structure in the rural Peruvian Altiplano is the peasant community; however, because of their indigenous status these communities have had little or no political participation until recently (UNDP, 2002).

The region presents two marked seasons. The rainy season runs from November to March with a concentration of precipitation in two months, January and February. The dry season runs from April to October, with September and October being critical, especially at the highest altitudes where almost no forage and little water are available at this time (Sperling *et al.*, 2008). Climatic conditions in the Atliplano in general are cold and dry. However, during the dry season, temperatures present more variability, registering the highest and lowest extreme temperatures, and the likelihood of frost and hail is higher.

The Peruvian Altiplano has three different agro-ecological zones, a function of distance from Lake Titicaca and altitude: the lakeside, the *suni*, and the dry *puna* zones. The lakeside is the lower zone surrounding Lake Titicaca, at 3,800 meters above sea level (m.a.s.l.), and average annual precipitation of 800mm. It presents mixed farming systems where crops are prevalent, especially potato and quinoa, along with fed livestock, mostly cattle and sheep. The *suni* zone is located between 3,800 and 4,000 m.a.s.l., has an average 600mm of annual precipitation, and combines cropping with grazing livestock (cattle and sheep). The dry *puna* in the upper zone above 4,000 m.a.s.l. receives less than 400mm of annual precipitation and is permanently exposed to frost. It experiences more climatic variability (Sperling *et al.*, 2008), and lately has been exposed to periods of dramatic drops in temperature known in the region as *friajes*.[2] Cultivation of crops is not possible in this zone. With clearly more difficult climatic conditions, this upper zone has fewer livelihood diversification options. The main livelihood here is grazing livestock, mostly South American camelids (alpacas and llamas) and sheep (Swinton and Quiroz, 2003).

In the Altiplano, the calendar of agricultural activities and the demand for labour are defined by the rainy season. Households from the lakeside zone intensify their agricultural activities during sowing just before the beginning of rainy season, and at the beginning of the dry season during the harvest. Households in the dry *puna* zone intensify their animal husbandry activities during the rainy season when shearing, mating and birthing take place; when the climate is more favourable and grasslands are more readily available. Agricultural production at the lakeside is for consumption and for market, while in the dry *puna* it is mostly for the market. Potato is the staple food with consumption at around 0.9kg per person per day in rural areas. Potato prices vary according to availability, so during the harvest season (March to June) prices are low, while in the pre-harvest months (November to February) prices rise. Because households in the dry *puna* lack the ability to produce crops, they rely on the market to purchase food. They are more vulnerable to price variability and to food insecurity, especially during the pre-harvest season of the lakeside zone. There is no evidence of chronic hunger, but there is marked malnutrition in the region, especially in the dry *puna* zone. There is also evidence of hunger during shock events, especially during droughts and the very cold spells (*friajes*), and people cope with these by depleting their animals and fibres (Sperling *et al.*, 2008). In other regions of the Altiplano, adults forgo consumption to feed their children or to purchase seeds (Valdivia and Quiroz, 2003) when there is a shock. The higher the altitude, the greater the degree of vulnerability to climate and food insecurity.

The lakeside zone is close to urban centres and markets, while the dry *puna* is distant and remote. Thus, lakeside households have more access to means of communication and better physical infrastructure (electricity, water, transport). Education and health services are also limited for rural households, but more so the higher the location. While most rural households live in poor conditions, those in the dry *puna* are among the poorest in the country, with incomes of less than one dollar per day (UNDP, 2002). Demographic growth has increased intensity of land use and land fragmentation, leading to the degradation of natural resources in all zones.

While the Peruvian Altiplano has been a target of government aid and international support for more than 30 years, success has been limited. Rural communities at the lakeside zone have been more exposed to these interventions than communities in the dry *puna*, and therefore have better institutional networks. However, interventions focused on agricultural development and modernization have had very little impact, other than to create aid dependency. Given the limited opportunities that rural households have to incorporate activities that keep them on the farm, migration has become a common income- and risk-reducing strategy. However, this is not only the result of natural and social constraints in the region, but is also the result of development policies implemented by various national governments.

Agricultural and rural development policy in Peru

Peru has three major geographic zones: the dry Pacific coast, the Andean region and the Amazon region. Major food production centres are located in the Andean region and the major urban centres are along the coast. After the structural adjustment programme in the 1980s, the public agricultural extension programme was eliminated. The policies of the 1970s and 1980s had systematically supported cheap food for urban centres at the expense of rural communities in the Andes (Valdivia, 1990). This dramatically affected rural households in the Andean region. The land reform converted workers on *haciendas*[3] into owners of cooperatives. In the 1980s a second reform pushed for privatizing the land from these cooperatives. Policies were liberalized, focusing on strengthening export capacity, mostly located on the coast (UNPD, 2002). This reform promoted the development of industrial agriculture. Public investment focused on the coastal region. Nevertheless, the expansion of agro-industry encouraged dependence on cheap imported agricultural inputs and consolidated the industrial agriculture sector (Shimizu, 2003).

It was expected that rural households from the surrounding areas would supply their extra labour to the emerging industrial agriculture. However, closeness to cities and improved physical infrastructure caused people to prefer getting jobs in the cities. Thus, migration is a response to demands from the cities for more labour. With the liberalization of the economy in the 1990s, mass production industrial agriculture and cheap imported food competed with small-scale rural households with high costs of production. Rural households vulnerable to seasonal availability of staple foods could smooth their consumption with cheap imported food. The latest agricultural development policy not only encouraged the expansion of industrial agriculture but also focused on exports, favouring the coastal region.

Andean rural households have been seen as aid recipients rather than agents of their own development (UNDP, 2002). Policies have mostly focused on poverty alleviation, not on development as in the coastal region. However, few attempts have been made in the last ten years. The programme Sierra Verde (1990–2000) attempted to improve dry season availability of grasslands in the Andean highlands. From 2001 to 2006, with the cold spells (*friajes*), aid was provided for livestock in the form of *cobertizos*[4] and forage. Unfortunately the response was from central government, often arriving late, or not at all. Recently, from 2007 to the present, the Sierra Exportadora programme (Export Sierra) was proposed to replicate the experience of coastal industrial agriculture in the Andes. But the natural (high diversity), geographical (inaccessibility, high transaction costs) and physical (inadequate road, electricity, water and communication systems) characteristics of the region are constraints.

An agricultural credit programme for Andean households was implemented. However, it was mostly for producers in the lakeside zone because their exposure to risk is lower. The government continues to provide assistance but the timing is still off. Policies have not been implemented to anticipate this type of hazard. Every year the *friaje* not only affects livestock production in the dry *puna*, it also affects people's health. However, the government still treats this as an unusual event. Poverty persists and agricultural production stagnates. Policies have failed to incorporate seasonal or geographic constraints.

The SANREM CRSP project in the Altiplano

The project 'Adapting to climate and market changes in the Altiplano', from the Sustainable Agriculture and Natural Resources Management (SANREM) collaborative research support programme (CRSP) sponsored by USAID, has been operating in the Peruvian Altiplano since 2006. The aim of the project was to understand how rural households of the Altiplano build their resilience in dealing with climatic and market changes, and to identify the bottlenecks they encounter in doing so. Using a household survey, participatory workshops and focus groups during 2006 and 2007, data were collected about household livelihood strategies and perceptions of change. Questionnaires were administered to 115 households from two communities. Data include household demographics, access to resources and livelihood strategies. Household heads were asked about where, when and in which activities they engage when working off-farm.

Off-farm work was defined as any type of activity that a member of a rural household participated in for income outside their own farm. Both survey communities are Aymara, located in the El Collao province in Puno. The Human Development Index ranking for this province is 133 of 142 (UNDP, 2002), indicating a high level of vulnerability. Apopata is in the upper *puna* zone and Santa Maria is in the lower lakeside zone, both in the Huenque watershed (see Figure 9.1).

Santa Maria belongs to the lakeside agro-ecological zone, at 3,860 m.a.s.l. Here, 130 families pursue a mixed farming system on an extension of 340 hectares. The main crops are potato and quinoa, but they also produce fava beans and other Andean tubers. Cattle and sheep are fed alfalfa, barley and oats. The main purpose of crop production is consumption, while livestock is produced for the market.

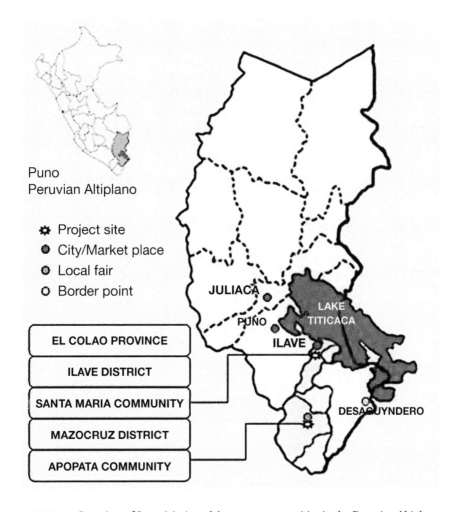

FIGURE 9.1 Location of Santa Maria and Apopata communities in the Peruvian Altiplano

This community is near Ilave, the main Aymara market in the region, and close to Puno city, the capital of the Department. This closeness to important urban areas provides good employment opportunities. Geographic location and favourable climatic conditions offer more options for income diversification. On-farm labour demand for sowing and harvesting intensifies between September to November and March to May respectively (see Table 9.1). The livestock calendar is more flexible. Many households access labour for agriculture through *ayni* (inter-familial labour exchange) and *minka* (communal labour). The community has had a women's handicraft association for many years. Off-farm work is a common livelihood strategy.

Apopata is situated between 4,070 and 5,300 m.a.s.l. in the dry *puna* agro-ecological zone. It has an extension of 11,500 hectares and around 70 families. The main source of livelihood is rainfed extensive grazing of alpaca, llama, and sheep. The community's main products are alpaca fibre and meat for the market. Apopata households depend solely on the market for their food security.

Apopata is in a remote area far from Ilave and Puno. However, the interstate highway to the coast crosses from northwest to southwest. The closest rural town, Mazocruz, has a weekly small local market on Saturdays. The community has few employment opportunities and few markets for their products. Moreover, because of Apopata's geographic location and unfavourable climatic conditions, there are limited options for income diversification. On-farm labour demands for livestock production intensify for shearing, mating and birthing from November to March (see Table 9.1). The sheep calendar adjusts to the alpacas'. A women's handicraft association was formed recently and is functioning. Off-farm employment is the main diversification strategy.

TABLE 9.1 Agricultural calendar of Santa Maria (lakeside zone) and Apopata (dry *puna* zone)

Community	Santa Maria	Apopata
Season\agro-ecological zone	Lakeside	Dry puna
January–February	Weeding/pest control	Mating/birth-shearing adults-cull
March	Harvest of quinoa	Mating/birth-shearing adults-cull
April	Harvest of quinoa/potato	Small shearing-cull for selling
May	Harvest of potato	Small shearing-cull
June–July–August	Fallow	Small shearing-cull
September	Sowing of quinoa	Small shearing-cull for selling
October	Sowing of quinoa/potato	Small shearing-cull
November	Sowing of potato	Shearing *tuis*[5]-cull
December	Weeding/pest control	Shearing *tuis*-cull

Off-farm work in the Peruvian Altiplano

Off-farm work is a common livelihood strategy for both communities, at the lakeside and in the dry *puna* zones. Table 9.2 shows the characteristics of household members who work off-farm and of their households. It also presents the characteristics of those who remain in the communities. In Santa Maria, 42.6 per cent of households reported working off-farm, as did 34.3 per cent in Apopata. In both communities, mostly men (either young or adult) with better education and command of Spanish work off-farm. Female adults and older people with little education or command of Spanish remain in the community, in charge of the house and farm chores. It seems that access to land, livestock holdings and sources of forage are not determinants for working off-farm. However, access to hired labour seems to be important in Apopata, especially because non-market access to agricultural labour like *ayni* and *minka* is not possible. Households that remain in both communities are those with less cash income, while those who work off-farm come from a diversity of economic backgrounds, ranging from wealthy to low-income. Poorer households in both communities remain and supply labour to households with members working off-farm. Hence, young people and adult men have better development opportunities when working off-farm. On the other hand, women (either young or adult), older people and the poor in the community have fewer or no opportunities to improve their lives. Moreover, because they do not generate cash income, they are the powerless in their households and communities.

Table 9.3 presents the destinations that rural households of the Altiplano choose when working off-farm. Within the region, these are the urban centres of Puno, Ilave, Desaguadero and Mazocruz. The city of Puno is the capital of the Department of Puno at the heart of the Peruvian Altiplano and is where government offices are located. The city of Ilave is the capital of El Collao province where local government offices are located, and also represents the capital of the Aymara culture. Desaguadero is the border town with Bolivia; it has an important informal import market of cheap Bolivian products. Mazocruz is a small town in the dry *puna* zone and has a local government office. Destinations beyond the region include Tacna, Moquegua, Arequipa and Lima. Apart from Arequipa, these are coastal cities (see Figure 9.2). Tacna is the most important city of the southern coast, bordering Chile. This coastal region has industrial agriculture. The Moquegua region has an emergent industrial agriculture and is an important growing urban area. Arequipa is the second most important city in the country after the capital Lima, and has an important agricultural valley close to the coast. The common destinations of households with members working off-farm in both communities are the cities of Puno and Ilave within the Altiplano region, and the departments of Tacna and Moquegua on the coast.

In the communities from both agro-ecological zones, the main destination for households working off-farm outside the Altiplano is Tacna; however, Tacna is more significant for Apopata (see Table 9.3). Santa Maria households have more destinations to choose from for off-farm work than Apopata, underscoring a favourable geographic location. These are Ilave (4km), Puno (54km), and the

TABLE 9.2 Comparison of household characteristics between those working off-farm and those who remain in both communities

Community (agro-ecological zone)		Santa Maria (lakeside) %		Apopata (dry puna) %	
Characteristic	Category	Off-farm work	Remain	Off-farm work	Remain
		42.6	57.4	34.3	65.7
Gender	Female	20	52	13	45
	Male	80	48	87	55
	Total	100	100	100	100
Age	20–35	35	12	26	11
	>35–65	45	44	70	59
	>65	20	44	4	30
	Total	100	100	100	100
Education	Illiterate	5	26	0	39
	Elementary	30	48	39	41
	Secondary	50	19	44	18
	Technical	15	7	17	2
	Total	100	100	100	100
Spanish	Only Aymara	0	11	0	25
	Little Spanish	30	48	0	34
	Good Spanish	70	41	100	41
	Total	100	100	100	100
Land	<3ha*/<100ha**	60	48	61	77
	>3ha*/>100ha**	40	52	39	23
	Total	100	100	100	100
Livestock	Cattle/alpaca				
	<2*/<80**	65	67	70	71
	>2*/>80**	35	33	30	29
	Total	100	100	100	100
	Sheep				
	<10*/<30**	95	89	48	64
	>10*/>30**	5	11	52	36
	Total	100	100	100	100
Forage	Alfalfa	100	96	--	--
	Barley	100	93	22	18
	Oats	65	33	--	--
Labour	Ayni (inter-familial)	55	56	13	5
	Minka (communal)	50	44	9	11
	Hired	10	7	26	9
Monthly income	< US$70	40	93	74	93
	> US$70–140	40	7	13	7
	> US$140	20	0	13	0
	Total	100	100	100	100

Note: * Santa Maria; ** Apopata

TABLE 9.3 Destinations, type of job and season of the year of rural households working off-farm in both communities

	Santa Maria (lakeside)%	Apopata (dry puna)%
Destinations within the region		
Puno	18	7
Ilave	20	10
Nearby community	17	–
Mazocruz	–	17
Desaguadero	4	–
Out of the region		
Tacna	23	56
Moquegua	9	10
Arequipa	5	–
Lima	4	–
Total	100	100
Type of job		
Agriculture	50	54
Construction	12	25
Commerce	23	11
Transport	10	–
Other services	5	10
Total	100	100
Season		
January–March	15	7
April–June	9	25
July–September	30	14
October–December	9	9
Any time	28	39
Almost whole year	9	6
Total	100	100

surrounding communities in the region and Tacna on the coast. Apopata has fewer destinations to choose from because of its geographic remoteness. These include Mazocruz (15km), Ilave (84km by road, 204km by highway) and Puno (138km by road, 258km by highway) in the region, and Tacna on the coast. Tacna is growing and there is demand for services, and therefore labour. In the rural area of Tacna, industrial agriculture demands labour permanently. Although Apopata is in a remote area, the interstate highway crosses it. However, transport is expensive, limiting the number of times per year that people can travel.

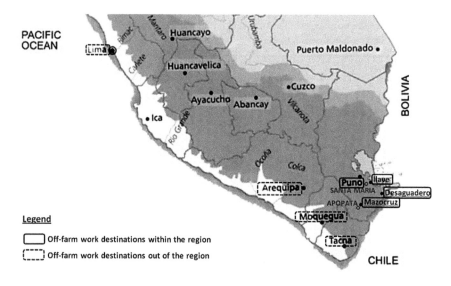

FIGURE 9.2 Destinations for off-farm work of Santa Maria and Apopata migrants

Similar jobs are performed in both agro-ecological zones (Table 9.3). Most migrants work in agriculture, in and out of the region; after this, migrants work mainly in commerce and construction. In the case of Santa Maria, most supply their labour to export-oriented agriculture in Tacna, and to nearby communities. Others work in construction and transport in Ilave and Puno, while others sell various products in Desaguadero. Most of the people from Apopata who travel out of the region work in agriculture in Tacna. Those who work in the region do so in construction and road maintenance in Mazocruz. The young travel to Tacna to work mostly as maids, cooks or waiters/waitresses in restaurants.

Agriculture in Tacna consists of olive farms on the coast, and oregano and corn farms in the hilly zone. Olives and oregano are export products, while corn is for local consumption. Most male adults work with export crops because wages are higher. Women work in corn production, and can also be paid in kind (corn), which is important for food security.

Labour for potato production is scarce in the Altiplano, especially when there are peak demands, due to opportunity costs. Poor households can only pay in kind (potato), and the most vulnerable in the community (women, older people, poorest) take on these chores. Young people and adult men work in construction in urban centres, while only a few women work off-farm where they are also engaged in agriculture and commerce.

Although households in both communities intensify their agricultural activities during the rainy season, they have different food and labour needs (Table 9.3), and thus different off-farm seasonal patterns. Households in Santa Maria demand more labour during sowing (September to November) and harvesting (March to May). Therefore, they are more willing to work off-farm during the fallow dry season from July to September. However, they also migrate during the rainy season (January–March) when children can help because they are on the school summer vacation. During peak labour demand seasons those who work off-farm have access to extra-familial labour – poor farmers who don't have resources to farm. Several households also indicated they could leave at any time of the year if there were good opportunities, highlighting the vulnerabilities faced in farming.

Apopata households require more labour during the rainy season. Thus, people are more willing to work off-farm during the dry season. However, some do leave during the rainy season because they have children who can work while school is out. Starting when they are six years old, children play a crucial role herding livestock during the rainy season. Other people can work off-farm during the shearing season (October–December) because young migrants return home to harvest the fibre. Most people in this zone work off the farm at any time of the year when employment opportunities are good. This is an indication of the vulnerability of Apopata's people, the conflicts between the community's seasonal demand for labour and that of export-oriented agriculture on the coast, and their ability to hire labour on-farm (Table 9.4).

TABLE 9.4 Comparative labour demands between coastal export-oriented agriculture and Altiplano agriculture

Community (Agro-ecological zone)	Export-oriented agriculture (Coast)	Santa Maria (Lakeside)	Apopata (Dry puna)
January– February	Oregano sowing	Weeding and pest control	Mating/birth-shearing adults-cull
March	Olive harvest	Quinoa harvest	Mating/birth-shearing adults-cull
April	Oregano and olive harvest	Quinoa and potato harvest	Small shearing-cull for selling
May	Oregano and olive harvest	Potato harvest	Small shearing-cull
June–July	Oregano and olive harvest	Fallow	Small shearing-cull
August	Oregano sowing	Fallow	Small shearing-cull
September	Oregano sowing	Quinoa sowing	Small shearing-cull for selling
October		Quinoa and potato sowing	Small shearing-cull
November	Oregano harvest	Potato sowing	Shearing *tuis*-cull
December	Oregano sowing and harvest	Weeding and pest control	Shearing *tuis*-cull

The export agriculture of the coast has a pull effect for people from the Altiplano. The olive and oregano industries demand labour throughout the year, as can be seen in Table 9.4. People can find work year-round by shifting from oregano to olives, and given that travel costs to this region are high, this is a likely scenario. In effect, this industry competes with the agricultural labour needs of the Altiplano.

Thus, there are different patterns of off-farm work in the Peruvian Altiplano. Generally, young people leave the community to make their living in the cities. Many of them return every year to harvest potato, fibre and meat. In this way, they keep the link with their households and with the community. Adults generally leave to work in agriculture in Tacna. The difference in migration is that Santa Maria people work off-farm for short periods of about 3 or 4 weeks, while Apopata's men mostly spend the entire dry season away due to the high cost of transport.

Key decision-makers are absent for short periods of time in Santa Maria, and therefore off-farm work does not interfere with household and community decision-making. On the other hand, the long periods of absence of key decision-makers in Apopata constrain household and communal decision-making. The constant mobilization of young people and adult men result in few permanent residents. Mostly women and the elderly remain behind to take care of production and reproduction activities. This permanent reduction of the rural population damages community governance. It also limits the opportunities for government to invest in infrastructure or development in the dry *puna* zone because such programmes rely both on labour and on the capacity to organize (Sperling *et al.*, 2008).

Conclusions

There are both similarities and differences in the migration patterns of each zone – a function of seasonality and geographic location. Young men from both zones work off-farm. Mostly women, older people and the poor remain in the community in charge of the house and farm chores. Those working off-farm are from the wealthy and middle-income households in the community. The poorest remain and are the labour supply to those who work off-farm. The main destination of those working off-farm in the southern part of the Peruvian Altiplano is Tacna, to work in agriculture.

People from the lakeside community who work off-farm have more destinations to choose from within and beyond the region, have access to more types of jobs, and migrate in different seasons of the year for short periods. These households have better climatic and geographic conditions, more on-farm diversification options and better labour market opportunities; they are therefore less vulnerable to food insecurity and less vulnerable to labour market conditions. On the other hand, people from the dry *puna* community who work off-farm have fewer destinations to choose from, mostly outside the region, have fewer job options, and leave the community once a year for a long period. Households in the dry *puna* experience less favourable climatic and geographic conditions, they have no on-farm diversification opportunities and fewer employment options; they experience more food insecurity and need to work off the farm.

The main type of work is casual labour in agriculture within and outside the region. Those who work in agriculture in the region do so in potato production, while those who migrate work in the export-oriented agriculture of Tacna. The latter is a pull effect on Altiplano labour. However, the labour they supply is not 'surplus'; their own on-farm labour demand cannot compete with the wages in export agriculture. In consequence, on their farms they hire women, children and older people, or the poorest who are not able to migrate; this is particularly true of the dry *puna* households. Thus, while export-oriented agriculture provides a good source of employment for surplus labour from Altiplano during the dry season, it may also limit the labour available during the rainy season.

Off-farm work as a livelihood strategy varies in the Altiplano. There are those who work in agriculture during the dry season. These are seasonal migrants, who return to their community to be in charge of their own agricultural production. Others are permanent off-farm workers who leave the community and only return every year during the potato, fibre and meat harvests. Most of these permanent migrants are young people. Push factors in both zones are the few education and development opportunities, difficult climatic conditions, few on-farm diversification options, food insecurity, and remoteness. These are more acute in the higher altitude zone. Labour market opportunities and export-oriented agriculture on the coast are pull factors.

Government policies today do not take into consideration the different seasonal and geographic conditions of the Altiplano zones. The export-oriented agricultural development policies of the coast attract workers from Altiplano rural communities. The pull effect is stronger in the dry *puna*. Members of the rural communities contribute to development on this coast, while those who remain in the dry *puna* communities are more vulnerable. Subsistence agriculture and the agriculture of staple foods have not been favoured by government policies. As a result, they remain stagnant. There are no investments to develop infrastructure that could help to diversify economic activities.

Moreover, communities' local organizations have been debilitated because of the absence of key decision-makers, and failed top-down aid interventions. Members from rural communities in the Altiplano, who are impacted by climate shocks every other year, identified specific needs to address the seasonal shocks they face. Among these, they included: timely information about labour market opportunities when seasonal migration is taking place; information and support in marketing fibre to negotiate better prices; school infrastructure suitable for the extreme temperatures; infrastructure that protects their livestock, as morbidity and mortality deplete their herds, an important asset (Sperling *et al.*, 2008). As Valdes and Foster (2010) underscore, pure income transfers to benefit children and older people are also employed as a way to alleviate poverty. An argument by Devereux (2010) that needs to be emphasized is that social protection is required for the vulnerable to address the market failures of meat, fibres and potatoes in the region, as well as those of labour markets. Liberalization and climate change are combining as an asset-depleting threat for Andean families that depend on agriculture for their livelihoods.

Policymakers need to understand the effect of export agriculture at the coast on the rural communities of the Altiplano. While cash income is generated by temporary migration, the costs are borne by those left behind, often women, children and older people. In cases where conditions are less favourable, such as in the dry *puna* zone, the prolonged absence of workers has a negative impact not only on the household, but also on the governance of the community and its ability to negotiate resources with the government. Some of these seasonal impacts are a reflection of the policies that have historically favoured an export-oriented economy, and have not valued the Andes, their people, and the services they provide as stewards of the environment.

Notes

1 Neotropical ecoregion comprising high plateaux and cliffs, 4,100–4,800m above sea level. It has low atmospheric pressure, little oxygen and extremely low temperatures. There is scarce precipitation and an average annual temperature of -7°C.
2 Annual period of dramatic temperature decrease in the dry season occurring in the last ten years, with considerable reduction in forage availability for livestock, so the alpaca population diminishes because of the cold weather and hunger.
3 Agricultural feudal system from 1920 to 1970, abolished by the land reform.
4 Shelters for livestock made of inexpensive material.
5 Alpacas born at the beginning of the year.

PART 3

Seasonal awareness

Ode to the Seasons conference (1978)

Assembled here in sunny Brighton,
we hope our meeting will shed light on
seasons. Is this good or bad?
Another conference? One *more* fad?

The answer is we're in a trap,
we don't have seasons on our map.
Our disciplines aren't trained to see
the range of seasonality.

First, anthropologists, I swear,
to seasons have been far too near.
Immersed in culture, rain or dry,
they have not seen the clouds pass by

And sociologists, even worse,
with questionnaires and questions terse,
snatch instant truths, one-off. It's rare
to find them survey all the year.

Nutritionists with careful plan
conduct their surveys when they can:
be sure the weather's fine and dry,
the harvest's in, food intake high.

Malariologists can claim
their pattern is not quite the same.
Superior in virtue they
migrate to *face* the rainy day.

Economists, that super breed
show seasonal supplies exceed
demand; result – the landless poor
for less and less work more and more.

And statisticians too declare
they have a seasonal nightmare.
An average is but a dream.
With seasons, means aren't what they seem.

Geographers – complacent crew –
will say – of course *they* always knew
what others now just come to know
that seasons come and seasons go.

Contrariwise plant breeders say
not seasons but the length of day
is critical; the key they've seen's
a photoperiodic gene.

Demographers now wonder why
we do it when it's cool and dry.
Conversely, when it's wet and hot,
it seems we tend to do it not.

Now epidemiologists
will say the worst is when it's poured
with rain, for that's when vectors vect
and swarms of small insects infect.

Then students seeking PhDs
believe that everyone agrees
that rains don't do for rural study;
suits get wet and shoes get muddy.

And bureaucrats, of urban type
wait prudently till crop be ripe
before they venture far afield
to ask politely: what's the yield?

The international experts' flights
have other seasons; winter nights

in New York, Paris, Brussels, Rome
are what drive them, in flocks, from home.

And Northern academics too
are seasonal in their global view.
For they are seen in Third World nations
only during long vacations.

The rural people – I forgot –
know what some others still know not:
long life and leisure, food and health
belong to those who have the wealth.

They do not need research to show
the troubles they already know;
oppressed by sickness, hunger, debt,
they know the worst is when it's wet.

But wealthy ones dislike life dry.
The poor may thirst but we'll get by,
eating and drinking (within reason)
steadily through the conference season.

Robert Chambers

(Originally published in Chambers, R., Longhurst, R. and
Pacey, A. (eds) (1981) *Seasonal Dimensions to Rural Poverty*,
Frances Pinter: London, pp248–9)

Sonnet for the Seasonality Revisited conference (2009)

And now we sup here after thirty years
and wonder what has happened in between.
And blame ourselves for all the needless tears
that fell because the seasons stayed unseen.
Though much has altered much remains the same;
those screws and ratchets still keep down the poor.
But global warming's changed the farmers' game,
with loaded dice that make the risks hurt more.
Our eyes are opened. No more season-blind,
our vision can be positive and green –
a world that's season-proofed for humankind;
in thirty more years let's transform the scene.

Let's go for change. By then may all have found
not pain but pleasure in the seasons' round.

Robert Chambers

10

Food affordability

Dealing with seasonal variation of purchasing power

Hélène Berton, Jennie Hilton and Anna Taylor

This chapter explores the two main reasons why access to food changes by season: the variability of the cost of food and the variability of available incomes. This chapter looks first at how much money is required to ensure that basic dietary needs are met. The second part describes the components of the cost of an adequate diet (local availability of food and local prices) through a methodology developed by Save the Children. The third part uses data from recent field surveys carried out by Save the Children to illustrate the variation of income available for food purchase. Finally, this chapter proposes some implications for decision-makers resulting from this more nuanced understanding of variable access to food.

This report compiles data from several livelihoods studies, including Household Economic Approach (HEA) analysis and Cost of the Diet studies, carried out in Kenya, Ethiopia, Niger, Burkina Faso, and Myanmar. Further research and improvement of methodologies would be required to complete this analysis and gain a more thorough understanding of the seasonal patterns of food affordability.

Introduction

The current economic recession has made purchasing power a topic of great interest in Western societies. The prospect of having to consume a few per cent less than in the recent past makes headlines, even though we are still able to afford far more than our most basic needs.

In the developing world the variation of purchasing power is on a completely different scale. The poorest people of the world not only struggle with very low incomes, they also have to cope with large variations in what they can afford for basic survival. Moreover, the reduction in their purchasing power is not just a matter of a few per cent; it can be halved between seasons.

The recent global events affecting the price of food commodities and the economic downturn have illustrated how dramatically the poorest can be affected by changes in the economic situation. It is estimated that more than 130 million people were pushed into poverty in 2008 because of soaring food and fuel prices, and an extra 100 million people were projected to be living on less than US$2 a day in 2009 as a result of the global economic crisis. Between 4 and 10 million children are estimated by Save the Children to have become malnourished as a result.

The current global situation has in many places reinforced the seasonal problems faced by the poorest people in developing countries. Large seasonal variations of purchasing power and therefore of access to food hinder the ability of families to afford an appropriate diet throughout the year. To tackle efficiently the problem of hunger we should therefore carefully consider how much the poorest rely on seasonal changes in local markets and the cash economy for their survival and wellbeing. These parameters have often been overlooked as these groups are typically believed to be small-scale farmers relying on a more or less food-sufficient economy – a view which is now understood to be less often the case.

Purchasing power: how much is needed throughout the year?

Survival threshold: a curve evolving through the seasons

To know how much income is required to access adequate food, we need to establish a threshold. The most commonly used indicator to express poverty and difficulty in accessing food is an income of US$1 a day (recently raised by the World Bank to US$1.25 a day) (World Bank Institute, 2005). This poverty line is, however, inadequate in expressing the affordability of food: it is not possible to purchase the same quantity and quality of food in India or Mali for US$1 a day. In the same way, US$1 does not give the same access to food throughout the year.

The World Bank has developed another indicator that is less commonly used, at least to communicate on hunger – the absolute poverty line. This poverty line is set on a yearly basis by country and represents what households require in order to meet their basic needs (World Bank Institute, 2005). The absolute poverty line gives a better idea of what is needed for survival, but it is still a static line. In reality, the threshold for basic needs is a moving curve that evolves to reflect changes in the price of staple foods (bold and dotted line, Figure 10.1). The threshold to access the cheapest *healthy* diet (bold line on top) also fluctuates seasonally according to market trends and local availability of nutritious food.

This example compares the annual variation of the five-year average cost of a staple ration with the variation of the 'survival cost' (staple food cost[1] + other basic expenditures estimated at 10 Fcfa pppd)[2,3] from 2004 to 2008 in Southern Niger (Zinder region). Over the four years, this survival threshold varied from less than 100 Fcfa per person per day at the harvest season (October) to over 200 Fcfa at the peak of the worst lean season (August 2005). This was due to the price of millet varying

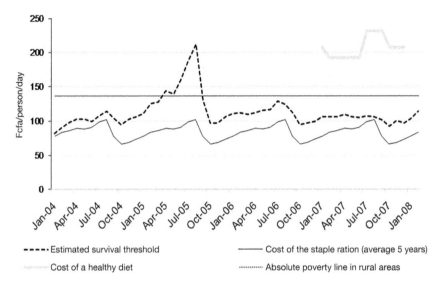

FIGURE 10.1 An evolving survival threshold in Niger

Notes:
The cost of staple food is calculated on the basis of the cost of millet as given by SIMA (Système d'information sur les marchés agricoles – Government of Niger) and the estimated 2,100kcal/day/person requirement. The cost of the diet has been calculated in the neighbouring region of Maradi in the same livelihood zone.

by about 50 per cent on average between these two seasons. Beyond this regular seasonal variation, additional shocks can exacerbate the seasonal trends dramatically, as was the case during the 2005 lean season in the example above (Figure 10.1).

The importance of seasonal changes to the rural cash economy

The importance of purchasing power when assessing the food situation will vary by season and by wealth group depending on the household's capacity to secure food, whether through their own production, or as gifts, in kind remittances, etc. However, Save the Children's field research has highlighted that the poorest households in developing countries rely heavily on markets (i.e. on cash economy) throughout the year for their food due to their very limited capacity to produce food (O'Connell, 2004; Muchambo and Sharp, 2007; Holt *et al.*, 2009). This is happening as resources are shrinking, less land is available and markets, even in remote areas of Africa, are increasingly linked to the global economy.

The example overleaf (Figure 10.2) illustrates the seasonal change in the poorest wealth group's level of dependency on markets for food at three different seasons: after the harvest, before the hunger gap and during the hunger gap. Unsurprisingly, we can observe an increasing dependency on the market while approaching the lean season. These data and complementary field surveys have confirmed that in this agricultural area there are only three months of the year (just after the harvest) during which the poorest households can rely on their own production as a main food source, and even then it only covers a third of their needs. Most of the year these households are largely dependent on their capacity to purchase food at the market, and this dependency on purchased food increases as they move beyond the harvest period.

Figure 10.2 also illustrates the difficulty with which the poorest households access enough food. Their purchasing power does not allow them to fulfil their most basic needs and the extent to which they meet their daily energy requirement decreases from 98 per cent in the post-harvest season, to 89 per cent in the pre-hunger gap and to 83 per cent at the beginning of the lean season.

A cash transfer project, focused on the poorest households during the lean season and piloted in the same area, has demonstrated that when the purchasing power of these households increases through additional cash availability, they can fulfil their basic food energy needs and also increase the diversity of their diet. By increasing the purchasing power of recipient households by about a third, their calorie requirement coverage increased within a month from 84 per cent of their

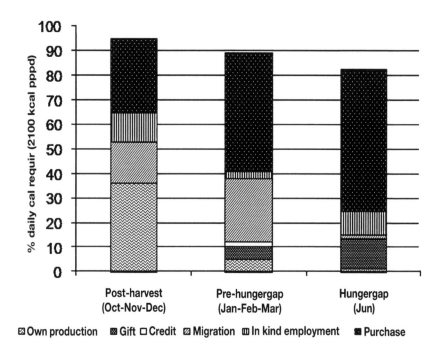

Sources: Berton (2009); Berton and Malam Dodo (2008)

FIGURE 10.2 Seasonal variation of food sources in a rainfed agricultural livelihood zone of southern Niger (Tessaoua and Kantche districts), 2007–08

daily needs[4] to 99 per cent. The consumption of pulses, meat, oil and milk also significantly increased (Berton, 2009).

The Niger case study is not an isolated example. Similar field research using the Household Economy Analysis methodology has demonstrated that very poor households rely heavily on purchasing power to meet their energy needs, and that in general the importance of having access to cash to meet food increases as the seasons move beyond the harvest period.

The seasonal variation of the cost of an adequate diet

The cost of an energy-sufficient food ration provides a reasonable estimate of the income required for survival, but in order to remain healthy and to prevent malnutrition a diet that provides the full range of macronutrients (carbohydrates, protein and fat) and micronutrients (vitamins and minerals) is necessary.

Save the Children UK has developed a new methodology to calculate the minimum amount of money a family will have to spend to meet its full nutritional requirements using locally available food. Named 'Cost of the Diet' (COD), this method has proven to be ground-breaking because it is the only tool currently available that can:

- calculate the minimum cost of a suitable diet for an individual child and the whole family
- take into account seasonal variations in food price and availability when costing the diet
- identify 'problem nutrients' which may be difficult to meet from a locally available diet.

The importance of the seasonal availability of nutritious foods in determining the cost of a healthy diet

A core determinant of a household's ability to access a sufficiently diverse diet is whether there are good quality foods available that will provide ample micronutrients and macronutrients to meet individual requirements. The change in seasonal availability of foods and the impact that this has on accessing a balanced diet is not just a result of the availability of locally harvested foods but also of indirect factors such as seasonal access to markets affecting the transportation of foods from other areas.

A CoD study in North East Kenya (Corbett and Chastre, 2007) showed that in the rainy seasons there were on average 38 per cent fewer food items available to purchase in the local market than in the dry season (Table 10.1). When the CoD analysis was conducted this lack of diversity of available foods meant that it was no longer possible to achieve a nutritionally adequate diet. There were no longer any fruits, vegetables and pulses available which resulted in iron and folate requirements not being met. To compound this, the cost of staples available in all seasons – maize, rice, wheat flour and potatoes – increased.

Box 10.1   Save the Children's Cost of the Diet (CoD) approach at a glance

Cost of the Diet came about as a response to research undertaken by Save the Children (Duffield, 2003) which demonstrated that the impact of traditional nutrition education programmes had been limited because of the economic constraints facing many households in low-income countries. In order to understand better the gap between the lowest cost of a diet and household income, the lowest cost of a nutritionally adequate diet is looked at in conjunction with HEA income data[5] from the same survey area and conclusions can be drawn about seasonal affordability.

In order to do this, monthly food price and availability data are collected from market traders and community group discussions for all locally available foods. The weight of units is measured in order to calculate a price per 100g and any seasonal change in the weight of the unit (for example a change in the number of pieces of fruit that are included in a portion) can be included.

In the simplest form of analysis (Tier 1) physiological diets that will meet nutritional requirements are calculated in order to identify whether a nutritionally adequate diet is achievable from locally available foods and how much it costs. Tier 1 (fairly theoretical) gives the cost of the cheapest diet that covers all nutrient needs that simply results from the software calculation of the household's members' needs versus available food items.

By collecting data on local food consumption patterns,[6] specifically for children aged 12–23 months, food pattern constraints can be set and a diet which more realistically resembles what is usually eaten is selected. These results, from Tier 2, demonstrate whether a good quality diet is still available when eaten in realistic amounts, how much it costs and if it is not available what the likely patterns of nutrient deficiency will be. In Tier 2, the rations proposed take into consideration what is realistically consumed by communities.

The seasonal calendar (Figure 10.3) demonstrates that, during the time when staples are most expensive in the *Hagay* and *Gan* (rainy seasons), there is a high milk yield which drives down the market price of milk and which, if included in the diet, can make a significant contribution to the overall nutrient content.

At times when there is a high milk yield but other food items are in short supply or expensive, it is crucial for households to consume milk to maintain a nutritionally adequate diet. Milk can be supplied from a household's own herd as well as being purchased. However, a CoD study in Legambo, Ethiopia found that the poorest families had no access to 'free' milk (that is milk produced by their own herds) and were therefore unable to meet their nutrient requirements in the seasons when other food items were most expensive.

TABLE 10.1 Food prices and availability in two seasons in north east Kenya

Food Item	Adolis (2nd dry season)	Hagay (2nd rainy season)
Maize flour	4	6
Rice	5	5.50
Sorghum	1.20	n/a
Wheat flour	4	5
Potato (Irish)	5	7
Kidney Bean	5	n/a
Cabbage	4	n/a
Tomato	5.41	n/a
Onion	8.70	n/a
Garlic	37.04	n/a
Lemon	17.86	n/a
Milk, camel	4.69	3.13
Milk, cow	6.25	4.69
Milk, goat	n/a	4.69

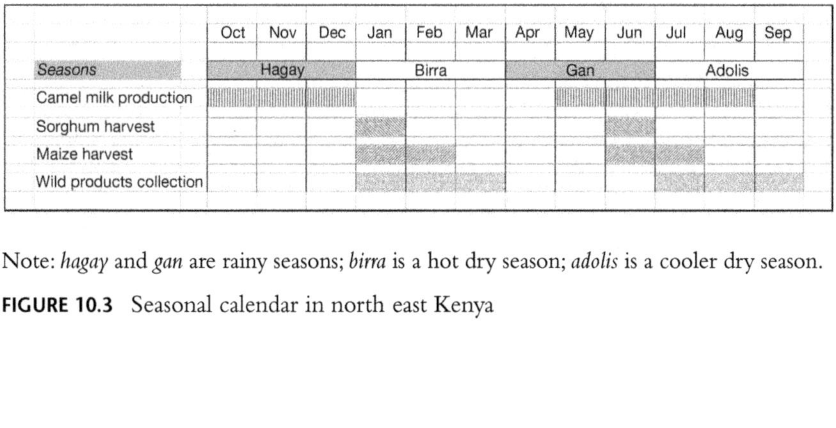

	Oct	Nov	Dec	Jan	Feb	Mar	Apr	May	Jun	Jul	Aug	Sep
Seasons		Hagay			Birra			Gan			Adolis	
Camel milk production	▓	▓	▓					▓	▓	▓	▓	
Sorghum harvest				▓					▓			
Maize harvest					▓	▓			▓	▓		
Wild products collection					▓	▓	▓				▓	▓

Note: *hagay* and *gan* are rainy seasons; *birra* is a hot dry season; *adolis* is a cooler dry season.

FIGURE 10.3 Seasonal calendar in north east Kenya

Crucially in the Kenya case study, wild or 'free' foods were not included, although we know that households from these communities consume leafy green vegetables which can be collected. Further investigation is needed to draw concrete conclusions about the impact such free foods have; however, it is reasonable to assume that consumption of these foods, which are high in iron and folate, would have a positive impact.

In Myanmar, where the same analysis of availability and cost was carried out and free foods were included, the study highlighted the importance of seasonal access to free foods, their contribution to meeting nutrient requirements, and the impact that this has on the cost of the diet (Chastre, 2007). In the rainy season, when free tamarind and gourd leaves cannot be collected, the diet was 32 per cent more expensive than in summer when those foods were available.

The delicate seasonal balance of the availability of free, wild and purchased foods is vulnerable to any shock which may influence the availability or cost of food types or access to the markets. Through CoD analysis it is clear that in each study location there are key food items or types which are heavily relied upon to meet nutritional requirements, such as cereals, pulses, leafy vegetables, and milk. Access to these is therefore essential and their prominence in meeting requirements leaves them vulnerable to shocks such as drought or a sharp increase in prices.

Pastoralist communities have previously shown resilience against normal seasonal changes in food availability and short-term food insecurity, through traditional coping strategies such as milk-sharing and movement to access better pasture (Sadler *et al.*, 2008). However longer-term food insecurity as a result of prolonged drought and increased settlement has led to poor access to good pasture, resulting in livestock loss and decreasing herd size and therefore lower milk production. A lack of free milk within the community is compounded by the increase in milk prices on the market as a result of generally lower milk yield. As was seen in Table 10.1, in a season when diversity is severely limited, milk provides essential nutrients, especially for the most vulnerable within the household – infants and young children.

The contribution of market trends to the seasonal cost of a diet

The CoD study in South Wollo, Ethiopia (Lejeune, 2007) found that as a result of changes in availability and prices, the cost of the cheapest diet that meets all micronutrient and macronutrient requirements can increase from one season to another by up to 125 per cent for a child aged 12–23 months. The season when the diet is cheapest is following the main harvest (*belg*), while the most expensive is in the months leading up to the main harvest, traditionally known as the cereal hunger gap.

Households are particularly vulnerable to seasonal price changes in staple foods. In Shinile, a pastoral area of Ethiopia, *injera* (a large sourdough flatbread) is eaten daily and therefore any seasonal fluctuation in the price of sorghum and wheat (the main ingredients) will have a negative impact on the money available to spend on more diverse food items. In the reference year January 2008 to January 2009, the price of sorghum went up on average 22.97 per cent between *jilaal* – the end of the dry season just following the local harvesting of sorghum, and the second *karaan* – the long rainy season; the price of wheat went up by an average of 23.4 per cent. The seasons when wheat and sorghum are most expensive are also the times of year when households are most reliant on purchasing cereals from the market.

Figure 10.4 demonstrates that in the early *jilaal* (dry) the cost of a diet is 79 per cent more expensive than in the *diraa* (rainy) season, which reflects the overall increase in cost of most food items between these seasons. Cereals and sugar are eaten on a daily basis. The results shown in Figure 10.4 are taken from analysis where the inclusion of these was forced, in order to reflect a more realistic cost. The horizontal line shows a daily income figure taken as an average across the whole year and demonstrates that achieving an appropriately diverse diet which reflects the usual dietary practices of most households would be largely unaffordable. This study would need to be further refined by calculating seasonal changes in incomes to determine seasonal affordability more precisely.

Being well informed about the seasonal variation in the availability and affordability of a nutritionally adequate diet and building this into an effective ongoing monitoring system can provide essential data to inform effective programming and policy decisions.

As the CoD assessment tool continues to be developed and the Tier 2 approach (proposing realistic nutritious diet rations) is used, the results can then be used to highlight the patterns of potential nutrient deficiencies and how these change across the seasons. Interventions, such as micronutrient fortification, Plumpy'doz or Sprinkles,[7] can be targeted to have an impact in the season when dietary diversity is most difficult to achieve.

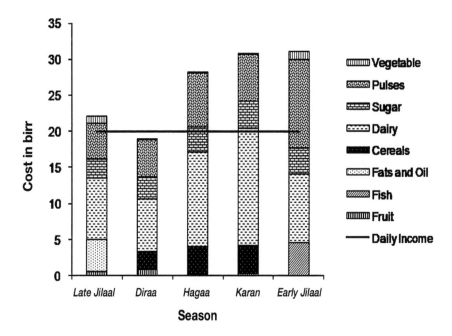

Notes: Cost of cheapest diet is estimated on the basis of local availability, not considering cultural preferences, but assuming a reasonable consumption of cereals and sugar; 1 *birr* = US$0.06.

Source: Lejeune and Hilton (2009)

FIGURE 10.4 Cost of an environmental diet for household of six in Shinile, Ethiopia

The seasonal variation of available incomes at the household level

The affordability of the diet is not solely determined by food prices; it is as much a matter of income being available to purchase it. And again, the poorest of the developing world are not only challenged by the variations in the cost of their diet, they also face great uncertainty in the level of income they can secure throughout the year.

Why are income sources of the poorest communities so insecure throughout the year?

The poorest of the developing world often rely on multiple sources of income as they lack a single economic activity that offers them a secure livelihood. These activities vary throughout the year according to local as well as more distant economic opportunities: casual agricultural labour, animal herding during pastoral migrations, activities such as brick-making, etc.

Identifying periods of high or low employment is therefore very important in understanding whether households can afford an appropriate diet. This knowledge also challenges the commonly held belief that in rural areas the hunger gap largely reflects the agricultural calendar. The food security of the rural poor is in fact often determined less by the level of food stock that can be produced directly by small-scale farmers, but instead by their success in securing casual wages. The pattern of wages can be quite distinct from the agricultural calendar (Box 10.2).

When the cost of staple foods rises, some adaptations in the level or type of remuneration can be observed, including increases in the length of the working day, changes in the amount of remuneration and payment in kind rather than in cash. To some extent therefore there are some mechanisms that mitigate the seasonal economic hardships. Overall, however, when the cost of food is highest, the availability and sometimes the level of remuneration of casual work tend to be lower than usual. Unregulated labour markets tend to work against those supplying the labour.

The following example (Figure 10.5) illustrates the purchasing power (for the staple food product, millet) of casual labourers in southern Niger from 2005 to 2008 in two different seasons: the lean season (July) and the harvest season (October).[8]

Normally the daily labour wage is estimated to cover at least the basic food needs of a typical household. This example shows that throughout this period the amount of food that could be purchased by the same amount of work fluctuated fourfold. During the 2005 and 2008 hunger gaps the daily wage was not enough to satisfy the most basic needs.

This study also highlighted the limited availability of casual work for rural labourers, who cannot find paid work every day. In this area, in times of crisis (such as in 2005), a typical family of two working parents and five children was unable to secure enough income to provide for the family's calorific requirements, much less other basic needs.

Box 10.2 Shifting the hunger gap period due to employment opportunities – a case study from Kantche district, Niger

Due to scarce natural resources, increasing pressure on land and low employment opportunities from January to June, the livelihoods of the rural population of Kantche district in Niger are increasingly dependent on the Nigerian economy, especially during these months. Young men from all wealth groups, but particularly from the poorest households, migrate for several months of the year (the length of migration varies according to the local food and economic situation) to large towns in northern Nigeria to seek casual labour. These sources of employment are essential to ensure that they can cover their basic needs. In 2008, the competition for employment increased due to the excess supply of labour as more people from the sub-region began looking for additional income in response to widespread price rises. At the same time, the casual work on offer decreased due to economic difficulties such as high prices of food and fuel. As a result, many Nigerien migrants failed to get adequate incomes from March to June. It was only at the beginning of the rainy season, which normally corresponds to the beginning of the lean season, that they started getting income through local agricultural work, which allowed them to cope slightly better with the difficult food situation. For them the usual pre-hunger period was in fact harsher than the hunger gap itself that preceded the harvest (Berton and Malam Dodo, 2008).

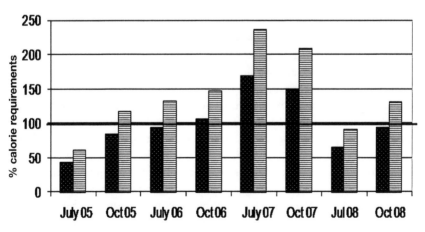

■ Weekly requirment (5 working days a week) ⊟ Daily requirement (1 working day)

Source: Save the Children (2009)

FIGURE 10.5 Variation of purchasing power of casual labourers in southern Niger, Tessaoua district – Chabaré village

The low purchasing power permitted by the level of remuneration and high food prices force the poorest households to use coping strategies that often have detrimental long-term consequences (child labour, harvest and sale of wild wood, sale of productive assets, etc). In the short term, they have to reduce the food ration to a level that compromises their health and particularly the health of their children.

Flexibility in expenditures: prioritizing food purchase

People in the developing world, regardless of wealth, require cash for purchases other than food, such as services and livelihood activities. But a characteristic of the poorest rural population is that their expenditure patterns evolve throughout the year. Purchasing staple food items is by far the highest priority in a poor household's budget. When cash is scarce and/or prices of staple items are high, other expenditures will be reduced. Therefore the change in the proportion of the household's budget spent on purchasing food is a fairly good indicator of its wealth and food security status. This indicator needs to be carefully interpreted according to the seasons.

The following case example (Figure 10.6) shows the expenditure patterns of different wealth groups in Kaya region in Burkina Faso, just after the harvest and then during the three following months.

For the poorest groups (Very poor and Poor) in the post-harvest period, the purchase of staple food items (mainly cereals) represented 54 per cent[1] of the total household budget, which allowed households also to invest in social services (health, education), clothing, etc. However, three months later staple food purchases represented almost 80 per cent of the total expenditures – a much heavier burden on the household's budget. These households had already stopped any expenditure on non-staple food items and social services, both of which made them more vulnerable to malnutrition and poor health. This situation is all the more concerning since the expenditure patterns observed in the pre-hunger gap are normally those found in the peak of the lean season.

The case study above also highlights the pressure that food purchase places on the budgets of different wealth groups. For the better-off, food expenditure does take a larger proportion of the household budget as the harvest period recedes, but this still represents less than 40 per cent of total expenditure during the pre-hunger gap period. This provides them with a margin for adapting their budgets during the coming hunger gap months, for example by reducing livelihood activities, without suffering from food shortages. Poorer households lack this margin in their budgets because of their limited purchasing power, and as a result they have very variable access to food throughout the year. Most of the year they cannot afford a healthy diet that fulfils their macronutrient and micronutrient needs; as a result they are at risk of chronic malnutrition and related health difficulties. At some times of the year the gap between their income and the cost of food does not allow them even to provide for their energy needs, which exposes them and particularly their children to acute malnutrition. And yet this financial barrier to a healthy diet is still poorly taken into consideration when designing responses to hunger and malnutrition.

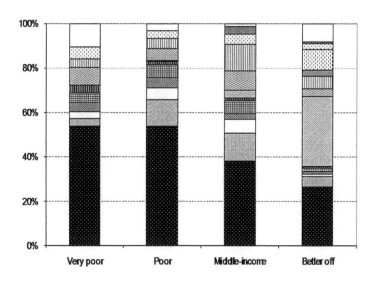

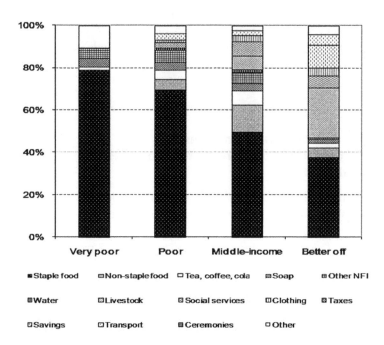

Source: Bernard (2008)

FIGURE 10.6 Expenditure patterns of different wealth groups in post-harvest and pre-hunger gap periods in a rainfed area of Kaya region, Burkina Faso, 2007–08

Implications for decision-makers of the seasonal changes in food affordability

Timely and appropriate monitoring of hunger

Understanding the gaps in food affordability and how they change across the year can help identify periods when households are particularly vulnerable as a result of reduced food availability, price changes, income fluctuations, or a combination of all of these. This understanding is essential to ensure effective monitoring of hunger and appropriate responses.

However, the affordability of food throughout the year is insufficiently taken into consideration in early warning systems. A systematic approach is required to measure and understand these factors that affect food access for poor families throughout the seasons and also to understand the nature of food-related crises that typically occur on a seasonal basis and to anticipate them. Save the Children has recently developed a Hunger Monitoring System which combines measurement of selected indicators, including economic access to food and the nutritional situation, to provide a clear grasp of the impact and causes of local and international shocks that affect families in developing countries.

Gaining an improved understanding of affordability is also fundamental if governments are to respond with policies that can support the real day-to-day challenges poor families face throughout each year in securing nutritious food. Social protection policies and programmes need to be based on the reality of vulnerabilities

---

Box 10.3 Save the Children's Hunger Monitoring System: Some indicators to measure food affordability

- Monthly market retail price per kilogram of main staple food
- Quantity of staple food in kilograms that can be purchased with the daily wage of an unskilled labourer
- Quantity of staple food in kilograms that can be purchased from the sale of an animal
- Daily cost of diet by season for a standard household
- Total annual/daily cost of diet as a proportion of total annual/daily income of a typical poor household
- Percentage of household income spent on food purchases
- Percentage of households whose food access meets or exceeds minimum food energy needs (2100kcals per person per day, seasonally and annually)
- Percentage of households whose income level meets the survival threshold (minimum food energy needs and minimum non-food needs)

that poor families face. This includes taking into account the cost of living, and in particular the ability to obtain nutritious food.

Conclusions

Food security analysis needs to take far more account of the cash economy. The poorest households rely less and less on natural resources for food and income as these resources dwindle under population pressure. The demands of a global economy with increasingly interconnected and unstable markets must also be considered. However, developing the means to measure and understand these issues is currently overlooked by programme planners and policymakers. Variations in prices remain perhaps the single most important factor in understanding hunger. The food price crisis in 2007/8 painfully illustrated this. Currently, for example, most studies that look at prices focus only on staple foods, while the cost and availability of other food items that are vital for a nutritious diet are neglected. Therefore, measuring a fuller basket of foods and the affordability of different types of diets is important.

Several immediate steps are necessary. Proper recognition of the existence of this gap in information systems should be followed by establishment of ways to monitor it. These steps could significantly strengthen the armoury of tools that will lessen the impact of emergencies. Information must help policymakers identify periods when households are becoming vulnerable as a result of reduced food availability, price changes, income fluctuations, or a combination of all three. Gaining early understanding is essential to ensure effective monitoring of hunger and appropriate responses.

Policymakers in the arena of disaster risk reduction, social protection and vulnerability analysis must heed the fluctuations that occur and should invest in means to ensure that good quality information on affordability is factored into decision-making. As we seek to strengthen the analytical tools they must be able to meet a number of objectives.

Detect drops in purchasing power

This would require an investment in early warning systems to develop methodologies and resources to understand and better capture the incomes of the poorest households, particularly income changes in local casual labour and migration. In order to make judgements about the impact of changes in income these systems would need to have established baseline information on the cheapest feasible nutritious diet in livelihood zones.

Offer systematic preventative measures and responses to a drop in purchasing power

This could be implemented through social protection measures such as insurance, strengthening the regulation of the labour market, price management of food products and social transfers, in an effort to allow the poorest to maintain a purchasing power that at least guarantees the ability to afford a nutritious diet.

Reduce the cost of a nutritious diet through the seasons

The development of the milk and agricultural sectors can also significantly contribute to improving the nutritional status of populations, if they are designed specifically to support the poorest and take into consideration their economic constraints. Micronutrient supplementation can also be more effectively used to fill the gap between needs and what is affordable/available in those seasons when a diverse diet is more difficult to achieve.

A fuller understanding of the seasonal fluctuations in accessing nutritious food and the importance of the real fluctuations in household incomes will make it possible to design more effective and appropriate policy and programming responses to tackle hunger.

Notes

1 The cost of staple food is calculated on the basis of the cost of millet provided by official SIMA (Système d'information sur les marchés agricoles – Government of Niger) data and assuming that on average people need to consume 2100kcal per day, i.e. 0.607kg of millet per day.
2 The cost of basic expenditures has been calculated according to the household economy assessment presented in Holt *et al.*, 2009.
3 1 Fcfa (or XOF) is about $US0.002, so 10 Fcfa is about US$0.02.
4 Based on the estimated average needs of 2100kcal per person per day.
5 For the methodology of collection of income data and other HEA findings, see Save the Children and FEG, 2008b.
6 Data on local food consumption patterns are collected through interviews with 30 mothers per zone and per wealth group. More details on the methodology of this data collection are available in Save the Children, 2009.
7 Plumpy'doz and Sprinkles are two innovative products designed to supplement food intake and reduce micronutrient deficiencies. Plumpy'doz is a nutritional supplement for growing children, in paste form, providing essential micronutrients plus protein and energy. Sprinkles are sachets of micronutrient powder which can easily be sprinkled onto foods prepared in the home.
8 The purchasing power is expressed as a ratio between millet prices (source: SIMA, government of Niger) and daily wages (collected by Save the Children's team in Tessaoua district).

11

Modelling seasonality in household income using the Household Economy Approach

Charles Rethman

This chapter illustrates the use of models to predict and analyse seasonality in income and food access. *Modelling* needs to be differentiated from *monitoring*; it aims to find a way of describing the variations in income and expenditure that households *are likely* to experience, given a set of reasonably good data on prevailing conditions and household livelihoods, while monitoring analyses and reports on actual situations that have occurred. Modelling, therefore, has a predictive ability and the resultant forecasting is useful for planning prevention, mitigation and reactive responses against future occurrences. Not only does modelling provide a predictive ability but it also helps practitioners try out different scenarios at relatively low cost; informed planners can then better devise and weigh up contingencies and programmes that are as efficient as possible in assisting those most in need. Seasonality, with its cyclical patterns, can fortunately be incorporated quite easily into the annual livelihoods models, giving the users and interpreters of the outcomes new temporal detail and resolution.

However, as models are usually built on parameters that are themselves often derived from assumptions, these parameters need to be checked as events unfold, so the model can be adjusted when assumptions are no longer valid or when the parameters change unexpectedly. Models of household income and food security using the Household Economy Approach (HEA) are able to provide a forecast that covers the period of the year ahead but, until recently, the results of these forecasts were always aggregated over the entire year, smoothing out seasonal variations.[1]

Monitoring data, on the other hand, are usually collected at specific intervals and represent the situation at a particular instant or over a short time interval (at most, a month). This makes it difficult to compare the outcomes of a forecast with actual occurrences reported from monitoring data, highlighting the need for the food security and income forecasts to be disaggregated at least into seasonal components. Clearly this will be very useful both for improving the models themselves and for informing the public when acting on the models' predictions, so that important seasonal issues can be examined and addressed.

The Household Economy Approach model for vulnerability over a whole year

The HEA model provides a relationship between household income and household needs, both of which vary seasonally and which are added together and compared. 'Income' can be actual income (money earned, food grown and consumed) and also potential income (such as assets and other 'capitals' that households may draw upon when required). Needs go from the most basic survival needs to those required to sustain and enhance a household's livelihood, to less necessary 'discretionary' or 'luxury' needs.

The Household Economy Approach has been very thoroughly described in two good publications: one for programmers, policymakers and users of the information (Save the Children UK and FEG Consulting, 2008a) and the other for practitioners and analysts (Save the Children UK and FEG Consulting, 2008b). Repeating this is beyond the scope of this paper, except for the sections on analyses that pertain to seasonality.

In practical terms, data for this model are usually some kind of aggregate, and different methodologies have been devised for collecting them. Both probability sample-based surveys and purposive key informant or focus group interviews have been used for this.[2] The model presented here has been designed to work with data collected using semi-structured key informant or focus group interviews. This data collection method usually begins with the definition of a 'livelihood zone', a geographic area defined as being of similar pattern of livelihood. Within each zone, households are clustered by 'wealth groups', which are differentiated primarily on assets. Examples of assets rural households list in their breakdowns are: land, livestock, labour, household goods and tools (this includes items such as carts, bicycles and farming equipment). Household assets determine productive options; for example, land provides for crop growing and pasture, livestock can be sold live, livestock also produce dairy and can be slaughtered for meat, labour (an important household asset) brings grain or cash through piece-work, petty trading or some form of self-employment (such as gathering firewood or making charcoal). Of course, there are inter-linkages between assets and production: livestock proceeds may be used to fund cropping inputs and labour is an essential input for both farming and animal husbandry.

Household production is converted into consumption either directly (when crops grown are consumed, for example) or through economic exchange. Exchanges for food and other essentials sometimes take place as direct barter but more usually they are done by converting production into cash and purchasing the desired items. The key to making the model work is to explore the relationships between assets, production, trade and consumption, paying particular attention to the *strategies* households employ to get the most out of these relationships, given the constraints of their capabilities and the environment. For example, environmental conditions such as soil types and climate, when combined with local capital expenditure and farming methods are only likely to yield a certain amount of production for a given size of land and input of labour, while trading conditions are likely to dictate prices for both sales of produce and purchases of needs.

The investigation is usually done for an annual household spending cycle, the most practical being a *consumption year* – the period running from one harvest to the next. The detailed study that results in a description of these livelihood strategies and the relationships between them is called a *baseline*.

While recognizing that human food needs are complex, the model considers food consumption in terms of *energy*, but makes allowances for other nutrients or food groups by including them in a *minimum non-staple expenditure basket*.[3] Each source of food produced or consumed by a household during the consumption year is then expressed as:

> the percentage of the minimum energy required by an average household for a whole year.

The model uses the average standard requirement of 2,100kcal of energy per person per day.[4] This factors in, approximately, the variations in requirements for different individuals within a standard household.

As an illustration of how a commodity can be converted this way, consider a household producing five standard 50kg sacks of dry maize. These sacks contain around 907,500kcal of food energy. The contribution of these sacks of maize to the household's annual requirement is derived as follows: a household of five people will comprise five consumption units each requiring on average 2,100kcal; hence, we obtain:

Food energy requirement $= 2,100 \times 5$ *people* $\times 365$ *days* $= 3,832,500kcal$

907,500kcal divided by 3,832,500kcal is 0.236 or approximately 24 per cent.

All food sources are expressed this way in order to bring them into a 'common currency' and allow for them to be added together.

In times of stress, which is usually seasonal, households look for ways of expanding their sources of food or cash income; they also reduce less essential consumption to ensure that they can cover their more necessary items, or they switch between consumption and sales of their own produced foodstuffs. Thus, if casual labour is paid for directly with food, households may seek out additional employment or travel further from home in order to get this employment, so that the 'casual employment' source of food is *expanded*. This *expandability* can be thought of as additional *potential* access that can be obtained through adaption or response by the household.

The sum of the baseline access and the expandability are referred to in this paper as 'entitlements' – the sum of the existing and potential income that can be used to meet all basic needs. Put algebraically:

$$E = B + X$$

where E is the projected entitlements of the household, B is their baseline or 'normal' access and X is their expandability. The degree of vulnerability is then the difference between entitlements and needs:

$$V = E - N$$

where V is the vulnerability of the household being analysed and N is the sum of their most essential needs. If V is found to be negative, then households have *missing entitlements* – a potential shortfall in their ability to make the most basic living. If V is positive, households have additional consumption or discretionary expenditure, which they may choose to invest or consume.

However, hazards affect both 'normal' access to food and other needs, as well as the expandability. Therefore, if the hazard is expressed as a *change*, it is multiplied by both baseline access and expandability. Putting this in an algebraic format gives the following formula:

$$E = (B + X) \times H$$

Or, using the algebraic distributive law:

$$E = B + H + X \times H$$

where E is the projected entitlement of the household, B is the baseline access, X is the expandability and H is the hazard or change.

These formulae describe vulnerability in very simple terms; in reality the equation is a much more complex algorithm, since there are multiple sources of food and income, which are interrelated. In addition to providing the sum of 'normal' access, the baseline also describes these important interrelationships and the linkages between different sources; it therefore is the basis of the *livelihood model* and describes households' *livelihood strategies* more completely.

An overriding assumption of any enquiry in household economy is that poor households have finite options for obtaining food and cash. These options almost always come from the following sources: own food crop production consumed or sold, cash crops, own livestock products consumed or sold (dairy and meat), cash or food from labour exchange, food and cash from gifts (including food aid and cash transfer programmes), food from barter, food purchased with cash, cash from livestock sales, cash from self-employment (e.g. collecting building materials, making charcoal, making artefacts, collecting firewood or water), cash from trading or petty trading (e.g. buying and selling), salaries and loans.

With spending, however, households' options are much broader and hence this chapter focuses on necessary spending by poorer households, which can be whittled down to a more manageable number of items. These are: food (staple and non-staple), clothing, small household assets (e.g. utensils), consumables such as soaps and paraffin, tools, inputs for cropping and livestock husbandry, transport (to markets, to outlets for public services such as health and education, to government offices for administrative functions or for public participation), education (where not freely provided), health (where not freely provided), taxes (where paid), repayments on loans, various capital expenditures (such as the purchase of a bicycle, or building materials) and entertainment. These expenditures are further grouped into four categories for analysis: staple, minimum non-staple, essential and discretionary.

Staple expenditure is money spent on the most popular and reasonably priced carbohydrate energy-rich food. This is usually either maize, sorghum, wheat, rice or a tuber such as cassava; occasionally it is a mixture of more than one of these.

Minimum non-staple expenditure includes all the basic minimum needs for survival that are not significant to providing food energy. This includes other macro- and micronutrient-rich foods that are absolutely necessary for survival (usually some greens, a little oil, and a protein food such as legumes), key basic household expenditures on hygiene, clean water (if needed) and, depending on obligations and locally accepted definitions for minimum basic rights, taxes and expenses for services like health and education.

Essential expenditure goes further than the raw survival needs listed in the staple and minimum non-staple categories. It includes: inputs and investments in livelihoods, schooling and health services, some basic assets such as clothing or household goods, and loan repayments.

Lastly, discretionary expenditure is spending on more 'luxurious' items, larger capital investments and entertainment.

How do all these disparate items then come together? Depending on the livelihood zone (which determines productive options and access to markets) and the wealth group being studied (which determines households' starting capital) these different sources and needs are combined with different weightings, but are assembled in more or less the same order.

Starting with food crops, production is either consumed directly into food energy, or is converted into cash and then summed into cash income. The consumed food crops are summed with food obtained from livestock products or obtained through exchange for labour, from gifts or through purchase, either as non-staple items or as the staple. As explained above, food consumption is expressed in terms of the percentage of minimum energy requirements; this way, different foodstuffs are easily summed together. Income sources are summed up and expenditure is broken down into its four main categories: minimum non-staple, staple, essential and discretionary, as explained above. Total income and expenditure must balance,[5] and the staple expenditure divided by the staple purchase price yields the amount of staple purchased in the food sources. If the households were surviving, they must have been eating at least close to or above 100 per cent of their required minimum energy intake.[6]

All of these sources of food and income may be affected simultaneously and to different degrees by hazard events. If they are affected, households are able to respond to these hazards; firstly, they adjust their strategies to minimize wasteful consumption and protect their livelihoods. If this is not enough they then adopt strategies that, although impacting on their livelihoods, will nevertheless protect their lives.

At the time that the analysis is carried out, the hazard for a particular source may be known or it may not be – if the analysis is a forecast, households may only access that particular source in the future. An example could be casual labour that is only available in a future season. Future prices are, of course, not known at present. To obtain the 'future' hazard, *assumptions* need to be made and these are collected together in a *scenario*. The assumptions themselves may be based on models developed for certain hazards; for example, future staple prices can be guessed at by looking at import cost parities if there is a recognized shortage of local staple production.

The model assumes that households maximize their access to food and other minimum requirements first and foremost (they have 'rational behaviour'). How do they do this?

1   Firstly, they can try to increase their direct access to food. They will do this by increasing the consumption of their own crop production (boosting their food intake).
2   Next, they will seek additional labour that is paid for in food.[7]

These two responses have a cost to the household: they lose income from the reduced crop sales and they have to spend extra time not only in doing the extra labour but in seeking it out. The latter is especially important if they are forced to travel further away.

3   Households reduce the consumption of food obtained from livestock products when they are under stress – this is because livestock food calories are worth considerably more than cereal calories (three to five times more), so it makes sense to switch consumption to sales and then to purchase cheaper cereal calories to meet food energy needs. This strategy has been observed with livestock keepers in Somalia and Ethiopia.
4   The same reasoning may apply to some high-value food crops such as legumes and vegetables and, indeed, increased sales of these sorts of crops are often a response to stress.
5   They may also resort to begging. Payment from this is often easier to obtain from community members in kind than as cash.

These five assumptions are summarized below in the first five rows in Table 11.1 on food sources. The options of switching livestock product sales as well as high-value and low-value crop sales are also summarized in Table 11.2.

Cash income from food crop sales and livestock product sales are summed with that from cash crop sales, asset sales and other sources. The amounts of cash

TABLE 11.1 Food sources, responses households can make to maximize those sources and the hazards each source may encounter

Baseline food source	Response to stress	Hazard
Own crops (low value)	Reduce sales, increase consumption	Reduced production due to climate factors, pests, lack of inputs
Own crops (high value)	Increase sales to use money to purchase cheaper calories from other foods	Reduced production due to climate factors, pests, lack of inputs. Lower producer prices, production affected by capital depletion because of previous hazards
Livestock production	Increase sales rather than consumption, because livestock commodities are more expensive and can be used to buy cheaper staples	Diseases, producer price drops, unsustainable off-take that took place previously
Food barter (usually for labour)	Seek more labour, possibly further afield	Reduced work opportunities, lower wage rates
Food from gifts	Increase begging and requests	Donors are unable to continue support, food aid programmes cut
Non-staple purchase	Reduce expenditure on expensive items to minimum	Price increases (common) and supply shortages (rare)
Staple purchases	Increase purchase of the cheapest energy source	Price increases and occasional supply shortages

obtained from each source are also each independently affected by the hazard events. Households respond to hazard events by increasing production from cash-earning sources. Again, there is usually a progression from strategies that have little cost to those that can be seriously destructive to livelihoods in the long run.

6   Hence, the preferred initial response options are activities such as seeking extra casual labour, collecting more firewood or making more charcoal – activities which require additional time and effort from the productive members. There are also hidden costs and restrictions, especially with the self-employment options: the trees lost in firewood or charcoal production result in serious environmental damage which can affect the whole community and governments may step in to limit these options. More seriously, prices in local markets for these products may fall dramatically with the glut caused by increased production and a fixed or inelastic demand. Households may also request assistance from relatives through remittances or they may increase the amount of petty trading they do.

7 Another option is the sale of livestock. This is an attractive option if house-holds have significant herds and the market is good. If, however, herd sizes are smaller there could be different levels of sales: sustainable sales where the number sold will not impact on overall herd size as reproduction rates will cover the off-take; stress sales where the number sold will reduce the overall herd size but nevertheless recovery will be possible as the main breeding stock are preserved; and distress sales where vital breeding stock are lost.

These two assumptions are summarized in Table 11.2 on cash income sources, which also summarizes the switching of food crops (low- and high-value), cash crop and livestock product sales, discussed in assumptions 1, 3 and 4 above.

8 Next, households can reduce all their expenditure on discretionary items, switching the money spent to staple purchase.
9 Lastly, if the use of all their discretionary expenditure is insufficient to enable them to meet their requirements, they will then have to use some of their essential expenditure to meet their staple food energy requirements. This has important implications in terms of the trade-off between short-term survival and longer-term livelihood security. Households may be sacrificing better-quality foodstuffs, access to education and health services or inputs for the next farming season in order to ensure their survival. When they use their essential expenditure in this way, we refer to the portion of essential expenditure switched to staple purchase as a *livelihoods missing entitlement* – meaning that their entitlements are insufficient to maintain or promote their livelihoods.
10 If the money used on discretionary expenditure and on essential expenditure is insufficient to meet their food energy needs, households have a missing entitlement. They cannot use their minimum non-staple because it is, like the staple requirement, a minimum.

These last three assumptions are summarized in Table 11.3, and they also link to the non-staple and purchase sources of food in Table 11.1.

Hence, when the model is applied to help forecast food insecurity, all necessary expenditure is channelled into staple purchase until minimum food energy needs are met. If the staple purchase, when added with other food sources, is unable to supply household energy needs, practitioners are able to pronounce the difference as a *missing entitlement*. As explained in the formulae above, 'entitlements' (the sum of items available for direct consumption plus income and potential income from assets and activities) are thus less than households' basic requirements.

This livelihood model has been conveniently condensed into an algorithm, which can be coded into a user-friendly format to allow practitioners to make the calculations quickly. The most popular example of this algorithm in practical use is the analytical spreadsheet developed by Mark Lawrence of the Food Economy Group.[8] Another sophisticated example is the RiskMap software, a standalone application that works with its own data file or database.[9]

TABLE 11.2 Cash income sources, responses households can make to maximize those sources and the hazards each source may encounter

Baseline income source	Response to stress	Hazard
Lower-value food crops	Reduce sales, increase consumption	Reduced production due to climate factors, pests, lack of inputs. Lower purchase prices during harvesting season, when household is more likely to sell.
Higher-value food crop sales	Increase sales for extra cash to buy cheap calories	Reduced production due to climate factors, pests, lack of inputs, etc. Purchasing prices may be low due to local gluts in sales
Cash crop sales	Usually nothing or very little can be done	Reduced production and low producer prices
Livestock product sales	Increase sales rather than consumption, because livestock commodities are more expensive and can be used to buy cheaper staples	Diseases, producer price drops, unsustainable off-take that took place previously that reduced herd size, low producer prices – sometimes due to local or temporal gluts
Livestock sales	Increase number of animals sold – there are different levels: balancing herds where the household can recover from the herd reduction within a year (livelihoods preservation) and unsustainable emergency sales (survival) where the household reduces its herd to the most minimal number of breeding stock	Crop hazards are often covariant with livestock hazards: poor condition of animals means they fetch a low price, market gluts caused by panic selling reduces prices, herds may not have recovered from the previous crisis
Casual labour for cash	Seek more labour, possibly further afield	Reduced work opportunities, lower wage rates
Cash from gifts, remittances	Increase begging and requests	Donors are unable to continue support, cash transfer programmes cut
Self-employment (collection and manufacture-type) activities	Increase intensity and duration of the activity to maximize production	Often the increase in the activity reduces availability of the raw materials so more time is required to collect them. Local and temporal gluts usually lower producer prices as well
Petty trading	Increase activities	Local markets squeezed by income shortages, purchase prices may rise and capital for goods purchases may be reduced. Overall margins reduced

TABLE 11.3 Expenditure, responses households can make to minimize waste and the hazards each source may encounter

Baseline food source	Response to stress	Hazard
Discretionary	Reduce it to zero, if need be	
Essential	Reduce to zero, if absolutely required for survival	Lack of availability of some items (because lower demand makes them unprofitable to supply) but more often purchase price rises
Minimum non-staple	None possible, although households may choose to reduce an item instead of reducing staple	Reduced availability and higher purchase prices
Staple (linked directly to staple purchases in Table 11.1 above)	Increase purchase of the cheapest energy source as much as possible	Price increases and occasional supply shortages

The analytical spreadsheets are in widespread use and have been used to great effect in forecasting hunger in a number of countries; these countries now include but are not limited to: Malawi, Swaziland, Lesotho, Botswana, Namibia, Tanzania, Somalia and Ethiopia. They come as Microsoft Excel workbooks that are readily copied and managed as files and present the analysis in a transparent and standardized format to trained practitioners. Since they are spreadsheets, they can be readily expanded and additional analysis can be added on to them without the need for specialized programming skills.

Household Economy Approach practitioners already collect information on seasonality

The model for the whole year that has been described above shows that vulnerability to hunger and food security is complex and that capturing information on it requires much more than just tracking variables. The Household Economy Approach recognizes this and, as a framework, helps practitioners identify the minimum dataset necessary for useful food security and vulnerability prediction and monitoring systems to be set up. Central to this is the construction of the baselines – the robustness of which influences many years of repeated modelling and analysis.

Practitioners in the field have found that for purposes of obtaining large-scale analyses of broad hazards and shocks, this complex information is more easily collected through purposively sampled semi-structured interviews with focus groups, rather than through random probability sampled individual respondents.[10]

Granted, respondents in a purposively sampled semi-structured interview do not have an equal chance of being picked for presenting their livelihoods, but this is compensated for by them quickly providing the enquiry with much detail and analysis upfront, which is difficult to obtain from a simple questionnaire-type survey.

To get the required quality of detail and analysis in semi-structured interviews for a good baseline requires skill; in particular the interviewer needs to triangulate the information collected by making things add up in different ways. Food must have added up to something close to or more than the 2,100kcal per person per day average energy requirement – otherwise the respondents would not be talking to the inquirer. Income must balance with expenditure and crop production figures must tie in with known yields and farming methods for that area. Significantly, household members' time and labour output must balance with production. Labour output is assigned to different activities and these activities all take place at different times of the year.

Practitioners collect this information on activities by drafting a *seasonal calendar*, an example of which is shown in Figure 11.1. Without the seasonal calendar, the rigour of the baseline study would be in question, so further analysis would be compromised. This chapter shows that the seasonal calendar can be made to do more: it allows skilled analysts to include a seasonality component in their forecasts of food insecurity.

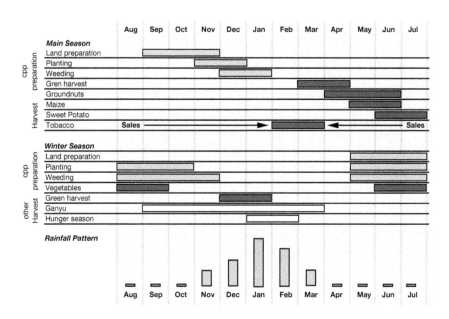

Source: Malawi Vulnerability Assessment Committee (2005: 37)

FIGURE 11.1 Example of a seasonal calendar from Malawi

Why include seasonality?

Seasonality can thus be incorporated into the analysis model using existing information. Presently, existing baselines are made for the entire consumption year, so the seasonal model breaks down the whole year's analysis into its constituent seasons.

This is useful enough for the following reasons:

- If there are missing entitlements, implementing agencies need to know when to act; sometimes the gaps may only appear after some months or sometimes they may be immediate. If the missing entitlements are early, this information will encourage faster action.
- Monitoring data that are collected continuously are rarely presented aggregated for a whole year because they are not held in much value this way.[11] Rather, data that become available at a particular time are compared with a forecast. More realistic comparisons will thus be made if the forecast is broken down into a set of discrete, shorter periods. Seasonal forecasts are thus a closer representation of current household access to food and income than forecasts that present an average for a whole year.
- Food aid responses are usually one-dimensional and are managed badly. Rations are fixed (at about 75 per cent of a beneficiary's needs) and often do not even vary with household size. As the year progresses and the tonnage delivered increases, more beneficiaries are added to the list, creating an impression of 'scaling-up'. Seasonality information shows that at a particular time, more beneficiaries may need less food or vice versa, and whether the 'scaling up' should be in terms of ration sizes or beneficiary numbers, or a mixture of the two.

Extending the HEA model

To keep the analysis simple and manageable the model splits the usual annual consumption year (consumption years are defined as running from the start of the main staple crop harvest in a year to just before the start of the next main staple crop harvest)[12] into four equal seasons of three months. A more detailed breakdown by, say, month, is possible and may in fact be easier to construct from the available data; however, the seasonal approach will be described for simplicity here.

The first part of extending the model is to split the staple purchase price into its seasonal variation. This is then used to calculate the *weighted average annual staple purchase price*, which is used in the annual analysis. This is shown in the following equation:

$$Py = (P_{s1}, P_{s2}, P_{s3}, P_{s4})$$

where Py is the weighted average staple purchase price for the whole year and $P_{s1}...P_{s4}$ are the average staple purchase prices for each of the four seasons.

Next, the average contribution of each source of food to the whole year is multiplied by four, since there are four seasons.

The sources of food are then placed into two categories: *lump-sum* sources and *stipend* sources. *Lump-sum* sources are those sources that the household obtains as a single lump sum once or twice a year. They may then draw down on the source at their discretion, carrying over the uncompleted balance to the next season, until the 'lump' is all finished. Examples of lump-sum sources are grains obtained from harvests; characteristically, lump-sum sources are relatively easily stored. *Stipend* sources are those sources that are available in smaller quantities for a limited time, and must be consumed or sold or else they will be lost. Dairy, non-grain vegetables and harvested tubers are typical of this category (they go bad if not consumed fairly quickly). Food obtained as payment for labour, although usually a grain, is treated in this analysis as *stipend*. This is because it is paid out in relatively small amounts at regular intervals; it is effectively rationed.

The same breakdown applies to sources of income; cash from livestock (or other large asset) sales and cash crop sales are examples of *lump-sum* sources, while cash from casual labour, gifts or remittances are usually *stipend* sources.

These are the steps for a seasonal breakdown:

1   The practitioner breaks down the stipend sources of food for the first three seasons according to the pattern of availability given in the seasonal calendar. The fourth season is calculated automatically. For example, milk production may be double during the wet season what it is during the dry. So, for example, if milk contributes 12 per cent of average annual food needs and the consumption year begins in the first dry quarter the breakdown will be as follows:

$$Milk_1 = \frac{12 \times 4}{6} = 8\% \ (dry \ season)$$

$$Milk_2 = \frac{12 \times 4}{6} = 8\% \ (dry \ season)$$

$$Milk_3 = \frac{2 \times 12 \times 4}{6} = 16\% \ (dry \ season)$$

The fourth quarter is calculated automatically from the average and the other three quarters; in this example it is also 16 per cent (it is also a wet season quarter).

If, when looking at a single quarter, the sum of all the stipend food sources is 100 per cent of food needs for that quarter, then the lump-sum food sources need not be used. They are thus carried forward to the next quarter. This, however, is rarely the case in real life.

2   To break down the lump-sum food sources, first check on the seasonal calendar when the harvest for each of the lump-sum sources actually begins. The main staple grain's harvest usually determines the start of the consumption year, so this is taken as being available from the beginning of quarter one. Multiply the yearly average of each of the lump-sum foods that are available from the first quarter and sum that product together with the first quarter's allocation of the stipend food sources. If this sum exceeds 100 per cent, then a proportion of each lump-sum food source must be removed to the next quarter until the total for all food sources in the first quarter is 100 per cent.

3   If the sum of both the stipend and lump-sum food sources is less than 100 per cent in the first quarter, the household will need to purchase food in that quarter.

In order to purchase, the household will need to have cash. This needs to be broken down seasonally as follows:

4   Break down the stipend sources of cash into each quarter.

5   Break down the minimum non-staple expenditure requirement into each quarter. The minimum non-staple expenditure items are all stipend expenditures.

6   Break down the essential expenditure requirement into each quarter. These are usually treated as stipend expenditures, although they may be lump-sum; that is to say, households may be able to defer larger payments (such as debt repayments, annual fees or taxes, etc.) to the next quarter.

The next step is tricky; it requires some judgement on options households may employ to maximize availability and access later on in the year versus the current season. To some extent this is governed by household behaviour and budgeting processes. There is an important assumption in the modelling process described in this chapter: *it is assumed that households have foresight to recognize future shortages and will take every means possible to eliminate them.* Households, therefore, are expected to follow the most rational choices that maximize their opportunities for meeting their needs. Of course, this is very hard for individual households to actually manage to do in practice.

7   If households have sufficient income to meet their minimum non-staple, essential expenditure and staple purchases for that quarter, then there is no need for them to bring in their lump-sum cash sources, so they will carry these over to the next quarter. In addition, the surplus cash will be carried over to the next quarter.

8   If the households have sufficient income to meet their minimum non-staple and staple purchases, but not their essential expenditure, then the lump-sum cash sources will need to be cashed in. Often, this is a large amount of income and so the excess will need to be carried over as expenditure to the next

quarter. However, if the sum of all the cash sources, stipends for the quarter and the lump-sums, are insufficient to meet their staple needs, minimum non-staple *and* essential purchases, households are then forecast to have a *seasonal livelihoods missing entitlement.*

9 If the households have insufficient income to meet their minimum non-staple and staple purchases, they are then forecast to have a *seasonal survival missing entitlement*, in addition to their seasonal livelihoods missing entitlement.

10 Repeat this process for the second and third quarter. Whatever food remains in the last quarter, if any, will be consumed.

The algorithm is transferred onto the analytical spreadsheet as an additional component. By doing so, the existing yearly analysis is broken down into four equal seasons. Some features of this extended spreadsheet are:

• The analytical spreadsheet seasonal component is self-zeroing. It automatically adjusts the staple purchase source of food to ensure households reach their needs, given that they have the cash available to do so. If they are able to exceed their needs from all the sources excluding staple purchases, then the staple purchase food source becomes negative (effectively, it becomes staple sales), giving households more income to carry over to the next quarter.

• As with the analytical spreadsheet for the whole year, the seasonality component models options and possibilities, it *does not model behaviour*. As such, it looks at what 'ideal' households would do to make ends meet and whether they are able to do so; it does not take into account the fact that households may over-consume one season (for example, after the harvest) and then be forced to under-consume later (due to behaviour or preferences).

• If there are no missing entitlements in the analysis for the whole year, then the seasonality extension makes sure that there are no missing entitlements during each season. The staple purchase source of food will adjust itself to make sure this is so. This may seem unrealistic because we know that households have seasonal shortfalls even in good years, but the point is to model households' options in future, not to describe a condition as it unfolds. Again the assumption is that households spread their consumption to meet their needs; this may not actually be the case in reality but the analysis is seeking to inform us on households' *options and possibilities, not behaviour.*

Some interesting outcomes

The most interesting result to come out of using this seasonality model of a household economy forecast analysis is that the timing of the periods of greatest vulnerability varies according to severity of the hazard. In a 'normal' year, households struggle the most or go hungry in the months just before the harvest. This is the usual hunger season and it is a period where the poorest households depend almost entirely on casual labour.

However, in hazard situations (and depending on the nature of the hazard), this hunger period may shift. In an area where people are dependent on rainfed agriculture and the rainfall pattern is unimodal, if crop production takes a particularly severe knock, both food and income at the start of the consumption year are heavily reduced. The consequence is that when food crops run out there is very little money for purchase, either. The ensuing dry season offers little in the way of prospects, as any potential employers and purchasers are protecting their expenditure and are less inclined to spend on home crafts, extracted or collected items like charcoal and firewood, casual labour or small livestock. These are some of the only things that can boost incomes for the poor. Selling prices for all these commodities and services supplied by the poor may tumble, tightening the pinch. After this difficult dry season, the start of the rains and the ensuing farming season with its attendant labour opportunities actually offer relief – even if wages may be depressed when compared with staple prices – at least there is something to be done.

The charts below illustrate what happens to sources of food when a progressively severe crop production hazard is applied to the livelihoods of two different wealth groups, described by key informants as the 'worse-off' and the 'middle' wealth groups, in the Central Region of Malawi. This is a region where cereal and tobacco farming are both very prominent. The percentages on the ordinates in the graph represent the proportions that each food source contributes towards 2,100kcal of energy requirement. This analysis includes adjustments to income prices and purchase prices as well.

Initially, a situation where there are no crop losses is considered. The 'worse-off' wealth group households run out of their own-produced food in the third quarter, replacing it with purchases and food from casual labour (called *ganyu* in Malawi). The 'middle' wealth group households still consume their own-produced food in the fourth quarter, supplementing it with purchases and some casual labour.

In a drought situation, cash crop performance may not be as bad as that of food crops; hence, in the following series of graphs, cash crop losses are roughly half of food crop losses.

In Figure 11.2, a mild failure of summer crops is considered. The 'worse-off' wealth group households run out of own-produced food from their summer harvest in the second quarter, while 'middle' wealth group households do so in the third quarter. Notice that up to this point, all households can, by maximizing their food and income sources, still reach their basic needs.

Things go below the minimum threshold for households in the 'worse-off' wealth group when they lose one third of their summer food crops and a sixth of their tobacco; casual labour and purchases dominate the last two quarters but they are not enough for them to make ends meet. Their own-produced summer food crops run out in the second quarter. Households from the 'middle' wealth group now rely entirely on casual labour and purchases (purchases are the greater share) in the last quarter, their own-produced summer food crops running out during the third quarter.

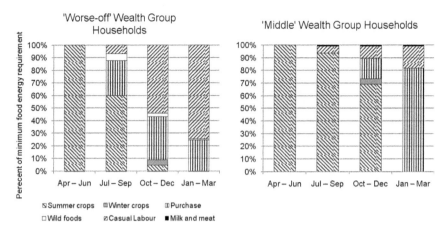

Source: Malawi Vulnerability Assessment Committee (2009a)

FIGURE 11.2 Mild failure: lose 13% tobacco and 25% main summer food crops

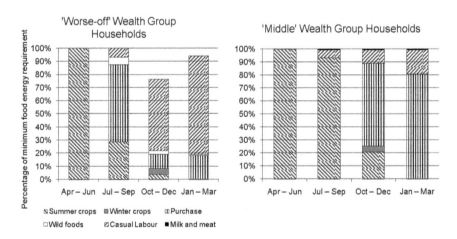

Source: Malawi Vulnerability Assessment Committee (2009b)

FIGURE 11.3 Heavy failure: lose 20% tobacco and 40% main summer food crops

In an extreme crop failure shown in Figure 11.4, households from the 'worse-off' wealth group are in serious trouble because their own-produced crops do not even last them through the first quarter – they are forced to purchase at that time. This drains what little money they have left and they have nothing during the cold, dry months from July to September. This is a time of the year of low economic activity and scarce employment opportunities. Weak demand for crafts or extracted products from self-employment activities will only heighten the entitlement shortfall.

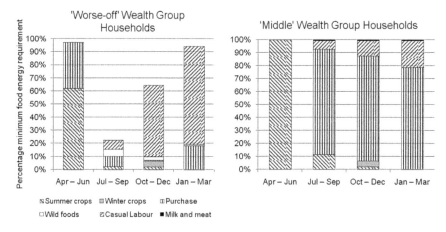

Source: Malawi Vulnerability Assessment Committee (2009c)

FIGURE 11.4 Extreme failure: lose 40% tobacco and 70% of main food crops

What is noticeable in the model is that as summer crop losses go from 'heavy' to 'extreme', the worst quarter is not the last; at least there is casual labour available during that season. As is shown in Figure 11.4, the second and third quarters – winter months – are when 'worse-off' wealth group households have the biggest entitlement shortfalls. The 'middle' wealth group households are still able to make ends meet, largely through purchases from their better income base.

The tendency of international relief agencies is to steadily build up the deliveries of food and other aid over the seasons, maximizing it during the last, so-called 'hunger season'. The reasons are often to do with the time it takes for drafting and securing appeals, moving bulky perishable commodities over the high seas and across difficult or expensive land corridors, as well as the belief that the worst will only come at the end. Unsurprisingly then, if food distributions do start but the amounts and the targeted beneficiaries are targeted very narrowly, there will be large numbers of hungry onlookers at the distribution sites. This is exactly what was reported in September 2005 in Malawi during the second, winter season of a year of extreme crop failure.[13]

The analysis therefore shows that in exceptionally bad years for certain types of livelihood the season of want is not what may typically be imagined. In the case of this livelihood system it is imperative to begin humanitarian assistance *early* and the current practice of 'scaling up over the year' is at best inadequate. The analysis also places an additional burden on information providers and analysts; in bad years, the situation forecast needs to take place *earlier* – well before the harvest – so that implementing agencies have time to react. Typically, forecasts in southern Africa are made around May–June (during the first quarter) but in an extremely bad year, such as the 2005–06 consumption year in southern Africa, this will need to be moved forward to February–March. Fortunately, the evidence of a pending large-scale disaster is normally strong early on as well.

Conclusion

The livelihood models developed using the Household Economy Approach do lend themselves well to seasonal breakdowns, thanks to the rich details routinely collected by practitioners during a baseline or reference enquiry on the different periods and quantities of activities undertaken by the households in the studies.

These data can be used to extend the model from presenting results as year aggregates into at least seasonal aggregates or even shorter periods, such as months. A variation on the year aggregate analysis spreadsheet has been developed that enables practitioners, using their existing seasonal datasets, to provide outcomes that are split over seasons. This spreadsheet has an algorithm that, once users have split up the *stipend* sources of food, income or expenditure into their seasonal components, then automatically adjusts the *lump-sum* sources to maximize access to food and the most basic needs. *Stipend* sources are those sources that are available at certain times but must be consumed immediately or within a short period (such as milk or dairy production), whereas *lump-sum* sources are those that can be stored and carried over. In this way, the model is auto-zeroing; if there is no missing entitlement on average for the whole year, the model 'finds' ways of getting one season to 'cover for another'. It does not try to model behaviour – it is looking for constraints and limitations for households; it assumes they make decisions on consumption that are in their best possible interests for the whole year.

Applying the model to existing livelihood patterns shows some interesting results regarding the seasons of hunger for progressively worsening hazards. When a hazard is not there or is mild, the 'hunger season' is usually at the end of the consumption year, just before the next harvest. However, as the hazard becomes more severe, the 'hunger' season also shifts. For example, when crop failure occurred in the Central Region of Malawi, the most hungry quarter of the year shifted from the fourth to the second, highlighting the need for relief programmes to be implemented quickly and not scaled up gradually through the year as is current practice.

Good seasonal breakdowns also help model outcome projections to be compared with real-time monitoring data a lot more easily. This helps to verify and calibrate the model.

Notes

1 Practitioners do keep seasonality in mind when conducting their analyses but this is normally lost when results are presented to the public and compared.
2 There has been much discussion about the reliability, rigour and usefulness of these different methods, but this discussion is beyond the scope of this chapter. See Save the Children UK and FEG Consulting (2008a: pp93–100; p127).
3 The minimum non-staple category also includes other critical non-food expenditure in addition to non-staple foods, such as health, education and some household items such as soap, fuel, etc.

4 2,100kcal is an internationally accepted minimum energy requirement per person per day. It is based on the nutritional energy requirements of a standard population with a standard distribution of ages and genders.

5 If income and expenditure do not balance, discretionary expenditure is adjusted in the model until they do. Loans count as additional income, while debt repayments count as expenditure. The 'softness' of the debt determines which category of expenditure the repayments are listed under – usually it is in the essential category.

6 In practice, poor households in the poorest countries have a food intake that is consistently about five to ten per cent below this minimum requirement. Elsewhere, or among wealthier households, intake may exceed the minimum by about twenty per cent.

7 Labour for food is usually preferred in times of stress as food prices often rise well above cash wage rates during times of shortage. However, households are often constrained by the amount of labour they can find and are usually condemned to accept whatever is offered to them.

8 The Household Economy Approach Analytical Spreadsheet, developed by Mark Lawrence of the Food Economy Group, is a spreadsheet 'template' with formulae already included so that users need only insert their baseline, expandability and hazard data to get a calculated outcome. The analytical spreadsheet also provides some useful graphs of the outcomes.

9 This has been constructed by John Seaman under Save the Children and further developed by Charles Rethman and Zangaphee Chimombo under Save the Children and the Malawi Vulnerability Assessment Committee. The latest version of this software can be downloaded from the Zombasoft website at www.zombasoft.com/node/21.

10 Of course, the information can be collected through random samples of individuals as well and the Approach does not specify which method should be used. The question of which method to use is best answered by looking at the *purpose* of the enquiry and practical considerations such as cost, speed of data collection and analysis and coverage. If precise figures in a histogram format are required and the coverage is smaller, then a random sample-type survey may be preferred.

11 Users are much more interested in 'peaks' and 'troughs', rather than single average values. This is because the peaks and troughs are much more likely to result in action.

12 This is the case for farmers. The main staple harvest usually comes at the end of the main rainy season – so the consumption year runs from the start of the main dry season after the harvest until the end of the next rainy season. It may differ for pastoralists and livestock-keepers as the consumption year begins when their animals fatten up and produce more dairy, that is, at the start of the rainy season not the end.

13 See Action Against Hunger Spain and the Ministry of Health and Population Nutrition Unit, *Sentinel Site Surveillance Monthly Bulletins* for the months of August 2005 up to March 2006. Also, the Ministry of Agriculture and Food Security, *Food and Nutrition Security Joint Task Force Plenary Committee Meeting* minutes, September (2005) and *Food and Nutrition Security Joint Task Force Humanitarian Response Sub-Committee Meeting* minutes (September 2005).

12

Re-tooling for seasonality

Seasonally sensitive disaster risk assessment in Ethiopia

Tanya Boudreau and Mark Lawrence

Introduction

Encoded in the definition of food security is an explicit requirement for seasonal analysis. In its simplest form the definition refers to ensured access to sufficient food for all people at *all times* (World Bank, 1986). The goal of humanitarian and development assistance – to protect and support lives and livelihoods – presupposes that we know when productive activities occur throughout the year so we can: ensure timely support; avoid imposing unsustainable labour or investment demands at critical times of the year; ensure aid is delivered during periods when it will be of most use; and create the biggest gains with the least harm. Achieving the first Millennium Development Goal – to eliminate extreme poverty and hunger – rests, therefore, on our capacity to be able to adequately address the analytical requirements associated with obtaining this understanding of seasonality.

Furthermore, we need to understand seasonal access in the context of a constantly changing external world, where multiple hazards such as price shocks, increasingly unpredictable weather patterns and conflict-induced market disruptions, are the new norm. Reaching Millennium Development Goal One thus also compels us to take into account seasonal fluctuations (intra-annual variability) in the context of ongoing disaster risks (inter-annual shocks). Seasonality determines people's access to food, and disasters undermine this access. There is general agreement on the need to make sure that our development interventions achieve their desired effects without putting people at additional risk by unintentionally increasing seasonal vulnerabilities to unforeseen hazards (UNDP, 2004, p15).

So why is it that seasonal variability typically fails to get addressed adequately in ongoing development and disaster risk programming? One answer is that the massive amount of information required to capture the complexity involved when we disaggregate livelihoods along seasonal lines exceeds the bandwidth of most existing analysis systems. Taking seasonal variability into account in the context of disaster risk assessment requires that we characterize people's vulnerability to different hazards not just on an annual basis but on an intra-annual basis. In the case of somewhere like Ethiopia, where there are at least 170 distinct livelihood zones, adding seasonality into the already complex mix required to track the effects of inter-annual shocks increases by a factor of 12 the amount of data that needs to be processed on an ongoing basis. This can overload the analytical capacity of any system unless appropriate tools for streamlining and managing these data are in place.

This chapter introduces a tool called the Livelihood Impact Analysis Spreadsheet (LIAS), developed in the context of Ethiopia's Disaster Risk Management and Food Security programme to help track changes in food and overall livelihood security on a seasonal basis. In the first part of the chapter we provide a brief background on the context in which risk assessment and analysis are taking place in Ethiopia. In this section we also introduce and discuss the LIAS and its use in this context. The second part of the chapter focuses on how seasonal analyses can improve decision-making in the disaster risk reduction sphere in Ethiopia, pointing out a number of seasonally specific programming conclusions.

Background

The Ethiopia context

Disasters in Ethiopia have been largely 'extensive' in nature, rather than 'intensive'. 'Extensive risk' is defined by the International Strategy on Disaster Risk (ISDR) as 'The widespread risk associated with the exposure of dispersed populations to repeated or persistent hazard conditions of low or moderate intensity, often of a highly localized nature, which can lead to debilitating cumulative disaster impacts' (UNISDR, 2009, p6). As a result, the disaster management system has had to orient itself around picking up on a wide range of potential threats, and sifting through the noise to distinguish between small hazards that have big effects, and big hazards that have small effects (Boudreau, 2009, p7).

What this means in practice is that a disaster risk assessment system in Ethiopia needs to take into account and make operational what Amartya Sen so clearly described in his ground-breaking work on famine – the fact that people's livelihoods are a complex web of interdependent pathways (Sen, 1981). Household economies are linked to community networks of social, political and economic exchange, which are further connected to an ever-widening set of regional, national and global systems. One disruption along the path can lead to unforeseen effects many miles away. Thus, food crises are almost never the result of production failures alone, but of a combination of 'entitlement' failures. And since people's access to food is mediated by their reliance on different means of ownership, which in turn are based on accepted entitlement relations, understanding who has access to food, and who will lose this access in the face of different threats, rests on a rigorous investigation of the network of pathways that connect households to each other and to these entitlements.

Furthermore, these entitlement systems frame the seasonal options people have for securing food and cash income, and it is the repeated breakdown in access at certain times of year that results in the type of famines that have affected Ethiopia. The relatively recent example of widespread food crisis in 2002/2003, when over 11 million people were identified as in need of food assistance, underscores this point. The crisis was brought on by the consecutive failures of both of the seasonal rains (*belg* and *meher*)[1] when households had not yet fully recovered from the drought in 1999/2000. With declining crop production, seasonal access to cash from agricultural labour contracted and seasonal migratory labour – an important stopgap measure for many poor households in the famine-prone areas of the country – dropped off (Government of Ethiopia/UN, 2002; FEWS NET, 2002).

This recognition of the importance of understanding access (as opposed to just recording availability) led the government of Ethiopia to engage in a five-year consultative process starting in 2000, resulting in the establishment of the Livelihoods Integration Unit (LIU) in 2006, a project funded by USAID. The objective of the unit is to build capacity within the government's early warning system to take into consideration the types of entitlements identified by Sen, and at the same time to analyse how the relative reliance on one or another entitlement changes households' vulnerability to various natural and man-made hazards. The analytical framework that was chosen to implement this decision is called the Household Economy Approach (HEA) (Save the Children and FEG, 2008b; see also Rethman, this book).

The LIU's analytical framework

A brief description of HEA is necessary in order to understand the role that the LIAS plays in improving the capacity of the government to carry out ongoing seasonally specific disaster risk assessment. HEA is an analytical framework developed over 15 years ago to help agencies better take into account the various ways that people are affected by different kinds of shocks and, more specifically, to understand how these shocks translate into seasonal crises of food access that can result in famine.

At the heart of HEA is the contention that in order to predict the effects of any hazard or set of hazards in a bad year, it is necessary to first be able to understand the ways that people piece together their livelihoods in normal years. Not every household will be vulnerable to every hazard, and in order to distinguish between those who will and will not be affected, we need to be able to understand the community structures and relationships that link households to their local economy, and the wider economic systems that link them to the outside world.

Three main components make up HEA:

1   livelihood baselines;
2   hazard analysis;
3   outcome analysis.

In HEA, quantified information from the livelihood baselines is linked to quantified data from the hazard analysis to generate projections about whether people will or will not be able to meet their basic needs. This process – of combining baseline and hazard information to make projections – is referred to in HEA as outcome analysis (LIU, 2009).

The LIAS was developed to facilitate the process of outcome analysis. In Ethiopia, where a complex set of agro-ecological and market factors result in at least 170 discrete livelihood zones, it is essential to have a tool that can organize and make accessible the vast amounts of baseline data, and also to link these data to the changing constellation of ongoing weather and market shocks. The LIAS, and in particular its seasonal functionality, is discussed further below.

The Livelihood Impact Analysis Spreadsheet

The Livelihood Impact Analysis Spreadsheet was developed within the context of the Ethiopian early warning system in response to a growing need to integrate an understanding of livelihoods into the emergency assessment process. The LIAS can be used to help identify the relative importance of different sources of food and income for rural households and to highlight the variable impact of hazards, depending on the household's location and wealth status. These functions are important for a large number of disaster risk assessment purposes. Relevant to note for this chapter, the LIAS also has a seasonal component, allowing analysts to view results month-by-month as opposed to just annually.

So why is it necessary to have a set of dedicated tools on hand to conduct seasonal risk assessment? The answer is found in the sheer amount of data that needs to be processed in a seasonal risk analysis. One *annual* outcome analysis involves roughly 100 calculations per wealth group in each livelihood zone within each district. For Ethiopia, with 600 districts and an average of around two livelihood zones per district, the typical outcome analysis for an annual projection involves approximately 120,000 calculations. With the seasonal dimension added in, the same process needs to be conducted monthly, which increases the number of calculations to 1,440,000. Without having the LIAS on hand to organize and logically link together these different sets of data, it is practically impossible to carry out ongoing risk analysis in Ethiopia on an annual basis, much less a seasonal one.

Quantifying seasonal access in a complicated setting

Seasonality in Ethiopia is a complex affair. Rainfall patterns are caused by both the north–south migration of the Inter-Tropical Convergence Zone and offshore winds originating in the Arabian Sea (LIU, 2010, p12). This results in three distinct rainfall patterns, with a July/August dominant bi-modal regime in the north-east and east, a uni-modal pattern in the southwest, and an April/May dominant bi-modal regime in the southeast. These rainfall patterns translate into four main, and one very minor, seasonal production patterns. It is precisely these seasonal production patterns that form the basis for the variability in the timing of three distinct patterns of hunger seasons across Ethiopia. In *meher*-dominant areas (the north, centre and east of the country), the main hunger season is from June to September/October. In the *belg*-producing areas (mainly in the south) it occurs earlier in the year, from February to May/June. In pastoral areas the main hunger season is from December to February/March. These differences suggest a need to plan more carefully appropriate responses in line with these time periods (LIU, 2010, p18).

It is important to note for the purposes of this chapter that the quantified information on livelihood strategies gathered in Ethiopia is seasonally specific. Every source of food and cash income is time-bound.

For instance, in Degahbur Agropastoral Livelihood Zone in Somali Region, there are two main rainy seasons. The first season occurs from April to May; the second is from October to November. This rainfall is crucial for pasture regeneration, which sustains the camel, cattle and goat/sheep herds upon which people depend. The food value generated by each of these seasons can be captured in quantitative terms. For example, camel milk from the first rainy season supplies 32 per cent of annual food needs for better-off households, 15 per cent of annual needs for middle-income households, and 2 per cent or less for poorer households. Second season camel milk covers 14 per cent, 7 per cent and 1 per cent or less of annual food needs for better-off, middle-income, and poorer households, respectively.

The implications of having these data on hand by season are that it is now possible to analyse how a failure in the *Gu* (April–May) or the *Deyr* rains (October–November) will translate into effects on access to food at the household level. Clearly, the failure of the April to May rains will have a much bigger effect on households' access to milk in this livelihood zone than a failure of the October to November rains. This is important for two reasons: it improves our monitoring precision, and it increases the accuracy and timing of emergency interventions. With a failure of first season rains, we know immediately that, at a minimum, better-off households will lose around a third of their annual food needs, and will have to make this up through livestock sales. Monitoring livestock-grain terms of trade will be particularly important in the subsequent months and a downturn in terms of trade may lead to a need for emergency food aid.

In addition, for each livelihood zone, a detailed seasonal calendar exists, documenting: the main cropping seasons and associated activities (preparation, planting, weeding, harvesting); livestock production seasons (birthing, milking, etc.); main marketing seasons (crops, livestock, labour, etc.); seasonal health risks; and other activities. Figure 12.1 provides an example of a seasonal calendar from Kedida-Badewacho Livelihood Zone in SNNPR. These seasonal calendars contain powerful insights into rural life. It is in their ability to convey something about the complexity of people's lives that we can see the hidden constraints and opportunities that regulate household activities. We are able to understand a little better why households with little labour would be hard pressed during January, February and March, when planting times coincide with the tail end of the coffee harvest, as well as migratory and local labour opportunities. We can see why the second sweet potato harvest is so critical, filling a March–April gap at the height of the hunger season. We can also see why an emergency food intervention, if deemed appropriate, would be a good time to hand out mosquito nets as well.

Putting dynamic risk analysis into action

It is important to be able to store the baseline livelihoods information in a quantified way, as discussed in the Degahbur example above, but in order to conduct a dynamic analysis, we need a tool that links up all the components of HEA. In the LIU, the tool that has been developed to do this is called the Livelihood Impact Analysis Spreadsheet.[2] The LIAS allows programme staff to enter a real or hypothetical problem specification

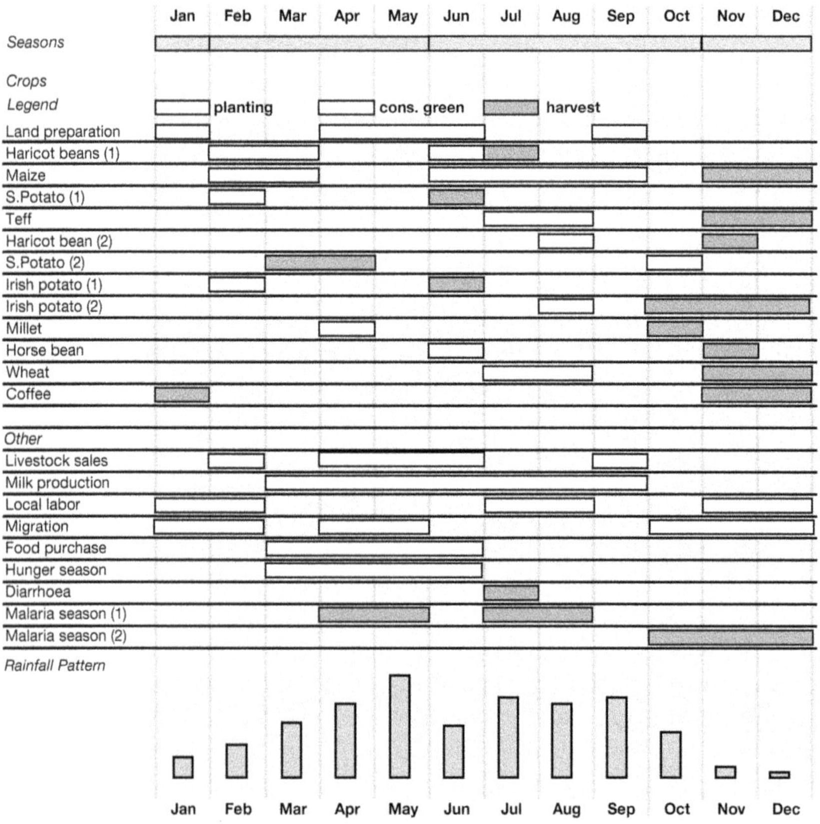

Source of rainfall data: National Meterorological Service Agency (NMSA) Data Archives (long-term average).

Source: Livelihoods Integration Unit, Disaster Risk Management Food Security Sector (DRMFSS), Ministry of Agriculture, Government of Ethiopia

FIGURE 12.1 Seasonal calendar for Kedida-Badewacho Coffee Livelihood Zone

(e.g. a climatic or market shock) and review the outcome in figures and in graphs. The analysis can be used for both emergency response and development planning.

The spreadsheet makes use of HEA protocols to estimate hazard impacts at household level. Three types of data are used for the analysis:

1   livelihoods baseline data, i.e. data on baseline food, income and expenditure;
2   coping strategy data, i.e. estimates of the amounts of additional food and cash income that can be accessed to help deal with a hazard;
3   hazard data, i.e. data that define the problem, including changes in crop and livestock production compared to the baseline, changes in market prices, etc. An annual projection is used to ensure sufficient resources are on hand before a crisis occurs; and in the best of worlds the projection encourages remedial action to avert the worst outcomes.

Seasonal functionality

The LIAS has a seasonal component that combines seasonal calendar data with quantitative food and cash data from the Livelihood Baseline Storage Spreadsheet (LBSS), making it possible to project the seasonal pattern of consumption. Figure 12.2 presents a seasonal consumption graph for a poor household in the Middle Tekeze Livelihood Zone in Tigray Region of Ethiopia. This graph shows the main seasonal output from the LIAS.

The graph also highlights the seasonal importance of own crop production from October through May, followed by exclusive reliance on the market until the harvest starts again the next October. Poor households in this zone meet their survival requirements in the reference year, but are unable, without external assistance, to cover costs to ensure a sustainable livelihood (e.g. agricultural inputs, school fees, health costs, etc.) for six months of the year. This inability to cover all their livelihood requirements even in a relatively good year puts them at enormous risk because they have no buffer to draw on in bad years, and no means of investing in a productive future. The graph also encourages programme planners to consider providing non-food livelihood interventions from February through June to help such households fill this seasonal gap.

The uses of seasonal analysis in Ethiopia

Five specific uses of the type of seasonal analysis facilitated by the LIAS are detailed in this chapter, including:

1   improved contingency and emergency response planning;
2   improved pastoral early warning systems;
3   better nutritional surveillance;
4   customized monitoring indicators and schedules;
5   identification of leverage points for development support.

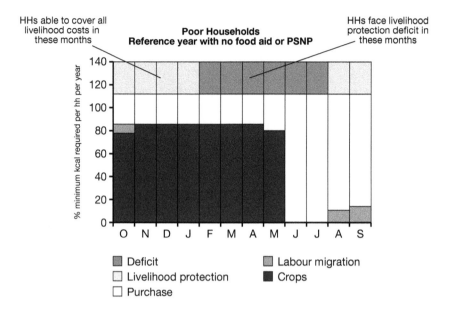

Source: Livelihoods Integration Unit, Disaster Risk Management Food Security Sector (DRMFSS), Ministry of Agriculture, Government of Ethiopia

Note: PSNP is the Productive Safety Net Programme.

FIGURE 12.2 Seasonal consumption graph for Middle Tekeze Livelihood Zone, Tigray, Ethiopia

Contingency and emergency response planning

The graph in Figure 12.2 illustrates a seasonal consumption graph for a reference year. The seasonal component of the LIAS can also be used in scenario analysis to help estimate when deficits are likely to occur, and when people will be able once again to meet their needs on their own – both crucial pieces of information for contingency and emergency response planning. It can also help explain how the timing of a specific hazard can affect the outcome of a household's entire year.

The series of graphs in Figure 12.3 illustrates this point. The first row shows the situation in the reference year for very poor households in Raya Valley Livelihood Zone, with the graph on the left indicating the seasonal pattern of cash income generation, and the graph on the right showing the pattern of seasonal consumption. There are two periods in which agricultural labour is important: weeding/preparation labour income is generated from June through September, while harvest labour contributes to households' cash pool in October and November. Very poor households are able to cover all of their survival requirements in the reference year, but can meet their livelihood protection costs in only one month – October.

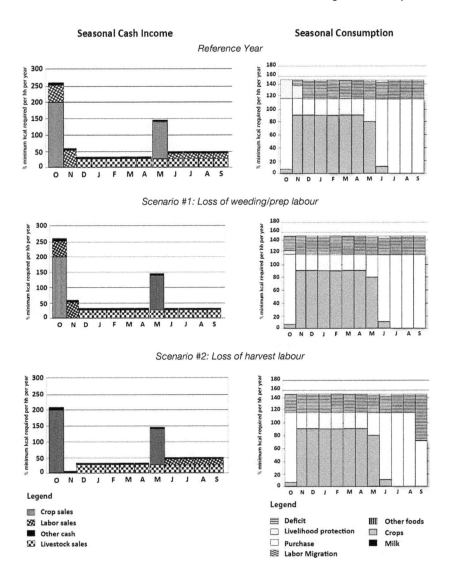

Source: Tanya Boudreau, FEG

FIGURE 12.3 The seasonal effects of income losses in Raya Valley Livelihood Zone, very poor households

Using the LIAS to analyse the effects of a labour disruption, it is possible to see the relative importance of weeding/preparation labour versus harvest labour. With a loss of weeding labour, households continue to cover their survival requirements, although they lose most of their livelihood protection expenditure. However, the picture changes if harvest labour in October/November is lost, resulting in a survival deficit that emerges months later towards the end of the next year's hunger season in September, when all savings and stocks have run out; here is evidence that the cash income households generate in one month can have critical implications for household welfare throughout the year.

While the example above is interesting from a theoretical point of view because it provides a method for isolating the impact of a single hazard, real-life hazards are rarely single events. Figure 12.4 provides an example of how the seasonal analysis was used to analyse the compounded effects of multiple hazards, helping to explain the severe food crisis experienced in parts of Southern Nations, Nationalities and Peoples Region (SNNPR) in 2008.

In this area, a failure of the *belg* rains can lead to rapid declines in nutritional status between January and June, often with very little warning. The seasonal analysis presented in Figure 12.4 shows how this can happen (LIU, 2009).

Failure of the *belg* rains not only resulted in a loss of sweet potatoes, but agricultural labour, upon which poor households depend. The demand for agricultural labour dries up if there are insufficient rains. It was due to this lack of income, in combination with a steep increase in staple prices (associated with the global food

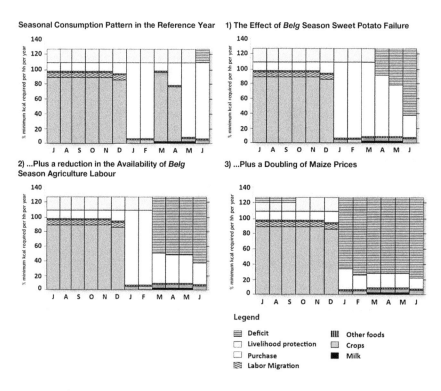

Source: Mark Lawrence, FEG

FIGURE 12.4 Seasonal analysis showing the effects of severe *belg* rain failure on poor households in the Wolayita Maize and Root Crop Livelihood Zone of SNNPR

price crisis) that malnutrition was emerging long before the sweet potato crop would normally have been harvested. The series of graphics shows the effects of this sequence of hazards on poor households in the Wolayita Maize and Root Crop Livelihood Zone in SNNPR, which is located in the *kremt*-dominant bi-modal area in the southwest of the country.

1   **Failure of *belg* season sweet potatoes.** Planted at the end of the *meher* season in October, *belg* season sweet potatoes mature during the *belg* rains and provide an important stopgap between March and May. A failure of this crop is by itself enough to create deficits from April–June, but not before.
2   **Reduced availability of agricultural labour.** Agricultural labour is the single most important source of cash income from January onwards. If the *belg* rains fail, there is less labour available, and the deficit gets larger.
3   **Increases in maize prices.** Once the *belg* season sweet potatoes have failed, purchase becomes the most important source of food. As prices rise, so less food can be purchased, and the bigger the deficit becomes.

Improving pastoral early warning systems

Pastoral areas in Ethiopia have experienced periodic severe food crises, especially since 2000. Recent climate projections to 2050 estimate that areas of Ethiopia where pastoralists currently reside will be among the worst affected by declining rainfall and subsequent pasture availability (Funk and Brown, 2009). Early warning of food crises in pastoral areas is particularly difficult, complicated by seasonal issues related to milk availability and the timing of conceptions. Figure 12.5 illustrates this seasonal complexity.

Milk production, which is critical for both consumption and cash income, is difficult to monitor because output depends not just on rainfall in the current season (which translates into current grazing conditions) but also on rainfall in previous

Source: Atlas of Ethiopian Livelihoods, page 61, Livelihoods Integration Unit, Disaster Risk Management Food Security Sector (DRMFSS), Ministry of Agriculture, Government of Ethiopia

FIGURE 12.5 Pastoral production factors

seasons, when livestock conceived and carried their unborn young. Drought in any of the critical periods (conception, gestation, birthing) can affect whether a mother carries her young to term and how much milk is produced when the offspring are born. In Ethiopia, where pastoralists raise cattle, goats, sheep, and camels, each with a different gestation period, monitoring pastoral food security requires a solid understanding of seasonal patterns of productivity (LIU, 2010).

The requirement to monitor multiple seasons over consecutive years suggests a need to reorient the current early warning system in pastoral areas. In addition, unlike in cropping areas, where there is a significant time gap between a rainfall failure and associated household food deficits, a failure of the rains in pastoral areas translates into immediate milk yield reductions. Since food deficits can occur with very little warning for pastoralists, a more refined policy in these areas might logically include pre-positioning of relief supplies.

Guiding nutritional surveillance

Seasonal outputs from the LIAS can also help guide nutritional monitoring schedules, because they indicate areas where nutritional stress is likely to be highest, and identify which households will be at risk and when. Figure 12.6 presents the results of the 2009 *belg* seasonal assessment for poor households in three different livelihood zones in SNNPR. The results strongly suggest that nutritional status should be monitored closely in Burji and Bena from October to May.

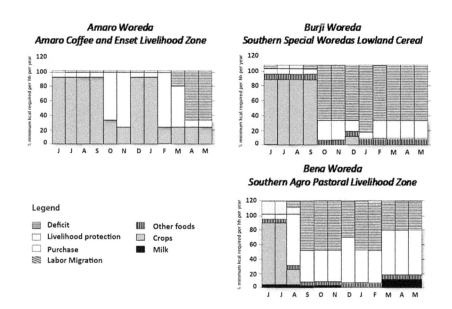

Source: Jane MacAskill, LIU

FIGURE 12.6 Seasonal consumption graphs, results from three *woredas*[3] in SNNPR, 2009 *belg* season scenario analysis

Customizing monitoring indicators and schedules

Seasonal assessments in Ethiopia are carried out twice a year – in June/July and in November. The June/July assessment checks on the status of the *belg* harvest as well as other key parameters (such as staple prices, livestock numbers and health, labour prices, etc.) and estimates the number of people who will require assistance in *belg*-dependent areas in the coming year. In November, the status of the *meher* harvest is assessed, along with other key parameters. At this time numbers from the earlier *belg* assessment are meant to be updated as well. In June/July the objective of the *belg* assessment is to assess the impact of the *belg* harvest together with other key parameters and to update the *meher* assessment in the *meher*-dependent areas if necessary.

A recent analysis of long-term rainfall trends conducted by the LIU provides evidence in support of a more refined approach to the timing of assessments. The analysis concluded that there is cause to revisit the current biannual June/July and November schedule, highlighting in particular the possibility of carrying out assessments in parts of SNNPR as early as September and in pastoral Afar up to a month earlier than currently. More importantly, the conclusions show that lead times between assessments and the start of the hunger season, which is typically the time when emergency interventions need to be launched, vary throughout the country. The longest lead times are in areas where the harvest occurs once a year, generally the *meher* areas. In these areas the harvest typically occurs in November and the hunger season begins the following June, providing a lead time of seven months. In these places crops can be stored and consumed for months after the harvest. Shorter lead times occur in parts of western Oromiya and Benishangul, where the harvest takes place later, and in areas where there are two harvests (e.g. large parts of SNNPR and agropastoral parts of Somali Region). The shortest lead times are in pastoral areas of Afar, Somali and southern Oromiya. There are limited possibilities for storing seasonal production (milk) and so the hunger season starts soon after the rains stop and animals lose condition (LIU, 2010, p21).

An especially sensitive monitoring system would also be calibrated to check – in a timely way – on the status of a larger set of seasonal activities as well, where relevant, such as labour migration, firewood sales, wild food collection and sales, fishing, petty trade, and so on.

Seasonal leverage points for development

New opportunities for targeting development assistance may also be suggested by careful analysis of seasonal activities and intra-annual patterns of food and cash income. If we know when and where households engage in livelihood-related activities, we are better able to find creative options for adding value to these pursuits.

Figure 12.7 highlights the importance of seasonal migratory labour for poor households in the Middle Tekeze Livelihood Zone in Tigray. Infertile soils and recurrent droughts have made a significant part of the population in this zone food insecure. Lack of oxen further inhibits the capacity of poor households to fully utilize the land resources available to them. Because of a paucity of local opportunities, the poor and very poor seek labour opportunities elsewhere. Many households in the less productive areas of Tigray travel every year to western Humera, where commercial sesame production generates a consistent demand for seasonal labour. Just what this seasonal opportunity provides in terms of income helps us understand the relative importance of this option for poor households.

As shown in the figure, approximately 1,000 of the 2,600 *birr* earned by very poor households each year comes from this labour migration. However, while nearly half of their cash comes from migratory labour, the net gain for households is significantly less, because around 8 per cent of earnings is spent on transportation to Humera. In addition, malaria, which is endemic in the western lowlands, takes its toll, with health, productivity and wages all at risk. With transportation and health costs both eating into potential profits, it is worth taking a look at how development interventions could help improve the odds.

By understanding the seasonal options that households have for securing food and income we can gain an insight into possible ways to lift constraints and expand opportunities. For instance, in the case of migrant labourers in Humera, are there ways to provide extra assistance to these households during these months? Is it possible to boost the health clinic budgets seasonally in the sesame harvesting areas to cover the health needs of an influx of upwards of 200,000 people? Could transportation to the sesame areas be subsidized during these months? Is there a need to establish institutions aimed at protecting the rights and welfare of migrant workers?

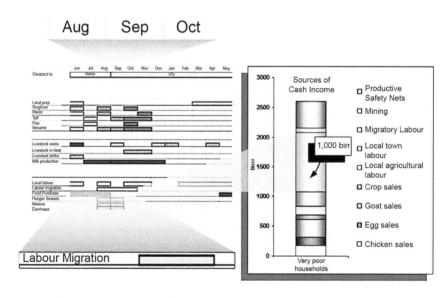

Notes: *teff* is a very fine grain with a grass-like stem, unique to Ethiopia as a staple; $US1 is approximately 17 *birr*.

Source: Tanya Boudreau, FEG

FIGURE 12.7 Seasonal cash income in Middle Tekeze Livelihood Zone, Tigray

As seen in this example, the detail provided by a seasonally textured description of local livelihoods stimulates debate and engagement that is directly relevant and specific to people's real needs.

Conclusion

A majority of the world's rural dwellers continue to depend on rainfed agriculture to fuel their livelihoods (either directly or indirectly). In this context, the norm is one of continual change. Natural hazards, such as drought, floods, and cyclones, and man-made hazards, like war, market disruption, and policy changes combine with the vulnerability of livelihood systems and households, resulting in either disasters or windfalls. The vulnerability of these livelihood systems is determined in part by intra-annual, or seasonal, cycles. Thus, seasonality, and the timing of hazards in relation to normal cycles, is a key factor in determining disaster outcomes.

If reducing poverty and hunger is contingent on the establishment of a set of policies and associated programmes that support people's livelihood systems and strategies and 'proof' these against ongoing expected and unexpected hazards, then we need to be able to characterize people's vulnerability to different hazards and ensure that an ongoing analysis of current (and projected) hazard effects is factored into the planning process on both the development and the emergency sides. People's livelihoods are a complex web of interdependent pathways. Capturing this complexity, and making it amenable to decision-makers' busy planning time-tables is an enormous challenge. In practice, leaving aside the seasonal complexi-ties, just managing to accomplish this on an inter-annual basis is daunting because of the enormous amounts of information that need to be managed, tracked and analysed. By adding in seasonal dimensions, we can easily overload the system unless we have appropriate tools to streamline and make sense of the data.

At the same time, it is clear from the evidence presented in the second half of this chapter that seasonality is a critical factor in early warning, emergency response, nutrition and development decisions. Therefore, if we expect to facilitate the use of seasonal information in the context of disaster risk reduction-oriented develop-ment planning, the onus is on analysts and practitioners to provide customized, dedicated tools for managing these complex streams of information and analysis.

Notes

1   *Belg* are the short rains between February and May in southern, north-eastern, eastern and north-central parts of the country; also used to describe the secondary agricultural season. *Meher* is the primary agricultural season, or main growing season, associated with the *kremt* rains (the long rains between June and September) but including long-cycle crops (sorghum, maize) which may be sown in the *belg* season. *Meher* is one of the words for 'harvest' in the Amharic language.
2   Mark Lawrence, of FEG, is the author of the LIAS, and designed the mapping, price, rainfall and livestock monitoring tools currently in use by the LIU.
3   A *woreda* is an administrative unit equivalent to a district.

13

Water-bound geographies of seasonality

Investigating seasonality, water and wealth in Ethiopia through the Water Economy for Livelihoods (WELS) approach

Lorraine Coulter, Zemede Abebe, Seifu Kebede, Eva Ludi and Belay Zeleke

Introduction

Precursors and linkages: Household Economy Approach (HEA)

Water Economy for Livelihoods (WELS) is a new approach that was designed in 2007–08 to bring analytical rigour to understanding the inter-linkages between water security and food security. Designed to build on approaches and methodologies that have already achieved buy-in and skills/capacity development, it has also aimed to link to and inform the livelihoods monitoring and early warning systems in place in Ethiopia.

Ethiopia's Disaster Risk Management and Food Security Sector (DRMFSS) and its Livelihoods Integration Unit (LIU) currently use the Household Economy Approach (HEA) as the analytical framework through which to assess food and livelihoods-based needs of populations affected by a range of hazards such as drought, floods, crop/livestock disease and pests, and market-based shocks. Agencies in a wide range of countries – particularly in sub-Saharan Africa, but also in Asia, Eastern Europe, and Latin America – have also incorporated HEA into their early warning frameworks, their monitoring and evaluation frameworks, or have used it to better understand the livelihoods and needs of their populations.

The premise behind both HEA and WELS is that an understanding of how people will be affected by shocks or hazards in a bad year is only possible if an understanding is achieved of how people piece together their livelihoods – and, in the case of WELS, how they secure access to sufficient water to meet livelihood needs – in 'normal' years. An analysis of household economy aims to determine systematically how people live, what puts different households at risk of food or non-food shortages, and what type of responses are most appropriate (Save the Children and FEG, 2008b).

More than simply relevant to emergency response, however, HEA rests at the core of Ethiopia's emerging disaster risk management system: a system capable of both *corrective* (current disasters) and *prospective* (future potential disasters) risk management (Boudreau, 2009). In Ethiopia, where emergencies are endogenous to the country and have posed a persistent threat to much of its population for centuries, the ability to bridge the emergency–development divide is particularly urgent.

The strength of HEA's ability to serve this task lies in its ability to transform a descriptive analysis into a predictive one, where scenario-based risk assessment provides dynamic, targeted recommendations for building resilience and reducing vulnerability – as well as responding to current shocks faced by populations (Boudreau, 2009).

The missing link: water

Much as the emergency–development divide is impossible to bridge without a systems-based (as opposed to a sector-based) approach to understanding how hazards and vulnerabilities interact to create disaster risks, the livelihoods picture is incomplete without a holistic understanding of the interdependencies of food security and water security.

Access to safe water in drought – one of the most common hazards in Ethiopia – is consistently a major problem, and water-related disease resulting from restricted water availability and access often causes more fatalities than starvation does in times of famine. Integration of water security into traditionally food-centred assessments contributes to the formulation of more effective and creative multi-sectoral responses. Because water interventions often have long-term impacts and consequences, if planned for properly, it would also strengthen prospective risk reduction.

This is where WELS aims to fill the gaps. Until recently, livelihoods analysis has under-appreciated how crucially water contributes to production, and to the ability of households to secure the resources they need to survive. In reality, access to food, income and water are linked in important ways, particularly during drought. WELS aims to link household economy with access to water at the household level – and strengthen our understanding of livelihoods and our responses to threats to livelihoods.

Methodology

Methodological components

The Water Economy for Livelihoods approach has three components:

1   **Water baselines** – which address both **water availability** and **water access** within each geographical unit of analysis, or livelihood zone.[1] Water access

baselines capture quantified data on access to sources of water by different wealth groups, across seasons, and across uses (e.g. domestic and productive). Hydrogeological data and mapping enable characterisation of groundwater potential – or the ability of aquifers (or sub-surface rocks) to store and transport water during normal conditions and during drought – in specific geographic areas, as well as identification of areas vulnerable to groundwater drought.[2] Water-point coverage lends to this information on local water availability.

2 **Hazards analysis** – which is based on periodic assessments that quantify shocks or hazards[3] and translates them into quantified economic and water access consequences at household level.

3 **Outcome analysis** – which projects the impact of the hazards in relation to survival and livelihood protection needs, or thresholds. See Annex 13.A for an explanation of these thresholds.

Quantified information on water access, and its importance in relation to specific livelihood strategies, forms the baseline datasets that provide the foundation of an analytical tool, the Water Impact Analysis Sheet (WIAS). The WIAS provides an interactive interface that allows for input of seasonal hazards information and which provides outputs in the form of data and graphs illustrating impact on water access and livelihoods at household level.

WELS assessments and research

Three WELS assessments and research projects are addressed in this paper. They are summarized briefly below.

WELS pilot assessment in pastoral areas of Bale Zone, Oromiya Region, Ethiopia

The assessment took place in March and April of 2008 under the LIU and MoARD alongside LIU HEA baseline data collection in Bale Pastoral (BPA) livelihood zone.

Rapid emergency water and livelihoods needs assessment in north-eastern Southern Nations, Nationalities and Peoples Region (SNNPR), Ethiopia, targeting vulnerable populations in Alaba-Mareko, Badewacho, and Gumer wredas

The assessment took place between May and June of 2008 and was commissioned by Community Housing Fund International (CHF). It aimed to assess water and livelihoods needs of vulnerable populations to inform emergency response and recovery activities by CHF and other agencies. Identification of innovative responses that paired non–food-based support with traditional food-based support was a central emphasis of the assessment.

RiPPLE-funded action-research WELS study in East and West Hararghe and Shinile Zones, Oromiya and Somali Regions, Ethiopia

The research is one component of RiPPLE's Growth Long-term Action Research Project (Growth LARS), which focuses on how investments in the Water and Sanitation Sector (WSS) contribute to poverty reduction, sustainable livelihoods and pro-poor growth. Within this, the WELS case study aimed to assess local water availability and household access to water by different wealth groups in a transect of lowland, midland, and highland livelihood zones, with a focus on how differential access to water affects livelihoods security and potential for resilience in different areas.

Quantifying seasonal access to water

Because water is a daily need for both humans and livestock (the latter are significant to household livelihoods in virtually every rural livelihood zone in Ethiopia), and access to water depends so heavily on seasonal changes in rainfall and groundwater flows, quantifying access to water must be done seasonally. Understanding seasonal access to water is imperative for understanding periods of resilience and vulnerability within the yearly production cycle.

There is perhaps no livelihood system for which this is more relevant than pastoralism, in which livelihood strategies are wholly dependent on access to water for livestock. Quantifying seasonal water access reveals important lessons for timing of monitoring, response targeting, and type of response in drought years. An illustration of how access to water for livestock is quantified is presented in Figure 13.1 for Bale Pastoral (BPA) livelihood zone (Oromiya Region, Ethiopia).

Fluctuations in seasonal access levels vary widely in pastoral Bale and are, broadly speaking, related to rainfall fluctuations. In the wet seasons (*gena* from March to May and *hagaya* from September to October), all households can access water at nearby ponds and seasonal pools that form after the rains. In the dry seasons, pastoralists must excavate water from dried riverbed pits – an arduous task – and migrate to perennial rivers during the second half of the long dry *bona* season (November–February) to secure enough water.

Notably, very poor and poor households are not able to secure enough water in the dry seasons of a *normal* year, falling far short of 100 per cent of minimum needs. All households see their water access drop by nearly 60 per cent from the wet to the short dry *adolesa* season (June–August).[4] However, wealthier households mobilize resources to ensure that their livestock obtain nearly 85–90 per cent of minimum water needs in the long dry *bona* season when water needs are highest due to depletion of grazing and its moisture content, hotter temperatures and high transpiration, and accumulating dehydration of animals.

While middle-income and better-off households increase water access for their livestock from the short dry *adolesa* season to the long dry *bona* season by 3 per cent and 8 per cent, respectively, poorer households have limited household asset bases

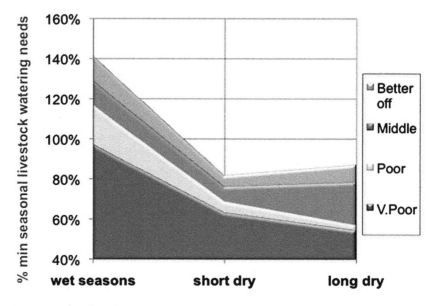

Source: Coulter (2008a)

FIGURE 13.1   Seasonal access to water for livestock in BPA livelihood zone

from which to draw. They see their livestock water access drop a further 10–15 per cent in the *bona*, facing productive water deficits of at least 40 per cent of minimum needs. This is illustrated in Figure 13.1.

The failure of the poorer wealth groups to secure enough water for their livestock in the dry seasons has significant implications for their ability to generate income and maintain assets. Such low seasonal access levels significantly undermine livestock condition and increase livestock susceptibility to disease, which is further compounded by lower expenditure on veterinary care. Indeed, the prices that poor wealth groups receive for their livestock are at least 15–20 per cent lower than those fetched by the wealthier households due to their poor condition. Finally, milk yields per animal are 50–75 per cent lower for stock of poorer households compared to better-off households.

The reasons behind these wealth-based disparities in seasonal access among wealth groups are related to asset and capital bases. Poorer households have smaller household sizes (approximately 6 compared to upwards of 9–11 for the better-off) which limits their ability to release labour to water livestock. Wealthier households also have higher cash reserves to pay labour to assist with or water their livestock herds. Labour is particularly important for water collection in this zone because extraction of water from excavated pits that are at least 5m deep requires more than one person in the long dry *bona*. Figure 13.2, which shows seasonal collection times, speaks to the huge time investment required to access water in the dry seasons.

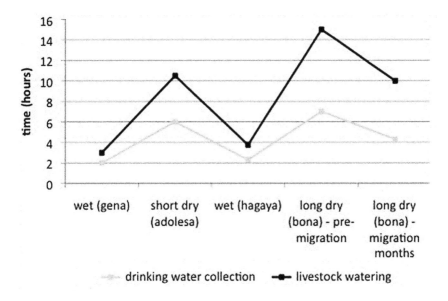

Source: Coulter (2008a)

FIGURE 13.2 Water collection times by season in BPA livelihood zone

Implications for emergency monitoring and response

Generating quantified seasonal access trend data is important for monitoring and response in drought periods. In this case, it suggests that, given the high deficits for poorer households in the dry seasons of a *normal* year, livestock of poorer households may need targeting earlier in the emergency cycle. Understanding seasonal deficits in the baseline year enables responses to reach the most vulnerable herds *before* their condition deteriorates past the point when interventions can still protect livestock assets.

Assessing seasonal conflicts of labour allocation: seasonal calendars of water access

For each livelihood zone assessed through WELS, a seasonal calendar of water access is generated. The calendar facilitates identification of times during the year when demand for labour, resources, and time compete against each other. Figure 13.3 is an example of a seasonal calendar of water access for Alaba-Mareko Lowland Pepper (AMP) livelihood zone, in SNNPR. It is paired with a hazard timeline of the emergency period during the 2008 *belg* season[5] in that area.

The seasonal calendar in Figure 13.3 takes traditional seasonal calendars one step further by plotting collection time for each source of water by month of access. Combined with charting other seasonal activities, the seasonal calendar suggests points of possible conflict over household-level labour allocation among domestic

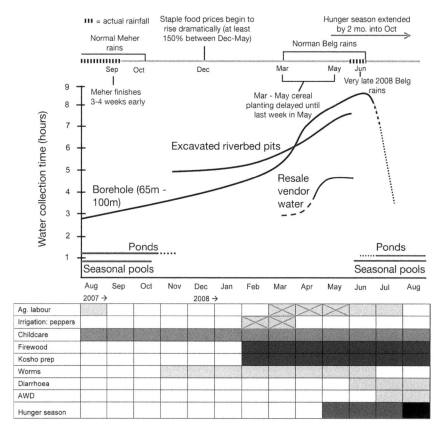

Source: Coulter (2008b)

FIGURE 13.3 Seasonal calendar of water access in a hazard year – Alaba-Mareko Lowland Pepper (AMP) livelihood zone, SNNPR

and productive activities. Comparing collection times and water source behaviour (e.g. yield, water quality) in normal years and in hazard years can also inform understandings of the likely impacts of hazards on household time and labour constraints.

The set of hazards indicated in Figure 13.3 for 2008 in SNNPR included: extremely high staple food price inflation (reaching 150–175 per cent of the previous year's prices), which reduced purchasing power dramatically; early termination of the 2007 *meher* rains (usually from July to October); and a very late start to the 2008 *belg* rains in the last week of May (usually from March to June). Drought conditions resulted in high rates of borehole breakdown in Alaba-Mareko, starting in March.

The calendar reflects the spike in collection time at boreholes – the only safe source of water in the livelihood zone. By March, when the rains were supposed to have arrived, collection time had risen to 5 hours at boreholes and rose sharply to 7–9 hours once boreholes started breaking down. Information on hydrogeology (see next section) and water-point management collected during the emergency assessment revealed two important and related trends. First, most boreholes in the zone that continued to have water during the drought had minimum depths of at least 80m. Second, those boreholes that were still functioning were placed under excessive and increasing stress as the number of borehole points declined. As borehole pump equipment became more and more stressed at a declining number of boreholes that had to answer demand from an ever-increasing population, the trend of borehole breakdown was exacerbated.

The calendar also highlights the conflict over allocation of scarce labour during the hazard period from March to August due to increased demands on the time of women and children required for water collection. Poor households in particular – with fewer household members, no donkeys to transport water, and fewer and smaller jerry cans – were forced to choose between allocating their labour to water collection, which required at least seven hours per day, and allocating it to collection and sale of firewood and/or *kosho* (*enset*)[6] preparation to generate extra cash for food purchase.[7] In the absence of labour opportunities for men due to the delay in the planting season, these activities were some of the only coping strategies available to households. Women reported that time allocated to childcare dropped to marginal levels.

The seasonal calendar in Figure 13.3 also highlights the linkages between the incidence of diarrhoea and water access at ponds and seasonal pools, which people turned to once the rains began in late May because, unlike the borehole, pools were free and required only an hour of collection time per day. Despite their convenience, these sources became heavily contaminated with polluted floodwater once the rains started at the end of May. Intestinal problems related to parasites, on the other hand, were linked to water collection during the dry season at excavated riverbed pits, where breeding conditions were favourable.

Understanding the geography of seasonality: hydrogeological investigations

The importance of groundwater

Groundwater is often the most important source of water during dry seasons, as well as drought. Long after surface water sources have dried up, groundwater can still be accessed through wells, springs, and boreholes. This 'buffering' capacity – or the capacity of aquifers to store and transport water once recharge to the aquifer (e.g. through rainfall) is reduced – can vary significantly across different areas, and in some places, under certain conditions, groundwater sources can fail (Calow *et al.*, 2002).

An important new component of the WELS methodology is assessment of groundwater availability through hydrogeological investigations, both through secondary data, and observations at the local level. This component of the methodology builds on extensive work done by the British Geological Survey (BGS), elaborated on in MacDonald *et al.* (2005). This component of the methodology allows for a more sophisticated understanding of the linkages between how seasonal water availability affects water access at household level during different periods of the year, and how these impact on livelihood opportunities and constraints and vice versa.

In addition to analysis of existing maps on geology and hydrology, rock samples at working and abandoned water source sites in each livelihood zone are collected and stored using GPS. Local observations on hydrogeology and water source functionality seasonally and in drought years, as well as community management and attitudes towards each source, are recorded during a 'hydrogeology walk'.[8]

This information is analysed and output into a series of maps and information that can be used to identify areas that are (a) vulnerable to groundwater drought – where water supply through groundwater is likely to be much reduced or unavailable during dry seasons and exacerbated during drought; (b) areas where groundwater is likely to be available during dry seasons and drought, and therefore where groundwater interventions may be effective; and (c) areas where groundwater quality is already a problem, or is likely to be in future groundwater schemes (e.g. high salinity or fluoride content). It also informs understandings of limitations to and opportunities for water use for productive and domestic activities in the livelihood zone. The maps and hydrogeological data can ultimately provide guidance on what types of groundwater interventions can be supported and are possible given the geophysical characteristics of the livelihood zone.

Seasonality of groundwater sources

Assessing (a) recharge to the aquifer, which occurs through rainfall or surface water flows (e.g. floods, rivers, ponds) and (b) aquifer type allows us to determine groundwater availability.

Rainfall data – relevant to recharge – show that long-term average mean rainfall levels generally decrease with altitude. The highland Wheat, Barley and Potato (WBP) livelihood zone receives a long-term mean of approximately 900mm of rainfall per year; the midland Sorghum, Maize and Chat (SMC) zone receives 750mm per year, and the lowland Shinile Agro-Pastoral (SAP) zone receives just over 600mm per year. Seasonal rainfall trends indicate October through February as months with the lowest rainfall levels in all zones.

Hydrogeological analysis allows for identification of aquifer properties. Figure 13.4, produced from secondary geological maps and village-level hydrogeological investigation and rock samples, presents the susceptibility of water table levels to changes in rainfall levels in the three livelihood zones. The higher the susceptibility, the higher the 'seasonality' of the aquifer – in other words, the greater the variation in groundwater table levels, and thus groundwater-fed water source yields, given a change in rainfall levels. From this map, we see that in these areas, response rate and 'seasonality' of groundwater-fed water sources increases with altitude.

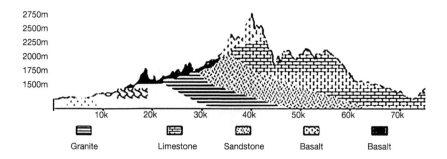

Source: EIGS (1993); EIGS (1996); Kebede and Zeleke (2009)

FIGURE 13.4 Vulnerability/speed of response to changes in environmental parameters as measured by aquifer storage properties in east/west Hararghe and Shinile

Highland seasonality and implications for responses

Due to steep slopes, small aquifer sizes, and high transmissivity (or ability to transport water) of the aquifer types, most highland areas, including those in WBP livelihood zone, have a response rate of 7 (Figure 13.5). Groundwater recharged by rainfall in the highland zone travels quickly away from the highlands into the midlands and lowlands, both through runoff and in groundwater flows. This suggests that in drought periods, groundwater-based responses may not be a viable option unless localized fractures can be found with pockets of groundwater.

This high level of seasonality also indicates that a drop-off in rainfall leads quickly to decreased spring yields. This trend is elaborated by household water access baseline data from household interviews and local observation, which reflect no 'transitional' water access period in between dry and wet. Households report a decline of spring yield within days of rainfall terminating. Dry season queueing time increases as some springs dry up and more people are forced to collect at the remaining perennial, but now lower-yielding, springs that are still fed by groundwater. Long-term rainfall data suggest that drought is not a frequent occurrence in the WBP zone. However, should a serious drought occur in this area – for instance, if climate trends shift in the next decades – the vulnerability of the zone to such conditions would be high in this traditionally water-secure area.

Midland seasonality and implications for responses

Seasonality is lower and groundwater potential slightly higher in midland SMC livelihood zone, which is characterized by moderate seasonality and response rates ranging from 4 to 6 (Figure 13.5).[9] Despite lower rainfall (recharge) levels, groundwater remains in the aquifer for longer periods of time in SMC – although spring sources are still characterized by seasonal variation in yield.

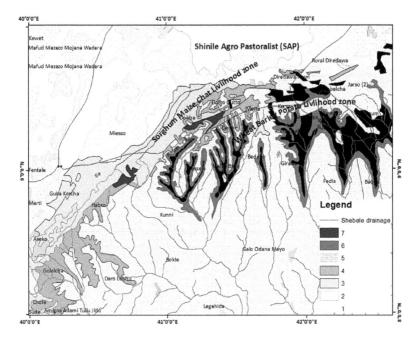

Source: EIGS (1993; 1996); Kebede and Zeleke (2009)

FIGURE 13.5 Speed of aquifer response

The higher groundwater availability and lower seasonality of groundwater flows in SMC zone may be a contributing factor to the higher water access levels of households in that zone compared to the highland zone, although relative wealth and related asset bases are relevant as well. Access levels for water for human consumption are presented in Figure 13.6.

Information on groundwater availability suggests two important points. First, water-point data tell us that shallow wells (<50m) and deep wells (>50m) are currently few in number in SMC livelihood zone. However, groundwater is present at shallow depths, as indicated by hydrogeological data and observations of water availability in shallow wells in the zone. Development of protected shallow wells is therefore possible. It is also desirable, particularly from a public health standpoint. Most of the population access water from unprotected springs, which are susceptible to contamination and are a source of water-related diseases.

Furthermore, population figures tell us that human population is only moderate in density, and livestock populations are not high; supported by the relatively good rainfall levels in the zone, development of shallow wells or boreholes is likely not to lead to over-abstraction and localized depletion of groundwater tables around wells. Rules concerning water use for irrigation (practised already by a small proportion of the population) would need to be instituted to prevent localized

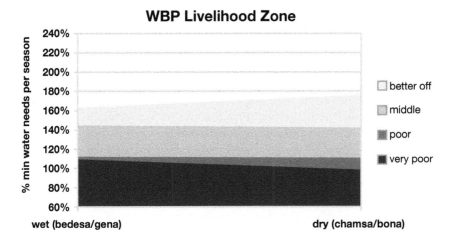

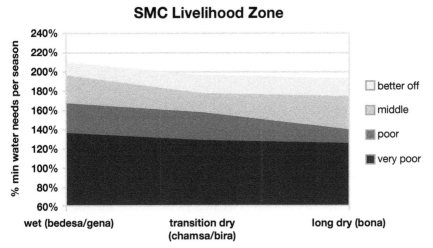

Source: Coulter (2008a)

FIGURE 13.6   Access to water for human consumption: Highland WBP and Midland
SMC livelihood zones

depletion, however. Second, boreholes and even properly sited shallow wells may
be effective options during serious drought periods.

Spring protection would also be an appropriate and important intervention in
both WBP and SMC zones, as most springs become highly contaminated, due
partly to their role in serving multiple water uses – domestic, livestock watering,
and also irrigation. Lastly, to reduce the seasonal decline in spring yields, construction of artificial recharge enhancement structures such as ponds may also be appropriate to increase the water retention in the zone. Ponds may also direct livestock

and irrigation users away from springs, which can then be limited to domestic use to reduce the risk of contamination.

Lowland seasonality and implications for responses

Seasonality and response rates in lowland SAP livelihood zone are low – ranging from 1 to 4 in most areas. This suggests that, despite lower rainfall levels, even in the dry seasons, water is still available from dug-out excavations in dried up riverbeds. It is also likely to be available during droughts as well, though at deeper depths. Households in SAP zone concur, reporting the continued presence of water in excavated pits through most drought periods (although water quality declines substantially, and the depth of pits must be increased).

The retention of water in excavated pits during dry seasons and drought suggests that construction of sub-surface dams to facilitate storage and extraction of water would be an effective preventative and resilience-building measure in this zone. This would be particularly useful given the high volumes of water required for livelihoods in this agro-pastoral zone.

Since groundwater is not found close to the surface in most areas, boreholes with submersible pumps are the only other option to tap groundwater in the lowland livelihood zone in the dry seasons.

Seasonality: a factor in improper siting of boreholes?

WELS collects, through its 'hydrogeology walks', information and data on why and when sources fail or are abandoned by the community. This kind of information is important in identifying interventions appropriate to both the physical characteristics of the zone and the social and economic motivations and interests of communities.

Information collected on abandoned boreholes in lowland SAP livelihood zone suggests that despite the relatively low seasonality of groundwater sources, it is imperative that siting of boreholes occurs during the dry season, rather than the wet season. A large number of abandoned boreholes had been drilled at the end of the fiscal year (the government budget deadline), which occurs in June – the middle of the wet season. Yet many of these boreholes were found to have been abandoned because they dried up during the dry seasons. This suggests that water tables were high when drilling took place and so crews stopped drilling when they reached water – but did not account for the drop of the water table during the dry seasons. Properly timed siting of water supply interventions and properly implemented hydrogeological surveys are necessary to ensure source behaviour is adequate for the population in the dry seasons and drought.

Scenario analysis: intensifying seasonality

Scenario analysis is at the heart of HEA's predictive capacity. Scenario analysis for both HEA and WELS uses baseline data on food, income, and expenditure (for

HEA) and access to water for human consumption, hygiene and sanitation, and productive activities (e.g. livestock watering, irrigation, for WELS) as the foundation from which to project impacts of hazards at household level.

For WELS, quantified data on coping strategies undertaken by households in bad years are used to assess the ability of different households to mobilize and secure additional water. Coping may mean increasing expenditure on water from boreholes, paying for water sold in water markets, migration or travel to other working or higher-yielding sources farther away.

Hazard data defining the problem are based on assessment of conditions or a projection of estimated future conditions. Such data can include information on changes in source yields or changes in availability of water during specific months, and water quality tests which indicate water as unsafe for consumption by humans in particular source types.

Scenario analysis for the 2008 *belg* emergency in Alaba-Mareko Lowland Pepper (AMP) livelihood zone in SNNPR (discussed above) from an 'integrated' assessment combining HEA and WELS data is discussed below to illustrate the importance of looking at the relationship between seasonal vulnerabilities restricting access to water and their impact on households' ability to protect livelihoods during hazard periods.

The drought in the *belg* of 2008 precipitated a continuation of the dry season in AMP livelihood zone that resulted in water scarcity and severe water shortages. Falling water tables and higher than normal demand from the population had exacerbated the breakdown of an estimated 30 per cent of previously functional boreholes, as discussed above. Communities from up to ten Peasant Associations, or communities, used the remaining functional boreholes (compared to one to two Peasant Associations in normal years), placing great stress on the remaining infrastructure, particularly in light of only moderate yields at these sources (1.5–3L/sec). Water availability at the only other dry season water sources – excavated riverbed pits – had declined by an estimated 20 per cent, with groundwater recharging pits at significantly lower rates.

The water scarcity problems of the drought also brought consequences for access to food and income by the population. Although the most serious impacts of the drought would not be felt until the *meher* harvest, which would be delayed by 1–2 months because of the late onset of the *belg* rains, income normally obtained from labour during the *belg* planting – significant to poor households in the hunger season – was not available. The sharp rise in staple food prices beginning in December of 2007 also substantially reduced households' purchasing power, compounding the labour problem.

HEA analysis indicated that, as a result of these hazards, significant survival deficits had begun to emerge in those areas in March, as indicated by seasonal consumption graphs. Figure 13.7, which reproduces the seasonal consumption graph for AMP livelihood zone, indicates that poor households began to experience survival deficits in April of 2007, with deficit levels peaking in May, June and July.

However, poor households had already been facing significant water-for-survival deficits since October, as they usually do in a normal year. Unlike in a

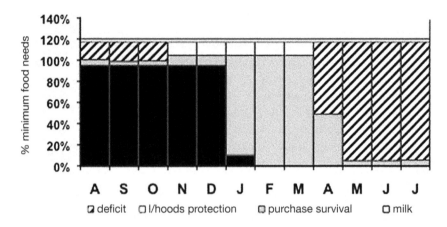

Source: Coulter (2008b)

FIGURE 13.7 Seasonal consumption for poor households in flooded areas of AMP livelihood zone, SNNPR, 2007–2008

normal year, however, deficits began to climb in April when the rains failed to resume, contributing to weakened household productivity during those months. Water-for-survival deficits reached over 60 per cent in May – right at the point when households were also facing significant survival deficits on the food side. Water deficits are shown in Figure 13.8.

Furthermore, although access in terms of *quantity* had resumed normal levels in June, *quality* was a significant concern due to the onset of the rains, which brought flooding and the transport of contaminants into ponds and seasonal pools that most poor households turned to once the drought had stopped. Cases of diarrhoeal disease, typhoid, and AWD (acute watery diarrhoea) peaked in June through August, as noted in the seasonal calendar of water access in Figure 13.3. Although wealthier households had enough cash to continue to resort to boreholes, poor households sought to reduce expenditure as much as possible and turned predominantly to accessing these ponds and seasonal pools despite the risk of disease.

Water-for-livelihoods deficits were also significant during the emergency period. Figure 13.9 indicates that poor households failed to secure nearly 80 per cent of their water needs for livestock and irrigation of pepper seedlings during May and June, with decreasing access levels running up to that seasonal peak.

These water-for-livelihoods-protection deficits had serious consequences for food security during the following *meher* of 2008. Typically, famers irrigate pepper seedlings prior to transplanting them into fields in late April and May. However, due to decreased access to water at excavated riverbed pits, conflicts over allocation of scarce labour across coping strategies (*kosho* production and firewood collection/sale), water collection for human consumption and irrigation activities, as

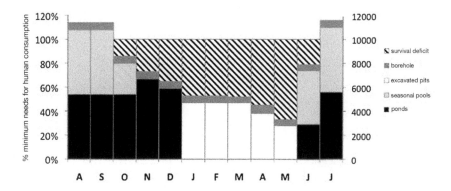

Source: Coulter (2008b)

FIGURE 13.8 Seasonal water access for survival for poor households in AMP livelihood zone, SNNPR, 2007–2008

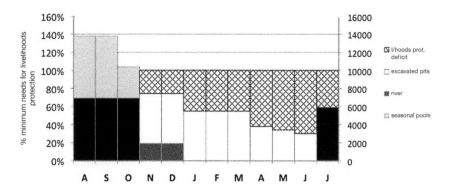

Source: Coulter (2008b)

FIGURE 13.9 Seasonal water access for livelihoods protection for poor households in AMP livelihood zone, SNNPR

well as the cessation of donkey-sharing arrangements by the better-off, the poor failed to irrigate their pepper seedlings in the *belg*.

Because the cash crop pepper is the single most important source of cash income for poor and wealthier households alike – forming up to 30 per cent of poor households' baseline income – the failure to irrigate was significant, and resulted in a 50–65 per cent loss of pepper production. This loss, along with the delayed harvest and inflationary constraints on the purchasing power for staple food, contributed to a 15–20 per cent survival deficit for poor households, as shown in Figure 13.10.

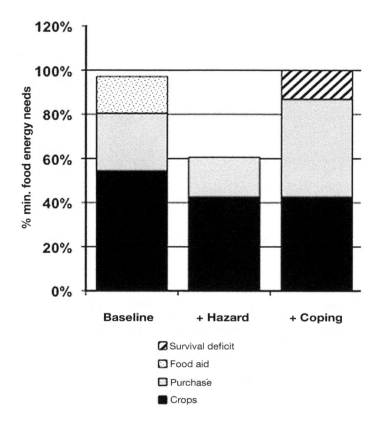

Source: Coulter (2008b)

FIGURE 13.10 Sources of food for poor households in AMP livelihood zone, SNNPR, 2008–2009

Conclusions

The water sector has long been concerned with the public health angle of poor water supply in communities, both for development and during emergencies such as drought. Partly due to the difficulty of measuring access, and an adherence to the traditional focus on 'developed' sources and public health concerns, many water sector assessments and data collection efforts have been limited to a focus on water-point density (e.g. number of improved water points per population unit in a given area) and epidemiological concerns. While important, these methods do not sufficiently inform our understanding of the significant linkages between water security and food security that are often at the heart of survival and livelihoods protection of populations in normal as well as bad years.

Furthermore, development practitioners have known for a while now that timing of responses is crucial to the effectiveness of their programmes and response systems. In practice, it has often been more difficult to identify and predict if and when a hazard will force households past the point when they can no longer rely on their own resources to sustain survival or livelihoods.

The HEA and WELS methods and tools discussed in this chapter can contribute to more sophisticated risk reduction as well as early warning systems tools. In addition, assessing food security and water security together in a way that allows for analytical linkages to be made between different sectors has the potential to strengthen our ability to creatively and more holistically address the root causes of vulnerability to particular hazards, as well as their immediate effects, and to develop appropriate responses.

Notes

1   A livelihood zone is a geographical area that shares similar agro-ecological characteristics, livelihoods strategies practised by the population and access to markets.
2   Groundwater drought is a term used to describe a situation in which groundwater sources fail as a direct consequence of drought (see Calow *et al.*, 1997). Groundwater is water stored below the surface in aquifers, which are subsurface rocks that store and transport water. The better the storage and transport properties of an aquifer, combined with adequate recharge from rainfall over the long term, the greater the potential that groundwater will be available during drought or during periods of high demand.
3   A shock or hazard is an event or process that significantly affects households' access to food, income, and water.
4   Water intake requirements for livestock are substantially lower in the wet season due to the moisture contained in fodder, which is estimated at 70–75 per cent during the wet seasons under Sahelian conditions. Moisture in forage drops to approximately 10 per cent in dry seasons with average temperatures of greater than 27°C (Taddesse, 2003).
5   The *belg* season rains run from March through May in most areas. They are the main rains for much of the southern areas of Ethiopia, as well as parts of a north–south corridor in eastern Amhara.
6   *Enset*, also known as 'false banana' plant, is a tuber that takes five years to mature and is cultivated in many areas in the Southern Nations, Nationalities and Peoples Region (SNNPR) as a staple crop. It is especially important in bad years, when households can harvest the tuber before it comes to maturity. One *enset* tuber can feed a household of five people for about one month.
7   Not only did better-off households have larger and a higher number of storage and transport assets, which enabled them to collect water less frequently – they also had more cash reserves to purchase water from vendors, at 30 *birr* (about 30 cents) per 20L jerry can – an expensive price. Purchasing from vendors involved the lowest collection time of all water sources.
8   Information on yield, quality, seasonality (i.e. the rate of response of the aquifer to changes in recharge levels) is taken across seasons at water sources within the livelihood zone (see MacDonald *et al.* 2005).
9   Hydrogeological data tell us that this is due to recharge from both rainfall and groundwater flow from the highlands, and a topography characterized by depressions (underlain by alluvial deposits, which have high storage properties) in which ground and surface water collects.

Annex 13.A: Survival and livelihoods protection thresholds for HEA and WELS

The Survival Threshold represents the total income required to cover:

a) 100% of minimum food energy needs (2100 kcals per person), plus

b) The costs associated with food preparation and consumption (i.e. salt, soap, kerosene and/or firewood for cooking and basic lighting), plus

c) Any expenditure on water for human consumption.

Note: Items included in categories b) and c) together make up the minimum non-food expenditure basket, represented by the min. non-food bar in the expenditure graphic.

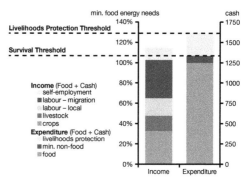

The Livelihoods Protection Threshold represents the total income required to sustain local livelihoods. This means total expenditure to:

a) Ensure basic survival (see above), plus

b) Maintain access to basic services (e.g. routine medical and schooling expenses), plus

c) Sustain livelihoods in the medium to longer term (e.g. regular purchases of seeds, fertilizer, veterinary drugs, etc.), plus

d) Achieve a minimum locally acceptable standard of living (e.g. purchase of basic clothing, coffee/tea, etc.)

FIGURE 13.A1 HEA survival and livelihoods protection thresholds

Water-for-Survival: Human Consumption Threshold represents the minimum volume and quality of water required for survival, specified by SPHERE as a minimum of 5 litres per person per day.

Hygiene and Sanitation Threshold represents the minimum volume of water required to maintain hygiene and sanitation activities, specified by SPHERE standards as 10 litres per person per day. This is not included in the Water for Survival Threshold above for the purposes of the assessments discussed in this paper.

Water-for-Livelihoods-Protection Threshold represents the minimum volume of water required to sustain household livelihoods activities so that food and income needs for livelihoods protection (see HEA Thresholds above) are met. Livestock protection needs are included as a livelihoods activity, as are other productive uses of water such as irrigation.

Each of the thresholds are measured as a percent of 100% minimum water needs.

FIGURE 13.A2 WELS thresholds

PART 4

Seasonal policies

Stabilizing food prices in the hungry season

It is 6am in late March, the start of the annual hungry season in northern Ghana. I am sitting on a bench in Pusiga village market, along with 15–20 market traders, watching the road to Bawku and Bolgatanga. A truck appears through the dust and early morning mist. The truck has 'GFDC' painted in yellow on its side. The traders stir. The truck pulls up and Seidu Konogini [*name changed*], Senior Commercial Assistant for the Ghana Food Distribution Corporation, jumps down. I greet him and introduce myself.

> Good morning, Mr Konogini. I was told you were coming today. My name is Steve. I am a researcher from England. I am interested in learning about what the government is doing to protect people here in northern Ghana against high food prices in the hungry season. So the traders told me I must talk to you.

Seidu smiles. Someone wants to talk about his job. This is a good start to the day. 'Okay, let's talk!' We sit and Seidu lowers his voice so the traders can't hear, but they are preoccupied with the sacks of rice being offloaded from the GFDC truck.

> Here in Upper East Region you have a problem with food shortage in the dry season. So the traders make big profits by buying millet and sorghum after the harvest and storing it until this time, when they can sell for double or even three times what they paid. Because at this time the farmers' granaries are running empty but they need food, so they will pay any price to get it, even if the traders are cheating them. So our job is to protect poor people from this profit-making by traders.
> And how do you do that?

Okay. I'm sure you know that down south we have big rice farms that produce surpluses every year. We also get more rain down south, so there is no problem with droughts and hunger like you get up here. So at harvest time we buy food crops for cheap prices, then we store them in our warehouse in Tamale until we see prices are starting to rise. This season we bought 46,000 bags of paddy rice and 1,000 mini-bags of millet and sorghum. Now that the dry season has come we travel non-stop around Upper East and Upper West, from market to market, selling our rice at much lower prices than the traders are charging. We only add 32 per cent over what we paid, to cover storage and transport, but we don't make any profit. Like now, we are selling for C6,700 a bag, but the market women are selling rice for C7,400. By June, just before the harvest, they will be charging C9,000 or C10,000 a bag, but we will still be selling for C6,700. At that time, people will be queuing up to buy from us.

And do you sell directly to the public or can traders also buy from you?

We won't ration our sales because we have so much rice in our stores. Today we have 180 bags to sell. So if we don't sell to whoever wants to buy we will be left with thousands of bags of rice rotting in our stores. It is quite common for a trader to buy up six or seven bags. Sometimes one trader will even buy up a whole lorry-load! But we do have time for those who want to buy only one bag. We also cater for those people.

But if you are trying to protect poor people shouldn't you sell only to them? Otherwise the traders can buy your supplies and re-sell at the same high prices they were charging anyway!

Look, the problem we face is that poor people usually buy only in bowls or maybe a basin – they can't afford to buy even one bag. But we can't sell in bowls. So we do sell to the traders but we tell them they should not add any mark-up, because this food is subsidized by the government.

Behind us, traders are loading bags of GFDC rice onto donkey-carts, while 'one-bag' customers are balancing their sacks on bicycles before cycling unsteadily homewards. Seidu goes to supervise sales. After the GFDC truck has departed to the next village market, one of the traders gossips about Seidu. 'Seidu left the Cotton Board to join the GFDC so that he can chop [eat] heavy and grow fat! He always takes home a bag of rice to chop as well as his salary'.

This reputation for corruption and inefficiency pervaded most of Ghana's parastatals. In the years after this interview (which was conducted over 20 years ago, in 1989), the GFDC and many other government agencies were scaled down, commercialized or closed, under structural adjustment conditionalities imposed by the World Bank and the IMF. In a context of fragmented markets and chronic food production deficits, northern Ghanaians were left exposed to food price seasonality with even less protection than the Ghana Food Distribution Corporation attempted to provide.

Stephen Devereux

14

How planning for seasonality can reduce extreme poverty

Lessons from the Chars Livelihoods Programme (2004–2010), Bangladesh[1]

Kate Conroy and Catherine Vignon

This chapter discusses successful responses to seasonality in the context of the DFID-funded Chars Livelihoods Programme Phase 1 (CLP) and the impact these interventions have had on achieving MDG1: namely reducing extreme poverty and increasing food security in the poorest households.[2] CLP was a £50 million integrated rural livelihoods programme based in five riverine districts of the River Jamuna in north-west Bangladesh.[3] Running from 2004–2010, CLP targeted extreme poor island char[4] households, who comprised the economically poorest 10 per cent of the Bangladeshi population but represented approximately 30 per cent of the wider char communities in CLP's working area.

Since 2004, over time and through trial, CLP developed a range of interventions, which adapted to seasonality and year-round pressures on chronically poor char dwellers. These interventions were developed through a progressive and learnt understanding of local livelihoods, varying household needs and the impact that seasonality has on the requirements of char households.

CLP's mutually reinforcing interventions included: significant asset grants to increase household wealth;[5] seasonal employment opportunities to buffer households against poverty shocks; infrastructure to protect against near-annual flooding and improve household sanitation; access to basic primary health and pilot-scale education services to limit intergenerational poverty transmission; and diverse cash safety nets to smooth seasonal fluctuations in household consumption, and environmental and health vulnerability.[6]

Seasonality on the chars

The River Jamuna chars are low-lying temporary sand islands, where approximately one million people have established their homes and livelihoods. These poor and remote agriculture-based communities lack basic infrastructure, healthcare and education services and other key sectors and markets. The isolation and remoteness of the region mean government and institutional resources are limited or absent. Living in a precarious, ecologically vulnerable area, char dwellers also face a tropical monsoonal climate characterized by a series of dry, hot and wet seasons. These seasons are both a blessing and a curse for households, providing peak harvest, employment and wage periods but also giving rise to dramatic overnight erosion and flooding that can prove disastrous for affected families (Chaudhury, 1981; Rahmen, 2002; Khandker, 2009).

Seasonality affects agricultural labour markets, impacts on communications between chars and the mainland limiting access to markets and service providers, influences household food security, and limits the ability to accumulate and protect assets as households make distress sales to meet consumption needs. However, it is the poorest char dwellers, those comprising the extreme poor, who are the least able to absorb and respond to seasonal shocks due to their limited physical, financial and productive asset base (Zug, 2006; Quisumbing, 2007 and Khandker, 2009).

Linkages between seasonality, vulnerability and needs

Rural char households, whether rich or poor, are affected by and must adapt to seasonal variations in their physical environment, employment opportunities and food production (Zug, 2006). Figure 14.1 summarizes seasonal occurrences on the chars, their impact at the household level and what this translates into for char dwellers' most important needs.

Subsequently, char households have specific needs according to the time of year and the intensity of season, with households requiring access to clean water and a safe place to live during the floods and access to food and income generation during *monga* (hunger season) (World Bank, 2008). Dependent on seasonal agricultural daily wages and the changing seasons, char dwellers also often temporarily

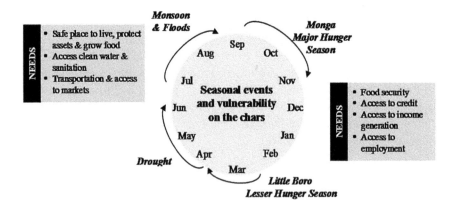

Source: Developed by authors

FIGURE 14.1 Seasonality and changing sources of vulnerability on the chars

and permanently migrate numerous times in their lifetime – a significant expense they can ill afford.

Poor sanitation, hygiene behaviour and inadequate diets on the chars mean under-nutrition is widespread. Under-nutrition results in poor cognitive development in children and those children born of malnourished mothers are likely to have children who are also malnourished. These children also go on to be less productive in later life (DFID, 2010). Incredibly, 61 per cent of the char children surveyed were shown to be undernourished prior to a CLP deworming and micronutrient pilot intervention (IML, 2010b).

Monga

Probably the most damaging of all the seasonality issues facing chronically poor char households is *monga*. *Monga* is a period of seasonal hunger that affects northwest Bangladeshi households and is associated with reduced employment opportunities between the planting and harvesting of the *aman* (rice) crop from September to November. A second, lesser hunger period 'little *boro*' (mid-February to end March) can also occur but is not preceded by flooding and so is not as severe as *monga* (Khandker, 2009). *Monga* used to be prevalent across Bangladesh but is currently only experienced in the more marginal and inaccessible areas of the country and is a predominant feature in the northwest.

Following Sen's (1981) classic argument, *monga* is not a lack of available food. Rather, *monga* is a consequence of seasonally limited work opportunities in a non-diversified rural labour market that results, for those households dependent on agricultural daily labour activities, in declining real wages, and reduced household income, consumption and purchasing power (Khandker, 2009).

Although an anticipated phenomenon, the severity of *monga* experienced at the household level is not only determined by the intensity of the near-annual pre-*monga* floods but is also linked to the household's ability to cope and manage risk (Kabeer, 2002; Holmes *et al.*, 2008). For example, elderly households or households headed by a single female with no working adult males may experience *monga* more severely and for longer periods as they have limited abilities to access work opportunities throughout the year and an often reduced initial asset base.

Furthermore, during *monga* many chronically poor families face not only the possibility of environmental disaster through flooding and erosion but also experience economic crisis and severe consumption constraints. This is reflected in the fact that the incidence of extreme poverty, using the Government of Bangladesh's (GoB) measurement of daily calorie intake of less than 1,805kcals, is comparatively higher in the region than elsewhere in the country (WFP, 2005).

Other seasonality issues

The drought period between April and June each year affects household food production and limits land productivity for those households who cannot afford nor have access to sufficient water supplies and irrigation technologies, with the later monsoon period limiting markets and communication.

During monsoon, the chars are affected by widespread floods. The impact of flood water and their seasonal timings for char dwellers should not be underestimated. Depending on their intensity, these floods have a dual nature for char dwellers, on the one hand stimulating land irrigation and fertility but on the other, seriously affecting the timing and availability of agricultural employment opportunities. Banerjee (2007) comments that July floods are positive (both for irrigation and more intensive intercropping activities) but those in September can be devastating, resulting in crop failure and a potential collapse in the rural labour market. Indeed, in 2007 two successive floods in the northwest destroyed or partially destroyed nearly 1.12 million hectares of cropland (GoB, 2007) – a catastrophe for agricultural daily wage-dependent households.

Accompanying the floods are seasonal peaks in water-borne infections, such as diarrhoeal disease, as families without access to safe water supplies use contaminated drinking water and often live, literally, amongst the floodwater. This can result in serious illness and sometimes death, which disproportionately affects children and the elderly (Chowdhury et al., 1981). Similarly, this period is also associated with an increase in livestock disease, resulting in ill health and the death of valuable household income-generating assets (Kunii et al., 2002).

With 50 per cent of the causes of under-nutrition attributed to a lack of access to a clean water supply and poor sanitation practices, and the long-term reduced cognitive and productive impact that food insecurity can have on children, the multiplier effects of responding to the seasonal needs of extreme poor households are powerful (Waddington et al., 2009; DFID, 2010).

Responses of 'extreme poor' households to seasonality

Clearly, seasonality in its many guises deeply influences char dwellers' lives, but on an individual level how do they respond to seasonal shocks? The focal point of most char families' coping strategies is consumption smoothing to meet the household's basic needs. There are certain 'guiding principles' regarding the use, timing, sequence and content of coping strategies that are employed by households under stress (Kabeer, 2002). This coping process often follows three key phases for the household: that of austerity, then preservation and finally destitution. Significantly, not all households can access or utilize each coping strategy in the same way; an already reduced productive asset or human capital base would mean that the household may face a shock and already be undertaking household preservation or destitution coping activities (see Figure 14.2).

The chronic poor employ a number of coping strategies to survive, often more intensively during seasonal crisis: in distress (and often loss) they sell off assets and labour; take high-interest loans and food credit; migrate for work and often accept reduced or in-kind wages (Conroy and Marks, 2008). Typically, as incomes decline during seasonal crisis 70–75 per cent of household income is spent

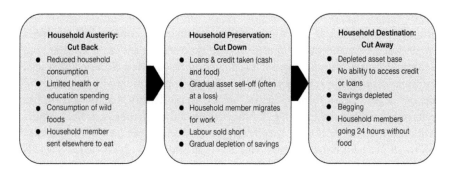

Household Austerity: Cut Back	Household Preservation: Cut Down	Household Destination: Cut Away
• Reduced household consumption	• Loans & credit taken (cash and food)	• Depleted asset base
• Limited health or education spending	• Gradual asset sell-off (often at a loss)	• No ability to access credit or loans
• Consumption of wild foods	• Household member migrates for work	• Savings depleted
• Household member sent elsewhere to eat	• Labour sold short	• Begging
	• Gradual depletion of savings	• Household members going 24 hours without food

Source: Adapted from Kabeer (2002)

FIGURE 14.2 Common coping cycle of chronically poor households

on food by poor families, compared to 56 per cent in non-crisis periods (WFP Bangladesh, 2002).[7] Indeed, seasonal trends in both wages and food prices result in seasonal food consumption patterns and nutritional status, with limited incomes resulting in a reduced ability to purchase food (Chowdhury *et al.*, 1981). Crucially, char households often decrease expenditure by reducing consumption in order to protect their asset base, as reducing consumption (quality, quantity and frequency) is often the most accessible (and sometimes only) crisis-coping strategy they are able to undertake (Conroy and Marks, 2008).

Male household members, if physically able, will migrate seasonally for employment, leaving their homes and families for work opportunities. Such work-related migration has now become part of the char household cycle (Zug, 2006). However, due to cultural and social restrictions, char women have limited livelihood opportunities. Floods also put increased constraints on women by reducing their already limited freedom of movement and moments of privacy (e.g. for defecation).

While these coping strategies enable families to survive in the short term, the longer-term trade-offs, both financially and physically, can result in these households moving much deeper into poverty (CPRC, 2010). Seasonal labour markets, and environmental and consumption shocks result in a constant churning of poor households throughout the year between the transient and chronic poor, resulting in a pushing and pulling of char households between the extreme poor and lower national poverty lines.[8]

Nonetheless, however severe seasonal variations are for households, they are predictable events. As such, they can be mitigated and controlled not only by the household through coping strategies but by seasonally responsive and sensitive interventions by donors and national governments: CLP sought to adopt such an approach. The Bangladesh policy background and subsequent lessons from CLP's interventions and their impact are presented next.

Bangladesh policy context

Although Bangladesh is an environmentally vulnerable country, which has a low resource base and high population density, over the last 20 years there has been significant economic growth and the country has been regarded as 'a lead performer among the least developed countries and considered as a successful example of graduation from traditional society to modernity at a low level of per capita income' (Sen *et al.*, 2004, p2). Nonetheless, although there was also a significant decline in national extreme poverty levels, from 34 per cent of the population to 25 per cent between 2000 and 2005 (World Bank, 2008), large pockets of poverty and deprivation still affect Bangladesh (Kotikula *et al.*, 2007). Over the last decade there has been a growing momentum from both donors and the GoB to tackle and broaden poverty reduction approaches; particularly since the 2005 Bangladeshi Poverty Reduction Strategy Paper (PRSP) explicitly emphasized the need to address extreme poverty, poverty seasonality and *monga* (IMF, 2005). CLP, and other programmes, such as Bangladesh Rural Advancement Committee's asset transfer Challenging the Frontiers of Poverty Reduction, the national food transfer programme Vulnerable Group Development, the Palli Karma-Sahayak Foundation's microfinance-based Programmed Initiatives for Monga Eradication, and CARE's large SHOUHARDO programme were all born of this drive.

In this context, CLP was co-sponsored by the GoB and supported the government's stated PRSP focus to reduce extreme poverty by approximately half by 2015 (IMF, 2005). Funded by DFID, CLP was overseen by a Programme Executive Committee that was chaired by the Ministry of Local Government, Rural Development and Co-operatives that was, in turn, advised by a steering committee of private sector, NGO and government stakeholders.

CLP: responding to the impact of seasonality

Against this backdrop, CLP took a multidimensional approach aimed at improving and meeting basic household needs (i.e. improving food security and stabilizing household income), in addition to supporting household economic growth. As such, CLP sought to challenge or *smooth* seasonal household shocks, by operationalizing a strategy that sought to break the cycles that can either push households into or keep them in extreme poverty. Had it not done so it risked any potential gains its participant households were making.

CLP: tools and governance

Originally beginning as a 'voice and choice' programme in 2004, by 2005 it was recognized that in the context of weak or 'missing' local and central government a large programme using this approach would not be achievable. After consultation with various stakeholders and the success of an experimental first phase of asset transfer to 3,174 households in 2006, the move towards this methodology emerged. This trial, learn and scale-up approach would continue throughout CLP: by the end of the programme in early 2010, 55,000 households had participated in the programme.

CLP learnt that week in, week out close contact and the proximity of the programme's offices to the chars were critical to respond effectively to seasonal crises and the real needs of char dwellers. Working from a secretariat based 200km northwest of Dhaka, CLP delivered its many activities and outputs through up to 21 contracted local implementing organisations (IMOs). In turn, IMOs employed a total of approximately 400 local Community Development Organizers (CDOs) who worked closely with CLP core participant households. Through weekly meetings over an 18-month period, CDOs delivered a 52-week training curriculum, provided monthly household cash stipends and monitored and supported the progress of individual households.

A particular and important characteristic of the relationship between CLP and its IMOs was the use of an accountable grant model, rather than the more popular partnership approach. This characteristic proved to be a key aspect in the ability of CLP to deliver high-quality services and goods to its participant households within agreed timeframes. If IMOs were unable to meet the terms of their contract or if performance was weak, contracts were curtailed and in some cases cancelled.

CLP monitored its transformational (programme outcomes) and transactional (programme outputs) impacts through a series of *ex-ante,* interim and *ex-post* anonymous and annual random surveys by independent contractors. This allowed CLP to respond to issues as they arose and to monitor household poverty transitions.

Adapting programme operations to seasonal climatic events

Programming interventions around the seasonal climatic events was at the core of CLP. Without responding to seasonality many of the hard-won achievements of the programme would have been lost.

A valuable lesson learnt from CLP field activities was the need to be local, flexible, proactive and, above all, timely in approach. This seasonal responsiveness resulted in many new innovations and adjustments to CLP policy, planning and programming. The success of these interventions was rooted in a field-based household-by-household approach. In addition to intensive CDO support, CLP adjusted its logistics, communication and service delivery systems to meet the needs of char dwellers. For example, the seasonal changes in travel times meant that both boats and motorbikes were required to get staff and inputs to participant households.

The near-annual flood cycle on the chars had a major impact on CLP's planning cycles and interventions. Whether it was the transfer of assets at a time of reduced livestock disease or the scheduling of a work programme to coincide with the hunger season, CLP sought to respond to seasonality, and to draw on its opportunities (see Table 14.1 overleaf).

TABLE 14.1 Overview of CLP 'seasonality smoothing' interventions

Bangladeshi seasons		Sheet		Barshanto		Grismo	Barsha		Sharat		Hemanto	
		J	F	M	A	M	J	J	A	S	O	N	D
Seasonal Climatic Events	Hunger Season			Little Boro						Monga			
	Drought												
	Monsoon/ Acute Floods												
CLP Response	Asset Transfer												
	Dry Season CFW												
	IEP												
	IEP Safety Net												

Source: Developed by authors

Transferring income generating assets

A key objective of CLP was to halve extreme poverty in the riverine Jamuna chars by 2015. Fighting seasonal income fluctuation was seen as critical to achieving this goal. Between 2004 and 2010, 55,000 households (approximately 225,000 men, women and children) received investment capital grants to purchase income-generating assets. This 18-month *asset transfer* pathway grew from an initial experimental phase of 3,174 households (Phase 1) in early 2006, with three further phases being added to the programme over three years: Phase 2 comprised 8,246 households (early 2007); Phase 3, 18,850 households (early 2008); with a final 24,730 households in the last CLP phase (Phase 4, late 2008/early 2009).[9] Supporting asset transfer was an intensive but finite package of investment capital, stipends, training and other inputs. The various complementary approaches that CLP employed over time to reduce poverty on the chars was felt necessary, given the multidimensional characteristics of poverty experienced by many targeted households.

Participant households were identified and targeted as *jobless, assetless and landless* through clear selection criteria, which were deemed as proxies for the household's wellbeing status. This non-traditional but operationally efficient approach proved successful as each cohort of households were shown to have the characteristics associated with the extreme poor (Conroy *et al.*, 2010).

Households were free to choose how to spend their asset grants but invariably they opted to buy cattle. Over the programme life cycle, experience showed that households spent approximately 80 per cent of their investment capital on cattle, further sums on small ruminants and any remaining monies used for consumption or the building of a livestock shelter. In addition to receiving investment capital, households were also assisted to support their livestock through a series of capacity building training sessions and the provision of two small monthly cash stipends supporting household consumption and asset support-related costs. To support seasonality and consumption smoothing the cash grants were offered for a period of 18 months, totalling Tk.600 monthly for the first six months and Tk.350 monthly for the remaining 12 months in the core programme.

Importantly, CLP sought to synchronize the transfer of assets to households to take place after the flood period to reduce the potential spread of diseases, like foot-and-mouth, and prevent livestock mortality. Livestock health was further supported through veterinary voucher subsidies and the training of Livestock Service Providers. The success of these combined and mutually reinforcing protection and promotion interventions was evident in the low mortality rates of livestock, at <3 per cent (Scott and Islam, 2010b).

CLP impact: increasing household income, assets and consumption

From an initial asset base of less than Tk.2000, by September 2009 average Phase 1 and 2 households had assets valued at Tk.46,024 and Tk.34,281 respectively (Scott and Islam, 2010b). While this figure includes the value of the original asset transfer, these are significant results for a finite transfer programme only a few years after inception, particularly since both phases had not been receiving assistance from CLP for two years and 18 months respectively. Over the same period, Phase 1 and 2 households had also seen 66 per cent and 59 per cent increases in their average monthly income (Scott and Islam, 2010a).

Food security also significantly improved for participating households. Monthly monitoring over a two-year period (October 2007 to October 2009) showed that there was a significant decrease from 34 per cent to 9 per cent of Phase 1 households reporting that they had reduced their food consumption due to household shortages. Indeed, over the entire reporting period across CLP phases there was a downward trend in household usage of this food coping strategy (see Figure 14.3). It is of note though that despite these clear positive trends, seasonal peaks in reported food insecurity, although decreasingly severe over time, can still be seen during the *monga* period. Nonetheless, research has shown that children and mothers from households recruited earlier in CLP have significantly lower levels of chronic under-nutrition than later phase households (Mascie-Taylor and Goto, 2009).

In addition to a tangible income-generating asset, each core participant household was given a homestead garden package of inputs and training. The package included winter and summer season vegetable seeds and fruit saplings to plant a 25m² garden – enough to allow the family to grow produce year-round on the homestead. The homestead garden initiative was particularly promising for CLP's overwhelmingly female core beneficiaries who had reduced opportunities to access income-generating activities. It also gave these women further control over food stocks and consumption, as men typically purchase household food at the market.

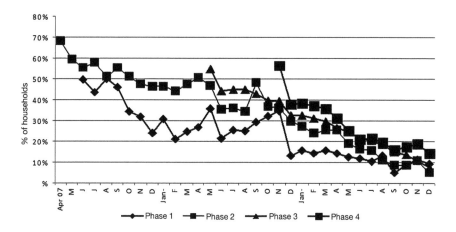

Source: Data taken from internal CLP monthly monitoring of households

FIGURE 14.3 Percentage of households across CLP reporting eating smaller meals due to a shortage of food between April 2007 and December 2009

This seasonally focused intervention was very successful in increasing the food security of participating households. In 2008, during the typically food-scarce *monga* month of October, earlier phase households with established gardens were producing vegetables, fruits and seeds worth, on average, over three times those of the latest phase of households who had just received their homestead garden inputs. Homestead garden produce consumed by households also represented an additional 10 per cent of average monthly food expenditure (Conroy and Islam, 2009). This indicates the real and verifiable impact that seasonally conscious interventions can have on the poorest households.

Responding to seasonal needs

Linked to the local need for seasonal employment opportunities and the lack of basic infrastructure, CLP undertook two major cash-for-work programmes each year. Both of these schemes were seasonally timed and adjusted over the years to meet the changing needs of char dwellers.

Seasonal employment opportunities

The Dry Season Cash for Work (CFW) scheme and the *monga* Infrastructure and Employment Programme (IEP) were specifically planned to take place in January to May and October to December each year, coinciding with the little *boro* and *monga* hunger seasons. This allowed char men and women access to local market-based employment opportunities, buoyed the rural labour market, reduced the need for migration and provided unskilled wages for much of the year.

IEP, in particular, was adapted over time to respond to the varying needs of house-holds during *monga*. In 2007, the start of IEP was delayed by one month due to succes-sive floods. To smooth consumption, mitigate potential asset depletion and offset the huge flood-related loss of agricultural employment opportunities, CLP increased its projected work days from 2 to 3 million, and offered every registered worker up to Tk.500 advance on their future earnings. This flexible and informed programming was successful: approximately 80 per cent of the IEP advance was used for food expenditure (Conroy et al., 2008). Wages were based on local private sector activities, with a 20 per cent premium added to account for the wet working conditions. Further, due to limited work opportunities available to female char dwellers, from 2007 CLP also set aside a guaranteed and non-transferable 30 per cent of IEP jobs for women and a set, five-day, working week was introduced to allow for domestic activities.

Environmental protection against erosion and floods

Built through these work employment schemes, earthen plinths on which to erect homes offered environmental protection against annual flooding by raising home-steads above the highest known local flood level. Once the plinths had been raised, households were then given access to improved sanitation facilities and safe, clean water. To reduce potential leakage and ensure that quality plinths were built, CLP developed a robust anti-corruption reporting framework and undertook regular independent audits of its outputs.

The impact of seasonal responses

The success of raised plinths was evident during the consecutive floods of 2007, with many providing shelter and safety to numerous char families (Marks and Islam, 2007). Participation on IEP was also shown to be associated with signifi-cantly reduced household loan-taking, distress sales and work-related migration, and improved women's and children's nutritional status (Conroy and Marks, 2008; Mascie-Taylor and Goto, 2009).

Preventative and responsive safety nets

Over its programme cycle, CLP offered a range of safety net stipends to quali-fying households to both enable and ensure their pathway out of extreme poverty. The need for programme flexibility to adjust established interventions or trial new approaches was critical to both reducing extreme poverty and ensuring that house-holds remained buoyant during seasonal shock. In addition to the monthly stipends offered to beneficiaries, one-off fixed grants were also offered to any char house-hold forced to move as a result of river erosion, which covered the cost of house rebuilding and the resettlement of families. All these cash transfers were delivered to beneficiaries through CDOs and, if necessary, were distributed to the household within a matter of days – essential when households are facing overnight shocks.

Adjusting established interventions

In response to the seriousness of *monga* in 2007, CLP offered Phase 2 and 3 households up to two months of these advance cash stipends. This response offset the need to draw down on assets or take high-interest loans for vulnerable households early in their CLP pathway. The success of this experimental approach meant that it was repeated in 2008. However, once set, cash transfers must be allowed to be adjusted to meet crisis or rising inflation; as such, inflationary adjustments were made both to the initial asset grant and to the accompanying cash stipends that core participants received.

Piloting initiatives and new interventions

Responding in time to severe seasonal shocks is critical in assisting poor households to cope. For example, when IMOs reported that the food price crisis was seriously affecting char dwellers, in August 2008 CLP responded with a monthly cash Temporary Food Transfer (TFT). The TFT was directly linked to the local price of *mota chal* (coarse rice), with the total cash transfer adjusted according to the number of women and children within each Phase 3 or 4 household. Initially set at Tk.50 per woman and child, this safety net was reduced over time and gradually phased out, as the price of *mota chal* fell back to pre-crisis levels, in mid-2009.

In the context of adopting seasonally responsive interventions, it should be recognized that not all households have the same needs. In 2007, CLP offered families who were not able to participate in the IEP scheme a small weekly time-bound cash transfer – the IEP Safety Net (IEP SN). Qualifying criteria included households with pregnant or nursing women, disabled or elderly with *no other* productive family member; elderly female-headed households made up the majority of IEP SN awardees. This 12-week grant provided the most vulnerable households with a regular and guaranteed cash flow during *monga*.

These initiatives worked. During *monga* 2007, IEP SN households took only a quarter of the food loans and a third of the food credit per capita that 'control' households sought over the same period (see Figure 14.4).[10] These households also begged for food/cash for significantly fewer days than similar households not receiving the grant (Marks, 2008).

The seriousness of the 2007 flood saw CLP move outside of its remit and undertake a significant humanitarian flood relief operation. Dramatic overnight flooding in the northwest saw a wide appeal by the GoB for assistance. Within a few days of the flood peak, a £1 million operation was delivered by CLP, through its local partners and their staff and logistic support. Covering 713 villages, 6.3 million person days of food was given to 128,000 households. In addition, nearly two million water purification tablets were distributed and almost 4,000 cattle and people were rescued. Field staff and local NGO networks were not only essential for this but the rapid approval and mobilization of funds by DFID were critical for the success of the project.

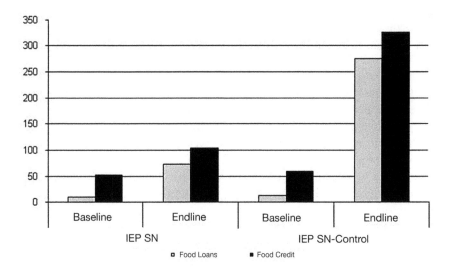

Source: Conroy and Marks (2008)

FIGURE 14.4 Per capita food loans and credit (Tk.) taken during *monga* (2007) by IEP SN and control households

Similarly, CLP realized the need to be continually responsive to the needs of households through the development and trial of new interventions, even late into its own programme cycle. During *monga* 2009, CLP trialled a three-month combined therapy of daily micronutrients and the provision of deworming tablets. For both adults and children, there were considerable short-term impacts. By the end of the three-month trial period, for children there was a 54 per cent reduction in wasting in the deworming and micronutrient group, 40 per cent reduction in the deworming only group and only 3.5 per cent in the control group. Adults who undertook the combined therapy over the period also experienced least weight loss (IML, 2010a).

Sustainability

Although the impacts of the CLP pathway have been shown in reducing both extreme poverty and food insecurity, as ever questions remain about sustainability and the replicable nature of the approach.

Unquestionably, CLP had significant resources and remit to undertake its multi-component approach. The CLP pathway required intensive input, costing approximately £557 in total per participant household (Conroy *et al.*, 2010). At the global level, will such significant resources be available in the new climate of financial austerity that many donor countries are experiencing? In this changing donor context, more research needs to be undertaken into whether different types and intensities of these various poverty reduction measures would achieve greater value for money and leveraging of impact results at the household level.

While it has been shown that participant households have increased income streams and been more resilient to shock, as CLP's presence and staff leave project areas will these households maintain their asset base and still be able to cope during future crises? Although the results to date show success, with just over four years since the initial asset transfers, it is still too early to know at the household level whether these apparent trajectories out of poverty will continue in the medium and longer term. CLP is continuing to monitor a representative cohort of households into the new CLP2 programme and will need to carefully analyse the various trajectories of differing households to understand fully its longer-term programmatic impact.

Although CLP ran a large successful pilot in health provision, improved household sanitation and drinking water access and gave emphasis to sanitation, nutrition and hygiene behaviour through various training sessions, more action is needed in this area. As a driver of downward poverty transitions, improving health services and provision will continue to be an area that needs to be urgently addressed. This is beyond a short-term donor-funded programme and needs wide-ranging support from the GoB, as well as significant funding.

Eradicating *monga* permanently in areas such as the chars will require more than a finite asset transfer programme such as CLP. While CLP may have helped to ameliorate the worst realities of extreme poverty beyond income and consumption stabilization, government, local markets and service provision need to be dramatically improved. This will be a huge challenge given the remote location and current failures in the adequate provision of basic services such as health, education and the rule of law. For this to happen, local government and institutions will need to be intensively supported and developed, financially and technically, to build their capacities and these systems. This will also take significant resources and time.

Policy recommendations

Despite the context-specific nature and idiosyncrasies of development problems and solutions, there are transferable lessons learnt from the CLP experience.

Understanding seasonality, locally and in time

Chronically poor households, dependent on agricultural daily wage employment, are the most vulnerable to price inflation and seasonal drops in income, employment and food security. Adopting flexible programming that allows for and can respond quickly to these needs in the context of local seasonality is needed. However, practitioners and programmes must go beyond known generalizations and understand what is actually taking place on the ground. This means undertaking close monitoring of participating households and their wider communities prior to and for the duration of their participant cycles and beyond. Furthermore, to achieve a truly seasonally responsive programme, offices and staff must be located in the field near participants and the programme management context should not be reliant on lengthy procurement processes or fixed budgets.

Programmes must have the flexibility to meet seasonal needs, either establishing or adapting programme interventions or through additional safety nets in real time, not weeks or months later. It is also critical to adjust cash safety nets and asset grants according to inflationary increases. Focus should also be given to complementary interventions which address the seasonal protection, promotion and transformation of livelihoods. Gender impacts cannot be forgotten and tailored employment opportunities should be designed that women and workers from female-headed households can undertake, specifically during periods of seasonal crisis.

Specific seasonal social protection interventions

In the context of agrarian-based societies, transferring income-generating assets has been shown to protect against and smooth the impact of seasonal fluctuations in household income and consumption. Nonetheless, to ensure that these gains are not lost, additional and temporary safety nets, such as small cash stipends, can prevent seasonal distress sale of assets and sustain household consumption. Furthermore, programming significant employment opportunities for the wider community during seasonal lean periods reduces the use of damaging household coping strategies and provides significant infrastructure to secure households against seasonal flooding and disease. To improve household health and productivity, these households also require seasonal pre-emptive health interventions that target and include a reduction in parasitic worms and increase micronutrient intake and absorption.

The lessons learnt from CLP are simple. Development assistance is most effective when tailored to the local seasonal context within which recipient participants live and work. Programmes and their sub-components must be able to adjust and respond, quickly, to the varying intensity of seasonal fluctuations and changing needs. Prior to and throughout a programme's cycle, this requires a learnt, context-specific, understanding of vulnerability, its multiple dimensions and variability throughout the year. Subsequently, interventions must be sequenced according to these requirements.

Finally, to pre-empt seasonality effects and pre-position programme responses, seasonal trends must be monitored and, if necessary, interventions adjusted, with findings disseminated to the wider development community. More research needs to take place reviewing the degree to which events linked to climate change may impact on seasonal trends: this will have to take place in the context of extreme poor households, if we hope to achieve MDG 1 globally.

Notes

1 Adapted from Conroy, K. and Vignon, C. (2009) 'How planning for seasonality can reduce Extreme poverty: Lessons from the Chars Livelihoods Programme, Bangladesh', briefing paper for the 'Seasonality Revisited' International Conference, Institute of Development Studies, July 2009.
2 The authors follow DFID's 2009 definition of extreme poverty of $1.25 per capita per day corresponding to the economically poorest 10 per cent of the population.
3 These districts were Kurigram, Gaibandha, Jamalpur, Sirajganj and Bogra.
4 Chars are low-lying temporary sand islands.
5 The asset grant was initially set at Tk.13,000 for the first phase of participant households (2006), inflation-adjusted to Tk.17,000 for the fourth and final cohort in 2009.
6 These included: erosion grants for households forced to permanently migrate following annual floods; a monthly asset maintenance grant and consumption smoothing stipend to buffer against distress sales and reduced household consumption; and a small cash allowance for households during *monga* (seasonal hunger) that could not participate in cash-for-work initiatives.
7 This figure is also supported by CLP internal monthly monitoring income and expenditure figures of its core beneficiaries (www.clp.bangladesh.org).
8 For further details on poverty thresholds in Bangladesh see Jackson, 2009.
9 See the CLP website (www.clp-bangladesh.org) for further information regarding each cohort of participants.
10 Control households met the qualifying criteria stated above but lived in villages where IEP activities were not present, so did not receive the grant.

15

Seasonality and capital in farm household models

Andrew Dorward

Introduction

Seasonality is a major feature of rainfed agriculture and plays a significant part in perpetuating poverty. One major feature of this is the way that people juggle peaks and troughs in highly seasonal agricultural labour demands and incomes with relatively constant consumption requirements and labour supply across the year. The problems of managing these seasonal peaks and troughs and their effects are much greater for poorer people in poorer economies than for less poor people in more developed economies. It is then both surprising and unfortunate that these problems are commonly overlooked in the widespread use of standard household models in the analysis of the impacts of policy and other changes on poor rural people's behaviour and welfare. This chapter describes a simple modification of standard household models to take account of seasonal imbalances in household consumption needs and resources, and associated seasonality in wages and prices. It then uses a graphical simplification of the model to show how allowance for seasonal factors can change model predictions of the welfare and behaviour of poor people.

Following this introduction, the paper provides a brief review first of key seasonal factors affecting poor rural people with significant dependence on farming and then of farm household models' common inattention to these factors. A relatively simple modification to the standard model is put forward. Insights and benefits from the wider use of models allowing for these seasonal factors are demonstrated by examining the effects of changes in prices, wages, and unsubsidized and subsidized technologies on households with different resource and consumption characteristics. Significant differences from (improvements over) predictions of the standard model are shown for some (generally poorer) households.

Seasonality and access to financial services

The particular seasonal nature of much agricultural production (particularly rainfed crop production) is one of the characteristics of agriculture that have traditionally set it apart from other industries or sectors, even in wealthier economies where agriculture is a relatively unimportant part of the economy.[1] This leads to seasonal troughs in pre-harvest demands for labour and working capital which precede seasonal peaks in income from post-harvest crop production. Labour supply and income demand for basic food and other expenditures are, however, more evenly distributed across the year – indeed higher pre-harvest morbidity and demands for health, school, festival and other expenditures may reduce pre-harvest labour supply and increase pre-harvest income demands. Without good access to financial and wider labour and produce markets, seasonal imbalances between supply and demand of labour and income can then interact to cause seasonal variations in prices, not only of labour and farm produce, but also of other assets that people use for saving (livestock, for example). The effects of this on farm household and sectoral behaviour and welfare are particularly severe among poorer farm households living in poorer rural areas due to thin and poorly functioning produce and asset markets which should otherwise smooth prices across the year, limited diversity and importance of non-farm income sources, and limited access to seasonal capital due to poverty and lack of personal assets and access to financial services and markets (for savings, borrowing and insurance). The nature and effects of these seasonal problems and of their interactions have been recognized in a long-standing literature identifying and describing seasonal constraints affecting different types of rural households and their responses to these constraints (Chambers *et al.*, 1981; Longhurst, 1986; Corbett, 1989; Davies, 1989; Gill, 1991; Ellis, 2000; see also the other chapters in this book). An important theme in this has been the extent and effects of seasonal poverty traps (Chambers, 1983) which is linked to consideration of more general asset poverty traps associated with resurgent interest in risk, uncertainty, vulnerability and social protection (for example, Carter and Barrett, 2006; Carter and Barrett, 2007; Barnett *et al.*, 2008).

Poor rural people's lack of access to saving, borrowing and insurance services is a core element of poverty traps. On the one hand, access to these services allows better exploitation of opportunities for people to invest their assets more productively. On the other hand, development of these services is inhibited by lack of productivity for individual households and for the economies in which they are located (see Newbery and Stiglitz, 1981; Feder *et al.*, 1985; Binswanger and Rosenzweig, 1986; Binswanger and McIntire, 1987; Dorward, 1996, 2006; Dorward *et al.*, 2005, 2009). Furthermore, seasonality in agriculture poses particular problems for microfinance services (Morduch, 1999), problems which have seriously restricted the spread of microfinance services in poor rural areas (Poulton *et al.*, 2010). The effects of seasonality and lack of access to financial services on poor rural people's behaviour, productivity and welfare analysis should therefore be an important element in modelling and analysis of poor farm households and their livelihoods.

Farm household models

General farm household models have provided a valuable theoretical basis for empirical and conceptual analysis of interactions between production and consumption resource allocations of poor rural people. Building on standard production economics and early twentieth-century analysis by Chayanov of peasant agriculture in Russia (Ellis, 1993), farm household models developed by Nakajima (1986) and by Barnum and Squire (1979) have been widely used to develop theoretical understanding of peasant farm households (by investigating theoretical properties of and inferences from these models) and for empirical investigation of the effects of different technical, market and policy changes on different peasant farm households' behaviour, welfare and interactions with produce and factor markets.

These models have been given significant attention by postgraduate agricultural and rural development textbooks. Ellis (1993), for example, provides a particularly accessible review of different models and of the insights they provide. Singh et al. (1986) presented an early and seminal collection of papers describing examples of development and empirical application of farm household models. Bardhan and Udry (1999) and Sadoulet and de Janvry (1995) are other examples of textbooks introducing students and analysts to the particular features of peasant households and to analytical techniques for investigating and describing the behaviour of peasant households and economies. Taylor and Adelman (2003) review these models with the explicit objective of providing a starting point for students and researchers to build models to investigate impacts of policy and market changes.

Unfortunately, a failure of the models presented in much of the dominant theoretical and empirical literature and exemplified in the texts discussed above (which both describe and influence theoretical and empirical work), is the lack of the integrated analysis of simultaneous production and consumption decisions (the focus of the farm household models discussed above) with the effects of seasonal capital constraints.[2] Singh *et al.* (1986) include no discussion of seasonal credit constraints or examples of models addressing this, although Iqbal (1986) allows for inter-year (not intra-year) borrowing and saving. Ellis (1993) makes no mention of credit market failures in his chapters on farm household models. Sadoulet and de Janvry (1995, pp164 ff) include discussion of a related literature that considers the effects of liquidity constraints on intertemporal household models looking at life cycle, inter-year liquidity constraints (again rather than intra-year liquidity constraints). Bardhan and Udry (1999), in a chapter on household models, discuss only land and labour market failures (not credit market failures) and in a subsequent chapter on credit markets explore credit market failures in terms of information economics, without reference to their impacts on household behaviour. Taylor and Adelman (2003) in their review mention a small literature on household models showing or describing credit market failures, but make no mention of seasonality, and do not consider credit market failures in further discussion of the application, development or weaknesses of models.

A general pattern is apparent in this, that financial market failures (including in some cases seasonal market failures) is a topic that is addressed in some of the farm/household model or related literature. However, this literature tends to have a relatively narrow focus on exploring variations in effective demand for, or supply of, different seasonal finance services: it has been less concerned with exploring the impacts of lack of access to financial services and severe seasonal finance constraints on wider aspects of poor farm household behaviour and welfare, and some models which do consider seasonal finance constraints lack other elements that are critical for examination of the wider issues addressed in this chapter (see, for example, Carter and Olinto, 2003; Feder *et al.*, 1990).

Models that do address these issues are rare, but welcome. Skoufias (1993) and de Janvry *et al.* (1992) present models that allow for seasonal (intra-year) credit constraints affecting production and consumption decisions within and between seasons. However, as demonstrated by the brief review of textbooks above, this approach is rarely cited or followed in other, particularly more recent, papers: very few studies using household models to examine the impacts of changes in other variables (for example input or output prices or technology) take account of the impacts of seasonal finance constraints on farm household responses to such change.

Absence of wider consideration of the effects of seasonal market failures on farm household behaviour leads to important failings in the general use of farm household models. The models' focus on future (harvest and post-harvest season) consumption from own production – not on consumption for current survival – ignores poor rural people's preoccupation with current survival at the expense of their ability to invest in future production, but this is a major feature of the seasonal poverty traps discussed earlier. This failing arises from the conflation of income from crop production at or after harvest with pre-harvest income and expenditure associated with buying and selling labour, but this conflation fails to describe capital constraints on livelihood options.

As compared with more generalizable econometric farm household models discussed above, these issues have been more commonly addressed in situation-specific linear and non-linear programming models (Holden, 1993; Dorward, 1996; Alwang and Siegel, 1999; Dorward, 1999, 2006). These models show the critical importance of seasonal finance constraints and production/consumption interactions in together constraining the behaviour and welfare of poor rural people. Dorward (2006), for example, shows widely differing responses to and welfare effects of maize price and wage rate changes for poor and less poor people in Malawi, with backward sloping supply responses to maize prices and wages for the poorest households, and more limited uptake of more productive technologies as a result of seasonal credit constraints.

The results of the common omission of seasonal finance constraints from general farm household models are therefore not merely academic and conceptual: these analytical mis-specifications can lead to serious errors (a) in diagnosis of the problems facing poor rural people and (b) in policy and other prescriptions to address these problems.

The remainder of this paper demonstrates the following:

- the standard farm household model as described by Sadoulet and de Janvry is easily extended to take account of seasonal finance constraints;
- such extensions can provide valuable analytical and policy insights where significant numbers of farm households do face serious seasonal finance constraints; and
- consequently, 'seasonal farm household models' should be the standard default that is routinely implemented.

A formal farm household model allowing for limited access to seasonal finance

The introduction of seasonal finance market failures into algebraic models is conceptually simple, involving the separation by season of consumption and income in the utility function, of leisure (or disutility of labour) in the utility function, and of labour equations. This must be accompanied by the introduction of a seasonal capital equation and of new variables in labour and income equations. A minimalist standard seasonal farm household model with pre-harvest and post-harvest seasons can then be represented as:[3]

$$\text{Max } U = u\ (C_1, C_2, V_2, L_R, H_R) \tag{1}$$

where u is the household utility function with utility U determined by pre-harvest and post-harvest consumption C_1 and C_2, value of post-harvest cash and stocks V_2, and harvest and pre-harvest 'leisure' (or disutility of household labour) L_R and H_R such that:

$$L_t = L_o + L_F + L_R - L_1 \tag{2}$$

$$H_t = H_o + H_F + H_R - H_1 \tag{3}$$

$$V_1 = p_1 C_1 + V_T + w_1 L_1 + V_F + V_S - B - w_1 L_o \tag{4}$$

$$V_2 = V_T + p_2(Y - C_2) + (1+i)\ V_S - (1+i)B + w_2 H_1 - w_2 H_o \tag{5}$$

$$Y = y(L_F, H_F, V_F, D) \tag{6}$$

where L_t = household pre-harvest labour supply; L_o = hiring out of pre-harvest labour; L_F = on-farm pre-harvest labour use; L_1 = hiring in of pre-harvest labour; H_t, H_o, H_F, H_R and H_1 defined as for L_t, L_o, L_F, L_R and L_1 but for harvest labour; V_1 = value of pre-seasonal cash and stocks (working capital); V_T = carry-forward of pre-seasonal cash and stocks; w = wages for labour hire; V_F = on-farm investment of pre-seasonal working capital; V_S = savings/lending of pre-seasonal working capital at interest rate i; B = borrowing of pre-seasonal working capital; p = price of farm produce; and Y is harvest-time production expressed as a production function y of pre-harvest and harvest farm labour use, on-farm investment of pre-seasonal working capital and land use.

This model can be extended in a number of ways, for example to allow seasonal and/or differential buying and selling wage rates and/or food prices, differentiation between pre-harvest time periods, land rental, separation of farm and purchased consumption, and different farm production activities (see Dorward, 2006). The standard farm household model presented by Sadoulet and de Janvry is a special case of the general seasonal farm household model presented above, where V_1 is large relative to $p_1 C_1$ and/or i is low such that equation 4 does not constrain equations 5 and 6, and equations 2 and 3 can consequently be conflated, as can equations 4 and 5, with removal of C_1 from equation 1 and the simple summation of L_R and H_R in equation 1.

The model in equations 1 to 6 should be amenable to econometric estimation from farm household data sets, subject to the normal difficulties of obtaining the necessary (reliable) data and of specifying and estimating tractable and appropriate functional forms.

Analysing change with limited access to seasonal finance

Dorward (2010) develops a graphical analysis and presentation of the model above describing key effects of seasonal finance constraints on farm household behaviour when producing a staple food crop. He then uses it to demonstrate differential effects of price, wage and input subsidy effects on household behaviour and welfare, depending upon households' access to and needs for seasonal capital. He begins by distinguishing between four different household types, with different ratios of pre-harvest consumption requirements to pre-harvest working capital and different ratios of pre-harvest working capital to land. These are shown in Table 15.1.

Household types A and B are both poorer households with lower labour and capital resources per consumption unit (with higher dependency ratios), and household type B is also land-poor. Both these households are prone to serious seasonal finance constraints as their pre-harvest capital is insufficient to provide for their consumption requirements, so their pre-harvest decisions may be constrained by their need to use capital for consumption rather than on-farm production. Household types C and D have more labour and capital resources per consumption unit (with lower dependency ratios), and household type D also has more land. Their greater pre-harvest capital stocks mean that these households are less prone to serious seasonal finance constraints, so their pre-harvest on-farm production is not affected by the need to use capital for meeting consumption requirements.

Dorward's graphical presentation of the seasonal model shows that although the analysis is clearly different from standard farm household analysis, the results it generates are similar in describing general comparisons between different

TABLE 15.1 Household types

		C:X ratio Pre-harvest ratio of consumption requirements (C_{1min}) to working capital (X_{max})	
		High (high dependency)	**Low** (low dependency)
X:land ratio Pre-harvest ratio of working capital (X_{max}) to land	**Low** (more land)	A	D
	High (less land)	B	C

Source: Dorward (2010)

household types as regards patterns of labour hire, on-farm labour use and welfare: poorer households hire out labour and have lower welfare achievements, less poor households hire in labour and have higher welfare achievements. Similarly, land-poor households hire in less labour or hire out more labour and have lower welfare achievements than households with more land.

Differences between this and standard farm household analysis arise, however, in examination of responses to and impacts of different types of change. Figure 15.1 compares the analysis of the effects of a change in wages for household types A and D using a seasonal model. Further explanation of the model may be found in Dorward (2010). The minimum pre-harvest consumption requirement of each household is shown by C_{1min}, and this requires X_0 of working capital (measured in labour days equivalent). Household D has greater stocks of capital and is able to meet this relatively easily from its total stocks of initial working capital of X_{max}, and then apply further capital to hiring in labour. Household A, however, has much more restricted initial working capital relative to C_{1min} and therefore has to hire out pre-harvest labour so that its earnings can meet minimum household consumption. This is despite much higher returns to labour from on-farm production than from wages.

The allocation of pre-season stocks and pre-harvest labour is shown along the top of the diagram for each household. Initial asset stocks are used for consumption, augmented by hiring out of labour if assets are insufficient to meet consumption needs. Further labour is then allocated to on-farm production up to the point where the total physical product (TPP) curve touches an indifference curve or wage line (bold circles in Figure 15.1). Comparison of the two households' initial situations shows that household A hires labour out to meet pre-harvest consumption requirements, and is only able to allocate a limited amount of labour to on-farm production, and has little labour and capital available for other uses, such as household tasks. Household D, on the other hand, is able to finance all its consumption

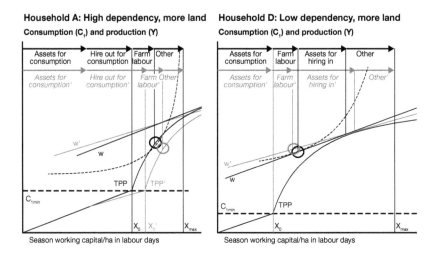

FIGURE 15.1 Graphical presentation of household model of change in wages with seasonal capital constraints

from its assets and then hire in labour on the farm to supplement household labour, with higher production per hectare, higher welfare (represented by achievement of a higher and 'flatter' indifference curve), and more resources for other uses.

We now consider the effects of a fall in wage rates, represented by a shallower wage line w'. The effect on household D is a relatively minor switch of resources to hire in more labour to both increase on-farm labour use per hectare and reduce the amount of household members' work on the farm. This analysis is no different from that of the standard household model without allowance for seasonal capital constraints. For household A, however, the fall in wages makes its seasonal capital constraints more severe, as more labour has to be allocated to meet its pre-harvest consumption needs. This reduces the labour available to on-farm production, effectively shifting the TPP curve to the right (TPP'). As a result, there is an increase in hiring out for consumption, a decrease in the household's on-farm labour, a reduction in its production per hectare, a reduction in the labour available for other uses (childcare, for example), and a reduction in welfare (with achievement of a lower indifference curve, which is not drawn). This analysis is different from that produced by a standard household model, as it leads to a backward sloping supply curve for pre-harvest labour, a reduction in on-farm labour use and farm production (not an increase), and a greater reduction in welfare and in labour available for other uses. This represents a less efficient use of land and labour by these households, and hence a fall in the overall productivity of the rural sector. The model therefore demonstrates the effects of seasonality on the behaviour of poor households constrained by seasonal capital (in terms of their hiring out of labour and on-farm work), on their welfare, on the productivity of their labour, and on the productivity of the agricultural and rural sectors if such households make up a significant proportion of the population and labour force and farm a significant proportion of cultivatable land.[4]

Similar results are obtained for rising food crop prices, provided that there are identical pre-harvest and post-harvest prices (a strict condition) as they both affect real wages evaluated in terms of food purchasing power. This leads to a backward sloping supply curve among poor households with severe pre-harvest capital constraints. This analysis is consistent with results from formal non-linear programming models reported in Dorward (2006) for different types of household in Malawi.

Table 15.2 summarizes the effects of falling wages on the four household types (analysis for households B and C are similar to those for A and D).

We now consider the effects of new technology on the different household types in Table 15.1. If adoption of the new technology requires no extra labour or other capital investments in the pre-harvest period then there are few differences in outcomes from standard farm household model analysis: production and welfare achievements increase across all households and hired labour demand increases for household types C and D (see Table 15.3). This applies if only direct and immediate household impacts are considered. If wider market effects are also considered then the increased production and demand for harvest labour should exert pressures that depress produce prices and/or increase wages (if these markets are to some extent separated from wider markets), and (as shown by the analysis of the effects of wage and produce prices changes) the impacts of these will be different where seasonal finance constraints are considered – with particular benefits for poorer households.

How is this analysis changed if the new technology requires some initial investment in, for example, extra labour, seed or fertilizer? Provided such investments are not too high, the ability of households C and D to benefit from adoption will not be affected. For households A and B, however, adoption of such technology reduces the working capital available for consumption and would need to be financed by an increase in the hiring out of labour, with a consequent fall in

TABLE 15.2 Impacts of rise in output prices or fall in wages

Farm/ hh type	C:X ratio	X:land ratio	Price increase/wage fall effects			
			Labour Hire		Production	Welfare
			In	Out		
A	High	Low	n/a	↑	↓	↓
B	High	High	n/a	↑	↓	↓
C	Low	High	↑	n/a	↑	↑
D	Low	Low	↑	n/a	↑	↑

Source: modified from Dorward (2010)

Note: '↑' represents an increase, '↓' a decrease. Only direct impacts and responses are identified.

labour available for on-farm work and reduction in on-farm production. Unless the consequent fall in production from reduced farm labour is more than compensated for by the benefits of technical change in increasing labour productivity (which is unlikely for many poorer households), investment in new technology leads to lower welfare, and the new technology will therefore not be adopted.[5]

This analysis explains variation between apparently similar households (similar in terms of land and labour endowments) regarding their technology choices and productivity and can be extended to consider the impacts of a subsidy that reduces the seasonal working capital requirements for the new technology. A partial subsidy is assumed that substantially reduces, but does not eliminate, the cost of inputs such as seed or fertilizer. The analysis is only relevant for household types A and B, since only these household types would not invest in the new technology without a subsidy. As compared to the unsubsidized situation, the reduction in seasonal working capital as a result of the subsidy reduces the need to divert labour from on-farm production to the hiring out of labour (to meet immediate investment and consumption requirements). If the opportunity cost of the reduced on-farm labour use is now smaller than the benefit of adopting the new technology, then the subsidy will allow household types A and B to achieve higher production and improved welfare with new technology. This result depends upon the size and nature of the subsidy, and the new technology's impact on land and labour productivity. If the subsidy is rationed and targeted, then subsidy recipients may also be able to sell some of their subsidized inputs, increasing their seasonal working capital and perhaps allowing them to invest their retained inputs without the need for any increased hiring out of labour.

The likelihood of changes in labour and produce demand and supply should again lead to lower output prices and higher local wages, benefiting poorer households, if these markets are separated to some extent from wider markets. Price and wage changes should be more marked as compared with the unsubsidized situation, as output and labour market effects should be greater, if there are large numbers of subsidy beneficiaries.[6]

TABLE 15.3 Impacts of technical change without and with investment or subsidy

Farm/ hh type	Pure technical change				Technical change with investment				Technical change with investment and subsidy			
	Labour Hire		Production	Welfare	Labour Hire		Production	Welfare	Labour Hire		Production	Welfare
	In	Out			In	Out			In	Out		
A	n/a	=	↑	↑	n/a	↓	↓	↓	n/a	↑/=	↑	↑
B	n/a	=	↑	↑	n/a	↓	↓	↓	n/a	↑/=	↑	↑
C	↑	n/a	↑	↑	↑	n/a	↑	↑	↑	n/a	↑	↑
D	↑	n/a	↑	↑	↑	n/a	↑	↑	↑	n/a	↑	↑

Note: '↑' represents an increase, '↓' a decrease, and '=' no change. Only direct impacts and responses are identified.

The analysis presented here and summarized in Table 15.3 is consistent with analysis of the impacts on different household types of the 2005/6 to 2008/9 large-scale agricultural input subsidy programme in Malawi (School of Oriental and African Studies *et al.*, 2008; Dorward and Chirwa, 2011) and supports emerging arguments regarding the role of subsidies in promoting the affordability of inputs rather than just their profitability where poor households face severe seasonal capital constraints (Dorward, 2009).

Conclusions

The stylized findings presented in this paper make two important contributions to the analysis of poor rural people's livelihoods and of the rural economies of which they are a part.

First, they provide a clear analytical demonstration of an important way in which seasonality leads to low productivity and locks poor rural people and poor rural economies into a poverty trap, and undermines ways in which traditional price and technology interventions might be expected to promote growth and poverty reduction. The damaging effects of seasonality examined formally here are exacerbated by other aspects of seasonality (such as seasonal asset price variability and morbidity). There is a clear message here: seasonality, at least with respect to seasonal capital constraints, should be given much more attention in rural livelihood analysis and policy formulation.

Second, the approach used in this chapter to examine these issues suggests a set of tools for the investigation of the effects of seasonal capital constraints in rural livelihood analysis and policy formulation. These tools may range from econometric model estimation with formal simulation of different interventions and changes on different households and markets, through to much more informal consideration of the cause and effect pathways linking seasonal capital constraints and poor rural people's behaviour, welfare and options for climbing out of rural poverty.

Notes

1   Other features of agriculture that set it apart from other sectors are the relatively inelastic demand for many agricultural (particularly food) products; the particular importance of food to human consumption; the dispersed nature of crop production; agriculture's dependence and effects on renewable natural resources; and, in poor agricultural economies, the large proportion of employment and GDP associated with agriculture (particularly in rural areas where poverty incidence and severity tend to be highest); the integration of consumption and production in subsistence and (more commonly) semi-subsistence farm households; and financial (savings, credit and insurance) market failures (particularly in poorer areas and among poorer households predominantly producing food crops).

2   There are of course other weaknesses with the farm household models, most importantly their failure to describe the nature and effects of intra-household relations and their limited ability to describe market linkage equilibrium effects. These issues are, however, widely recognized by analysts and in the textbooks discussed earlier, and a range of formal models have been developed to address these issues – see McElroy and

Horney (1981), Smith (1998), Quinsumbing (2007) and Seebens and Sauer (2007) on intra-household relations and Taylor and Adelman (2003) on market linkage effects.

3   The model presented here is similar in many ways to those presented by Skoufias (1993) and Dorward (2006) – extension to more seasons is conceptually very simple with more seasonal subscripts and equations.

4   These effects, and seasonal capital constraints, will be diminished if there is a flourishing market for land rental (or indeed sale, though distress sales carry many risks for poor people), with enough capitalized buyers to offer reasonable prices and cultivate the land effectively.

5   This analysis only takes account of direct responses and impacts. Increased hired labour demand and higher production should lead to indirect, market effects lowering output prices and raising local wages (if these markets are to some extent separated from wider markets and if there are sufficient numbers of producers able to adopt the new technology) and this may offer benefits to poorer households that are unable to adopt the new technology themselves.

6   It should be noted that output price effects may however be dampened somewhat if the 'profit effect' (see Ellis, 1993) increases output consumption. Wage effects, however, may be heightened if increased real incomes increase demand for non-tradeable goods and services. Falling output prices and rising wages should themselves also lead to positive impacts on poorer households' welfare in subsequent seasons and thus raise the possibility of a virtuous circle of growth.

16

Seasonality and access to education in sub-Saharan Africa

Sierd Hadley[1]

Introduction

Improved education is associated with higher socioeconomic status, lower fertility rates, improved health, reduced mortality rates and greater gender equality and mobility. Investment in primary education is especially crucial, as it offers the greatest private social returns to investment of all education spending. However, despite continued investment in education in sub-Saharan Africa, the net primary enrolment rate for the sub-continent remains the lowest in the world at 67.2 per cent (Huebler, 2006). Dropout rates and gender disparities have also tended to be greater than in any other developing region (Fentiman *et al.*, 1999).

Research is limited, but there is evidence to suggest that access to education may have seasonal dimensions. For example, school attendance in Malawi falls during the hungry season, particularly in years of greater food insecurity (Kadzamira and Rose, 2003). This is significant because children who drop out of primary school are unlikely to return (Lewin, 2007). The discussion that follows draws together literature on seasonality and education in sub-Saharan Africa to inform how a seasonal approach to education may provide effective tools for improving primary school participation rates and reduce the burden of education on poor households. There is a particular emphasis on fluctuations in expenditure and income and demand for child labour, followed by a discussion of seasonal migration and health.

Seasonal dimensions to access to education

Seasonality of income and expenditure

Income, expenditure and consumption are highly seasonal in many regions of the developing world – varying both within and between years – with particularly damaging consequences for poor rural households. As income and expenditure fluctuate, so do purchasing power and the relative cost of goods and services faced by households. This means that while many direct private costs of education – such as school fees (official or not), uniforms and learning materials – may remain constant in cash terms, they become relatively more expensive in periods when prices of necessities (such as food) are high or income is low. However, the reality is that many direct costs are not distributed evenly throughout the year: for example, unpublished research conducted by ACF International[2] in 2008 in Malawi found that school fees were levied twice annually, around January and April. Other expenses like building fees and transport costs may be more directly tied into the seasonal calendar, although evidence is largely anecdotal and rarely documented.

School uniforms and school fees are often regarded as two of the principal barriers to education, leading to policies such as free primary education. Removing school fees in Kenya in 1974 increased Grade One enrolment by 150 per cent (Somerset, 2007). However, schools in many countries that have introduced free primary education continue to require fees to cover a range of costs from phone line installation to teachers' funerals, and in-kind payments such as collecting firewood or providing labour for construction (Mehrotra and Delemonica, 1998; Kadzamira and Chibwana, 2000; UNESCO, 2006). Learning materials, exam fees, school meals and other direct costs also come at significant expense to families living on the lowest incomes, and can raise barriers to education.

Figure 16.1 shows the expenditure patterns of participants in a cash/food transfer programme in Swaziland, where school fees are due in January. Devereux and Jere (2008) describe how expenditure on schooling was greatest as a proportion of expenditure in January and February, the peak of the hunger season – with education accounting for 15–20 per cent of household expenditure among recipients of cash transfers. The proportion of expenditure going on clothing – including school uniforms – was also highest in January (9 per cent of expenditure). Households financed these costs largely by reallocating expenditure, often away from food, which can increase the risk of children developing micronutrient deficiencies. However, only 4 per cent of households withdrew their children from school, despite 16–22 per cent migrating and 10 per cent selling their livestock (Devereux and Jere, 2008). This is probably because households exhaust other coping strategies before withdrawing their children from school, and it is generally children from poorer households who drop out (Hunt, 2008). This may include searching for alternative sources of income, as evidenced by families in Cameroon gathering and selling African plums in the lean season to pay school fees and purchase uniforms (*New Agriculturalist*, 2001). Research from Ethiopia suggests that children who can afford to enrol in school may drop out later in the year due to seasonal changes in household income or hunger as food stocks are depleted, especially in the second semester (Orkin, 2009).

Research from outside sub-Saharan Africa provides further insights. Participatory research from Palawan Island, Philippines, shows that school costs were greatest in March and June (Chambers, 1995). In June, the middle of the rainy season, the principal source of income was debt, followed by labour. Lewin (2002) found that potato farmers in Papua New Guinea were required to pay school fees in January when the potato harvest happens in September; people generally did not seek income in the lean season except when needed, to pay for school fees or to cover the costs of healthcare. The effects of inter-annual seasonality (or income shocks) are also documented; for example, evidence from India shows that harvest losses can lead families to withdraw their children from school (Jacoby and Skoufias, 1997; Beegle *et al.*, 2005). It is likely that similar pictures exist elsewhere, including in sub-Saharan Africa.

Seasonality of demand for child labour

Seasonality also has a bearing on indirect private costs of education, particularly on the opportunity costs of attending school. Poor families often rely on the labour of their children to top up household income, assist in agricultural activities or look after younger children while parents work. Where labour markets are poorly developed, richer families have also been found to rely on child work because hiring labour is unpractical, too expensive or simply not feasible – sometimes referred to as the 'wealth paradox' (Woldehanne *et al.*, 2005). Though child work does not necessarily prevent access to education (conversely, it may even be used to pay for schooling in some cases), heavy workloads can lead to regular absenteeism and temporary withdrawals and reduce children's ability to engage adequately in the learning process, increasing the risk of dropout (Hunt, 2008).

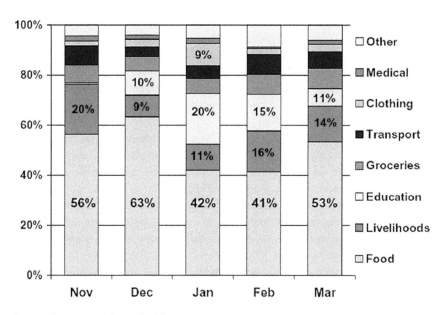

Source: Devereux and Jere (2008)

FIGURE 16.1 Monthly spending of households of 'food and cash' recipients, 2007/08

Overall, more than 40 per cent of under-fourteens in Africa are engaged in the labour market (Admassie, 2002). However, the extent and impact of child labour on education in sub-Saharan Africa varies substantially. While conclusions should ideally be embedded in local contexts, generalizing across the literature it is found that older girls from poorer, rural families with younger siblings are most likely to see their access to education restricted by work (Fuller *et al.*, 1995; Urwick, 2002; Admassie, 2003; Edmonds, 2006). The type of work a child engages in is also an important determinant of access to education. Admassie (2003) finds that certain activities, like herding, farm work, fetching water and collecting firewood, are less of a barrier to school attendance than other activities in Ethiopia. Guarcello *et al.* (2006) suggest that household chores and family-based work are less damaging to educational access than work outside the household, though most studies find that childminding is a substantial barrier to school participation. In Ethiopia and Botswana, for example, children who mind younger siblings are less likely to attend school (Admassie, 2003; Fuller *et al.*, 1995). HIV/AIDS prevalence in southern Africa may further restrict girls' schooling in the region by increasing the demand for domestic help and childminding (Kadzamira and Rose, 2003).

History reveals that seasonal child labour was an important factor behind school attendance in Europe in the early 1900s; for example, school log books frequently noted patterns of absenteeism because children took part in agricultural activities or housework (Rahikainen, 2004). Llop (2005) provides a detailed account of the interaction between child labour and education in 1930s Spain which showed similar patterns to those in Africa today. For example, children were only regarded as 'proper' labourers in their early teens, and school attendance fell rapidly for those aged over 10 years old to around 18 per cent for 12-year-olds. School attendance was also significantly lower in provinces characterized by small farms and estate agriculture than in urban centres. More significant to the current discussion is that absenteeism exhibited a clear seasonal pattern in provinces such as Lugo, where families depended more on child labour with high attendance rates in the winter (over 60 per cent in January) and lower attendance in late spring and early autumn (between 20 and 30 per cent) (Llop, 2005).

In contemporary sub-Saharan Africa, demand for labour is often greatest in the hungry season when most agricultural activities take place, as documented by Hopkins *et al.* (1994) in Niger. Seasonal child labour in Malawi is closely linked with adult labour patterns, with demand peaking in the *ganyu* season (Kadzamira and Rose, 2003). Research is limited, but it is likely this is also true elsewhere on the continent. Additionally, the type of work children engage in may also vary, affecting access to education differently throughout the year. Fentiman *et al.* (1999) and Kadzamira and Rose (2003) find that seasonal absenteeism is common in Malawi and Senegal respectively during the planting and harvesting seasons, when children are required to look after livestock and mind younger siblings to allow adults to undertake income-generating activities.

The discussion to this point (as with the bulk of the available literature) has predominantly focused on how child labour interferes with educational development. However, there may also be instances where demand for schooling affects the livelihoods or behaviour of the rural poor. Huss-Ashmore (1993, pp202–19) and Moris (1989, pp209–34) describe how policies to universalize education, combined with high demand for education from rural peoples in Sukumaland, Tanzania, resulted in an accelerated move to growing hybrid maize instead of sorghum and millet, because children were unavailable for bird-scaring. Farmers explained that maize is less prone to bird damage, and with their children in school it became risky to grow sorghum and millet which require bird-scarers – traditionally children – at key stages of the growing season (Moris, 1989). However, maize is less drought-resistant than sorghum and millet, meaning households are more vulnerable in dry years.

There are other seasonal dimensions of child labour which are not discussed in this chapter. Income shocks, for example reduced harvests following floods and droughts, can increase the number of children engaging in work, restricting school participation (Hunt, 2008). Adult labour patterns may also play a role in children's access to education, through the capacity of parents to take time to look after their children, but also where regular teacher absenteeism comes about because teacher salaries are supplemented by agriculture. More research is needed to gain a greater understanding of the relationship between seasonality, child labour and education, including the seasonal dimensions of the different types of work that children engage in.

Seasonal distress migration

Seasonal migration is a common coping strategy in sub-Saharan Africa and has been widely reported in West Africa and the Sahel in particular. Migration patterns vary by industry and type. Sometimes only adult men migrate, while at other times the whole family or only the children will move to find work. Girls in Ghana, for example, frequently migrate to become housemaids in urban areas, often for family and kin (Fentiman *et al.*, 1999). Destinations may be local, but are often in neighbouring countries or distant urban and agricultural centres. Few statistics are available on the scope of this coping strategy, though Alderman and Sahn (1989, pp81–107) estimated that seasonal rural–urban migration in Senegal involves as much as 40 per cent of the active population. There is a danger that seasonal migration could become permanent migration and homelessness, with whole families travelling between work sites, never returning home.

Comprehensive studies that examine the impact of seasonal migration on primary education in sub-Saharan Africa are sparse. However, unpublished research from Malawi finds that school terms fail to match up with seasonal migration patterns, resulting in regular periods of under- and over-enrolment (Namphande, 2007). Outside Africa, Smita (2008) investigated the relationship between seasonal distress migration and educational access in India where agricultural labourers migrate for short periods, often several times per year, while migrants to industrial and agro-industrial employment follow a single cycle beginning after the monsoon, and lasting for six to eight months until April or June. The study identifies a number of ways that seasonal distress migration prevents access to education, particularly in the primary age group (Smita, 2008). Here, listed, are some:

- The disconnect between the migration cycle and school calendar: as adults migrate, so do children, taking children away from school and only returning after the next school year has already started (see Figure 16.2). Children who start school late and are required to catch up are more likely to drop out or simply be excluded.
- School availability and discrimination: schools are often unavailable near worksites, and even where schools are present, migrant children are often intentionally prevented from enrolling and discouraged from attending by the resident society.
- Labour commitments at home: older girls are often required to look after their siblings while the parents work and so are unable to attend classes. School participation can be restricted or irregular, even if adult males migrate without their families, because children are required to help with domestic chores and household income-generating activities.
- Labour commitments at the worksite: some forms of labour require migrant workers to have children work with them, preventing parents from leaving children in hostels or boarding schools. When child migration is unaccompanied, child labour becomes an even more serious barrier to school participation as children on worksites often work in excess of 14 hours per day. Many of these tasks are highly gendered, with a preference for girls.
- Lack of political voice: migrant labourers have little or no democratic voice and are rarely able to vote, limiting space for change and empowerment. In addition, children of seasonal migrants are rarely captured in government statistics, excluding them from public services and government interventions.

The social, environmental and economic context of South Asia is different from much of sub-Saharan Africa and more research is needed to establish whether seasonal migration in sub-Saharan Africa is having a similar impact on children's education.

Seasonality of health and nutrition status

Health and nutritional status are often highly seasonal. In Madagascar, child mortality triples between the harvest and the hungry season largely because of diarrhoea and malnutrition (Dostie et al., 2002). Table 16.1 broadens work by Tomkins (1993), tabulating seasonality of infection, diseases and disorders in West Africa by adding dimensions observed in other studies.

Fentiman et al. (1999) described that the leading cases of absenteeism and dropouts in rural Uganda were underachievement, inability to concentrate, hunger and malaria. Some of these could be interrelated, and nearly all are seasonal. Overall, Pridmore (2007) provides a comprehensive review of recent literature discussing

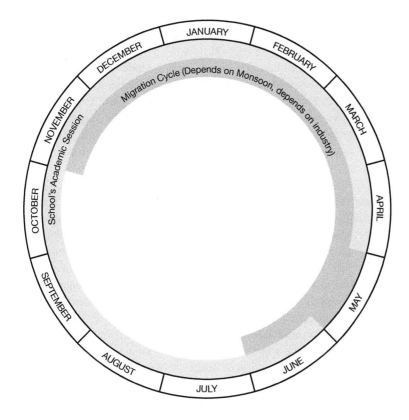

Source: Smita (2008)

FIGURE 16.2 Overlap of the seasonal migration cycle and the school calendar in India

TABLE 16.1 Seasonality of ill-health in West Africa

Dry season	Wet season
Measles	Low birth weight
Meningitis	Lessened capacity to lactate
Pneumonia	Malnutrition
Tetanus	Intestinal worms
Scabies	Malaria
Acute respiratory diseases	Typhoid
	Diarrhoea
	Guinea worm
	Iron deficiency anaemia
	Vitamin A deficiency

Source: Tomkins (1993); Steenbergen *et al.* (1980); Rowland *et al.* (1981, pp164–75)

the importance of good health to educational access. Importantly, the impact of health on children's education begins with maternal health. Prenatal health and birth weight, both of which can be seasonal (Gill, 1991), are linked to the long-term cognitive ability of children (Pridmore, 2007). Mothers' labour requirements could further impact children's health through their ability to lactate and by reducing time available for breastfeeding (Steenbergen *et al.*, 1980; Chowdhury *et al.*, 1981), though the evidence is not conclusive (Jukes, 2005). Maternal health can also be adversely impacted by man-made seasons – for example, Gambian women showed significant weight loss over the course of a month when fasting during Ramadan (Cole, 1993).

Children's health, cognitive ability and schooling can also be affected more directly. Hunger can reduce concentration, excluding children from an adequate learning experience (Hunt, 2008). Malaria and diarrhoeal disease rates generally peak in the wet season and can lead to absenteeism and reduce enrolment, as noted by Orkin (2009). Both may also result in reduced cognitive performance (Holding *et al.*, 1999; Boivin, 2002). Acute malnutrition and micronutrient deficiencies – particularly deficiencies in iron and vitamin A – can also have long-term consequences for cognitive development, as well as other health complications, with implications for school achievement and completion (Pridmore, 2007). These deficiencies, as well as diarrhoeal diseases, are exacerbated or caused by worms that are also most prevalent in the wet season and affect around 40 per cent of children aged five to fourteen years old, worldwide (Sommer, 1982; Awasthi *et al.*, 2000; Alderman *et al.*, 2006). Though debate continues, there are suggestions that tropical entreropathy may also contribute significantly to child undernutrition and growth in developing countries (Humphrey, 2009). Linked to faecal ingestion this may have a strong seasonal dimension.

The dimensions of seasonality may be compounding and mutually reinforcing. Palmer (1981, pp195–201) explains that women in Bangladesh wean children off the breast in December just after the main rice harvest, when labour demands are greatest. Women then resume ovulation in January or February with a peak in conception in March and births around December, when the time needed for childcare and labour are in direct competition with one another, perpetuating the cycle. Understanding these patterns is crucial for designing effective interventions.

Other dimensions

Child labour, health, migration and private costs of education are only a few of the multitude of barriers to schooling faced by children in sub-Saharan Africa, and their relative contribution to the low enrolment and high dropout rates is not clear. Other barriers to educational access like transport may also have a seasonal dimension, as noted by Fentiman *et al.* (1999) and the Jesuit Centre for Theological Reflection (2009). The latter explains how specific transport routes in Masaiti, Zambia collapse each year in the rainy season, making it impossible for children to make their way to school. The seasons can also have other effects on school attendance: a field note by Robert Chambers reveals the story of a seven-year-old girl who had missed three of the previous ten days of schooling because she only had one uniform that got wet when it rained, leaving her with no uniform for the following day. Though anecdotal, this example is important for highlighting that there are other seasonal complications surrounding access to education. It is also possible that man-made seasons, such as Christmas and Eid, could have a bearing on the ability of children to attend school, financially or due to other priorities, though available quantitative research fails to draw out these details. Initiation ceremonies may also play a part in parts of Africa, including in Guinea and Malawi (Kadzamira and Rose, 2003; Hunt, 2008). The next section gives some examples of seasonally sensitive education policies, and suggests potential spaces for further reform of school calendars.

Implementing a seasonal approach

In 1997, the Government of Malawi initiated a change in the school calendar. The school year previously began in October and ran until July, but was shifted to a January–November calendar. The motivation behind the reform was to enable tertiary institutions and boarding schools to close during periods of more acute water shortages. As a result, the academic year begins after Christmas (Malawi is a predominantly Christian nation) in the peak hungry season, which stretches between December and April. Lack of consideration of the livelihoods of the rural poor appears to have had several negative implications for educational attendance (Kadzamira and Rose, 2003), though these were not well documented. Household income and savings are seriously depleted around January, especially after Christmas, and schooling costs are likely to be an added burden or simply unaffordable. This is an example of a seasonally insensitive reform.

The seasonal dimensions of access to education lend themselves to a variety of seasonally sensitive interventions that bridge a number of disciplines – including agriculture, education, food security and health – providing a platform for joined-up thinking. For example, in a world of limited resources, interventions to reduce malaria rates (such as spraying) or malnutrition (such as building up food stocks) could be implemented in and around peak seasons, with positive knock-on effects for school attendance and completion in both the short run and the long run. To narrow the scope of discussion, this section will examine one facet of education policy – the school calendar. As evidenced in the case of Malawi, poorly planned school calendars may have unintended consequences for poor households and children's education.

Examples of seasonally sensitive education policy

Many developing countries have school calendars that follow a similar schedule and pattern to those in Europe and the USA. It is also assumed that the current school schedule in the North is closely linked to the old agricultural calendar.

However, the educational systems and school schedules of the United States and Western Europe changed rapidly at the turn of the twentieth century. The demographic shift from a rural to an urban-centred population and the increased mobility of labour led to changes in the school calendar in the United States, which previously followed the local agricultural calendar. School holidays, previously timed in conjunction with the planting and harvest seasons, were unified to help migrant families, and moved to the summer when it was easier and more comfortable to move home (Fischel, 2006). The failure to understand this development in the North has restricted progress in boosting education in regions like sub-Saharan Africa. However, a number of 'good practice' examples led both by government and non-government organizations have emerged. Here are a few.

Colombia's Escuela Nueva has become the most renowned of the state-led reforms, by adapting the curriculum to local contexts and developing a multi-grade system with a flexible calendar designed through a participatory process that allows children to halt their education temporarily without being required to repeat a year. Children of the Escuela Nueva perform better than children in other rural schools and exhibit greater confidence (Watkins, 2000). Brazil initiated a simpler shift in the school calendar, including moving the start date, so it did not clash with child labour demands in the sowing and harvest seasons (Lucas, 2001). In rural areas education participation rates increased by 300 per cent, while literacy and dropouts halved, though this was part of wider reform and it is difficult to assess how much of this gain resulted from the calendar shift. The Gambia moved school fee due dates to the post-harvest period to make them more affordable, following participatory rural appraisal conducted between 1993 and 1995 (Kane *et al.*, 1998, pp31–43), though anecdotal evidence suggests that seasonal absenteeism from child labour remains a problem. Ethiopia has decentralized decisions over the school calendar, providing some flexibility to adjust to seasonal absenteeism (Colclough *et al.*, 2003). Table 16.2 shows how the school calendar in Bale, Ethiopia, has been changed to better match the key agricultural seasons; however, it is argued that the school schedule remains too inflexible for children labouring on commercial farms (Orkin, 2009).

The Bangladesh Rural Advancement Committee (BRAC) operates a rural education programme consisting of over 35,000 non-formal primary schools in Bangladesh. These schools target poor rural children, mostly girls, using a highly participatory school schedule designed through consultation with parents and local communities. Graduates of BRAC schools are able to rejoin state schools at grade level five or six (Watkins, 2000). Some of Mali's community schools have implemented flexible schedules and school calendars. The calendar starts at the end of the harvest season and runs six days week per week for between two and three hours each day. As a result, more girls are attending these schools (Colclough *et al.*, 2003). Chambers and Maxwell (1981, pp226–38) briefly reference other examples from Uganda and Kenya, which have not been discussed in more recent journals and books.

TABLE 16.2 *Agricultural seasons and the school calendar in Bale, Ethiopia*

Month	Agricultural activity	School calendar
Jan–Feb	Vegetable harvest (*Belg* crop)	School opens in mid-January
Mar	Main fishing season	
Apr–May	Maize planted (*Belg* rains)	School moves to the afternoon
Jun	Teff planted in late June (*Keramt* rains begin)	Examinations School closes
Sep	Maize harvested (*Meher* crop) (*Keramt* rains end)	School opens in early September
Oct	Maize and teff harvested Vegetables planted	School closes for two weeks and then moves to the afternoon
Nov		School moves to the morning
Dec		School closes

Source: Orkin (2009)

Space for seasonal interventions

Employing participatory and flexible timetabling in African schools, as in the Escuela Nueva and BRAC programmes, would give children the greatest control in deciding whether to attend school, without the risk and cost of repeating years or increasing household vulnerability. However, such a system may not always be appropriate (Kadzamira and Rose, 2003). A number of areas of the school calendar are open to reform that could potentially improve enrolment, lessen the burden of education on households, or both.

School holiday periods offer a clear possibility for seasonally sensitive reforms. Changes in the school schedule should consider the different types of seasonal labour, seasonal changes in household vulnerability and traditional/religious festivals. For example, there may be different policy implications resulting from analysis of child labour in the bird-scaring season when children will be in the fields at certain times of the day or night compared to analysis of domestic and childminding duties.

The school start date is generally linked to school holiday periods, but is also a space for seasonal reform. School should not start in a period of high demand for children's labour, nor when the significant costs associated with beginning school (such as books, pens and uniforms) represent a particularly large percentage of income or expenditure for that time of year.

School days and hours can also be adjusted. The traditional US/European schedule of five days per week, eight hours per day is often not appropriate in the circumstances discussed in this paper – in fact, many (even most) schools in Africa run much shorter days. School hours could be designed to allow children to complete domestic chores as well as attend school at certain times of the year (as evidenced in Ethiopia in Table 16.2). The customary Saturday and Sunday weekend could also be reconsidered (Eagle, 2006).

Considerable support exists for seasonally adjusting school fee due dates, usually proposing that they are postponed until after the harvest, as initiated in the Gambia. Participation of local communities, parents and even children in this process is vital. Exam fees have not been discussed in this paper, but will also be a significant part of education costs in many countries. The supply of learning materials and uniforms may also offer an opportunity for seasonally sensitive reform, though it is difficult to determine what form such an intervention would look like.

There are other non-seasonal dimensions that can be implemented to reduce the effects of seasonality and improve access to education. For example, school enrol-ment age could be adjusted to improve enrolment, attendance and completion, as the opportunity cost of education generally rises with age. Participatory research in the Gambia resulted in the government lowering the primary school enrolment age for girls (Holland and Blackburn, 1998). However, local context is vital for success – in Ethiopia, many children under ten years of age are not sent to school because they are regarded as too young (Woldehanne *et al.*, 2005). Seasonality is a lens for adapting policy and understanding poverty, and a tool for bringing together diverse disciplines to focus on a common goal – seasonally sensitive interventions outside education policy could play a significant role in promoting access to education, including those that target health (e.g. sanitation projects and mosquito spraying) and reduce hunger (e.g. school feeding and work programmes).

Areas for further research

The literature on seasonality, education and child labour is characterized by several major information gaps, including household expenditure, child labour and private costs of education (discussed below). Building the knowledge base and embedding seasonality in future studies will be key for building the profile of seasonality and designing effective policies in the future.

Appropriate income and expenditure data for sub-Saharan Africa are rare, though some data doubtless exist outside the public domain. The World Bank's Household Budget Surveys compile information through multiple visits to each household throughout a year and so may provide a picture of seasonal expenses and income (World Bank, 2008). Living Standard Measurements Surveys may show some variation within the month they are conducted. Ideally, household data would be recorded frequently and evenly across the year, and again across several years to give a clearer longitudinal picture of seasonality.

There are two major gaps in the child labour literature: scope and seasonality. Admassie (2003) claims that little is known about the extent and character of child labour in rural sub-Saharan Africa – though the literature is growing rapidly. Seasonality is regularly neglected and it is important that future research reveals the seasonal character of restrictive types of work. The same is required of studies examining the opportunity costs of education.

Mehrotra and Delemonica (1998) note the lack of availability of data on private costs of primary education. Despite a growing literature, no study clearly assesses the timing of the various costs of education, nor how they are distributed throughout the year. Studies connecting fluctuations in household income and expenditure on school payments are also rare. Participatory research in the Gambia and Zambia shows how useful this information can be for driving policy (Holland and Blackburn, 1998). Further research is needed to determine whether unofficial or hidden costs also exacerbate periods of seasonal stress, whether the costs associated with national exams fall at appropriate times for poor households, and when families are most likely to buy school uniforms.

To begin, there are a number of cases of calendar reform in the world, such as those initiated by BRAC and Colombia. Impact assessments of these reforms could examine effects on health, stress, expenditure, food security and other aspects featuring pronounced seasonality. Other areas of interest would be seasonal enrolment, seasonal absenteeism and seasonal dropouts. The Gambia's experiment with postponing school fee due dates until after the harvest appears to be successful, but how successful? Are fees still restricting access to education, or causing unnecessary stress, for certain groups? What is the effect of direct private costs on livelihoods? Does HIV have an impact? Other questions will undoubtedly arise – and should be welcomed.

Conclusion

Altering school schedules and fee due dates is not a panacea. Private costs of education and the need for children to contribute to household income are only a small part of a larger picture. There are many factors constraining education outside the scope of seasonality, and there are dimensions of seasonality which will not be helped by matching school calendars to agricultural calendars (some of which have been discussed here). However, this chapter has revealed opportunities that, if acted upon, can be taken to improve access to education for children in sub-Saharan Africa, particularly those in poor rural areas, at relatively little fiscal cost. A concerted effort must be made to incorporate seasonality into thinking behind education policy and research, but also for development practitioners to recognize the inter-linkages between dimensions of poverty, and work together. With adequate research and consideration for seasonality, it is possible to take strides to improve school participation and lessen the burden of education on poor, rural households in Africa and elsewhere.

Notes

1   This chapter is based on the Consortium for Research on Educational Access, Transitions and Equity (CREATE) Pathways to Access, Research Monograph 31, published in 2010. CREATE is a research programme consortium undertaking research designed to improve access to basic education in developing countries.
2   ACF International is an NGO that specializes in malnutrition. In England and the USA it is known as Action Against Hunger. However, there are five branches in the network, including offices in Spain and France, hence the organization has branded itself ACF International (derived historically from the French, Action Contre la Faim).

17

From seasonal lives towards a-seasonal living

Building seasonality into risk management response

Rachel Sabates-Wheeler and Stephen Devereux

Seasonality, risk and livelihoods

A prominent feature of rural livelihoods in tropical countries is their exposure to a variety of processes of change associated with shocks, seasonal cycles and long-term trends. Furthermore, they face 'normal' random variation occurring in many different dimensions of the environment, concurrently interacting with prices, resource availability and productivity. Some of these changes and their effects are predictable in their occurrence (such as seasonality) while others are not. Changes also occur within livelihoods, at times being the direct result of changes in exogenous conditions, such as the economic context, physical environment or policy reforms. Other changes are more endogenous (for example, accumulation or loss of assets as a result of household members' actions; or births, marriages, growing up and ageing processes affecting household demographics).

Interactions between multiple objectives, livelihood activities and dimensions of predictable and unpredictable change mean that rural livelihoods tend to be extraordinarily complex, such that any single change might have multiple effects that are difficult to predict and manage. For instance, since farmers and pastoralists are simultaneously producers and consumers of crops and livestock, interactions between 'productive' livelihood activities and 'reproductive' domestic activities mean that each domain is vulnerable to shocks and stresses affecting the other. Poor health (whether caused by accident, disease or ageing), food shortages or major expenditures to meet social obligations (such as weddings and funerals) can reduce household labour capacity and divert resources away from investment in productive activities, with damaging short- and long-term effects. The stresses caused by these predictable and unpredictable changes have profound implications for livelihood security, poverty reduction and economic growth. Understanding the sources and impacts of these changes and stresses is critical for the design and implementation of policies to support agriculture and to put in place effective social protection programmes.

Seasonality is a process of continuous change in multiple dimensions. It is predictable and regular in its occurrence, but its precise timing, severity and impacts vary from year to year and may be changing over time. The seminal works on seasonality (Chambers *et al.*, 1981; Longhurst, 1986; Sahn, 1989; Gill, 1991) all point to the integrated nature of seasonality and poverty, and assert that rural livelihoods and rural poverty cannot be fully comprehended unless seasonality is incorporated into the analysis. Yet as recently as 2008, Robert Chambers argued that:

> Of all the dimensions of rural deprivation the most neglected is seasonality. Vulnerability, sickness, powerlessness, exploitation, material poverty, under- and malnutrition, wages, prices, incomes … these are recognised, researched and written about. But among them again and again seasonality is overlooked and left out. Yet seasonality manifests in all these other dimensions and in how they interlock.
>
> (Chambers, 2008, pxvi)

The impacts of seasonality, as well as the effects of changes in seasonal variability, depend fundamentally on individual, community and national 'coping mechanisms'. The nature and effectiveness of portfolios of coping and insurance mechanisms are highly wealth-dependent. People with more income, assets, savings, education and connections are better protected against negative shocks and cycles. For this reason, the negative effects of seasonality are felt disproportionately by poor people.

Why has seasonality not figured more prominently in risk management response?

Social risk management and shock typologies

The World Bank's 'Social Risk Management' framework (SRM) has been a dominant approach for conceptualizing and operationalizing social protection for the past ten years (though it will be superseded in 2012 by the World Bank's new 'Social Protection and Labour Strategy'). Social risk management 'consists of a collection of public measures intended to assist individuals, households and communities in managing risks in order to reduce vulnerability, improve consumption smoothing, and enhance equity while contributing to economic development in a participatory manner' (Holzmann and Jørgensen, 1999). This framework provided an analytical toolkit to identify alternative strategies and arrangements for dealing with risks, and it has four basic elements. First is the *type of risk incurred,* which also traces the impacts of shocks and risks on various livelihood assets. Second are *strategies to address income shocks,* which include risk reduction, risk mitigation and risk coping. Third are *risk management instruments by formality of arrangements,* which range from informal or personal arrangements such as savings or community support, to market-based arrangements such as insurance and credit, to formally mandated or publicly provided arrangements such as welfare transfers. Fourth are the *type of institutions and actors involved* in providing risk management.

Although 'seasonal price increases' and 'seasonal variations in household income' are mentioned in chapter 8 – 'Helping Poor People Manage Risk' – of the *World Development Report 2000/2001*, seasonality is conspicuously absent from the typology of shocks listed in that chapter, and appears in the table of 'Mechanisms for managing risk' only in the form of 'seasonal or temporary migration', under informal household coping mechanisms (World Bank, 2001, p141). No policy responses to seasonality are discussed under 'risk reduction' and 'risk mitigation' interventions.

To be fair, seasonality is only mentioned once in the inception paper on 'Transformative Social Protection' – another framework for analysing poverty and vulnerability and operationalizing policy responses – by the authors of this chapter (Devereux and Sabates-Wheeler, 2004). Yet 'adverse seasonality' would appear to fit squarely within the remit of social risk management and social protection policies and programmes. Why then is it absent from these agendas? We believe the oversight can be attributed to:

1 the framing of shocks and risks as unpredictable events rather than regular stresses;
2 the inability of standard risk management frameworks to incorporate complex livelihoods that keep people in chronically vulnerable situations;
3 the simplistic focus on climate as the fundamental driver of seasonal vulnerability.

We elaborate on these points below.

Seasonality as a predictable stress

Risk management frameworks deal with unpredictable shocks, not predictable stresses. This might be because predictable stresses are, paradoxically, more complex and complicated to model and to devise 'technical fixes' for. Social Risk Management implicitly defines shocks as sudden changes that are unpredictable but relatively straightforward to manage. 'Rapid onset' shocks such as death, floods or price spikes undermine one or more livelihood 'capitals' (financial, physical, natural, human, social) so the appropriate policy response is to protect or replenish these capitals – if a flood destroys the rice harvest, give the affected people food aid or insure vulnerable populations against future floods. However, the SRM framework does not easily accommodate 'slow onset' shocks such as AIDS or steadily declining rainfall, 'chronic stresses' such as discrimination or political marginalization, or 'cyclical stresses' such as seasonality.

Moreover, risk management frameworks rarely recognize the structural and political dimensions of shocks and stresses. Since the effects of seasonality are obviously played out through a maze of social and political relationships and systemic rigidities in specific local contexts, seasonality can never be accommodated within risk management analysis and policies, currently conceived as generic technocratic responses to natural disasters or market failures.

An observation about the links between seasonality and famines illuminates the distinction between unpredictable shocks and predictable stresses. According to Hauenstein Swan (2008), 'seasonality represents the "father of all famines", but it is predictable, analysable, and there are tested solutions to deal with its effects'. So seasonality refers to events that are cyclical, periodic, repetitive, and generally follow regular and predictable patterns. Famines magnify the worst of the negative consequences of seasonality, but they occur less frequently and less predictably – often being triggered by dramatic deviations in regular patterns of temperature and rainfall from their seasonal norms. In terms of their adverse impacts, the difference between the stress of seasonality and the shock of famine is that the former can be better planned for and 'coped' with than the latter, because of differences in their predictability and severity. On the other hand, for poor and vulnerable people with limited coping capacity, a 'regular' hungry season can have similar impacts on resources and wellbeing as a minor famine. If the hungry season was understood as a 'seasonal food crisis' affecting millions of poor rural families every year, it might receive more attention from policymakers nationally and globally.

The complexity of a seasonality-sensitive response

So why do risk management frameworks not deal with predictable stresses and risks such as 'adverse seasonality'? Probably because predictable stresses are more messy to explain and address or 'manage'. They are often the result of complex interactions between structural conditions and exogenous changes, as well as having historical and sociocultural significance. Chronic and predictable livelihood stresses generated by social exclusion, demographic transitions or seasonality require fundamentally different analyses and policy responses than are offered by standard responses to risk, because both the analysis and the response must recognize and deal with the structural determinants of vulnerability.

Frequently absent from risk management responses is attention to chronic poverty, and its negative synergies with risks and shocks. The 'chronic poor' include people who have never recovered from severe shocks, such as a disabling illness or loss of key productive assets. Due to their lack of resources and limited options, cyclical stresses such as seasonality perpetuate and entrench their poverty. In their analysis of chronic poverty and social protection, Barrientos and Shepherd (2003, p7) state that:

> Although risk and vulnerability are key factors in explaining the descent into poverty, it is not clear ... how important they are in maintaining people in poverty, transmitting poverty from one generation to the next, and in preventing the interruption of poverty.

Importantly, Barrientos and Shepherd highlight structural reasons related to 'social, political and economic structures and relationships, and processes of exclusion and adverse incorporation' (Barrientos and Shepherd, 2003, p3) that prevent many poor people from benefiting from development interventions and market opportunities. The chronic poor 'have fewer options, less freedom to take up available options, and so remain stuck in patterns of life which give them low returns to whatever few assets they have maintained' (Hulme, Moore and Shepherd, 2001, p8). Social, political and economic structures are the defining characteristics of livelihood risk, with the possible exception of some natural disasters – though even in these cases, the contribution of sociopolitical factors has persistently been underappreciated (Bankoff *et al.,* 2004). Seasonality, as one contributor to livelihood stress, should be central to the analysis of chronic poverty, because it is a driver of the vulnerability that produces and reproduces rural poverty.

Vulnerability is typically defined as a function of exposure to a hazard or shock, and the ability to manage the consequences. A robust capacity to manage shocks signifies resilience, the antidote to vulnerability. In order to understand fully the nature of vulnerability to shocks, whether the consequences are likely to be immediate and minor or permanent and irreversible, if the nature of shocks and vulnerabilities are changing over time, and which groups of the population are most vulnerable, it is crucial to understand what is meant by a shock and what is meant by ability to manage.

Income and assets are crucial for overcoming poverty and managing livelihood shocks – as the risk management literature asserts – but we would argue that the ability to manage risk is more complex than a simple focus on household income and asset portfolios. It is instead a complex function of individual and household behaviour, reflected in: livelihood profiles that themselves represent long-term or structural adaptation to predictable stresses; crisis response behaviour (such as the ability to call on formal and informal insurance and networks in times of crisis); and external (policy) responses to predicted and actual crises. Provision of consumption, income and asset insurance is only a partial response to vulnerability. An expanded view of social protection must incorporate responses to both chronic poverty and structural vulnerabilities. The adverse effects of seasonal stress, such as increased malnutrition, poverty and food insecurity, depend on a complex array of factors that all need to be considered in policy formulation for risk and vulnerability reduction.

People respond to livelihood stress by engaging in 'coping strategies' that balance the objective of smoothing immediate consumption (e.g. borrowing to buy food) against that of retaining key productive assets (e.g. eating less rather than selling the family's plough) to protect their future livelihoods. Nonetheless, these behaviours often compromise the household's resources, elevating their vulnerability to future stresses and shocks. Over time, the decreasing ability of poor households to meet their subsistence needs and retain their assets can push them down a declining spiral into deeper poverty, hunger and ultimately destitution. Repeated episodes of seasonal stress can act as a kind of 'poverty ratchet', because the damaging 'coping' behaviour that people affected by seasonality are forced to adopt leaves them slightly worse off after each hungry season than before. However, seasonality per se is not the problem. Rather, it is the interaction of cyclical stress with limited livelihood opportunities, chronic deprivation and weak fall-back positions.

This analysis from a risk and vulnerability perspective resonates with work by Gill (1991), who conceptualized seasonal poverty through a simple mean–variance model which pivots on mean consumption, critical consumption thresholds, and inter-seasonal and inter-annual variation. Gill (1991, pp14–15) wrote that:

> The full significance of a critical minimum level of consumption lies in the interaction between intra-seasonal and inter-seasonal variation in income around a low mean, since the critical level is clearly most likely to be reached in the hungry season of a bad year.

Gill's analysis focuses on the interaction between rains, illness and poverty, and other shocks that cause variation around a threshold that can push households towards catastrophic consequences and actions. However, his analysis does not fully investigate the structural and persistent nature of these variations.

Climate as the overriding determinant of seasonal impacts

Much of the seasonality literature frames the relationship of the rural poor to the seasons in terms of changes in the weather (especially rainfall), which is seen as the underlying driver of most seasonal effects, from disease vectors to food price fluctuations. In other words, although rainfall cycles interact with other dimensions of seasonality to generate both good and bad outcomes, cyclical weather patterns are understood as the fundamental binding constraint that compromises the wellbeing of rural people.

In the past, many technical innovations and policy interventions were designed specifically to counteract the negative consequences of weather seasonality, with the objective of smoothing seasonal variations in production, income and consumption for the rural poor. These 'solutions' were tailored for specific population segments, but most focused on smallholder farmers and, to a lesser extent, on other agriculture-based livelihoods such as pastoralism or agricultural labour. Scientific analyses of 'low input, low output' agriculture identified seasonal effects on crop *production* and proposed appropriate technological interventions to overcome seasonal constraints. Some of the classic responses to overcome water constraints include irrigation infrastructure (see Masset, this volume), new seed varieties that are drought-resistant or enable multiple cropping on an annual basis, and new energy-efficient technologies.

Alternatively, governments intervened with policies to counteract the adverse consequences of seasonality on *consumption*. The 1970s and 1980s saw the replication in numerous countries of counter-seasonal initiatives such as grain reserve management and pan-territorial pricing, with the objective of stabilizing food availability and prices throughout the year. More recently, these umbrella responses have been superseded by group- or household-level responses such as cash transfers, targeted input subsidies and seasonal public works programmes, reflecting a policy shift from direct government intervention in agricultural production and marketing towards a social protection agenda dominated by individualized transfers (Devereux, 2010).

We would question this climate-centred approach to seasonality analysis and response, based on the striking evidence from wealthy countries that weather cycles do not necessarily translate into seasonal fluctuations in food availability, prices and consumption. The explanation is that farmers in high-income countries enjoy preferential access to agricultural technologies that raise and stabilize crop yields (especially mechanization and irrigation). At the same time, consumers in wealthy countries enjoy preferential access to alternative sources of food through international markets. Thus while the seasons are very distinct in the northern hemisphere, consumption is largely a-seasonal, reflecting the differential ability of affluent people to access food both domestically and from around the world throughout the year. This leads us to critique the notion that changes in climate are the primary driver of downside seasonal impacts. Instead, we suggest that inequalities in wealth, underpinned by the politics of access and distribution, are the fundamental drivers of 'adverse seasonality'. Poverty, not the weather, is the binding constraint.

The dependence of low-income economies on 'subsistence' agriculture is a defining theme of much of the work on seasonality (Chambers et al., 1981; Gill, 1991; Sahn, 1989; Devereux et al., 2008). Indeed, poor rural people do tend to get poorer seasonally, but the proposed responses are not drawn out for rich and poor or North and South alike. Putting considerations of access and distribution at the centre of a seasonality analysis leads us to differentiate the impacts of seasonality by location, wealth, gender and a range of other factors. Recognizing the varied impacts across groups and socioeconomic status also implies that we need to acknowledge the interconnectedness of prosperous a-seasonal living by one group in one location with poor and vulnerable seasonal lives by another group in another location (see Chambers, this volume). This approach to seasonality moves the discussion away from technical responses to alleviate production and consumption deficits to a call for a holistic response to addressing the many other interrelated effects of seasonality, such as health, labour, migration, malnutrition and education.

Several implications for seasonally sensitive policy follow from these reflections:

1 Seasonality is about the multiple impacts – both positive and negative – of regular, cyclical fluctuations on lives and livelihoods.
2 Seasonality introduces predictable stresses, and as such needs to be built into risk management or social protection programmes in ways that are long-run, sustainable and appropriately timed.
3 Seasonal effects are highly complicated, reflecting the intricate interconnections and interdependencies of different spheres of lives and livelihoods.
4 The ways in which the impacts of seasonality are felt are location- and group-specific, but are also mediated by systems of distribution and access.

In the next section we draw on the case of the Productive Safety Net Programme in Ethiopia as an illustration of an initiative that recognizes and addresses some aspects of seasonality, while also illuminating some challenges of building these considerations into programme design.

Case study: seasonality and social protection in Ethiopia

Seasonality has significant negative impacts on wellbeing in rural Ethiopia, where livelihoods depend heavily on rainfed agriculture. Ethiopians are acutely aware that seasonality is a major determinant of their poverty and food insecurity. During the World Bank's 'Consultations with the Poor' in Ethiopia, 'Both urban and rural households listed seasonal variance in rainfall as the major cause of vulnerability' (World Bank, 2006, p25).

Empirical evidence on the contribution of seasonal variability to fluctuations in wellbeing comes from the Ethiopian Rural Household Survey (ERHS), a multiple-round panel survey that was implemented three times in 1994 and 1995, specifically to capture seasonal effects (Dercon and Krishnan, 2000). Across the panel of 1,411 households, food and non-food consumption were virtually constant in the first and third rounds – administered during two consecutive hungry seasons – but average consumption was higher by 25 per cent in the second round – just after the main annual harvest. These variations in consumption resulted in measurable seasonal fluctuations in undernutrition. The percentage of adult males with a body mass index (BMI) below 18.5 (a threshold for undernourishment) fell from 28 per cent to 22 per cent between rounds 1 and 2, but rose again to 26 per cent in round 3. Mirroring these trends, the poverty headcount among the 1,411 households fell from 34.1 per cent in the first hunger season to 26.9 per cent around harvest time, then rose again to 35.4 per cent in the next hungry season. The authors noted that, 'These seasonal fluctuations are striking and not confined to a particular poverty line' (Dercon and Krishnan, 2000, p32). The implications for the measurement of poverty – globally, not only in Ethiopia – are obvious, but have yet to be adopted as standard practice in poverty assessments and reporting.

The Government of Ethiopia has introduced various social protection measures to address seasonal (as well as chronic and transitory or acute) food insecurity. Every year since 2005, the government has delivered cash and/or food transfers to 7–8 million Ethiopians through the donor-supported Productive Safety Net Programme (PSNP). After South Africa's extensive social grants system, this is the largest social protection programme in sub-Saharan Africa. A remarkable feature of the PSNP is that no mention of 'seasonality' can be found in any programme documentation, yet even if it was not conceptualized as a seasonal safety net, it is clearly seasonal in its design and implementation. For instance, the Programme Implementation Manual (PIM) does not specify when the PSNP should be implemented, but in practice it is scheduled to run from January through June each year, stopping before the heavy rains – and peak on-farm labour requirements – of July to August.

The PSNP illustrates several points about seasonality and risk management that have relevance to social protection in Ethiopia and elsewhere, but are often over-looked. Several of these points are discussed below. Our key finding about season-ality can be summarized in a sentence. *Seasonality is relatively predictable in its timing and regularity, but not in the severity of its impacts across either individuals or places.* Our evidence from two evaluations of the PSNP, which we led in 2006 and 2008, provides several lessons for the design of counter-seasonal food security and social protection inter-ventions. *Social protection interventions can mitigate the adverse impacts of seasonality, but only if they are sensitively designed, well-targeted, and delivered at the right time.*

Finding 1: Seasonality is relatively predictable in its timing and regularity

The main (*Meher*) rains in Ethiopia fall between June and August, while many farming areas also have a second (*Belg*) rainy season between March and May. Household food security in rural Ethiopia depends on good *Meher* and/or *Belg* rains, but in recent years the *Belg* rains have become particularly erratic and there have been several failed harvests in the past decade.

Seasonality in rainfall translates directly into seasonality in food availability and, especially in unimodal systems, seasonal hunger. Figure 17.1 illustrates the preva-lence of self-reported food shortages by month in rural Ethiopia, disaggregated by PSNP participation status (Public Works participant/Direct Support beneficiary/ non-participant in 2005/06; current beneficiary/past beneficiary/non-beneficiary in 2007/08). Figure 17.1a presents the results for 2005/06, while Figure 17.1b shows responses to the same question for 2007/08. Both figures illustrate that the experience of food insecurity in rural Ethiopia is markedly cyclical, peaking in mid-year (May–August) and being lowest around the turn of the year (October–January). The similarity in the shape of the graphs across the two periods confirms that cyclical food insecurity is predictably seasonal in nature, and is related to the timing of rains and harvests.

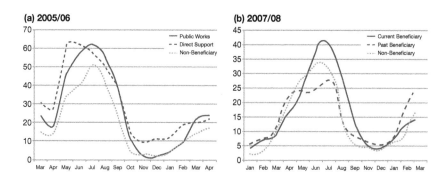

Source: Devereux *et al.* (2006, 2008)

FIGURE 17.1   Self-reported food shortage in rural Ethiopia, by month and PSNP status

The shape of the graphs also varies by programme participation status. In almost every month of 2005/06, Public Works participants and Direct Support beneficiaries reported higher rates of food shortage than non-beneficiaries. In 2007/08, when overall levels of self-reported food shortage were lower, the highest rates were recorded among current beneficiaries, while rates among non-beneficiaries and past beneficiaries (or PSNP 'graduates') were significantly lower. Since the PSNP is targeted at the most food-insecure households, this confirms that targeting was accurate and that the adverse effects of seasonality are felt most by the poorest.

Finding 2: Seasonality impacts differently in different areas

Just because seasonality is 'predictable' does not mean that the cycle is identical everywhere. Across Africa, the shifting Inter-Tropical Convergence Zone (ITCZ) brings rains at different times of year, so that (for instance) the main annual harvest occurs in March–April in Malawi but in August–September in northern Ghana. Even within a single country, rainfall patterns can vary from north to south. Figure 17.2 illustrates the consequences of variability in rainfall regimes on the timing of the annual harvests (and hence of the pre-harvest 'hungry season') in different parts of rural Ethiopia. In most areas, as noted, the *Meher* rains fall between June and August and the main annual harvest occurs towards the end of the year (November–December). In areas that have *Belg* rains (March–May), however, the harvest – or the first of two harvests – occurs in mid-year (June–July). As a result, the 'hungry season' occurs as early as April–May in some areas, but as late as July–August in others.

Differences in seasonal rainfall cycles translate into different impacts – or different severity of impacts – in different places. This is strikingly evident in Ethiopia by comparing seasonal trends in food prices across different regions. Figure 17.3 reveals a pronounced seasonality in prices of staple food crops (averaged across the four most widely consumed food grains – barley, maize, sorghum

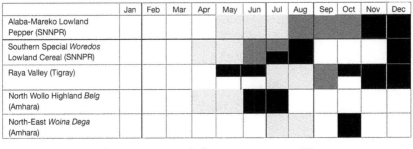

Hungry period ▨ Some harvesting ■ Main harvest periods

Source: Save the Children UK (2008, p8)

FIGURE 17.2 Hungry periods and harvest periods in selected livelihood zones of Ethiopia

and wheat) throughout rural Ethiopia, with prices being highest during the hungry season in mid-year, and lowest in the harvest period towards the end of each year. However, disaggregation by region reveals that grain prices are consistently highest in northern Ethiopia (Tigray), lower in central Ethiopia (Oromiya) and lowest in southern Ethiopia (SNNPR).

The combination of seasonality in rainfall and in food prices generates differences in the timing of food insecurity across regions. Disaggregating self-reported food shortage by region reveals that the most food-insecure months in northern Ethiopia (Tigray) are July–August, but in southern Ethiopia (SNNPR), food insecurity peaks earlier in the year, in March–April (Figure 17.4). Also interesting is the evidence that households in Tigray experience substantially lower rates of food shortage (and hence of hunger) than households in any other region. Since Tigray is widely recognized as the wealthiest (or least poor) of these four regions, Figure 17.4 provides further confirmation that people with more resources are better able to smooth their consumption across seasonal cycles.

Finding 3: Seasonality affects different people differentially

People who are poor and lack 'asset buffers' – including savings and social networks (Swift, 1989; Moser, 1998) – are more vulnerable to the worst consequences of seasonality. Our findings from Ethiopia confirm that female- and older-headed households – two widely recognized 'vulnerable groups', in Ethiopia and elsewhere – face consistently higher levels of food insecurity than do male-headed households (Figure 17.5). Even though all household types face deteriorating levels of food insecurity during the annual 'hungry season' (May–August), households headed by women and older persons are more likely to go hungry (in every month of the year). Female-headed households also suffer most intensely, followed by older-headed households, as is evident (from other survey data) in the 'coping strategies' they are forced to adopt, including rationing food consumption more

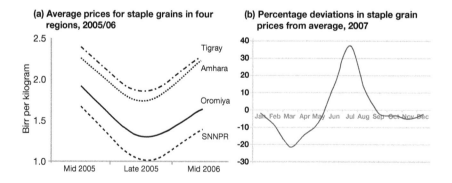

Source: Devereux *et al.* (2006, 2008)

FIGURE 17.3 Food price seasonality in Ethiopia, 2005–2007

severely. For instance, during the peak of the hunger season in 2005, average meals per day dropped to 2.0 in male-headed households, but to just 1.9 in female- and older-headed households (Devereux *et al.*, 2006). Nonetheless, male-headed households are almost as badly affected by seasonal hunger, and should not be overlooked since they comprise the majority of food-insecure households.

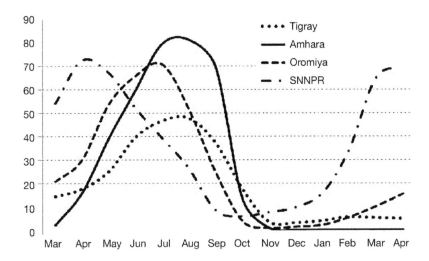

Source: Devereux *et al.* (2006)

FIGURE 17.4 Self-reported food shortage in rural Ethiopia by regions, 2005/06

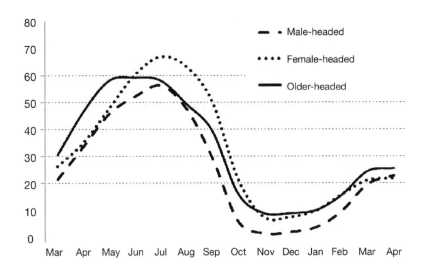

Source: Devereux *et al.* (2006)

FIGURE 17.5 Self-reported food shortage in rural Ethiopia by household head, 2005/06

Lesson 1: Well-timed interventions can mitigate the worst consequences of seasonality

The PSNP functions as a seasonal safety net, providing public works employment for poor rural Ethiopians who can work and unconditional transfers for those who cannot work, between January and June each year. The logic for this timing is that food insecurity is high in the first half of the year but generally lower towards the end of the year (as seen in Figure 17.1 above) – so the PSNP intervenes to provide social assistance to households that face seasonal food deficits, until the next harvest. This seasonality can be clearly seen in Figure 17.6b – PSNP households worked between 14 and 21 days on public works projects every month between January and June in 2007, but this fell to 10.5 days in July and 8.6 days in August. From September to December the PSNP was closed, and days worked on public works fell to zero, before the next cycle began in January 2008. A similar employment cycle was followed in 2005/06. Figure 17.6a overlays days worked on PSNP public works with percentage of households reporting food shortage by month, and finds a striking correlation. The peak hunger period in these households is April–June, and these are also the months of peak PSNP activity each year.

Lesson 2: Work requirements can undermine the effectiveness of seasonal safety nets

The hungry season in tropical countries peaks during the pre-harvest months, which is also the farming season when on-farm labour demands are highest. For this reason, delivering social protection through public works programmes is problematic, because the work requirement means that farmers have to choose between working for food or cash on public works, or tending their fields to secure a good harvest – effectively a choice between food today or food tomorrow.

The PSNP delivers 'seasonal social protection' through two modalities: Public Works (which delivers transfers with a work requirement to over 80 per cent of

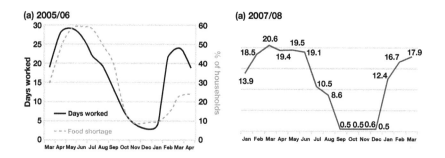

Source: Devereux *et al.* (2006, 2008)

FIGURE 17.6   Average days worked on PSNP public works by household per month, 2005/06 and 2007/08

programme participants) and Direct Support (unconditional transfers of cash or food to eligible beneficiaries who have no labour power). Public Works are supposed to stop before the farming season, but in both 2006 and 2008 PSNP participants in our survey complained that Public Works overlapped with their farming activities and with opportunities for paid agricultural work on other farms, for two reasons. Firstly, in 2005, when the PSNP had just started, public works projects were slow to get going, and activities continued in many places until as late as October (Figure 17.7a). Secondly, in 'Belg-dependent' areas, PSNP public works competed directly with family labour needs for farming during the March–May rainy season.

Unconditional transfers do not compete with on-farm labour requirements, but Direct Support has also been adversely affected by the timing of PSNP Public Works projects. Because Direct Support and Public Works payments are made at the same time, delays in payments affect both categories equally. In the early years of PSNP, payments were often late by several weeks or even months, so food rations or cash wages were disbursed until November or even December – i.e. during or after the harvest, when the need for food or cash is considerably less urgent than during the hungry season.

By 2007 this competition for household labour had receded to some extent, as programme efficiency improved and most Public Works activities finished earlier (by August). PSNP officials also built some flexibility into the schedule: Public Works stopped for a few days at times during the *Belg* rains to allow farmers to work in their fields. Moreover, the lag between working and being paid had been almost eradicated. No food or cash payments were reported after August until the PSNP restarted in January 2008 (Figure 17.7b).

Delays in payments are significant quite apart from their impact on farming and other livelihood activities, because they undermine the consumption smoothing objective of the PSNP. As noted above, seasonal food insecurity in Ethiopia manifests in reduced consumption and high rates of seasonal undernutrition, and the timing of the PSNP is intended to bolster food consumption precisely during these

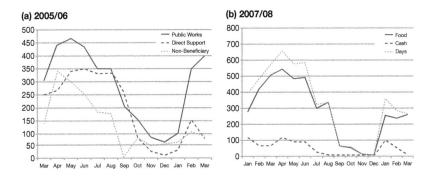

Source: Devereux *et al.* (2006, 2008)

FIGURE 17.7   PSNP participation and payment by month, 2005/06 and 2007/08

months. Late disbursements mean that PSNP cash or food transfers fail to address household food deficits at the most critical time of the year.

Figure 17.8 shows how the time lag in disbursement of PSNP cash transfers shortened each year between 2006 and 2008, from a very poor performance in 2006 to slightly better in 2007, to approaching the goal by 2008. This improvement likely resulted in enhanced household food security, through positive impacts both on farming and on consumption smoothing.

Lesson 3: Design flaws can undermine the effectiveness of seasonal safety nets

One objective of the PSNP was to shift humanitarian assistance programming in Ethiopia away from food aid towards cash transfers. In *woredas* (districts) with sound administrative capacity and well-functioning markets, PSNP participants were paid in cash rather than food. The intention was to allow cash recipients to make their own choices about their food and other purchases, thereby allowing them to meet a wider range of basic needs while stimulating local production and trade. While these are powerful arguments in favour of cash transfers, there are problems associated with cash transfers that PSNP managers did not foresee.

Firstly, we saw above (Figure 17.3) that average food prices vary significantly across Ethiopia. The PSNP cash transfer was set at 6 birr – enough to buy 3kg of staple cereal, the same as the World Food Programme (WFP) food ration – at prices

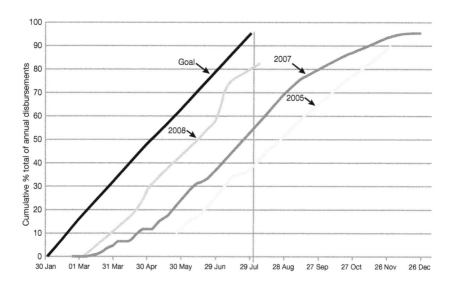

Source: Save the Children UK (2008, p10)

FIGURE 17.8 Timing of PSNP cash transfer disbursements, 2006–2008

prevailing in 2005. Because of localized price variability, 6 birr could purchase 3.5kg of grain in southern Ethiopia (SNNPR) in mid-2005, but only 2.5kg in northern Ethiopia (Tigray) (Figure 17.9). So the PSNP objective of ensuring household food security was achieved in SNNPR and Oromiya regions, but was not achieved in Tigray and Amhara regions. Seasonal price fluctuations meant that 6 birr was more than enough to buy 3kg at harvest time in late 2005, making it appear that the transfer was adequate on average over the year – but seasonality makes 'averages' irrelevant. The critical issue is that during the hungry seasons of mid-2005 and mid-2006, PSNP participants could not meet their subsistence food needs through PSNP cash transfers.

Secondly, on top of seasonal cycles, food prices tend to increase over time, and this natural inflation was compounded, in Ethiopia as elsewhere, by the global food price crisis of 2008. By mid-2008 staple grain prices in Ethiopia had trebled since 2005, but the PSNP cash transfer had been raised by only 33 per cent, from 6 birr to 8 birr per day. Failure to adjust cash transfers to account for either seasonal price variability or food price inflation undermines the purchasing power of the cash, especially at times of year when food is scarcest and hunger is most severe.

Rising and fluctuating food prices contributed to a substantial shift in beneficiary preferences against cash transfers and in favour of food (which the Government of Ethiopia was hoping to phase out). PSNP cash transfers were blamed for fuelling price inflation and for losing their purchasing power over time and during the hungry season, whereas food aid was credited with stabilizing prices and retaining

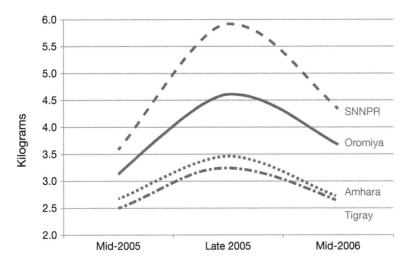

Source: Devereux *et al.* (2006)

FIGURE 17.9 Purchasing power of PSNP cash transfer by region, 2005/06 (kg of staple grain for 6 birr per day)

its value irrespective of market prices (Sabates-Wheeler and Devereux, 2010). Government and donors have responded by reverting to food transfers in some areas, or by paying beneficiaries partly in cash (when food prices are low) and partly in food (when prices are high).

It should also be noted that the Productive Safety Net Programme is complemented by the Household Asset-Building Programme (HABP), which aims to provide access to productive assets that will generate future streams of income and ultimately 'graduate' PSNP beneficiaries out of vulnerability and chronic dependence on transfers. The two interventions are complementary, in that the PSNP stabilizes consumption and protects assets while the HABP promotes livelihoods and builds assets and incomes. This integrated approach has the virtue of addressing both a defining symptom of chronic poverty (low consumption) and a fundamental cause of chronic poverty (lack of assets), potentially breaking the cycle of seasonal poverty ratchets and enabling the seasonally affected poor to move towards a-seasonal living.

Summing up, commendable attempts have clearly been made by the Productive Safety Net Programme to address the seasonal nature of poverty and food insecurity in Ethiopia. Providing transfers in the most food-insecure months of the year is one example of seasonal awareness in design, while delivering livelihood packages to generate complementary streams of income is another. On the other hand, seasonally sensitive outcomes are compromised by competing labour requirements between public works and the family farm, by a failure to account for location-specific seasonal price variations, and by lengthy delays in transfer payments (though this has improved over time), all of which undermine the PSNP's effectiveness as a 'seasonal safety net'. Some of these problems are design features or implementation challenges that could be rectified. For instance, better coordination between food and cash donors could enhance the PSNP's ability to respond promptly to shifting market conditions and beneficiary preferences. Seasonal food price variability can be accommodated by adjusting cash transfers to ensure constant purchasing power as prices rise and fall. (This has been trialled successfully in Malawi, though on a smaller scale.) The Employment Guarantee Scheme in India allows people to register for public works when they need it, not when administrators think it is needed. The evidence from these innovative programmes suggests that even minor modifications in design and implementation could have significant positive impacts on chronic poverty and seasonal vulnerability.

Conclusion

Few would deny the striking and sometimes devastating effects of seasonality on the lives and livelihoods of poor rural people. However, attempting to draw general lessons for the design of seasonally sensitive risk management interventions from the established literature leaves much to be desired, for the reasons discussed above. First, traditional rural risk analysis and response deal with unpredictable shocks – and tend to model seasonality, if at all, as a climate-triggered shock – whereas seasonality is a predictable stress requiring longer-term, tailored interventions. Second, seasonality manifests in multiple dimensions of people's livelihoods – food availability, health, prices, employment, access to services – making accurate diagnosis and comprehensive response a challenging task, which may explain why policies and programmes tend to neglect seasonality in their design and implementation.

Important lessons emerge from this reflection on the literature and evidence from Ethiopia, not only for risk analysis and management, but for social protection interventions and agricultural and rural development policies. Most fundamentally, seasonality must be acknowledged and accommodated as a primary determinant of rural livelihoods and wellbeing outcomes, but it should also be understood as complex, multidimensional and differentiated in its impacts. To minimize seasonal blind spots, policymakers must explicitly recognize that: (1) seasonality is a predictable stress and driver of rural 'poverty ratchets'; (2) seasonality is embedded within all aspects of rural lives and livelihoods; and (3) the impacts of seasonality are mediated by systems of access and distribution – which makes seasonality a political, not just a technical, issue.

As for risk management and social protection programmes, these interventions might partially smooth income and consumption over the year, but they do not provide enough resources to enable poor rural households to live a-seasonal lives in highly seasonal environments. Tackling fundamental inequalities in resource distribution will have more sustainable long-term impacts on the adverse effects of seasonality than social transfer programmes can ever achieve alone.

REFERENCES

Adair, L. and Guilkey, D. (1997) 'Age-specific determinants of stunting in Filipino children', *Journal of Nutrition*, vol 127, no 2, pp314–20

Admassie, A. (2002) *Explaining the High Incidence of Child Labour in sub-Saharan Africa*, African Development Bank, Blackwell Publishers, Oxford

Admassie, A. (2003) 'Child labour and schooling in the context of a subsistence rural economy: Can they be compatible?', *International Journal of Educational Development*, vol 23, no 2, pp167–85

Aho, G., Lariviere, S. and Martin, F. (1998) *Poverty Analysis Manual with Applications in Benin*, Université Nationale du Benin and Université Laval, UNDP

Alderman, H. and Garcia, M. (1994) 'Food security and health security: Explaining the levels of nutritional status in Pakistan', *Economic Development and Cultural Change*, vol 42, no 3, pp485–507

Alderman, H. and Lokshin, M. (2009) 'Tall claims: Mortality bias and the heights of children', mimeo, The World Bank, Washington, DC

Alderman, H. and Sahn, D. (1989) 'Understanding the seasonality of employment, wages and income', in D. Sahn. (ed.) *Seasonal Variability in Third World Agriculture*, Johns Hopkins University Press, Baltimore, MD, pp81–107

Alderman, H., Conde-Lule, J., Sebuliba, I., Bundy, D. and Hall, A. (2006) 'Effect on weight gain of routinely giving albendazole to preschool children during child health days in Uganda: Cluster randomised controlled trial', *British Medical Journal,* vol 333, pp122–7

Alderman, H., Hoddinott, J. and Kinsey, B. (2006) 'Long-term consequences of early childhood malnutrition', *Oxford Economic Papers*, vol 58, no 3, pp450–74

Alderman, H., Hoogeveen, H. and Rossi, M. (2005) 'Reducing child malnutrition in Tanzania: Combined effects of income growth and program interventions', *Economics and Human Biology*, vol 4, no 1, pp1–23

Ali, T. (2004) 'Crime and poverty: Thefts in Domar, Nilphamari', mimeo, Dhaka: BRAC Research and Evaluation Division

Alwang, J. and Siegel, P. B. (1999) 'Labor shortages on small landholdings in Malawi: Implications for policy reforms', *World Development*, vol 27, no 8, pp1461–75

Amano, T., Smithers, R. J., Sparks, T. H. and Sutherland, W. J. (2010) 'A 250-year index of first flowering dates and its response to temperature changes', *Proceedings of the Royal Society B: Biological Sciences*, vol 277, no 1693

Appleton, S. (2002) '"The rich are just like us, only richer": Poverty functions or consumption functions?', *Journal of African Economies*, vol 10, no 4, pp433–69

Ashfaq, M., Shi, Y., Tung, W., Trapp, R. J., Gao, X., Pal, J. S. and Diffenbaugh, N. S. (2009) 'Suppression of south Asian summer monsoon precipitation in the 21st century', *Geophysical Research Letters*, vol 36, L01704, doi:10.1029/2008GL036500

Awasthi, S., Pande, V. K. and Fletcher, R. H. (2000) 'The effectiveness of albendazole in improving the nutritional status of preschool children in urban slums', *Indian Paediatrics*, vol 37, pp19–29

Banerjee, L. (2007) 'Flood disasters and agricultural wages in Bangladesh', *Development and Change,* vol 38, no 4, pp641–64

Bang, A. T., Reddy, H. M., Baitule, S. B., Deshmukh, M. D. and Bang, R. A. (2005) 'The incidence of morbidities in a cohort of neonates in rural Gadchiroli, India: Seasonal and temporal variation and a hypothesis about prevention', *Journal of Perinatology*, vol 25, S18–S28

Bankoff, G., Frerks, G. and Hilhorst, D. (eds) (2004) *Mapping Vulnerability: Disasters, Development and People*, Earthscan, London

Bardhan, P. and Udry, C. (1999) *Development Microeconomics*, Oxford University Press, Oxford

Barnett, B. J., Barrett, C. B. and Skees, J. R. (2008) 'Poverty traps and index-based risk transfer products', *World Development*, vol 36, no 10, pp1766–85

Barnum, H. and Squire, L. (1979) 'A model of an agricultural household: Theory and evidence', Occasional Paper, no. 27, World Bank, Washington, DC

Barrera, A. (1990) 'The role of maternal schooling and its interaction with public health programs in child health production', *Journal of Development Economics,* vol 32, pp69–91

Barrientos, A. and Shepherd, A. (2003) 'Chronic poverty and social protection', paper prepared for the international conference 'Staying Poor: Chronic Poverty and Development Policy', University of Manchester, 7–9 April

Barrios, S., Ouattara, B. and Strobl, E. (2005) 'The impact of climatic change on agricultural production: Is it different for Africa?', *Food Policy*, vol 33, pp287–98

Beegle, K., Dehejia, R. H. and Gatti, R. (2005) 'Child labour, crop shocks and credit constraints', Centre for Economic Policy Research, Discussion Paper No. 4881, http://ideas.repec.org/p/cpr/ceprdp/4881.html

Behrman, J. and Deolalikar, A. (1988) 'Health and nutrition', in H. Chenery and T. Srinivasan (eds) *Handbook of Development Economics*, Vol. 1, Elsevier Science, Amsterdam 631-704

Behrman, J. and Deolalikar, A. (1989) 'Agricultural wages in India: The role of health, nutrition, and seasonality', in D. E. Sahn (ed.) *Seasonality in Third World Agriculture*, The Johns Hopkins University Press, Baltimore, MD and London

Behrman, J. and Rosenzweig, M. (2004) 'Parental allocations to children: New evidence on bequest differences among siblings', *The Review of Economics and Statistics*, vol 86, no 2, pp637–40

Bernard, J. (2008), 'Burkina Faso: Impact des prix sur les moyens d'existence des ménages', London, Save the Children

Berton, H. (2009) 'How cash transfer can improve the nutrition of the poorest children: Evaluation of the pilot safety net project in Southern Niger', London, Save the Children

Berton, H. and Malam Dodo, A. (2008) 'Enquête rapide sur la sécurité alimentaire des ménages, département de Kantché, région de Zinder', Save the Children (unpublished)

Binswanger, H. P. (1981) 'Attitudes towards risk: Theoretical implications of an experimental study in rural India', *Economic Journal*, vol 91, pp867–90

Binswanger, H. P. and McIntire, J. (1987) 'Behavioral and material determinants of production relations in land-abundant tropical agriculture', *Economic Development and Cultural Change*, vol 36, no 1, pp73–99

Binswanger, H. and Rosenzweig, M. (1986) 'Behavioural and material determinants of production relations in agriculture', *Journal of Development Studies*, vol 22, pp503–39

Boivin, M. J. (2002) 'Effects of early cerebral malaria on cognitive ability in Senegalese children', *Journal of Developmental and Behavioural Pediatrics*, vol 23, pp353–64

Boko, M., Niang, I., Nyong, A., Vogel, C., Githeko, A., Medany, M., Osman-Elasha, B., Tabo, R. and Yanda, P. (2007) *Africa. Climate Change 2007: Impacts, Adaptation and Vulnerability*, contribution of Working Group II to the Fourth Assessment Report of the Intergovernmental Panel on Climate Change

Boudreau, T. (2009a) 'Livelihoods impact analysis and seasonality in Ethiopia', paper presented at the conference 'Seasonality Revisited', Institute of Development Studies, Brighton, 8–10 July

Boudreau, T. (2009b) 'Solving the risk equation: People-centered disaster risk assessment in Ethiopia', Humanitarian Practice Network Paper 66, Overseas Development Institute, London

Bronson, H., (1995) 'Seasonal variation in human reproduction: Environmental factors', *The Quarterly Review of Biology*, vol 70, pp141–65

Brown, K., Black, R. and Becker, S. (1982) 'Seasonal changes in nutritional status and the prevalence of malnutrition in a longitudinal study of young children in rural Bangladesh', *American Journal of Clinical Nutrition*, vol 36, pp303–13

Browne, W. (2003) *MCMC Estimation in MLwiN, Version 2.0*, Centre for Multilevel Modelling, University of Bristol, Bristol

Bruce, J. and Clark, S. (2004) *The Implications of Early Marriage for HIV/AIDS Policy*, The Population Council, New York

Bryceson, D. F. (2002) 'The scramble in Africa: Reorienting rural livelihoods', *World Development*, vol 30, pp725–39

Bryceson, D. F. (2006) 'Ganyu casual labour, famine and HIV/AIDS in rural Malawi: Causality and casualty', *Journal of Modern African Studies*, vol 44, pp173–202

Bryceson, D. F., Fonseca, J. and Kadzandira, J. (2004) *Social Pathways from the HIV/AIDS Deadlock of Disease, Denial and Desperation in Rural Malawi*, CARE International, Lilongwe

Burbano, C. and Gelli, A., (2009) 'School feeding, seasonality and schooling outcomes: A case study from Malawi', paper presented at the conference 'Seasonality Revisited', Institute of Development Studies, Brighton, 8–10 July

Caldwell, J. C. (1979) 'Education as a factor in mortality decline: An examination of Nigerian data', *Population Studies*, vol 33, no 3, pp395–413

Calow, R. C. et al. (1997) 'Groundwater management in drought-prone areas of Africa', *International Journal of Water Resources Development*, vol 13, no 2, pp241–61

Calow, R. C. et al. (2002) 'The struggle for water: Drought, water security and rural livelihoods', *British Geological Survey Commissioned Report*, CR/02/226N

Cameron, A. C. and Trivedi, P. K. (2005) *Microeconometrics*, Cambridge University Press, Cambridge

Cardenas, J. C. and Carpenter, J. (2008) 'Behavioural development economics: Lessons from field labs in the developing world', *Journal of Development Studies*, vol 44, no 3, pp311–38

Carroll, C. D. (2001) 'A theory of the consumption function, with and without liquidity constraints', *Journal of Economic Perspectives*, vol 15, no 3, pp23–45

Carroll, C. D. and Kimball, M. S. (2007) 'Precautionary savings and precautionary wealth', *New Palgrave Dictionary of Economics*, 2nd edition

Carter, M. and Barrett, C. B. (2006) 'The economics of poverty traps and persistent poverty: An asset-based approach', *Journal of Development Studies*, vol 42, no 2, pp178–99

Carter, M. and Barrett, C. B. (2007) 'Asset thresholds and social protection: A "think piece"', *IDS Bulletin*, vol 38, no 3, pp34–8

Carter, M. and Olinto, P. (2003) 'Getting institutions "right" for whom? Credit constraints and the impact of property rights on the quantity and composition of investment', *American Journal of Agricultural Economics*, vol 85, no 1, pp173–86

Chambers, R. (1982) 'Health, agriculture, and rural poverty: Why seasons matter', *Journal of Development Studies*, vol 18, no 2, pp217–36

Chambers, R. (1983) *Rural Development: Putting the Last First*, Longman, London

Chambers, R. (1995) 'Seasonal variations in household expenditure and income, Palawan, Philippines', slide, Institute of Development Studies, Brighton

Chambers, R. (2006) *Poverty Unperceived: Traps, Biases and Agenda*, IDS Working Paper 270, Institute of Development Studies, Brighton

Chambers, R. (2008) 'Foreword', in S. Devereux, B. Vaitla and S. Hauenstein Swan, *Seasons of Hunger*, Pluto Press, London

Chambers, R., Longhurst, R. and Pacey, A. (1981) *Seasonal Dimensions to Rural Poverty*, Frances Pinter, London

Chambers, R. and Maxwell, S. (1981) 'Practical implications', in R. Chambers, R. Longhurst and A. Pacey (eds), *Seasonal Dimensions to Rural Poverty*, Frances Pinter, London

Chastre, C. (2007) 'Case study – Cost of the cheapest adequate diet and households' ability to afford it, Kangyidaunt Township/Myanmar', Save the Children (unpublished)

Chatterji, A. K. (1992) *Monsoons, Cyclones and Floods in India*, Sangam Books, London

Chaudhuri, S. and Paxson, C. (1994) 'Consumption smoothing and income seasonality in rural India', Discussion Paper 173, Woodrow Wilson School of Public and International Affairs, Princeton University

Chaudhury, R. H. (1981) 'The seasonality of prices and wages in Bangladesh', in Chambers (ed.) *Seasonal Dimensions to Rural Poverty*, Francis Pinter, London

Chen, M.A. (1991) *Coping with Seasonality and Drought*, Sage Publications, New Delhi

Chibuye, M. (2009) 'Understanding seasonality implications on quality of life through the innovative JCTR Rural Basket: The case of select rural areas of Matushi, Saka and Malama of Zambia', paper presented at the conference 'Seasonality Revisited', Institute of Development Studies, Brighton, 8–10 July

Chirwa, E. W. (2009) 'Sustained increases in food prices: Effect and policies in Malawi', draft report submitted to the Food and Agriculture Organisation, Rome

Chirwa, E. W., Dorward, A. and Vigneri, M. (2009) 'Investigating seasonality and poverty: The 2004/05 Malawi Integrated Household Survey', paper presented at the conference 'Seasonality Revisited', Institute of Development Studies, Brighton, 8–10 July

Chiwona-Karltun, L., Lemenih, M., Tolera, M., Berisso, T. and Karltun, E. (2009) 'Soil fertility and crop theft: Changing rural dimensions and cropping patterns', paper presented at the conference 'Seasonality Revisited', Institute of Development Studies, Brighton, 8–10 July

Chowdhury, A.A.K.M., Huffman, S.L. and Chen, L.C. (1981) 'Agriculture and nutrition in Matlab Thana, Bangladesh', in R. Chambers, R. Longhurst and A. Pacey (eds) *Seasonal Dimensions to Rural Poverty*, Frances Pinter, London

Christensen, J. H., Hewitson, B., Busuioc, A., Chen, A., Gao, X., Held, I., Jones, R., Kolli, R. K., Kwon, W.-T., Laprise, R., Magaña Rueda, V., Mearns, L., Menéndez, C. G., Räisänen, J., Rinke, A., Sarr, A. and Whetton, P. (2007) 'Regional climate projections', in S. Solomon, D. Qin, M. Manning, Z. Chen, M. Marquis, K. B. Averyt, M. Tignor and H. L. Miller (eds) *Climate Change 2007: The Physical Science Basis*, contribution of Working Group I to the Fourth Assessment Report of the Intergovernmental Panel on Climate Change, Cambridge University Press, Cambridge, UK and New York, NY

Christiaensen, L. and Boisvert, R. (2000) 'On measuring household food vulnerability: Case evidence from Northern Mali', Working Paper 2000-05, Department of Applied Economics and Management, Cornell University, New York

Chuma, J., Thiede, M. and Molyneux, C. (2006) 'Rethinking the economic costs of malaria at the household level: Evidence from applying a new analytical framework in rural Kenya', *Malaria Journal*, vol 5, p76

Colclough, C., Al-Samarrai, S., Rose, P. and Tembon, M. (2003) *Achieving Schooling for All in Africa: Costs, Commitment and Gender*, Ashgate, Aldershot

Cole, T. J. (1993) 'Seasonal effects on physical growth and development', in S. J. Ulijaszek and S. S. Strickland (eds) *Seasonality and Human Ecology*, Cambridge University Press, Cambridge

Conroy, C. (2005) *Participatory Livestock Research: A Guide*, ITDG Publishing, Bourton-on-Dunsmore

Conroy, K. and Islam, R. (2009) 'Homestead gardens. Improving food security: Results from a one-year study', www.clp-bangladesh.org, accessed 7 May 2010

Conroy, K. and Marks, M. (2008) 'The use of coping strategies by extreme poor households on the Jamuna chars during *monga*', www.clp-bangladesh.org, accessed 6 April 2009

Conroy, K., Goodman, A. R. and Kenward, S. (2010) 'Lessons from the Chars Livelihoods Programme, Bangladesh', www.chronicpoverty.org, accessed 1 October 2010

Conroy, K., Marks, M. and Islam, R. (2008) 'The impact of the 2007 CLP Infrastructure and Employment Programme', www.clp-bangladesh.org, accessed 1 April 2009

Corbett, J. (1989) 'Poverty and sickness: The high cost of ill health', *IDS Bulletin*, vol 20, no 2, pp58–62

Corbett, M. and Chastre, C. (2007) 'A causal analysis of malnutrition, including the minimum cost of a healthy diet, ElWak, northern Kenya', Save the Children (unpublished)

Coulter, L. (2008a) 'Household water economy analysis in Bale Pastoral livelihood zone, Oromiya Region, Ethiopia: Baseline report', Livelihoods Integration Unit, Ethiopia

Coulter, L. (2008b) 'Rapid emergency assessment, May–June 2008: Water and livelihoods in Southern Nations, Nationalities and People's Region (SNNPR)', Community Housing Fund International, Silver Spring, MD

CPRC (Chronic Poverty Research Centre) (2010) 'The Chronic Poverty Report 2008–09: Escaping Poverty Traps', www.chronicpoverty.org, accessed 5 April 2010

Cruz, R. V., Harasawa, H., Lal, M., Wu, S., Anokhin, Y., Punsalmaa, B., Honda, Y., Jafari, M., Li, C. and Huu Ninh, N. (2007) *Asia. Climate Change 2007: Impacts, Adaptation and Vulnerability'*, contribution of Working Group II to the Fourth Assessment Report of the Intergovernmental Panel on Climate Change

Dabi, D. D. and Nyong, A. (2005) 'Nigeria: Incorporating community-based adaptation strategies into rural development policies in a developing economy', presentation at UNFCCC climate change conference, Montreal, www.iisd.org/pdf/2005/climate_cop11_daniel_dabi.ppt

Datt, G. and Ravallion, M. (1998) 'Farm productivity and rural poverty in India', *Journal of Development Studies*, vol 34, no 4, pp62–85

Datt, G., Simler, K., Murkherjee, S. and Dava, G. (2000) 'Determinants of poverty in Mozambique: 1996–97', FCND Discussion Paper No. 78, International Food Policy Research Institute, Washington DC

Davies, M., Guenther, B., Leavy, J., Mitchell, T. and Tanner, T. (2009) 'Climate Change Adaptation, Disaster Risk Reduction and Social Protection: Complementary Roles in

Agriculture and Rural Growth?', IDS Working Paper 320, Institute of Development Studies, Brighton

Davies, S. (1989) 'Are coping strategies a cop out?', *IDS Bulletin*, vol 28, no 4, pp 60–72

de Haan, A. (1999) 'Livelihoods and poverty: The role of migration: A critical review of the migration literature', *Journal of Development Studies*, vol 36, no 2, pp1–47

de Haan, A. (2002) 'Migration and livelihoods in historical perspective: A case study of Bihar, India', *Journal of Development Studies*, vol 38, no 5, pp115–42

de Janvry, A., Fafchamps, M., Raki, M. and Sadoulet, E. (1992) 'Structural adjustment and the peasantry in Morocco: A computable household model', *European Review of Agricultural Economics*, vol 19, pp427–53

de Merode, E., Homewood, K. and Cowlishaw, G. (2003) 'Wild resources and livelihoods of poor households in Democratic Republic of Congo', Wildlife Policy Briefing No. 1, Overseas Development Institute, London

Deaton, A. (1997) *The Analysis of Household Surveys*, World Bank, Washington, DC

Deaton, A. and Zaidi, S. (2002) 'Guidelines for constructing consumption aggregates for welfare analysis', *Living Standard Measurement Study Working Paper* 135

Decosas, J., Kane, F., Anarfi, J., Sodii, K. and Wagner, H. (1995) 'Migration and AIDS', *Lancet*, vol 346, pp826–8

Dercon, S. and Krishnan, P. (1998) 'Changes in poverty in rural Ethiopia 1989–1995: Measurement, robustness tests and decomposition', Working Paper Series, 98-7, Centre for the Study of African Economies, Oxford

Dercon, S. and Krishnan, P. (2000) 'Vulnerability, seasonality and poverty in Ethiopia', *Journal of Development Studies*, vol 36, no 6, pp25–53

DES (Department of Economics and Statistics of Hyderabad) (2005) *Golden Jubilee of Andhra Pradesh: 50 Years*, DES, Hyderabad

Deshingkar, P. and Start, D. (2003) 'Seasonal Migration for Livelihoods in India: Coping, Accumulation and Exclusion', Working Paper 220, Overseas Development Institute, London

Devereux, S. (1992) 'Household Responses to Food Insecurity in Northeastern Ghana', doctoral dissertation in Economics, University of Oxford, Oxford

Devereux, S. (2002) 'The Malawi Famine of 2002', *IDS Bulletin,* vol 33, no 4, pp70–8

Devereux, S. (2009a) 'Seasonality and social protection in Africa', Growth and Social Protection Working Paper 07, Centre for Social Protection, Institute of Development Studies, Brighton, Future Agricultures Consortium, www.future-agricultures.org

Devereux, S. (2009b) 'Social protection for agricultural growth in Africa', FAC Working Paper, No. SP06, Future Agricultures Consortium, Brighton

Devereux, S. (2010) 'Seasonal food crises and social protection in Africa', in B. Harriss–White and J. Heyer (eds) *Comparative Political Economy of Development: Africa and South Asia*, Routledge, London

Devereux, S. and Jere, P. (2008) '"Choice, dignity and empowerment"? Cash and food transfers in Swaziland: An evaluation of Save the Children's Emergency Drought Response, 2007/08', Save the Children Swaziland, Mbabane

Devereux, S. and Longhurst, R. (2009) 'Seasonal neglect? Aseasonality in agricultural project design', paper presented at the conference 'Seasonality Revisited', Institute of Development Studies, Brighton, 8–10 July

Devereux, S. and Sabates-Wheeler, R. (2004) 'Transformative social protection', IDS Working Paper, 232, Institute of Development Studies, Brighton

Devereux, S. and Tiba, Z. (2007) 'Malawi's first famine, 2001–2002', in S. Devereux (ed.) *The New Famines: Why Famines Persist in an Era of Globalization*, Routledge, London

Devereux, S., Chilowa, W., Kadzandira, J., Mvula, P. and Tsoka, M. (2003) 'Malawi food crisis impact survey: A research report on the impacts, coping behaviours and formal responses to the food crisis in Malawi of 2001/02', Institute of Development Studies, Brighton, UK and Centre for Social Research, Lilongwe, Malawi

Devereux, S., Sabates-Wheeler, R., Tefera, M. and Taye, H. (2006) 'Ethiopia's Productive Safety Net Programme (PSNP): Trends in PSNP transfers within targeted households', report commissioned by DFID Ethiopia, Institute of Development Studies, Brighton

Devereux, S., Sabates-Wheeler, R., Slater, R., Tefera, M., Brown, T. and Teshome, A. (2008) 'Ethiopia's Productive Safety Net Programme (PSNP): 2008 Assessment Report', report commissioned by the PSNP Donor Group, Institute of Development Studies, Brighton

Devereux, S., Vaitla, B. and Hauenstein Swan, S. (2008) *Seasons of Hunger*, Pluto Press, London

DFID (2010) 'The neglected crisis of under-nutrition: Evidence for action', www.dfid.gov. uk, accessed 6 April 2010

Dhawan, B. D. (1988) *Irrigation in India's Agricultural Development: Productivity, Stability, Equity*, Sage, New Delhi

Dibley, M., Goldsby, J., Staehling, N. and Trowbridge, F. (1987) 'Development of normalized curves for the international growth reference: Historical and technical considerations', *American Journal of Clinical Nutrition*, vol 46, pp736–48

Dorward, A. and Chirwa, E. (2011) 'The Malawi Agricultural Input Subsidy Programme: 2005–6 to 2008–9', *International Journal of Agricultural Sustainability*, vol 9

Dorward, A. R. (1996) 'Modelling diversity, change and uncertainty in peasant agriculture in northern Malawi', *Agricultural Systems*, vol 51, no 4, pp469–86

Dorward, A. R. (1999) 'Modelling embedded risk in peasant agriculture: Methodological insights from northern Malawi', *Agricultural Economics*, vol 21, no 2, pp189–201

Dorward, A. R. (2006) 'Markets and pro-poor agricultural growth: Insights from livelihood and informal rural economy models in Malawi', *Agricultural Economics*, vol 35, no 2, pp157–69

Dorward, A. (2009) 'Rethinking agricultural input subsidy programmes in a changing world', paper prepared for FAO, School of Oriental and African Studies (SOAS), London, (http://eprints.soas.ac.uk/8853/)

Dorward, A.R. (2010) 'Conceptualising seasonal financial market failures in applied rural household models', Working Paper, Centre for Development Environment and Policy, School of Oriental and African Studies, http://eprints.soas.ac.uk/10806/

Dorward, P., Galpin, M. and Shepherd, D. (2009) 'Exploring farmers' practices and the factors influencing them during production seasons in Ghana and Zimbabwe through the use of participatory budgets', paper preseted at the conference 'Seasonality Revisited', Institute of Development Studies, Brighton, 8–10 July

Dorward, A. R., Kydd, J. G. and Poulton, C. D. (2005) 'Beyond liberalisation: "Developmental coordination" policies for African smallholder agriculture', *IDS Bulletin*, vol 36, no 2, pp80–5

Dorward, A. R., Kydd, J. G., Poulton, C. D. and Bezemer, D. (2009) 'Coordination risk and cost impacts on economic development in poor rural areas', *Journal of Development Studies*, vol 45, no 7

Dostie, B., Haggblade, S. and Randriamamonjy, J. (2002) 'Seasonal poverty in Madagascar: Magnitude and solutions', *Food Policy*, vol 27, no 5–6, pp493–518

Drèze, J. and Sen, A. (1989) *Hunger and Public Action*, Clarendon Press, London

Dutta, B. and Ramaswami, B. (2001) 'Targeting and efficiency in the public distribution system. The case of Andhra Pradesh and Maharashtra', *Economic and Political Weekly*, vol 36, no 18, pp1524–32

Duffield, A. *et al.* (2003) 'Thin on the ground, questioning the evidences behind World Bank-funded community nutrition projects in Bangladesh, Ethiopia and Uganda', London, Save the Children

Duflo, E. (2003) 'Grandmothers and granddaughters: Old-age pensions and intra-household allocation in South Africa', *World Bank Economic Review*, vol 17, no 1, pp1–25

Eagle, W. (2006) 'Africa's "community school" movement brings education to rural areas', *Voice of America News*, www.voanews.com/english/archive/2006-04/2006-04-27voa24.cfm?CFID=15160057&CFTOKEN=41322095

Edmonds, E.V. (2006) 'Child labour and schooling responses to anticipated income in South Africa', *Journal of Development Economics*, vol 81, no 2, pp386–414

Egashira, K., Matsushita, Y., Virakornphanich, P., Darmawan, Moslehuddin, A. Z. M., Al Mamun, M. A. A. and Do, N. N. H. (2003) 'Features and trends of rainfall in recent 20 years at different locations in humid tropical to subtropical Asia', *Journal of the Faculty of Agriculture*, Kyushu University, vol 48, pp219–25

EIGS (1993) *Hydrogeological Map of Ethiopia at 1:2000000 Scale*, Ethiopian Geological Survey, Ethiopia

EIGS (1996) *Geological Map of Ethiopia at 1:2000000 Scale*, Ethiopian Geological Survey, Ethiopia

Ellis, F. (1993) *Peasant Economics*, Cambridge University Press, Cambridge

Ellis, F. (1998) 'Household strategies and rural livelihood diversification (a survey article)', *Journal of Development Studies,* vol 35, no 1, pp1–38

Ellis, F. (2000a) 'The determinants of rural livelihood diversification in developing countries', *Journal of Agricultural Economics*, vol 51, no 2, pp289–302

Ellis, F. (2000b) *Rural Livelihoods and Diversity in Developing Countries*, Oxford University Press, Oxford

Ellis, F., Kutengule, M. and Nyasulu, A. (2003) 'Livelihoods and rural poverty reduction in Malawi', *World Development*, vol 31, pp1495–510

Escobal, J. (2001) 'The determinants of nonfarm income diversification in rural Peru', *World Development*, vol 29, no 3, pp497–508

Fafchamps, M. (2003) *Rural Poverty, Risk and Development*, MPG Books, Bodmin

Fan, S. G. and Hazell, P. (2001) 'Returns to public investments in the less-favored areas of India and China', *American Journal of Agricultural Economics*, vol 83, no 5, pp1217–22

Feder, G., Just, R. and Zilberman, D. (1985) 'Adoption of agricultural innovations in developing countries: A survey', *Economic Development and Cultural Change*, vol 33, pp255–98

Feder, G., Lau, L., Lin, J. and Luo, X. (1990) 'The relation between credit and productivity in Chinese agriculture: A model of disequilibrium', *American Journal of Agricultural Economics*, vol 72, no 5, pp1151–7

Fentiman, A., Hall, A. and Bundy, D. (1999) 'School enrolment patterns in rural Ghana: a comparative study of the impact of location, gender, age and health on children's access to basic schooling', *Comparative Education*, vol 35, no 3, pp331–49

Ferro-Luzzi, A., Morris S. S., Taffesse S., Demissie, T. and D'Amato, M. (2002) 'Seasonal undernutrition in Rural Ethiopia: Magnitude, correlates, and functional significance', *Food and Nutrition Bulletin*, vol 23, pp227–8

FEWSNET (2002) 'FEWSNET Food Security Warning, Ethiopia, October 31, 2002', www.fews.net/Pages/countryarchive.aspx?pid=100&gb=et&I=en

FEWSNET (2005) 'Malawi Food Security Update November 2005', www.fews.net/Pages/countryarchive.aspx?pid=500&gb=mw&l=en

FEWSNET (2008) 'Malawi Food Security Update January 2008', www.fews.net/Pages/country.aspx?gb=mw&l=en

FEWSNET (2009) 'Malawi Food Security Update January 2009', www.fews.net/Pages/country.aspx?gb=mw&l=en

FEWSNET (2010) 'Malawi Food Security Update August 2010', Famine Early Warning Systems Network, Lilongwe

Fischel, W.A. (2006) '"Will I see you in September?" An economic explanation for the standard school calendar', *Journal of Urban Economics*, vol 59, no 2, pp236–51

Frankenberger, T., Luther, K., Fox, K. and Mazzeo, J. (2003) 'Livelihood erosion through time: Macro and micro factors that influenced livelihood trends in Malawi over the last 30 years', CARE Southern and Western Africa Regional Management Unit, Johannesburg, www.sarpn.org/documents/d0000344/index.php (accessed 26 November 2008)

Freeland, N. (2009) 'Seasonality and social protection: A bridge too far?', paper presented at the conference 'Seasonality Revisited', Institute of Development Studies, Brighton, 8–10 July

Fuller, B., Singer, J.D. and Keiley, M. (1995) 'Why do daughters leave school in Southern Africa? Family economy and mothers' commitments', *Social Forces*, vol 74, no 2, pp657–81

Funk, C. and Brown, M. (2009) 'Declining global per capita agricultural capacity production and warming oceans threaten food security', *Food Security*, vol 1, pp271–89

Garnett, G. P. and Anderson, R. M. (1996) 'Sexually transmitted diseases and sexual behavior: Insights from mathematical models', *Journal of Infectious Diseases*, vol 174, Suppl 2, ppS150-61

Geda, A., de Jong, N., Kimenyi, M. S. and Mwabu, G. (2005) 'Determinants of poverty in Kenya: A household-level analysis', Department of Economics Working Paper No. 2005-44, University of Connecticut

George, C. K., Kavitha, B. S., Reddy, N. S. and Srikanthi, B. (2005) *Frontiers Prevention Program Outcome Evaluation: Qualitative Baseline of the India Program*, Institute of Health Systems, Hyderabad

Gill, G. (1991) *Seasonality and Agriculture in the Developing World: A Problem of the Poor and Powerless*, Cambridge University Press, Cambridge

Gill, G. J. (undated) *But How Does it Compare with the Real Data?*, Winrock International, Kathmandu

Gillespie, S. and Drimie, S. (2009) 'Seasonal dimensions of the HIV-hunger nexus in eastern and southern Africa', paper presented at the conference 'Seasonality Revisited', Institute of Development Studies, Brighton, 8–10 July

Gillespie, S., Jere, P., Msuya, J. and Drimie, S. (2009) 'Food prices and the HIV response: Findings from rapid regional assessments in eastern and southern Africa in 2008', *Food Security*, vol 1, pp261–9

Gillespie, S., Kadiyala, S. and Greener, R. (2007) 'Is poverty or wealth driving HIV transmission?', *AIDS*, vol 21 (suppl. 7), ppS5–S16

Glewwe, P. (1999) 'Why does mother's schooling raise child health in developing countries: Evidence from Morocco', *Journal of Human Resources*, vol 34, no 1, pp124–36

Glewwe, P. and King, E. (2001) 'The impact of early childhood nutritional status on cognitive development: Does the timing of malnutrition matter?', *World Bank Economic Review*, vol 15, no 1, pp81–113

GoB (Government of Bangladesh) (2007) 'Consolidated damage and loss assessment, lessons learnt from the flood 2007 and future action plan', www.dmb.gov.bd/Flood%20Report.pdf, accessed April 2010

Goswami, B. N., Venugopal, V., Sengupta, D., Madhusoodanan, M. S. and Xavier, P. K. (2006) 'Increasing trend of extreme rain events over India in a warming environment', *Science*, vol 314, pp1442–5

Government of Ethiopia, United Nations (2002) *Emergency Assistance Requirements and Implementation Options for 2003*, Addis Ababa

Government of Malawi (2000) *Sexual and Reproductive Health Behaviours in Malawi*, National AIDS Commission and Ministry of Population and Health, Lilongwe

Government of Malawi (GOM) and World Bank (2007) *Poverty and Vulnerability Analysis: Investing in Our Future*, World Bank, Washington, DC

Green, D. (2008) *From Poverty to Power: How Active Citizens and Effective States Can Change the World*, Oxfam International, Oxford

Greenland, S. (1987) 'Interpretation and choice of effect measures in epidemiologic analyses', *American Journal of Epidemiology*, vol 125, pp761–8

Groisman, P.Y., Knight, R. W., Easterling, D. R., Karl, T. R., Hegerl, G. C. and Razuvaev, V. N. (2005) 'Trends in intense precipitation in the climate record', *Journal of Climate*, vol 18, pp1326–50

Grooteart, C. (1997) 'The determinants of poverty in Côte d'Ivoire in the 1980s', *Journal of African Economies*, vol 6, no 2, pp169–96

Guarcello, L., Lyon, S. and Rosati, F. C. (2006) 'Child labour and education for all: An issue paper', Understanding Children's Work Project Working Paper Series, University of Rome, Rome

Gujarati, D. N. (2003) *Basic Econometrics*, McGraw Hill, Boston

Haddad, L. and Zeitlyn, S. (eds) (2009) 'Lifting the curse: Overcoming persistent undernutrition in India', *IDS Bulletin*, vol 40, no 2, Institute of Development Studies, Brighton

Hadley, S. (2010) 'Seasonality and access to education in sub-Saharan Africa', CREATE, Pathways to Access Monograph no 31, Institute of Education, University of London

Haggblade, S., Longabaugh, S. and Tschirley, D. (2009) 'Spatial patterns of food staple production and marketing in South East Africa: Implications for trade policy and emergency response', MSU International Development Working Paper 100, Michigan State University, East Lansing

Halperin, D. T. and Epstein, H. (2004) 'Concurrent sexual partnerships help to explain Africa's high HIV prevalence: Implications for prevention, *Lancet*, vol 364, pp4–6

Hampshire, K. (2002) 'Fulani on the move: Seasonal economic migration in the Sahel as a social process', *Journal of Development Studies*, vol 38, no 5, pp15–36

Harris, J. R. and Todaro, M. P. (1970) 'Migration, unemployment, and development: A two-sector analysis', *American Economic Review*, vol 60, pp126–42

Haswell, M. (1975) *The Nature of Poverty: A Case History of the First Quarter-Century after World War II*, Macmillan, London and Basingstoke

Hauenstein Swan, S., (2008) www.odi.org.uk/events/report.asp?id=300&title=food= shocks-food-stress-seasonality-hunger-debate, accessed 17 May 2011

Hauenstein Swan, S., Vaitla, B. and Devereux, S. (2009) 'An integrated intervention framework for fighting seasonal hunger', paper presented at the international conference, Seasonality Revisited, 8–10 July, Institute of Development Studies, Brighton

Hazell, Peter B. R. (1984) 'Sources of increased instability in Indian and U.S. cereal production', *American Journal of Agricultural Economics*', vol 66, no 3, pp302–11

Hellmuth, M. E., Moorhead, A., Thomson, M. C. and Williams, J. (eds) (2007) *Climate Risk Management in Africa: Learning from Practice*, International Research Institute for Climate and Society (IRI), Columbia University, New York, NY

Hoddinott, J. and Kinsey, B. (2001) 'Child growth in the time of drought', *Oxford Bulletin of Economics and Statistics*, vol 63, no 4, pp409–36

Holden, S. T. (1993) 'Peasant household modelling: Farming systems evolution and sustainability in Northern Zambia', *Agricultural Economics*, vol 9

Holding, P.A., Stevenson, J., Peshu, N. and Marsh, K. (1999) 'Cognitive sequelae of severe malaria with impaired consciousness', *Transactions of the Royal Society for Tropical Medicine and Hygiene*, vol 93, pp529–34

Holland, J. and Blackburn, J. (1998) *Whose Voice? Participatory Research and Policy Change*, Intermediate Technology Publications, London

Holmes, R., Farringdon, J., Rahman, T. and Slater, R. (2008) 'Extreme poverty in Bangladesh: Protecting and promoting rural livelihoods', www.odi.org.uk/resources/download/1586.pdf, accessed 18 January 2011

Holt, J. *et al.* (2009) 'Understanding household economy in rural Niger', Save the Children, London

Holzmann, R. and Jorgensen, S. (1999) 'Social protection as social risk management: Conceptual underpinnings for the Social Protection Sector Strategy Paper', Social Protection Discussion Paper No. 9904, World Bank, Washington, DC

Hoorweg, J., Foeken, D. and Klaver, W. (1995) *Seasons and Nutrition at the Kenya Coast*, African Studies Centre, Leiden

Hopkins, J., Levin, C. and Haddad, L. (1994) 'Women's income and household expenditure patterns: Gender or flow? Evidence from Niger', *American Journal of Agricultural Economics*, vol 76, no 5, pp1219–25

Huebler, F. (2006) 'International education statistics: Primary school enrollment in 2004', http://huebler.blogspot.com/2006/09/primary-school-enrollment-in-2004.html

Hulme, D., Moore, K. and Shepherd, A. (2001) 'Chronic poverty: Meanings and analytical frameworks', *CPRC Working Paper 2*, University of Manchester, Manchester

Humphrey, J. (2009) 'Child undernutrition, tropical enteropathy, toilets, and handwashing', *The Lancet*, vol 374, pp1032–35

Hunt, F. (2008) 'Dropping out from school: A cross-country review of literature', Pathways to Access, Research Monograph No 16, *CREATE*

Huss-Ashmore, R.A. (1993), 'Agriculture, modernisation and seasonality', in S.J. Ulijasek and S.S. Strickland (eds) *Seasonality and Human Ecology*, Cambridge University Press, Cambridge

IDC (International Development Committee) (2003) *The Humanitarian Crisis in Southern Africa. Third Report of Session 2002–2003*, House of Commons, International Development Committee, London, www.parliament.the-stationery-office.co.uk/pa/cm200203/cmselect/cmintdev/116/11602.htm (accessed 26 November 2008)

IEG (2007) *An Impact Evaluation of India's Second and Third Andhra Pradesh Irrigation Project. A Case of Poverty Reduction with Low Economic Returns*, World Bank, Washington, DC

IFAD (2001) *Assessment of Rural Poverty: Western and Central Africa*, International Fund for Agricultural Development, Rome

ILO (2004) *Consumer Price Index Manual: Theory and Practice*, International Labour Organization, Geneva

IMF (International Monetary Fund) (2005) 'Bangladesh Poverty Reduction Strategy Paper 2005', www.imf.org/external/pubs/ft/scr/2005/cr05410.pdf, accessed 1 October 2010

IML (Innovation, Monitoring and Learning Division: CLP) (2010a) 'Impact of deworming treatment and daily micronutrient supplementation on adult and child nutritional status during *monga* (hungry) season', www.clp-bangladesh.org, accessed 6 April 2010

IML (Innovation, Monitoring and Learning Division: CLP) (2010b) 'Impact of earlier recruitment into the CLP programme on mother and child nutritional status among chars dwellers', www.clp-bangladesh.org, accessed 6 April 2010

IPCC (Intergovernmental Panel on Climate Change) (2007) *Climate Change 2007: Impacts, Adaptation and Vulnerability*, The Intergovernmental Panel on Climate Change, Geneva

Iqbal, F. (1986) 'The demand and supply of funds among agricultural households in India. Agricultural household models: Extensions, applications and policy', in I. Singh, L.

Squire and J. Strauss (eds) *Agricultural Household Models: Extensions, Applications and Policy*, Johns Hopkins University Press, Baltimore, MD

Jackson, A. (2009) 'DFID Bangladesh Information Note: Poverty Thresholds and Reporting', www.dfid.gov.uk/bangladesh, accessed 5 April 2009

Jackson, C. and Palmer-Jones, R. (1999) 'Rethinking gendered poverty and work', *Development and Change*, vol 30, no 3, pp557–83

Jacoby, H. and Skoufias, E. (1997) 'Risk, financial markets, and human capital in a developing country', *Review of Economic Studies*, vol 64, no 3, pp311–35

Jacoby, H. and Skoufias, E. (1998) 'Testing theories of consumption behavior using information on aggregate shocks: Income seasonality and rainfall in rural India', *American Journal of Agricultural Economics*, vol 80, no 1, pp1–14

Jairath, J. (2000) 'Participatory irrigation management in Andhra Pradesh', South Asia Regional Poverty Monitoring and Evaluation Workshop, New Delhi

JBIC Institute (2007) 'Impact assessment of irrigation infrastructure development on poverty alleviation: A case study from Pakistan', JBICI Research Paper No. 31

Jennings, S. and Magrath, J. (2009) 'What happened to the seasons?', paper presented at the conference 'Seasonality Revisited', Institute of Development Studies, Brighton, 8–10 July

Jesuit Centre for Theological Reflection (2009) *JCTR rural basket: Saka area, Masaiti, February 2009*, JCTR, Lusaka, Zambia

Jukes, M. (2005) 'The long-term impact of preschool health and nutrition on education', *Food and Nutrition Bulletin*, vol 26, pp193–200

Jupp, D. (2003) *Views of the Poor: The Perspectives of Rural and Urban Poor in Tanzania as Recounted Through their Stories and Pictures*, Swiss Agency for Development and Cooperation, Berne

Kabeer, N. (2002) 'Safety nets and opportunity ladders: Addressing vulnerability and enhancing productivity in South Asia', www.odi.org.uk/resources, accessed 6 April 2009

Kadzamira, E. and Rose, P. (2003) 'Can free primary education meet the needs of the poor? Evidence from Malawi', *International Journal of Educational Development*, vol 23, no 5, pp501–16

Kadzamira, E.C. and Chibwana, M P. (2000) *Gender and Primary Schooling in Malawi*, Institute of Development Studies, Brighton

Kale, P., Andreozzi, V. and Nobre, F. (2004) 'Time series analysis of deaths due to diarrhoea in children in Rio de Janeiro, Brazil, 1980–1998', *J Health Popul Nutr*, vol 22, no 1, pp27–33

Kamawa, O. (2002) *Living in the Abyss: Hunger in Mchinji*, Save the Children, Lilongwe

Kane, E., Bruce, L. and de Brun, M.O. (1998) 'Designing the future together: PRA and education policy in the Gambia', in J. Holland and J. Blackburn (eds) *Whose Voice: Participatory Research and Policy Change*, Intermediate Technology Publications, London

Kar, K. with Chambers, R. (2008) *Handbook of Community-led Total Sanitation*, Plan International, London

Kassouf A. and Senauer, B. (1996) 'Direct and indirect effects of parental education on malnutrition among children in Brazil: A full income approach', *Economic Development and Cultural Change*, vol 44, no 4, pp817–38

Kebede, S. and Zeleke, B. (2009) 'Hydrogeology in a transect of three livelihood zones in East and West Hararghe and Shinile zones, Oromiya and Somali regions, Ethiopia', RiPPLE, Ethiopia

Key, N., Sadoulet, E. and de Janvry, A. (2000) 'Transaction costs and agricultural household supply response', *American Journal of Agricultural Economics*, vol 82, pp245–59

Khaila, S., Mvula, P. M. and Kadzandira, J. M. (1999) 'Consultations with the poor. Country synthesis report, Malawi', prepared for the Global Synthesis Workshop, September 22–23, Poverty Group, Poverty Reduction and Economic Management Network, World Bank, Washington DC

Khandker, S. R. (2009) 'Poverty and income seasonality in Bangladesh', World Bank Policy Research Working Paper No. 4923, World Bank, Washington, DC, www.wds-world-bank.org, accessed 7 March 2010

Kinabo, J. (1993) 'Seasonal variation of birth weight distribution in Morogoro, Tanzania', *East African Medical Journal,* vol 70, pp752–5

Klein Tank, A. M. G., Peterson, T. C., Quadi, D. A., Dorji, S., Zou, X., Tang, H., Santhosh, K., Joshi, U. R., Jaswal, A. K., Kolli, R. K., Sikder, A. B., Deshpande, N. R., Revadekar, J. V., Yeleuova, K., Vandasheva, S., Faleyeva, M., Gomboluudev, P., Budhathoki, K. P., Hussain, A., Afzaal, M., Chandrapala, L., Anvar, H., Amanmurad, D., Asanova, V. S., Jones, P. D., New, M. G. and Spektorman, T. (2007) 'Changes in daily temperature and precipitation extremes in central and south Asia', *Journal of Geophysical Research*, vol 111, D16105, doi:10.1029/2005JD006316

Kost, K., Landry D. and Darroch, J. (1998) 'The effects of pregnancy planning status on birth outcomes and infant care', *Family Planning Perspectives*, vol 30, no 5, pp223–30

Kotikula, A., Narayan, A. and Zaman, H. (2007) 'Explaining poverty reduction in the 2000s: An analysis of the Bangladeshi Household Income and Expenditure Survey', www.worldbank.org, accessed 7 June 2009

Krishna, A. (2010) *One Illness Away: Why People Become Poor and How They Escape Poverty*, Oxford University Press, Oxford

Kunii, O., Nakamura, S., Abdur, R. and Wakai, S. (2002) 'The impact on health and risk factors of the diarrhoea epidemics of the 1998 Bangladeshi floods', *Public Health*, vol 116, no 2, pp68–74

Lejeune, S. (2007) 'The cost of the cheapest adequate diet and a household's ability to afford it – Legambo, South Wollo, Ethiopia', Save the Children UK (unpublished)

Lejeune, S. and Hilton, J. (2009) 'The minimum cost of an adequate diet and a household's ability to afford it – Shinile Region, Ethiopia', Save the Children (unpublished)

Lewin, K. (2002) 'Microfinance in the Pacific – mipela katim bus! The experience of Putim na Kisim', http://devnet.anu.edu.au/online%20versions%20pdfs/57/2357Lewin.pdf

Lewin, K. (2007) 'Improving access, equity and transitions in education: creating a research agenda', CREATE, Pathways to Access, Research Monograph No 1, www.create-rpc.org/pdf_documents/PTA1.pdf, accessed 2 February 2009

Lipton, M. (1977) *Why Poor People Stay Poor: A Study of Urban Bias in World Development*, Temple Smith, London

Lipton, M., Litchfield, J. and Faures, J-M. (2003) 'The effects of irrigation on poverty: A framework for analysis', *Water Policy*, vol 5, pp413–27

LIU (Livelihoods Integration Unit, MOARD/DRMFSS) (2009) *The Livelihoods Integration Unit: Uses of the Information and Analysis*, LIU, Addis Ababa

LIU (Livelihoods Integration Unit, MOARD/DRMFSS) (2010) *An Atlas of Ethiopian Livelihoods*, LIU, Addis Ababa

Llop, J.M. (2005) 'Schooling and child farm labour in Spain, circa 1880–1930', *Community and Change,* vol 20, no 3, 385–406

Loevinsohn, M. (2006) 'AIDS and watersheds: Understanding and assessing biostructural interventions', in S. Gillespie (ed.) *AIDS, Poverty, and Hunger: Challenges and Responses,* IFPRI, Washington DC, www.ifpri.org/pubs/books/oc50.asp

Loevinsohn, M. (2009) 'Seasonal hunger, the 2001–03 famine and the dynamics of HIV in Malawi', paper presented at the conference 'Seasonality Revisited', Institute of Development Studies, 8–10 July

Lokshin, M., Das Gupta, M. and Ivaschenko, O. (2005) 'An assessment of India's integrated child development services nutrition program,' *Development and Change*, vol 36, no 4, pp613–40

Longhurst, R. (ed.) (1986a) 'Seasonality and poverty', *IDS Bulletin*, vol 17, no 3, Institute of Development Studies, Brighton

Longhurst, R. (1986b) 'Household food strategies in response to seasonality and famine', *IDS Bulletin*, vol 17, no 3, Institute of Development Studies, Brighton

Longhurst, R. and Kgomotso, P. (2009) 'Planning to address seasonal poverty: Some experiences of the last 30 years', paper presented at the conference 'Seasonality Revisited', Institute of Development Studies, Brighton, 8–10 July

Longhurst, R. and Payne, P. (1981) 'Seasonal aspects of nutrition', in Chambers *et al.*, *Seasonal Dimensions to Rural Poverty*, pp45–52

Lucas, K. (2001) 'And the meek shall occupy the Earth', *UNESCO: The Courier*, vol 54, no 1, http://unesdoc.unesco.org/images/0012/001215/121514e.pdf

Lurie, M. N., Williams, B. G. and Zuma, K. (2003) 'The impact of migration on HIV-1 transmission in South Africa: A study of migrant and nonmigrant men and their partners', *Sexually Transmitted Diseases*, vol 30, pp149–56

MacDonald, A. *et al.* (2005) *Developing Groundwater: A Guide for Rural Water Supply*, ITDG Publishing, Bourton-on-Dunsmore, Warwickshire

Macours, K. and Vakis, R. (2010) 'Seasonal migration and early childhood development', *World Development*, vol 38, no 6, pp857–69

Maddala, G. S. (1983) *Limited-dependent and Qualitative Variables in Econometrics*, Cambridge University Press, Cambridge

Magombo , T., Magreta, R. and Zingore, S. (2009) 'Seasonality and profitability of rice value chains for smallholder farmers at Nkhate Irrigation Scheme in southern Malawi', paper presented at the conference 'Seasonality Revisited', Institute of Development Studies, Brighton, 8–10 July

Malawi Vulnerability Assessment Committee (2005) 'Malawi Livelihood Profile – Kasungu Lilongwe Plain', Malawi Baseline Livelihood Profiles, MVAC, Lilongwe

Malawi Vulnerability Assessment Committee (2009a) 'MWKAS_1_s1.xls', Kasungu Lilongwe Plain – Malawi Analysis Spreadsheets, MVAC, Lilongwe

Malawi Vulnerability Assessment Committee (2009b) 'MWKAS_2_s1.xls', Kasungu Lilongwe Plain – Malawi Analysis Spreadsheets, MVAC, Lilongwe

Malawi Vulnerability Assessment Committee (2009c) 'MWKAS_3_s1.xls', Kasungu Lilongwe Plain – Malawi Analysis Spreadsheets, MVAC, Lilongwe

Malawi Vulnerability Assessment Committee (MVAC) (2005) *Malawi Food Security Monitoring Report*, Ministry of Economic Planning and Development, Lilongwe

Maleta, K., Virtanen, S. M., Espo, M., Kulmala, T. and Ashorn, P. (2003) 'Seasonality of growth and the relationship between weight and height gain in children under three years of age in rural Malawi', *Acta Paediatrica*, vol 92, pp491–7

Mandala, E. C. (2005) *The End of Chidyerano: A History of Food and Everyday Life in Malawi, 1860–2004*, Heinemann, Portsmouth, NH

Marks, M. (2008) 'Infrastructure and Employment Programme. Safety Net Grant: Initial Impacts', www.clp-bangladesh.org, accessed 1 April 2009

Marks, M. and Islam, R. (2007) 'CLP flood relief activities: Summary of relief efforts and customer satisfaction survey', www.clp-bangladesh.org, accessed 20 May 2009

Martorell, R. (1999) 'The nature of child malnutrition and its long-term implications', *Food and Nutrition Bulletin*, vol 20, no 3, pp288–92

Mascie-Taylor, N. C. G., and Goto, R. (2009) 'A cash for work programme improved nutritional status, food expenditure and consumption of poor rural Bangladeshi women and children in the hungry season', www.clp-bangladesh.org, accessed 1 April 2010

Masset, E. (2009) *Food Demand, Uncertainty and Investments in Human Capital. Three Essays on Rural Andhra Pradesh, India*, Institute of Development Studies, Brighton

Masudi, A., Ishumi, A., Mbeo, F. and Sambo, W. (2001) 'Investigating the Worst Forms of Child Labour, No. 9. Tanzania: Child Labour in Commercial Agriculture – Tobacco: A Rapid Assessment', International Labour Organization, International Programme on the Elimination of Child Labour (IPEC), Geneva

McElroy, M. B. and Horney, M. J. (1981) 'Nash bargained household decisions', *International Economic Review*, vol 22, no 2, pp333–50

McKay, A. and Lawson, D. (2002) 'Chronic poverty in developing and transition countries: Concepts and evidence', CREDIT Research Paper, No. 02/27, Centre for Research in Economic Development and International Trade, University of Nottingham, Nottingham

McSweeney, C., New, M. and Lizcano, G. (undated) 'UNDP Climate Change Country Profiles: Malawi', http://country-profiles.geog.ox.ac.uk

Medora, N. (2003) 'Mate selection in contemporary India', in R. Hamon and B. Ingoldsby (eds) *Mate Selection Across Cultures*, Sage, Thousand Oaks, CA

Mehrotra, S. and Delemonica, E. (1998) 'Household costs and public expenditure on primary education in five low-income countries: A comparative analysis', *International Journal of Educational Development*, vol 18, no 1, pp41–61

Moestue, J. and Huttly, S. (2008) 'Adult education and child nutrition: The role of family and community', *Journal of Epidemiology and Community Health*, vol 62, pp53–9

Morduch, J. (1995) 'Income smoothing and consumption smoothing', *Journal of Economic Perspectives*, vol 9, pp103–14

Morduch, J. (1999) 'Between the state and the market – can informal insurance patch the safety net?', *World Bank Research Observer*, vol 14, no 2, pp187–208

Moris, J. (1989) 'Indigenous versus introduced solutions to food stress in Africa', in D. Sahn (ed.) *Seasonal Variability in Third World Agriculture*, Johns Hopkins University Press, Baltimore, MD

Morris, M. and Kretzschmar, M. (1997) Concurrent partnerships and the spread of HIV, *AIDS*, vol 11, pp641–8

Mortimore, M. (2009) 'Adaptation to seasonality, drought, and climate change in the West African Sahel', paper presented at the conference 'Seasonality Revisited', Brighton, Institute of Development Studies, 8–10 July

Moser, C. (1998) 'The Asset Vulnerability Framework: Reassessing urban poverty reduction strategies', *World Development*, vol 26, no 1, pp1–19

Mubiru, D. N., Angona, A. and Komutunga, E. (2009) 'Micro-level analysis of seasonal trends, farmers' perception of climate change and adaptation strategies in Eastern Uganda', paper presented at the conference 'Seasonality Revisited', Institute of Development Studies, Brighton, 8–10 July

Muchambo, E. and Sharp, B. (2007) 'Southern Sudan Livelihoods profile', Southern Sudan Centre for Census, Statistics and Evaluation and Save the Children UK

Mukherjee, S. and Benson, T. (2003) 'The determinants of poverty in Malawi, 1998', *World Development*, vol 31, no 2, pp339–58

Munthali, A. (2006) 'The impact of the 2001/2002 hunger crisis on child labour and education: A case study of Kasungu and Mchinji Districts in Central Malawi', in T. Takane (ed.) *Current Issues of Rural Development in Malawi*, Institute of Developing Economies, Chiba, Japan

MVAC (2002) *Malawi Emergency Food Security Assessment Report (September)*, Lilongwe, http://sarpn.org/documents/d0000046/index.php

MVAC (2003) *Malawi Food Security Assessment Report (August)*, Malawi Vulnerability Assessment Committee, Lilongwe

MVAC (2007) *Malawi's 2007 Bumper Harvest: Is Everyone Food Secure?* Malawi Vulnerability Assessment Committee, Lilongwe, http://ochaonline.un.org/rosea/Home/tabid/6327/language/en-US/Default.aspx

Nakajima, C. (1986) *Subjective Equilibrium Theory of the Farm Household*, Elsevier, Amsterdam

Namphande, P.N.W. (2007) 'Choice or deprivation? Primary school drop outs in Malawi: The case of Kasungu District', MPhil thesis, University of Science and Technology at Trondheim, Norway

Narayan, D., Chambers, R., Shah, M. K. and Petesch, P. (2000) *Crying Out for Change: Voices of the Poor*, Oxford University Press for the World Bank, Oxford

National AIDS Commission (2003) *HIV Sentinel Surveillance Report 2003*, Ministry of Health and Population, Lilongwe, Malawi

National Statistical Office (NSO) (1998) *Population and Housing Census: Final Report*, National Statistical Office, Zomba, Malawi, www.nso.malawi.net (accessed 9 December 2008)

National Statistical Office (NSO) (2005) *Integrated Household Survey 2004/05*, National Statistical Office, Zomba, Malawi

National Statistical Office (NSO) (2006) *Welfare Monitoring Survey 2005*, National Statistical Office, Zomba, Malawi

National Statistical Office (NSO) (2007) *Welfare Monitoring Survey 2006*, National Statistical Office, Zomba, Malawi

National Statistical Office (NSO) (2008) *Welfare Monitoring Survey 2007*, National Statistical Office, Zomba, Malawi

National Statistical Office (NSO) (2009) *Welfare Monitoring Survey 2008*, National Statistical Office, Zomba, Malawi

National Statistical Office (NSO) (2010) *Welfare Monitoring Survey 2009*, National Statistical Office, Zomba, Malawi

Neogi, M. G., Khair, A. and Samsuzzaman, S. (2009) 'Adjustment of short duration rice variety in rice-based cropping pattern and agro-techniques to mitigate seasonal food insecurity (*monga*) in northern districts of Bangladesh', paper to conference on 'Seasonality Revisited', Institute of Development Studies, Brighton, 8–10 July

New Agriculturalist (2001) 'Cultivating "Cinderella trees"', Issue 3, www.new-ag.info/01-3/index.html

New, M., Hewitson, B., Stephenson, D. B., Tsiga, A., Kruger, A., Manhique, A., Gomez, B., Coelho, C. A. S., Masisi, D.N., Kululanga, E., Mbambalala, E., Adesina, F., Saleh, H., Kanyanga, J., Adosi, J., Bulane, L., Fortunata, L., Mdoka, M. L. and Lajoie, R. (2006) 'Evidence of trends in daily climate extremes over southern and west Africa', *Journal of Geophysical Research*, vol 111

Newbery, D. and Stiglitz, J. E. (1981) *The Theory of Commodity Price Stabilization: A Study in the Economics of Risk*, Clarendon Press, Oxford

NSO and ORC Macro (2001) *Malawi Demographic and Health Survey 2000*, National Statistical Office and ORC Macro, Zomba, Malawi and Calverton, MD

Nwosu, A. B and Anya, A. O. (1980) 'Seasonality in human hookworm infection in an endemic area of Nigeria, and its relationship to rainfall', *Tropenmed Parasitol*, vol 31, no 2, pp201–8

O'Donnell, M. (2004), 'Household Economy Assessment report, Thar Desert Livelihood Zone Tharparkar District, Sindh Province, Pakistan', Save the Children UK, Thardeep Rural Development Programme (TRDP), Oxfam Novib

Okwi, P. O., Ndeng'e, G., Kristjanson, P., Arunga, M., Notenbaert, A., Omolo, A., Henninger, N., Benson, T., Kariuki, P. and Owuor, J. (2007) 'Spatial determinants of poverty in rural Kenya', *PNAS*, vol 104, no 43, pp16769–74

Olango, P. and Aboud, F. (1990) 'Determinants of mothers' treatment of diarrhea in rural Ethiopia', *Social Science and Medicine*, vol 31, pp1245–49

Omamo, S. (1998) 'Farm-to-market transaction costs and specialisation in small-scale agriculture: Explorations with a non-separable household model', *Journal of Development Studies*, vol 35, no 2, pp153–63

Orkin, K. (2009) 'Child work and schooling in rural Ethiopia', conference paper for UKFIET Conference, Department for International Development and Oxford University, Oxford

Orr, A., Mwale, B. and Saiti-Chitsonga, D. (2009) 'Exploring seasonal poverty traps: The "Six-Week Window" in southern Malawi', *Journal of Development Studies*, vol 45, no 2, pp227–55

Osborne, H. (2000) 'The seasonality of nineteenth-century poaching', *Agricultural History Review,* vol 48, no 1, pp27–41

Oxfam (2008) 'Viet Nam: Climate change, adaptation and poor people', http://policy-practice.oxfam.org.uk/publications/vietnam-climate-change-adaptation-and-poor-people-112506

Oxfam (2009) 'Bolivia: Climate change, poverty and adaptation', http://policy-practice.oxfam.org.uk/publications/bolivia-climate-change-poverty-and-adaptation-111968

Oxfam (Abbass, Z.) (2009) 'Climate change, poverty and environmental crisis in the disaster-prone areas of Pakistan: Community-based research', http://policy-practice.oxfam.org.uk/publications/climate-change-poverty-and-environmental-crisis-in-the-disaster-prone-areas-of-111982

Oxfam (Emmett, B.) (2009) 'Even the Himalayas have stopped smiling: Climate change, poverty and adaptation in Nepal', http://policy-practice.oxfam.org.uk/publications/even-the-himalayas-have-stopped-smiling-climate-change-poverty-and-adaptation-i-112507

Oxfam (Jennings, S. and Magrath, J.) (2009) 'What happened to the seasons?', http://policy-practice.oxfam.org.uk/publications/what-happened-to-the-seasons-changing-seasonality-may-be-one-of-the-major-impac-112501

Oxfam (Magrath, J.) (2008) 'Turning up the heat: Climate change and poverty in Uganda', http://policy-practice.oxfam.org.uk/publications/turning-up-the-heat-climate-change-and-poverty-in-uganda-112505

Oxfam (Magrath, J.) (2009) 'The winds of change: Climate change, poverty and the environment in Malawi', http://policy-practice.oxfam.org.uk/publications/the-winds-of-change-climate-change-poverty-and-the-environment-in-malawi-112508

Oxfam (Pettengell, C.) (2010) 'Climate change adaptation, enabling people living in poverty to adapt', http://policy-practice.oxfam.org.uk/publications/climate-change-adaptation-enabling-people-living-in-poverty-to-adapt-111978

Palmer, I. (1981) 'Seasonal dimensions of women's roles', in R. Chambers, R. Longhurst and A. Pacey (eds) *Seasonal Dimensions to Rural Poverty*, Frances Pinter, London

Palmer-Jones, R. and Sen, K. (2003) 'What has luck got to do with it? A regional analysis of poverty and agricultural growth in rural India', *Journal of Development Studies*, vol 40, no 1, pp1–31

Panter-Brick, C. (1996) 'Proximate determinants of birth seasonality and conception failure in Nepal,' *Population Studies*, vol 50, no 2, pp203–20

Paxson, C. (1993) 'Consumption and income seasonality in Thailand', *Journal of Political Economy*, vol 101, pp39–72

Pender, J. L. (1996) 'Discount rates and credit markets: Theory and evidence from rural India', *Journal of Development Economics*, vol 50, pp257–96

Pison, G., Le Guenno, B., Lagarde, E., Enel, C. and Seck, C. (1993) 'Seasonal migration: A risk factor for HIV infection in rural Senegal', *Journal of Acquired Immune Deficiency Syndromes*, vol 6, pp196–200

Pitt, M. M. and Khandker, S. R. (2002) 'Credit programmes for the poor and seasonality in rural Bangladesh', *Journal of Development Studies*, vol 39, no 2, pp1–24

PLA (2007) 'Immersions: learning about poverty face-to-face', *Participatory Learning and Action*, vol 57, December

Potter, R. B., Binns, T., Elliott, J. A. and Smith, D. (2008) *Geographies of Development: An Introduction to Development Studies*, third edition, Pearson Education, Harlow

Poulton, C. D., Dorward, A. R. and Kydd, J. G. (2010) 'The future of small farms: New directions for services, institutions and intermediation', *World Development*, vol 38, no 10

Pradhan, B. K., Salulja, M. R., Roy, P. K. and Shetty, S. L. (2003) *Household Savings and Investment Behaviour in India*, NCAER, Mumbai

Pridmore, P. (2007) 'Impact of health on educational access and achievement: A cross-national review of the research evidence', Pathways to Access, Research Monograph No 2, CREATE

Quisumbing, A. R. (2007) 'Poverty transitions, shocks, and consumption in rural Bangladesh: Preliminary results from a longitudinal household survey', Chronic Poverty Research Centre Working Paper 105, International Food Policy Research Institute, Washington, DC

Quizon, J. and Binswanger, H. (1986) 'Modeling the impact of agricultural growth and government policy on income distribution in India', *World Bank Economic Review*, vol 1, no 1, pp103–48

Rahikainen, K. (2004) *Centuries of Child Labour: European Experiences from the Seventeenth to the Twentieth Century*, Ashgate, Aldershot

Rahmen, R. I. (2002) 'Rural poverty, patterns and processes', in K. A. Toufique and C. Turton (eds) *Hands Not Land: How Livelihoods are Changing in Rural Bangladesh*, Bangladesh Institute of Development Studies/DFID, Dhaka

Rajagopalan, S., Kymal, P. and Pei, P. (1981) 'Births, work and nutrition in Tamil Nadu, India', in R. Chambers, R. Longhurst and A. Pacey (eds) *Seasonal Dimensions to Rural Poverty*, Frances Pinter, London

Rasbash, J., Steele, F., Browne, W. and Prosser, B. (2005) *A User's Guide to MLwiN, Version 2.0*, Centre for Multilevel Modelling, University of Bristol, Bristol

Ravi, C. and Indrakant, S. (2003) 'Food security and public distribution system', in *Andhra Pradesh Development Economic Reforms and Challenges Ahead*, Center for Economic and Social Studies, Hyderabad

Reardon, T., Berdegue, J. and Escobar, G. (2001) 'Rural nonfarm employment and incomes in Latin America: Overview and policy implications', *World Development*, vol 29, no 3, pp395–409

Reardon, T., Delgado, C. and Matlon, P. (1992) 'Determinants and effects of income diversification amongst farm households in Burkina Faso', *Journal of Development Studies*, vol 28, no 2, pp264–96

Rosenzweig, M. and Schultz, T. (1982) 'The behavior of mothers as inputs to child health: The determinants of birth weight, gestation, and rate of fetal growth', in V. Fuchs (ed.) *Economic Aspects of Health*, University of Chicago Press, Chicago

Rowland, M.G.M., Paul, A., Prentice, A.M., Müller, E., Hutton, M., Barrell, R.A.E. and Whitehead, R.G. (1981) 'Seasonality and the growth of infants in a Gambian village', in R. Chambers, R. Longhurst and A. Pacey (eds) *Seasonal Dimensions to Rural Poverty*, Frances Pinter, London

Sabates-Wheeler, R. and Devereux, S. (2010) 'Cash transfers and high food prices: Explaining outcomes on Ethiopia's Productive Safety Net Programme', *Food Policy*, vol 35, no 4, pp274–85

Sabates-Wheeler, R. and Feldman, R. (eds) (2011) *Migration and Social Protection: Claiming Social Rights Beyond Borders*, Palgrave Macmillan, London

Sachs, J. (2005) *The End of Poverty: How We Can Make it Happen in Our Lifetime*, Penguin Books, London

Sadler, K., Kerven, C., Calo, M. and Manske, M. (2008) *Milk Matters*, London, Save the Children

Sadoulet, E. and de Janvry, A. (1995) *Quantitative Development Policy Analysis*, Johns Hopkins University Press, Baltimore, MD

Sahn, D. (1987) *Causes and Implications of Seasonal Variability in Household Food Security*, International Food Policy Research Institute, Washington, DC

Sahn, D. (1989) *Seasonal Variability in Third World Agriculture: The Consequences for Food Security*, Johns Hopkins University Press, Baltimore and London

Salahuddin, A., Neogi, M. G. and Magor, N. (2009) 'Addressing *monga* through a collective regional forum response in the northwest of Bangladesh', paper presented at the conference 'Seasonality Revisited', Institute of Development Studies, Brighton, 8–10 July

Samuelsson, U. and Ludvigsson, J. (2001) 'Seasonal variation of birth month and breast-feeding in children with diabetes mellitus', *Journal of Pediatric Endocrinology and Metabolism*, vol 14, no 1, pp43–6

Save the Children (2008) 'Livelihoods and vulnerabilities: An understanding of livelihoods in Somali Regional State, Ethiopia', Save the Children

Save the Children (2009) 'Cost of healthy diet guidelines', Save the Children, London

Save the Children UK (2008) *Cash, food, payments and risk - a review of the Productive Safety Net Programme*, Save the Children Ethiopia, Addis Ababa

Save the Children UK and FEG Consulting (2008a) *The Household Economy Approach – A Guide for Programme Planners and Policy-makers*, Save the Children and FEG Consulting, London

Save the Children UK and FEG Consulting (2008b) *The Practitioners' Guide to the Household Economy Approach*, Save the Children, FEG Consulting and Regional Hunger and Vulnerability Programme, Johannesburg and London

Schofield, S. (1974) 'Seasonal factors affecting nutrition in different age groups and especially pre-school children', *Journal of Development Studies*, vol 11, no 1, pp22–40

School of Oriental and African Studies, Wadonda Consult, Overseas Development Institute and Michigan State University (2008) 'Evaluation of the 2006/7 Agricultural Input Supply Programme, Malawi: Final Report', School of Oriental and African Studies, London

Scott, L. and Islam, R. (2010a) 'Have recipients of asset transfer seen an increase in their income and expenditure?', www.clp-bangladesh.org, accessed 1 June 2010

Scott, L. and Islam, R. (2010b) 'Moving out of material poverty? The current status of assets of CLP core beneficiaries', www.clp-bangladesh.org, accessed 6 July 2010

Seebens, H. and Sauer, J. (2007) 'Bargaining power and efficiency – rural households in Ethiopia', *Journal of International Development*, vol 19, no 7, pp895–918

Sen, A. (1981) *Poverty and Famines: An Essay on Entitlement and Deprivation*, Clarendon Press, Oxford

Sen, B., Mujeri, M. and Shahabuddin, Q. (2004) 'Operationalizing pro-poor growth: Bangladesh as a case study', http://siteresources.worldbank.org/INTPGI/Resources/342674-1115051237044/oppgbangladesh(Nov).pdf, accessed 1 October 2010

Shah, M. K., Osbourne, N., Mbilizi, T. and Vilili, G. (2002) 'Impact of HIV/AIDS on agricultural productivity and rural livelihoods in the Central Region of Malawi', CARE International in Malawi (Lilongwe)

Sheikh, M. M., Ahmed, A. U., Kolli, R. K., Shrestha, M. L. and Dharmaratna, G. H. P. (undated) 'Development and application of climate extreme indices and indicators for monitoring trends in climate extremes and their socio-economic impacts in south Asian countries', report for the Asia-Pacific Network for Global Change, www.apn-gcr.org/newAPN/resources/resources.htm

Shimizu, T. (2003) 'Development of small-scale farmers under a liberalized economy', in C. Trivelli, T. Shimizu and M. Glave (eds), *Economic Liberalization and Evolution of Rural Agricultural Sector in Peru*, L.A.S. Series No. 2., Institute of Developing Economies, Japan External Trade Organization

Singh, I. J., Squire, L. and Strauss, J. (eds) (1986) *Agricultural Household Models: Extensions, Applications and Policy*, Johns Hopkins University Press, Baltimore, MD

Skoufias, E. (1993) 'Seasonal labor utilization in agriculture: Theory and evidence from agrarian households in India', *American Journal of Agricultural Economics*, vol 75, no 1, pp20–33

Smita (2008) 'Distress seasonal migration and its impact on children's education', CREATE, Pathways to Access Research Monograph no 28, Centre for International Education, University of Sussex and National University of Educational Planning and Administration, New Delhi

Smith, L. C. (1998) 'Macroeconomic adjustment and the balance of bargaining power in rural West African households', American Agricultural Economics Association Annual Meeting, Salt Lake City, Utah

Somerset, A. (2007) 'A preliminary note on Kenya primary school enrolment trends over four decades', Pathways to Access, Research Monograph No 9, CREATE

Sommer, A. (1982) *Nutritional Blindness*, Oxford University Press, Oxford

Sparks, T. (2007) 'Harmless pastime or serious science? What does phenology tell us about the impacts of a changing climate?', www.bbk.ac.uk/ce/environment/ecssociety/documents/BirkbeckTimSparks.Phenology20071012.pdf

Sperling, F., Valdivia, C., Quiroz, R., Valdivia, R., Angulo, L., Seimon A. and Noble, I. (2008) *Transitioning to Climate Resilient Development – Perspectives from Communities of Peru*, Climate Change Series No. 115, World Bank, Environment Department Papers, Washington, DC

Spicker, P. (2007) *The Idea of Poverty*, The Policy Press, University of Bristol, Bristol

Spicker, P., Alvarez Leguizamon, S. and Gordon, D. (eds) (2007) *Poverty: An International Glossary*, second edition, Zed Books, London

Stark, O. (1993) *The Migration of Labour*, Blackwell, Oxford and Cambridge, MA

Stark, O. and Fan, C. S. (2007) 'The analytics of seasonal migration', *Economics Letters*, pp304–12

Steenbergen, W.M. van, Kusin, J.A. and Rens, M.M. van (1980) 'Lactation performance of Akamba mothers, Kenya: Breast feeding behaviour, breast milk yield and composition', *Journal of Tropical Pediatrics and Environmental Child Health*, vol 27, no 3, pp155–61

Stillwagon, E. (2006) *AIDS and the Ecology of Poverty*, Oxford University Press, Oxford

Stott, P. (2010) 'Odds for extreme events are shortening', *The Guardian*, 10 August

Strange, R. (2009) 'Avoiding seasonal food deprivation in poor countries', paper presented at the conference 'Seasonality Revisited', Institute of Development Studies, Brighton, 8–10 July

Susser, M. (1981) 'Prenatal nutrition, birthweight, and psychological development: An overview of experiments, quasi-experiments, and natural experiments in the past decade', *American Journal of Clinical Nutrition*, vol 34, pp784–803

Swift, J. (1989) 'Why are rural people vulnerable to famine?', *IDS Bulletin*, vol 20, no 2, pp8–15

Swinton, S. and Quiroz, R. (2003) 'Poverty and the deterioration of natural soil capital in the Peruvian Altiplano', *Environment, Development and Sustainability*, vol 5, nos 3–4, pp477–490

Syroka, J. and Toumi, R. (2002) 'Recent lengthening of the south Asian summer monsoon season', *Geophysical Research Letters*, vol 29, no 10, p1458, doi:10.1029/2002GL015053

Taddesse, G. (2003) 'Increasing water productivity: Livestock for food security and poverty alleviation', International Livestock Research Institute (ILRI), Ethiopia

Tadross, M. A., Hewitson, B. C. and Usman, M. T. (2005) 'The interannual variability of the onset of the maize growing season over South Africa and Zimbabwe', *Journal of Climate*, vol 18, pp1356–72

Taylor, J. E. and Adelman, I. (2003) 'Agricultural household models: Genesis, evolution, and extensions', *Review of Economics of the Household*, vol 1, no 1, pp33–58

Thomas, D. (1994) 'Like father, like son; like mother, like daughter. Parental resources and child height', *Journal of Human Resources*, vol 29, no 4, pp950–88

Thomas, D., Strauss, J. and Henriques, M. (1991) 'How does mother's education affect child height?', *Journal of Human Resources*, vol 26, no 2, pp183–211

Timmer, P. (1998) 'The agricultural transformation', in C. K. Eicher and J. M. Staatz *International Agricultural Development*, 3rd edition, Johns Hopkins University Press, Baltimore, MD

Tomkins, A. (1993) 'Environment, season and infection', in S.J. Ulijaszek and S.S. Strickland (eds) *Seasonality and Human Ecology*, Cambridge University Press, Cambridge

Townsend, P. (1993) *The International Analysis of Poverty*, Harvester Wheatsheaf, New York and London

Ukoumunne, O. C. and Thompson, S. G. (2001) 'Analysis of cluster randomized trials with repeated cross-sectional binary measurements', *Statistics in Medicine*, vol 20, pp417–33

Ulijaszek, S. and Strickland, S. (eds) (1993) *Seasonality and Human Ecology*, Cambridge University Press, Cambridge

Un Nabi, R., Datta, D., Chakrabarty, S., Begum, M. and Chaudhury, N. J. (1999) 'Consultation with the poor: Participatory poverty assessment in Bangladesh', prepared for the Global Synthesis Workshop, September 22–23, Poverty Group, Poverty Reduction and Economic Management Network, World Bank, Washington, DC

UNCT (United Nations Country Team) (2002) *Reproductive Health and HIV/AIDS Vulnerability Assessment*, United Nations Country Team, Lilongwe

UNDP (2002) 'Informe sobre Desarrollo Humano Perú 2002. Aprovechando las potencialidades', PNUD, Lima, Peru

UNDP (2004) *Reducing Disaster Risk: A Challenge for Development – A Global Report*, Bureau for Crisis Prevention and Recovery, New York

UNDP (2008) 'Población: las cuencas articulan la convivencia', Human Development Report 2008, PNUD, Lima, Peru

UNESCO (2006) 'Education: The price of school fees', http://portal.unesco.org/education/en/ev.php-URL_ID=32571&URL_DO=DO_PRINTPAGE&URL_SECTION=201.html

UNISDR (United Nations International Strategy for Disaster Risk) (2009) *UNISDR Terminology on Disaster Risk Reduction*, ISDR Secretariat, www.unisdr.org/eng/terminology/terminology-2009-eng.html

Urwick, J. (2002) 'Determinants of the private costs of primary and early childhood education: Findings from Plateau State, Nigeria', *International Journal of Educational Development*, vol 22, no 2, pp131–44

Valdez, A. and Foster, W. (2010) 'Reflections on the role of agriculture in pro-poor growth', *World Development*, vol 38, no 10, pp1362–74

Valdivia, C. (1990) 'The impact of government policies on the small ruminant sector of Peru', PhD thesis, Department of Agricultural Economics, University of Missouri-Columbia

Valdivia, C. (2004) 'Andean livelihoods and the livestock portfolio', *Culture and Agriculture*, vol 26, nos 1 & 2, pp19–29

Valdivia, C. and Gilles, J. (2001) 'Gender and resource management: Households and groups, strategies and transitions', *Agriculture and Human Values*, vol 18, no 1, pp5–9

Valdivia, C. and Quiroz, R. (2003) 'Coping and adapting to increased climate variability in the Andes', paper presented to Annual Meeting of the American Agricultural Economics Association, Montreal

Valdivia, C., Dunn, E. and Jetté, C. (1996) 'Diversification as a risk management strategy in an Andean agropastoral community', *American Journal of Agricultural Economics*, vol 78, no 5, pp1329–34

Valdivia C., Jiménez, E. and Romero, A. (2007) 'El impacto de los cambios climáticos y de mercado en comunidades campesinas del Altiplano de La Paz' ('The impact of climate and market changes in peasant communities of the Altiplano of La Paz'), *Umbrales, Revista del Postgrado en Ciencias del Desarrollo (Journal of the Post Graduate Program in Development Sciences)*, Ediciones Plural, La Paz, Bolivia, pp233–62

von Braun, J., Teklu, T. and Webb, P. (1998) *Famine in Africa: Causes, Responses and Prevention*, Johns Hopkins University Press, Baltimore and London

Waddington, H., Snilstveit, B., White, H. and Fewtrell, L. (2009) 'Water, sanitation and hygiene interventions to combat childhood diarrhoea in developing countries', www.who.int/entity/pmnch/topics/child/2009_3ie.../index.html, accessed 10 January 2010

Walsh, R. P. D. (1980) 'Drainage density and hydrological process in a humid tropical environment: The Windward Islands', PhD thesis, University of Cambridge, Cambridge

Watkins, K. (2000) *The Oxfam Education Report*, Oxfam GB, London

Weiser, S. D., Leiter, K., Bangsberg, D. R., Butler, L. M., Korte, F. P., Hlanze, Z., Phaladze, N., Iacopino, V. and Heisler, M. (2007) 'Food insufficiency is associated with high-risk sexual behavior among women in Botswana and Swaziland', *PLoS Medicine*, vol 4, pp1589–98

Welch, J. R., Vincent, J. R., Auffhammer, M., Moya, P. F., Dobermann, A. and Dawe, D. (2010) 'Rice yields in tropical/subtropical Asia exhibit large but opposing sensitivities to minimum and maximum temperatures', *Proceedings of the National Academy of Sciences*, www.pnas.org/content/early/2010/07/26/1001222107.abstract?sid=fl16865b-4e70-4ef1-abea-e5b209a3bbb8

WFP (World Food Programme Bangladesh) (2002) 'Food security assessment in Bangladesh', www.wfp.org, accessed 6 April 2009

WFP (World Food Programme Bangladesh) (2005) *Bangladesh Food Security Brief*, Vulnerability Analysis and Mapping Unit, Dhaka, www.wfp.org, accessed 6 April 2009

Whiteside, M. (2000) '*Ganyu* Labour in Malawi and its Implications for Livelihood Security Interventions – An Analysis of Recent Literature and Implications for Poverty Alleviation', Agricultural Research and Extension Network (AgREN) Network Paper No. 99, Overseas Development Institute, London

WHO (2002) 'Cholera in Malawi: Disease outbreak reported', www.who.int/csr/don/2002_03_26/en/index.html (accessed 12 January 2011)

Wiggins, S., Kirsten, J. and Llambi, L. (2010) 'The future of small farms', *World Development*, vol 38, no 10, pp1341–48

Woldehanne, T., Tefera, B., Jones, N. and Bayrau, A. (2005) 'Child labour, gender inequality and rural/urban disparities: How can Ethiopia's national development strategies be revised to address the negative spill-over impacts on child education and well-being?', Young Lives Working Paper No. 20, Save the Children

Woolf, L. (1913) *The Village in the Jungle*, Eland, London

World Bank (1986) *Poverty and Hunger: Issues and Options for Food Security in Developing Countries*, World Bank, Washington, DC

World Bank (2001) *World Development Report 2000/2001*. World Bank, Washington DC

World Bank (2005) *India's Water Economy: Bracing for a Turbulent Future*, World Bank, Washington, DC

World Bank (2006) *Ethiopia: Risk and Vulnerability Assessment*. World Bank, Washington DC

World Bank (2007) *Malawi Poverty and Vulnerability Assessment: Investing in Our Future*, World Bank report no. 36546-MW, Washington, DC

World Bank (2008a) 'Poverty Assessment for Bangladesh: Creating Opportunities and Bridging the East-West Divide', Bangladesh Development Series Paper No. 26, http://sitere-sources.worldbank.org/BANGLADESHEXTN/Resources/295759-1240185591585/BanglaPD.pdf, accessed 1 October 2010

World Bank (2008b) 'Standardised welfare indicators: Source of data', www4.worldbank. org/afr/poverty/measuring/Indicators/source_en.htm

World Bank Institute (2005) 'Introduction to poverty analysis', Washington, DC

World Food Programme (2003) *Full Report of the Real-Time Evaluation of WFP's Response to the Southern Africa Crisis, 2002–2003 (EMOP 10200)*, World Food Programme, Rome

World Health Organization (2006) 'Child growth standards: Length/height-for-age, weight-for-age, weight-for-length, weight-for-height and body mass index-for-age: Methods and development', WHO, Geneva

Zeller, M. and Sharma, M. (2000) 'Many borrow, more save, and all insure: Implications for food and microfinance policy', *Food Policy*, vol 25, pp143–67

Zhao, Y. (1999) 'Labor migration and earnings differences: The case of rural China', *Economic Development and Cultural Change*, vol 47, pp767–82

Zug, S. (2006) 'Monga – seasonal food insecurity in Bangladesh – Bringing the information together', *The Journal of Social Studies,* No 111, July–Sep 2006, Centre for Social Studies, Dhaka

INDEX

Pages containing relevant figures and tables are indicated in *italic* type. Differences in terms or capitalisations between chapters have been standardized to the majority usage.